THE
FANTASTIC
LABORATORY
OF
DR. WEIGL

ALSO BY **ARTHUR ALLEN**

*Vaccine: The Controversial Story of Medicine's
Greatest Lifesaver*

Ripe: The Search for the Perfect Tomato

THE FANTASTIC LABORATORY OF DR. WEIGL

HOW TWO BRAVE SCIENTISTS BATTLED TYPHUS

AND SABOTAGED THE NAZIS

ARTHUR ALLEN

W. W. NORTON & COMPANY

New York | London

For information about permission to reproduce selections from this book,
write to Permissions, W. W. Norton & Company, Inc.,
500 Fifth Avenue, New York, NY 10110

For information about special discounts for bulk purchases, please contact
W. W. Norton Special Sales at specialsales@wwnorton.com or 800-233-4830

Manufacturing by Courier Westford
Book design by Fearn de Vicq
Production manager: Louise Parasmo
Map of Central Europe created by Jamin Hoyle

Library of Congress Cataloging-in-Publication Data

Allen, Arthur, 1959–
The fantastic laboratory of Dr. Weigl : how two brave scientists battled typhus
and sabotaged the Nazis / Arthur Allen. — First edition.
pages cm
Includes bibliographical references and index.
ISBN 978-0-393-08101-5 (hardcover)
1. Weigl, Rudolf, 1883–1957. 2. Fleck, Ludwik, 1896–1961.
3. Typhus fever—Poland—History. 4. Scientists—Poland—Biography.
5. World War, 1939–1945—Underground movements—Poland.
6. Anti-Nazi movement—Poland. I. Title.
RC199.6.P6A44 2014
614.5'26209438—dc23
2014003246

W. W. Norton & Company, Inc.,
500 Fifth Avenue, New York, N.Y. 10110
www.wwnorton.com

W. W. Norton & Company Ltd.,
Castle House, 75/76 Wells Street, London W1T 3QT

1 2 3 4 5 6 7 8 9 0

To Margaret, Ike, and Lucy

CONTENTS

Contents

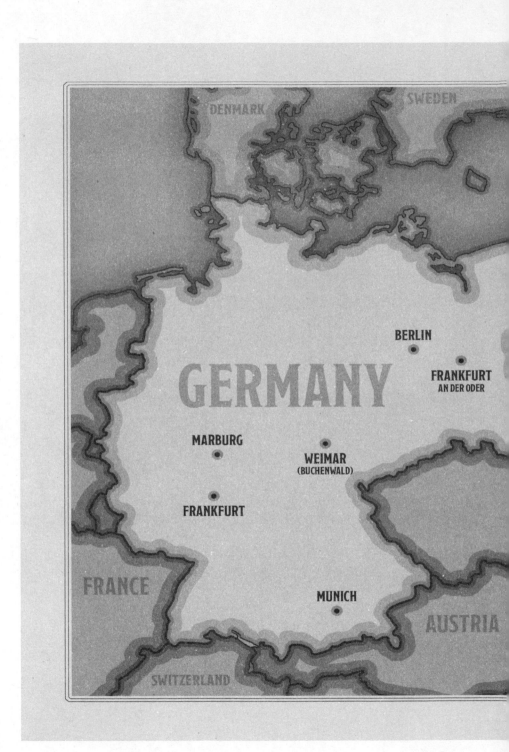

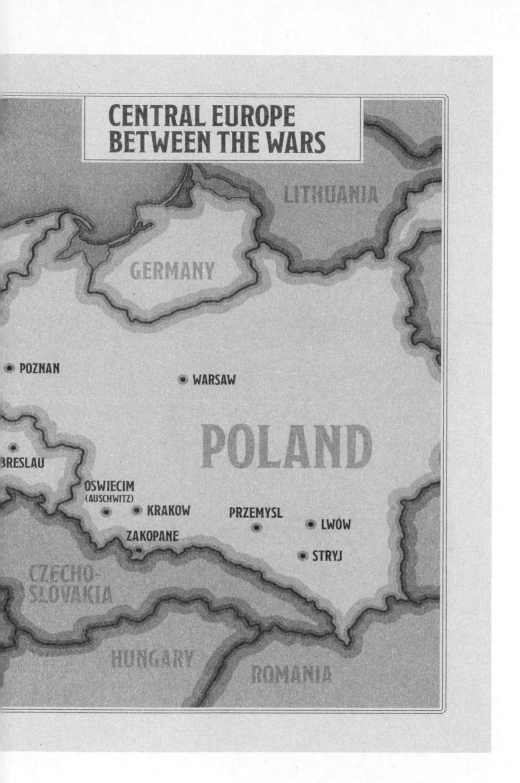

CENTRAL EUROPE
BETWEEN THE WARS

LITHUANIA

GERMANY

POZNAN

WARSAW

POLAND

BRESLAU

OSWIECIM
(AUSCHWITZ)

KRAKOW

PRZEMYSL

LWÓW

ZAKOPANE

STRYJ

CZECHO-
SLOVAKIA

HUNGARY

ROMANIA

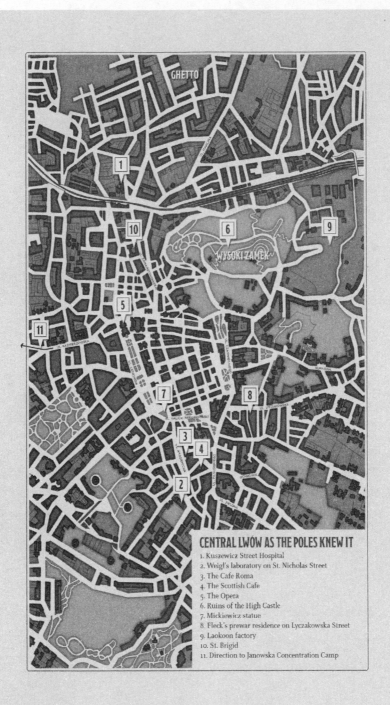

GHETTO

WYSOKI ZAMEK

CENTRAL LWÓW AS THE POLES KNEW IT

1. Kuszewicz Street Hospital
2. Weigl's laboratory on St. Nicholas Street
3. The Cafe Roma
4. The Scottish Cafe
5. The Opera
6. Ruins of the High Castle
7. Mickiewicz statue
8. Fleck's prewar residence on Lyczakowska Street
9. Laokoon factory
10. St. Brigid
11. Direction to Janowska Concentration Camp

THE
FANTASTIC
LABORATORY
OF
DR. WEIGL

PREFACE

Afew years ago I found myself in a dim corridor at the Institute of Epidemiology and Hygiene in Lviv, Ukraine, trying to persuade Dr. Oleksandra Tarasyuk, the institute's polite but recalcitrant director, to let me watch the feeding of the lice.

Why, one might ask, would anyone come all the way to Ukraine to look at lice? They are, after all, common loathsome insects, synonymous everywhere with disease and filth, wretchedness and neglect. To the naked eye, Dr. Tarasyuk's lice were no different from the ones that I and millions of other parents combed from the scalps of our children during elementary school infestations. I had once or twice examined my children's cohabitants under a microscope and found them to be surprisingly intricate, greasy-brown creatures whose guts contained tiny but distinct canals of blood.

But the lice of 12 Zelena Street, Lviv, were not quite ordinary creatures. For one thing, they were body lice (*Pediculus humanus humanus*) rather than head lice (*Pediculus humanus capitis*). The two insects, varieties of a single species, are remarkably similar; even geneticists have trouble parsing their essential difference. Both nourish themselves by poking an exoskeletal needle into the warm skins of humans and employing the musculature of their tiny proboscides to extract our blood. But for reasons that biologists have yet to understand, there is one fundamental distinction between head lice and body lice: head lice are a nuisance, but only body lice transmit one of humankind's most fearsome diseases, typhus. Body lice are thus players, in a way that head lice have never been, in some of the great tragedies and most horrendous pages of history. Few organisms have been as deadly to doctors and medical researchers as typhus. This is perhaps not surprising, because the sick shed lice, which are fussy about heat and cold and abandon the body once temperatures fall below 98 degrees Fahrenheit or rise above 102 degrees, desperately searching for a new home. Each laboratory in the fight against typhus had its martyrs, and publications about the disease were inevitably dedicated to fallen colleagues. This explains why the lice of Lviv led such a charmed existence, spending most of their lives swarming together in the comfort of heated wooden cabinets, unlike the rootless lumpen proletarians that burrow, for a brief while, in the hair of schoolchildren.

Like many scientists who spend careers in close proximity to lab animals, Dr. Tarasyuk felt quite protective of hers. "It's very difficult to keep this population alive," she told me in a remorseful tone. "They need particular temperature levels at different stages of their lives. They feed only once a day. And we have to make sure that the feeders are healthy."

And what do these lice eat? Human blood, of course. And how do they procure it? Why, by being placed in cages on the legs of human beings. The feeders at the institute, each paid a small sum for their sacrifice and blood donation, were mostly lab technicians. The idea of letting me, a stranger who didn't even speak Ukrainian, into the lab filled Dr. Tarasyuk with horror. I could give the lice a disease! I could threaten the survival of the colony! She could lose her job! "Come back the next time you are in Lviv, but give us more warning," she told me with a frown. "We would love to see you again."

Afterwards I stood outside the rather plain, five-story, Bauhaus-influenced building for a few moments and tried to conjure up a picture of its past. The lice of 12 Zelena Street are the descendants of a colony bred seven decades ago by the zoologist Rudolf Weigl, who

Preface

crossed lice picked from the bodies of Russian prisoners of World War I with those nestled in the robes of Ethiopian highlanders. With these lice and a lot of ingenuity, Weigl in the 1920s created the first effective vaccine against typhus, a disease that terrorized the world, inspired the creation of Zyklon B gas, and provided a pretext for the worst human crimes in history. Weigl's discovery drew global notice. Nobel laureates trod the corridors of his institute to study his techniques and pay homage to him. Agents from the Nazi SS and the Soviet NKVD sniffed around the halls of his institute; Nikita Khrushchev, later the Soviet premier, and Hans Frank, the Nazi governor of Poland, appeared at his doors, soliciting Weigl's services.

The lice were all that remained of a fantastic research laboratory where Weigl had devised his vaccine with an almost surrealistic series of manufacturing techniques. During World War II, Weigl's laboratory became the spiritual center of the city, protecting thousands of vulnerable people who worked in it. Weigl was a bit like Oskar Schindler, the real-life hero of Steven Spielberg's film *Schindler's List*, except that to get on Weigl's list, you had to strap many matchbox-size cages to your leg with a thick rubber band. In each cage, there were hundreds of lice that fed on your blood. The survivors of Weigl's laboratory became famous mathematicians and poets, orchestra conductors and underground fighters.

The one who most captured my imagination was Ludwik Fleck, a biologist in his own right, and also a philosopher of science. While working as Weigl's assistant, Fleck had incubated a captivating theory of scientific knowledge and laid it out in a 1935 book, *Genesis and Development of a Scientific Fact*. Today, Fleck is well known to sociologists and historians of science. Thomas Kuhn, the famous theoretician of knowledge who gave us the term "paradigm shift," borrowed heavily from Fleck's thought in writing his 1962 classic, *The Structure of Scientific Revolutions*.

Preface

Fleck's writing drew me because of his penetrating analysis of the human at work, his observations enlivened by clarity, humor, and earthiness. He showered empathy upon his subjects, whether they were medical researchers, women besotted with Parisian fashions, or medieval astrologers. Reading Fleck gave me a sudden sense of intimacy with the thought patterns of ancient and otherwise inscrutable people. He made the past bubble to life by showing the integrity of its thought systems, however wrong or bizarre they seemed to us. And he made me realize that although we live in a world separated by an almost infinite number of different mindsets, recognition of this fact can enable us to understand one another. In his day job, Fleck practiced traditional scientific reductionism, limiting the variables in order to resolve diagnostic problems. His job was to detect the invisible particles that lurked behind the familiar events of everyday life—the bacteria and antibodies that helped explain a cough, a fever, a sickly child. His philosophy, by contrast, did just the opposite: it cast a familiar light on the arcane thought patterns of the strangers who surround us in the present and the past.

Fleck's anthropological observations of science had allowed him to rise above tragedy, to gain an almost spiritual perspective amid a storm-tossed life. He had served the Habsburg Empire as a medical officer during the Great War, endured anti-Semitic discrimination in the 1920s and 1930s, then survived the Holocaust, the intrigues of postwar communism, and the hush-hush of a Cold War bioterrorism lab in Israel.

Fleck's medical specialty was immunology, or, as it was known in the first part of the 20th century, serology—the changes in the blood that helped doctors diagnose and treat infections. Blood had always been a mysterious and therefore a symbolic substance—"a humor with distinctive virtues," as Mephistopheles says in Goethe's *Faust*. That book intrigued Fleck, who believed that the immunological paradigm of his time—blood as a battleground in which cells and antibodies fought off germs—was only the latest, culturally influenced understanding, one that reflected the period's nationalistic quarrels. He predicted that more nuanced insights would open the way to calmer metaphors in the future. He was right, as demonstrated by recent studies of the multifaceted role of bacteria in our individual "microbiomes," which show that we are walking superorganisms whose life processes depend on interactions with trillions of bacteria inside of us.

In short, more than just lice had drawn me to Lviv. So much decision and thought and sacrifice had taken place here in this far-off corner of Europe near the Carpathian Mountain chain. The city had been occupied by ten different powers during eight decades. Its population had been murdered and expelled by the hundreds of thousands in the 1940s, and the remarkable accomplishments of these forgotten people had faded along with their bones. Now I watched its streets fill with buses and trams and with Ukrainian citizens, each individual possessing a feeling of belonging, no doubt, though they inhabited a city formed by people of languages and faiths that were absent now. It was as if Lviv's human population was fungible, its lice the only permanent colony.

The setting of this book is the fight against typhus during World War II. Nazi ideology had identified typhus, which is spread by lice, as a disease characteristic of parasitic, subhuman Jews. The Nazi medical profession whipped itself into a terror of typhus and took outrageous measures ostensibly to combat it. These included the walling in or closing off of Jewish ghettos in cities like Warsaw, Kraków, and Lviv, assuring that the disease would indeed spread, but only among Jews. Learned German doctors convinced themselves that it was better to kill the Jews than to allow them to contaminate others.

Weigl and Fleck thus found themselves fighting on two fronts. The Third Reich kept them alive because it needed their expertise on typhus, but in keeping them alive, the Nazis could not stop them from helping others. Fleck and Weigl found the calm to practice medical science—and to sabotage the goals of the oppressor. For their German bosses, meanwhile, the fight against typhus became a theater of medicine gone wrong. But there were degrees of wrongness and moral failure. Weigl's boss was a pragmatic army doctor, Hermann Eyer. Fleck, meanwhile, had to work for the notorious Dr. Erwin Ding of the SS, who ruled over a fiendish corner of the Buchenwald concentration camp, a laboratory of ethical choices that would go on trial at Nuremberg.

In Lviv, there are no statues of Weigl or Fleck, and no monuments to their work. The lice colony is nothing more than a scientific curiosity. After World War II, a thick layer of neglect settled upon the subjects of this book. What Fleck would have called the "thought collectives" of typhus research, and those of Polish and Jewish Lviv in general, no longer exist. This book attempts to clear away the dust and bring them back to life.

INTRODUCTION

L
ate afternoon at the Buchenwald concentration camp, on a mountainside six miles northwest of Weimar, Germany. A cloudless day: August 24, 1944. As always, the wind sweeps ceaselessly down the slope, buffeting the barracks, the Gestapo bunker, the hospital, and the typhus experimental station, blustering through the parade ground and the ditches where road crews of matchstick inmates lift pick and shovel accompanied by the capo's cruel barking of orders. It is a hostile wind that penetrates every fold in the clothing "as if it they had placed it there with the purpose of making people feel miserable," one prisoner will say. In the winter it "seemed to come direct and unimpeded from the North Pole." In this, the eighth summer of the concentration camp's existence, it tosses grit into the eyes and mouth.

On the second story of Block 50, a stone-and-stucco building toward the bottom of the hill upon which the camp stands, Ludwik Fleck runs tests on a series of blood samples sent over from the experimental block. He is one of a few dozen scientists from around Europe who have been captured and brought to this building in Buchenwald to help the SS produce typhus vaccines for the protection of German troops at the eastern front. For two years the news from the front has been bad for the Nazis, and the trenches are past lousy. Fleck is 48, a slight, myopic, balding man with an expression of skeptical con-

7

fidence. His slave scientist colleagues respect his skilled hands and knowledge of the world that swims under the microscope lens. So do the Nazi doctors who hold his life in their hands. From his lab bench, copiously appointed with all the equipment that the looted universities of Europe have to offer, Fleck can see through a window and double barbed wire to the Little Camp, where the truly doomed inmates live. Many of them are Jews like him, stumbling along on skeletal legs amid the dirt, lice, and shit.

He hears the faint hum of the planes, a hopeful sound that is more common now that the Luftwaffe, the German air force, has surrendered the skies. Then the air-raid sirens sound and unexpectedly, the shriek of explosions batters his eardrums and he falls, tossed to the wooden floor. At last, vengeance and a direct hit! The force of the blast blows open doors and shatters windows. Beakers and petri dishes tumble off laboratory shelves, fire and mud and hot metal leap into the sky. Electricity stops, silencing the lab's centrifuges; with panicked shouts, the SS duck and run and pitch themselves into their bomb shelters. The prisoners, with nowhere to hide, jump into trenches at the edge of the camp. D-day is two months past, Paris is on the verge of liberation, and SS control of the concentration camps finally seems to be weakening. Forty bombers of the Eighth U.S. Air Force have raided the military industries adjacent to Buchenwald. Their primary target, the Gustloff-II factory, where 3,500 camp inmates make carbines for the German army, lies in rubble after the hourlong strike. A few incendiary bombs land on the camp itself, and one sets fire to the *Effektenkammer*, the building where the stolen possessions of the prisoners are washed and sorted, along with the camp laundry. From there, the fire catches in the dead limbs of a large gray tree called the Goethe oak.

This spot in central Germany was called the Ettersberg, after the French, *hêtre*, for beech. In the early 19th century it was a wild and woolly forest, 1,500 feet above sea level, part of a royal hunting ground where German poets could commune with the inner Visigoth of their

Inmates walk in front of the Goethe oak in June 1944, with the
Effektenkammer in the background. (Photo by Georges Angeli.
Copyright Buchenwald Gedenkstätte.)

tree-worshipping past. But that all changed in the summer of 1937,
when the SS bused in a hundred of its political enemies and ordered
them to tear down the trees and rip out the stumps. A concentration
camp took shape on the wind-swept slope—crude barracks and whip-
ping posts for the prisoners; villas, gardens, and a private zoo for the
SS and their children. The Nazis renamed the place Buchenwald—the
beech wood.

Having done so, they maliciously removed all the beeches, but preserved a single tree, a great oak six feet in diameter. Under this tree,
Johann Wolfgang von Goethe was said to have composed the Walpur-
gis Night scene of his *Faust*. The camp commandant erected a bronze
plaque on the tree, an opportunity for the slaves to get a little culture
while they worked themselves to death. "Here Goethe rested," it read,
"during his wanderings through the forest."

As the war dragged on and the suffering of the prisoners passed
beyond any understanding, a legend began to circulate that the
destruction of the Goethe oak would augur the downfall of Germany.

And so, as fire spread from the laundry to the oak, some wondered whether deliverance was at hand. There were many literate prisoners in the camp, but any affection for the German Romantics had been replaced with an animal sensitivity to signs and portents. The glowing embers reflected glee in the faces of the inmate bucket brigades. The bombing raid had killed 600 inmates—along with 200 SS men and their family members. But it was the symbolic oak of Buchenwald that burned now, and not Paris. Ludwik Fleck captured the mood later in an unpublished essay that was found among his papers. "Die, die you beast, symbol of the German empire," he wrote. "Goethe? For us, Goethe doesn't exist. Himmler killed him."

The gift of Goethe, Germany's best-loved poet, the flower of a thinking, creative, generous world of art and science, came close to bitter extinction in Nazi Germany. It survived, among other places, in the mind of Ludwik Fleck, the Buchenwald laboratory slave, who had elaborated a marvelous and prescient philosophy of science in the happier days of his life. Science, he wrote, was a culturally conditioned, collective activity bound by traditions that were not precisely logical and were generally invisible to those who carried them out. Scientific disciplines, such as the ones he belonged to, operated by the same arcane rules as a tribe in the Amazon or a group of government clerks. The members of each thought collective saw and believed what they had been trained to see and believe. Pure thought and logic were illusions—perception was an activity bound by culture and history.

The ideas and thinkers of the past were not wrong, Fleck wrote, but they had built their ideas upon "shapes and meanings that we no longer see." This was not to say there was no progress, nor that one could not distinguish good science from bad. The idea of an "Aryan" or a "class-conscious" form of science, Fleck wrote in 1939—with Hitler and Stalin, champion corrupters of science, preparing to pounce on his homeland—"would be laughable if they weren't so dangerous." But Nazi medicine was a thought collective with peculiar fixed ideas.

Introduction

Fleck, as a sociologist of science, penetrated its weak points and put his insights to good use.

Arriving at Block 50 in Buchenwald in late 1943, he joined a group of prisoners who were trying to grow typhus germs in the lungs of living, immune-compromised rabbits. This was a task of great importance, for if they could cultivate the germs, the cultures would be used to make a vaccine, which would be immensely valuable to the German military. As long as the lab was contributing to the immunological defense of its soldiers, the Nazi regime would presumably keep the lab open and refrain from murdering its staff. The boss, the SS Dr. Erwin Ding, would be happy, too, because producing a vaccine would secure his position, keeping him far away from battle duty at the eastern front. And after the war, he hoped, the vaccine would win him a university professorship.

But there were problems with producing a sophisticated vaccine within the thoroughly corrupted confines of a concentration camp. *Rickettsia*, the intracellular bacteria that cause typhus, had bedeviled biologists for decades. Indeed, their somewhat mysterious existence—for no one knew just what they were—is one of the keys to understanding how Fleck developed his questioning, skeptical view of science. These germs were extremely difficult to grow artificially, though they thrived in lice and sick people. The prisoners in Block 50 knew nothing about how to prepare rickettsial cultures of the type one used to make vaccine. Yet everyone was desperate for success—Ding to further his career, the inmates in order to survive. Those in the thought collective of Block 50—a biologist, a baker, a politician, and a physicist, among others—convinced themselves that they were making a vaccine, and put the fluid substance into vials that were sent off to Hamburg and Paris, where German scientists, men of renown, responded with words of praise. How was this possible? Like 1,000 monkeys with typewriters and time, a group of desperate amateurs had learned how to prepare a devilishly complicated vaccine in the space of a few months. Or had they? Fleck, who arrived when the group was well advanced in its labors, was the only one among them with the appropriate specialized knowledge. He was the only one who knew whether the vaccine they were making was real.

To most of the inmates of Buchenwald, in any case, the vaccine was not the most interesting thing about the rabbits that were used to grow it. On the night of the big raid, as the Goethe oak burned, the prisoners—French scientists from the Pasteur Institute, tough Polish resistance men, German Communists, Russian peasants, Dutch Jews, and Fleck—all joined in singing the "Marseillaise." Then they had a feast of rabbit stew.

CHAPTER ONE

LICE/WAR/TYPHUS/MADNESS

Typhus is an unfamiliar disease to most everyone alive today, but it left an indelible mark in past centuries, shaping the fate of empires from Napoleon to Lenin. And no one who has lived through a typhus epidemic will ever forget it. The disease is transmitted by tiny arthropods that live snugly in the seams of warm clothing, which they do not leave, unless evicted, except to suck blood or--when the body they occupy has gone cold, or too hot with fever—to find a new human host. Lice have been seen crawling as far as five feet in an hour. Head lice lay their nits, or eggs, on hair; body lice, in underwear and shirts. The body louse evolved from the head louse when people started wearing clothes and is distinguished from its progenitor by its dislike for the temperatures of the head, our hottest surface.

Humans and lice have a long, intimate relationship. In one of the earliest sections of Exodus, Aaron "stretched out his hand with his rod and smote the dust of the earth, and it became lice on man and on beast. All the dust of the land became lice throughout all the land of Egypt." Expressions such as "nitwit" (for those who feel dull, sullen, and "lousy," after scratching their infected or allergic skin through sleepless nights) and "nitpicking" attest to this, as does the "fine-toothed comb" we use to examine things with care. It has even been hypothesized that the seven-day week and the Sabbath arose in recognition of body louse reproductive patterns—for if clothes are changed each week consistently, a person's lice and their eggs will die. Yet until a few centuries ago, people in colder climates nearly always carried lice in their clothes and rarely bathed. An account of the 12th-century funeral of Thomas à Becket notes that as his body cooled, the vermin living in the archbishop's many layers of clothing began to crawl out and "boiled over like water in a simmering cauldron, and the onlookers burst into alternate weeping and laughter."

In the modern world, though, the body louse is the louse of refugees, soldiers, and other desperate people. Typhus epidemics occur when a population is at the end of its tether. Starvation, cold, fear, and exhaustion are the normal prerequisites. Typhus corresponds with social collapse. Typhus "will continue to break into the open," wrote Hans Zinsser, author and Harvard typhus researcher, "whenever human stupidity and brutality give it a chance." By the time Zinsser wrote these lines in his famous book *Rats, Lice and History*, published in 1935, typhus was a distant memory to most Americans and Western Europeans, who were too clean for permanent louse infestation. Yet there were parts of the world where it was still an acute danger. At the end of World War I, the worst epidemic in history swept across Russia from Siberia all the way through Poland, causing 30–40 million cases of disease, and killing perhaps three million people. It was in the anteroom of this great catastrophe that Dr. Rudolf Weigl and his assistant Ludwik Fleck earned their stripes as typhus researchers. Working on the basis of new evidence that lice were the vectors of the disease, Fleck and Weigl were on the cutting edge of scientific efforts to tame it.

When the Austro-Hungarian Empire called up its male subjects to fight in 1914, Weigl was 31 years old, Fleck just 18. Both left their homes in the city of Lviv—which was known to the Poles as Lwów, to German speakers as Lemberg—to become medics in the kaiser's army. After some training in Vienna, they quickly joined the fight against typhus, which they encountered mostly in Russian prisoner-of-war camps in Bohemia and in western Galicia—around the cities of Lwów, Tarnów, and Przemyśl. From 1917 to 1921, Weigl was in charge of a military laboratory—at first under the Habsburgs, and from 1919 for the Polish state—in Przemyśl, which straddled the San River. This was a fortress town, now located at the border between Poland and Ukraine, and by some cultural maps a dividing line between Eastern and Western Europe. The Przemyśl complex of forts, the third largest in Europe in 1914, fell to the czar's army in March 1915, after a six-month siege that led to starvation among the poor Jews who lived there. It was retaken three months later, then lost its strategic significance and became something of a warehouse and a way station for troop movements and a center of military medicine, including a modern microbiological laboratory.

Rudolf Stefan Weigl was born in 1883 in Přerov, a picturesque Moravian town now located in the Czech Republic, and was the child of ethnic Germans. His father, who designed and produced vehicles of various sorts, died after crashing a large-wheeled bicycle of his own invention when Weigl was seven. His mother remarried a few years later to a Polish schoolteacher named Józef Trojnar. The family moved frequently from town to town until Trojnar became director of a middle school in Stryj, a wealthy town south of Lwów. The marriage was a happy one, and Rudolf, his older brother, Friedrich, and sister, Lilly, grew up in an atmosphere in which Polish language and culture predominated. After passing his examinations, Weigl enrolled at the University of Lwów, where in 1907 he received his doctoral degree under the zoologist Józef Nusbaum-Hilarowicz, a leading Polish proponent and translator of Darwin's ideas.

In the waning years of the Habsburg realm, the monarch had granted Polish autonomy to Galicia, a district stretching from Kraków in the west to east of Lwów and including areas of plains, forests, and mountains. The majority of peasants in the countryside were Ukrainians, the cities inhabited mostly by Poles and Jews. Those who chose to assimilate often learned Polish, the language of government and culture. This contrasted with the Russian- and Prussian-occupied areas of Poland, where assimilated Jews tended to speak German. Perhaps because of the light hand of the Austrian kaiser, the anti-Semitism and ethnic conflict that would characterize Poland following its independence in 1919 were not as close to the surface in wartime Galicia. Anti-Semitism was evident in the professions, but had not been codified, and was not universal. Thus Weigl was simultaneously a Czech, an Austrian, and a Pole, while his doctorate adviser, Nusbaum-Hilarowicz, was a Jew who had decided to accept a Catholic baptism in 1907, viewing it as a necessary step to achieve promotion to full professor. Weigl's boss in the military service, Filip Pincus Eisenberg, was also Jewish. A Pasteur Institure–trained bacteriologist, Eisenberg ran a laboratory that was as multiethnic as the empire it served. In 1919, Weigl hired Fleck, who had begun his studies of medicine in Lwów before the war, as his assistant in Przemyśl. Fleck was also from an assimilated background. He was the son of Sabina Herschdörfer and of Maurycy Fleck, a craftsman with socialist tendencies who owned a small house-painting business. Though not rich, the Fleck parents were ambitious for their children and sent them to Polish rather than Hebrew high schools, with hopes of offering them a way into the mainstream of Polish society. Maurycy earned enough money to send Fleck and his two sisters, Antonina and Henryka, to university. While Fleck earned his doctorate at Lwów University under Weigl, the girls studied arts and pedagogy in Vienna.

Eisenberg's expertise was microscopy, and he was skilled at identifying bacteria in their confusingly variable forms. Weigl, who was extremely adept in the laboratory arts, had already invented a device for improving microscopic lenses—a secondary focus adjustment knob. Fleck would also gain a reputation as a razor-sharp practitioner. In visible terms, the three of them represented the evolution of fashions in facial hair. Eisenberg was balding, with a long beard of the type seen on the waistcoat-with-tails-wearing professors in movies like *The Cabinet of Dr. Caligari* and *The Blue Angel*. From his 20s, Weigl had sported a distinctive goatee in the manner of *The Three Musketeers*, and sartorially he favored open-necked, wide-collared shirts. Fleck liked to dress in neatly pressed suits. He was clean-shaven, increasingly the style as the century went on, in part because of the nascent popular obsession with germs, which were thought to favor beards over smooth skin (an idea encouraged by Gillette and other razor makers).

Their prey, typhus, was an extremely difficult organism to understand and manipulate. Most successful human pathogens are relatively benign. Cold viruses, to give a classic example, spread far and wide because the humans they infect remain hardy enough to distribute them among their fellow men and women. Malaria doesn't kill mosquitoes, and *Borrelia* bacteria, the cause of Lyme disease, harm neither the deer tick nor the deer. Over time, pathogenic organisms generally become less virulent, or they fade away, or have limited success. (Or, as in the case of HIV and tuberculosis, they infect slowly, giving the patient plenty of time to transmit the germ before becoming incapacitated.) The deadly Ebola virus sowed terror when it appeared in Africa in the 1980s, but has proven of little global significance because it infects and kills quickly, before the patient has time to spread it efficiently. This trait is characteristic of new pathogens that haven't yet adapted to their hosts. At the other end of the spectrum is, for example, *Streptococcus pyogenes*, known also as Group A strep, which can cause strep throat, toxic shock, rheumatic fever, and scarlet fever, but usually colonizes, quietly, the throats of healthy three- to five-year-old children—at least 15 percent of whom harbor the organism in any given year.

Rickettsia prowazekii, according to this logic, must be a young disease, for it has not "learned" to occupy a sturdy ecological niche. Experts believe that American natives may have transmitted the disease to Spanish colonists in the 16th century, although some argue it was already present in Europe. *R. prowazekii* has definite shortcomings. Although it generally kills fewer than 20 percent of the humans it infects, leaving plenty of others alive to transmit it, typhus relies upon a single avenue—the louse—for its spread. And lice not only spread typhus—they are its victims. Sick insects can transmit the disease to humans for up to 10 days. Then they die, and they do not pass along the disease to their eggs. When there are no typhus patients around to sicken the lice, they stop transmitting the disease. The end of a typhus epidemic should thus mean the end of typhus. However, the germ has a few more survival tricks. First, a contaminated louse's feces contain high concentrations of *R. prowazekii* and remain infectious for several months. More importantly, human typhus survivors sometimes maintain latent infections for years. Just as a case of chicken pox in childhood can reappear as shingles in old age, typhus patients sometimes experience recurrences as their immune systems weaken. An American physician, Nathan Brill, first discovered such cases among Eastern European immigrants in New York's Lower East Side in 1913. They seemed especially common among elderly men and women mourning the death of a spouse, which led Brill to call it "bereavement disease." Hans Zinsser isolated the organism and indentified it as typhus. As old typhus patients die off, Brill-Zinsser disease becomes increasingly rare. But a senior with Brill-Zinsser who became lousy could infect his or her lice, and thus begin the cycle once again. This mechanism keeps typhus alive between epidemics. And if, as scientists believe, these are the only ways that typhus spreads, then the disease will disappear from earth when the last person who ever had it passes away.

A century ago, typhus's unique life patterns posed a thorny challenge to researchers. How were they to maintain a steady supply of the organism for study? It was hard to keep typhus bacteria alive in artificial cultures or in the bodies of mice or guinea pigs; there was no way to infect lice with typhus other than to feed them on the bodies of people sick with the disease. But patients were generally available only during typhus epidemics. Even the wobbly medical ethics of those days forbade intentionally infecting people with typhus. After many discussions with Eisenberg about this problem, Weigl hit upon an idea in 1916. Out of concern for his assistant's future career, Eisenberg had been urging Weigl to drop typhus research and concentrate on cholera, an organism that was easier to culture and grow.

"Tell me, Sir, where are you going to get the cultures?" Eisenberg asked. "You won't have access to the typhus organism until you have patients. And you won't get patients when there is no disease. So how is this going to work?"

Weigl thought for a moment, then with characteristic earthiness replied, "Well, if we can't get the louse to eat the germs, we'll stick them up its ass."

Eisenberg did not understand and was not amused. Weigl told him, "Have a look."

Whereupon he strode to his workbench and, using a bunsen burner, drew out a long, thin glass pipette. After pinning a louse down on a piece of blotting paper, he proceeded to stick the pipette into its

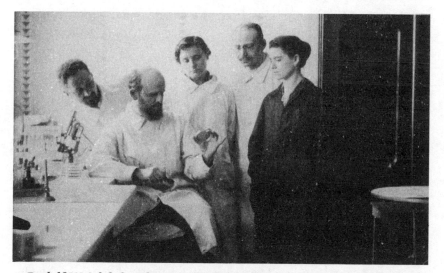

Rudolf Weigl, left, Filip Eisenberg, seated, with other lab workers in Przemyśl, around 1916. (Courtesy of National Museum, Przemyśl. Photograph of original by S. Kosiedowski.)

anus, and injected the louse with a tiny droplet of water. Weigl knew from his anatomical work that the insect's rectum was made of a stiff, chitinous material that would not be easily damaged, if the tube was carefully inserted and its tip carefully rounded.

And thus a new experimental animal was born—the louse. Grotesque though it was, this was one of the true eureka moments in typhus research, and an important one for the expansion of research into viruses as well. Never before had an insect been used as an experimental animal; Weigl owed his ability to take advantage of this idea to a marvelous manual dexterity. "To watch him tenderly section an insect or create a microscope slide was an intense aesthetic pleasure," one colleague noted.

For Weigl, as well as Fleck and the scores of other medics in the employ of the Austrian crown, there was considerable urgency in the work. Austria was largely free of typhus before the war, and the troops of the empire, lacking natural immunity, were ripe for contagion. The crown lands whose health they defended soon burned with typhus, which erupted first in the Balkans, then in Ukraine and Russia.

The word "typhus" comes from the Greek *typhos*, which means "smoky" or "hazy," and refers to the hallucinatory symptoms that arise in the sick mind. The disease is distinct from typhoid fever, whose symptoms can be similar but are caused by an intestinal bacterium present in contaminated food or water. Typhoid fever (in the early days of bacteriology, scientists tended to add the suffix "-oid" or the prefix "para-" to name a "new" organism that they had previously mistaken for another) was distinguished from typhus in the mid-19th century, but the original mistake left a linguistic muddle. In German, for example, *Tyfus* describes the disease that English speakers call typhoid fever, while the German word for typhus is *Fleckfieber*, literally "spotted fever." In English, "spotted fever" may refer to typhus or to Rocky Mountain spotted fever, caused by similar bacteria spread by the bite of certain ticks. To add to the confusion, epidemic louse-borne typhus has less deadly cousins—murine typhus and scrub typhus—

spread by fleas and chiggers and ticks in parts of Asia and the Americas, including Texas.

The body louse bites in order to attach itself to the skin, then feeds by poking a tiny tube called a stylet through the outermost layer. It uses a mechanical pump to draw out blood, and as it eats, it excretes. The bite of the typhus-infected louse does not transmit typhus; rather, the bite and the bug's saliva cause itching, which leads the human to inoculate himself with the typhus-laden feces by scratching where the louse bit. Typhus germs can live in human cells contained in dried louse waste for up to four months, and some unknown but small percentage of infections occur when the excrement infects people through the lungs, eyes, and nose.

Rickettsia are very tiny, primitive bacteria. Recent genetic analyses have shown that they share a common ancestor with mammalian mitochondria, the energy-producing organelles of the cell. Typhus bacteria live in the cells of the host, which they rely upon to metabolize the sugars they need to exist. Typhus germs colonize the cells that line blood vessels in tissues throughout the body, including the brain. The immune system's attack on the infected cells floods the lungs and other organs with fluid, and like a lighted match in a box of firecrackers, sets off a cascade of immune responses that contribute to the memorable and horrific symptoms of the disease.

Sickness typically begins around a week after the louse bite, with fatigue and a bad headache or backache. Soon the patient begins to appear pale and absent, and his or her reflexes fail. Around the fifth day, red circles pop out on the shoulders, torso, and arms resembling tiny jewels embedded in the skin. This is called petechial rash. Long before doctors knew what caused typhus, they diagnosed it on the basis of the spots and the delirium that typically emerges soon after their appearance. For a week or more, a severely ill patient will lie muttering and inert, with sporadic flashes of anger or frustration accompanied by spastic movements, incontinence, and loss of bowel control. Temperature can rise to 108 degrees Fahrenheit; the heart beats at 120 beats per minute. Complications include bronchitis, deafness, numb extremities, swollen testicles, or gangrene of the toes, penis, labia, or fingers. Deafness and memory loss occur and can be permanent.

At the peak of illness, many patients become profoundly distressed. "A ward full of typhus patients in the second week of the disease bears more resemblance to an acute mental ward in an asylum than to a hospital ward," one doctor wrote. "Some patients lie in a drowsy, comatose condition, others shout incoherently at the top of their voices, while still others, nearing the critical period, lie with very shaky hands outside the bedclothes and exhibit marked carphology and *subsultus tendinum* [twitching, plucking, and grasping]." The better typhus hospitals had table straps to keep patients from attacking the staff, throwing themselves out windows, or fleeing down flights of stairs to plunge into traffic or bodies of water. Suicide, if it can be called that, was a common

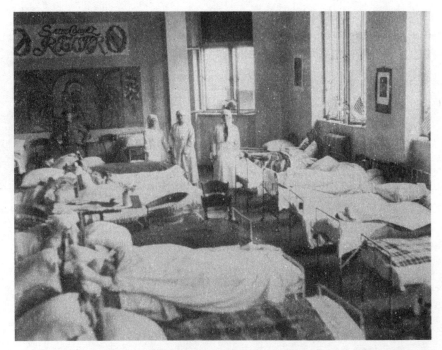

Typhus ward of Grace Hospital in Warsaw, 1921. (Library of Congress.)

sequela of typhus, because the patients were driven mad by pain and terrible visions that sent them hurtling through windows.

An entire literature could be created from the visions of typhus sufferers. An American volunteer who had been put in charge of 6,000 sick Austrian, Turkish, and Russian prisoners of war on a six-week train meander through Siberia in 1920 fell ill himself and lay down on a patch of straw. He was engulfed by an unforgettable vision. "It seemed there were two couches next to me and upon them reposed dark bodies, monsters of indefinite form and at the same time parts of my own body," he said later. "At other times, I was able to see myself from outside in a relatively logical way." Another American, a volunteer serving in the Italian army during World War I, suddenly was struck by the not-so-crazy inspiration that war was wrong, and thereafter refused to return to the front and preached pacifism among his fellow patients. Doctors responded to this feverish inspiration by placing him in a mental asylum for the remainder of the war.

Some patients temporarily gained marvelous mental powers, or lost the most basic skills. "Although my memory is not the sort that can normally capture verse, I recited three poems that I had read shortly before my illness," a Russian patient recalled. "Two days after this exaltation, my mind was a complete blank."

Some hallucinatory motifs were characteristic of different cultures: during World War II, German soldiers at the eastern front often imagined that the Führer had personally pinned medals on them and promoted them for brave deeds in battle. American famine relief workers, delirious in their camp hospital in Ufa in 1922, entertained fantastic escape dreams in which they boarded comfortable, pillow-cushioned airplanes and flew around the world. The journalist John Reed, who spent his last days in the Moscow typhus hospital after watching his beloved revolution fall to tatters, retreated into an idyll of beautiful visions and dreams of his long-lost boyhood in Portland, Oregon. "He would tell me that the water he drank was full of little songs," wrote Reed's widow, Louise Bryant, who sat with him in his dying days.

"He told me, 'You know how it is when you go to Venice. You ask people—Is this Venice?—just for the pleasure of hearing the reply.'"

Those who recovered described a ravenous convalescent hunger and a vivid sense of rebirth. In Chekhov's 1887 short story "Typhus," the character Klimov awakens in a stream of light: "His whole body from head to foot was overcome by a sensation of infinite happiness and joy in life, such as the first man must have felt when he was created and first saw the world. Klimov felt a passionate desire for movement, people, talk. . . . He rejoiced in his breathing, in his laughter, rejoiced in the existence of the water-bottle, the ceiling, the sunshine, the tape on the curtains." When his aunt tells Klimov that his sister, Katya, has died of typhus and that he had infected her, "this terrible, unexpected news . . . startling as it was, could not overcome the animal joy that filled the convalescent. He cried and laughed, and soon began scolding because they would not let him eat."

Lice-borne typhus has been known under many names: jail fever, malignant fever, spotted fever, but surely the most apt name, at least for latter centuries, is "war fever." Typhus followed soldiers and refugees into bombed-out houses and mud hovels, burrowed into their trenches and encampments, shrouded their train yards and horse-drawn wagons. The disease played a decisive role in many military campaigns, among them Napoleon's catastrophic invasion of Russia. The Grand Army marched to Moscow with 500,000 men and returned with 3,000. It is likely that 20 percent of the casualties were typhus deaths.

Napoleon's benighted soldiers had no idea what hit them, but scientists ascertained the primacy of the louse in typhus just in time for World War I. The French scientist Charles Nicolle, a methodical protégé of Pasteur's aide, Émile Roux, was the first to prove louse transmission of typhus. After taking over the Pasteur Institute's branch in Tunis in 1903, Nicolle noticed that at the city hospital, admission workers often fell ill with typhus, but nurses on the typhus ward did not. After learning that patients entering the hospital were stripped and washed, Nicolle reasoned that the agent spreading the disease was in their clothes. He carried out a few decisive experiments, using lice to transmit the human disease to a chimpanzee, from the chimp to a macaque, and from the macaque to another chimp. His study, published in 1909, was enormously influential and won Nicolle the Nobel Prize in Medicine in 1928.

As World War I began, doctors now knew that the louse spread typhus, and armies, accordingly, started to take action against the louse. Each country had a corpus of medical men whose sights were trained on typhus, and many tried, and failed, to create vaccines. France had a group at the Pasteur Institute, Britain physicians such as Arthur Bacot of the Lister Institute, the Americans Hans Zinsser and Richard Strong, both from Harvard. The hygienic corps of the Prussian army was the best organized of the lot, with a strong tradition dating to the previous century. Prussia in 1870 had been the first power to thoroughly vaccinate its army against smallpox. In 1914, German medical institutes sent top scientists into the field to study and combat infectious diseases. In Turkey, where the enfeebled Ottoman army had put German officers in charge of its military staff, scientists such as Ernst Rodenwaldt, Claus Schilling, and Heinz Zeiss of the Institute for Maritime and Tropical Diseases—each would be associated with Nazi medicine during World War II—found opportunities to study typhus in prisoner-of-war camps. German doctors carried out typhus experiments on Armenians, and when 50,000 Armenian refugees at Aleppo were suspected of carrying typhus and other diseases, German doctors urged they be removed from contact with soldiers. The Turks herded the refugees into concentration camps and murdered most of them.

German military doctors first became keenly aware of the threat of typhus to their troops after the 1914 Battle of Tannenberg, in which an outmanned German force destroyed two czarist armies and captured 92,000 Russians by capitalizing on the obtuseness of the czarist commanders, who transmitted their orders in plain code. ("Russia," a Russian officer told the relief worker and writer S. Ansky, "is fighting three enemies: The Germans, lice and our own generals—the last is the most dangerous.") Typhus was always lurking in parts of Russia. It traveled wherever the czar's conscript armies went, in the lice that clung to their unwashed clothes. One German doctor found 6,000 lice on a single Russian prisoner. Typhus broke out quickly in the POW camps.

The Germans, with characteristic punctiliousness, took extreme measures against the vermin. The army set up delousing columns where soldiers stripped and waited for hours in drafty tents or concrete buildings while their clothes were exposed to high-pressure steam or creosote baths designed to kill the lice. Prisoners faced the same treatment. Even Aleksandra Piłsudska, wife of Józef Piłsudski, the leader of the Polish independence movement, was forcibly deloused after being taken into custody in 1915. She and her compatriots had to disrobe outside in winter and bathe in a tub full of powerful disinfectant that "stung our skins until we were the color of lobsters." Her hair was washed with a strong carbolic lotion "which left it as hard and brittle as straw and so sticky and unmanageable that it took weeks to recover." The Germans deloused 3.5 million prisoners during the war, and while the system was certainly brutal, it brought results. Of the 33,000 German military deaths of infectious disease during the war, fewer than 1,500 were caused by typhus.

German disease control probably prevented typhus from spreading to the western front. This was quite an achievement, for the western trenches was every bit as lousy as those on the eastern side. In Erich Maria Remarque's *All Quiet on the Western Front*, the narrator describes German soldiers tossing their lice into a boot polish tin placed over a candle to kill them. British soldiers called the bugs "cooties"; a characteristic shrug of the shoulders and a careworn appearance told officers that their men were lousy and hadn't slept well. Lice are nocturnal creatures that like warm, dark, quiet spots, and one had to go to sleep sometime. "The only way to obtain relief was to get out of the dugout, put a rifle barrel between the belt and rub up and down like a donkey at a gatepost," one soldier wrote. "This stopped it for a bit, but as soon as one got back into the dugout, and was getting reasonably warm, so would the little brutes get going again." The poet Robert Graves, an officer in the Royal Welsh Fusiliers, said that lice were a source of bitter humor among his men. "Young Bumford handed me one: 'We was just having an argument as to whether it's best to kill the old ones or the young ones, sir. Morgan here says that if you kill the old ones, the young ones die of grief; but Parry here, sir, he says that the young ones are easier to kill and you can catch the old ones when they go to the funeral.' He appealed to me as an arbiter: 'You've been to college, sir, haven't you?'"

Though no typhus was reported in the West, the troops did get trench fever, a louse-carried illness that the Germans called Wolhynian fever, the Poles "Quintana" (the causative agent was eventually named *Rickettsia quintana)*. It rarely killed but was very unpleasant and extremely common, accounting for more than a third of British casualties. Fever spiked every five days and sometimes recurred years later. Hundreds of thousands of cases occurred among Allied and German armies at the western front.

German soldiers delousing at the eastern front, 1917. (Corbis.)

The Fantastic Laboratory of Dr. Weigl

Typhus broke out in Serbia following the Austrian invasion of August 1914 that began World War I. One bloody maneuver after another over a Balkan landscape already battered by Serbia's wars with Turkey and Bulgaria ended when the Serbs seized 60,000 Austrian prisoners in December. Many of them died of typhus before the year was out. The epidemic was sudden and extraordinarily deadly, and before long neither side had the stomach to launch an offensive, leading to a six-month cease-fire. Of the estimated 500,000 cases during the epidemic, 120,000 were fatal. More than half of Serbia's 450 medical doctors died or were incapacitated. Volunteer doctors from around the world rushed in to help, including a Polish immunologist named Ludwik Hirszfeld, who would later earn fame as a creator of the ABO blood-typing system. On any given day at the small rural hospital where Hirszfeld worked in February 1915, there were 100 new patients, he wrote, "half of them so sick you couldn't get their names out of them." Fifty died every day. Caravans of horses carried off the dead but couldn't keep up, leaving piles of corpses all around the hospital.

During the Great War, nearly every medic or scientist who had anything to do with the disease could recount a gruesome experience. Each laboratory had its martyrs, and typhus publications of the era were inevitably dedicated to fallen colleagues. Doctors and biologists walked a razor's edge treating and studying the disease in an era without prophylaxis or cure. This is evident in the final missives of the Czech aristocrat Stanislaus von Prowazek—a scientist based at the Hamburg Institute for Naval and Tropical Diseases—from his work station at a Russian POW camp in Cottbus, Germany, in January 1915. Lice had burrowed so thickly into the prisoners' barracks that the creatures rained down from the straw mattresses whenever someone slammed a door. Prowazek and his scientific partner, the Brazilian aristocrat Henrique da Rocha Lima, were fighting their colleagues' refusal to accept the evidence that lice were the vector of typhus. They were prevailing, in wretched circumstances. "Of 39 Russian doctors who did not believe in the louse theory, and who instead thought they could protect themselves with facemasks and *Mummenschanz*, 21 have fallen ill and five died," Prowazek wrote to the Austrian medical command. "Only three of the German doctors have sickened." Prowazek protected himself from lice with a tight coat, rubber gloves, and shoes smeared with creosote, but this was not enough. Three weeks after submitting this report, he died of typhus. Rocha Lima, who fell ill but recovered, honored his colleague by naming the causative organism *Rickettsia prowazekii*, thereby also paying homage to the American scientist Howard Ricketts, who had died in 1910 while studying typhus in Mexico.

One of the few typhus specialists who stayed well (though he did infect himself with a different form of typhus in 1929) was Hans Zinsser, the Harvard microbiologist. To avoid contamination with lice in a typhus region required great care. This is how Zinsser described his precautions at a grubby bordello where he was forced to overnight in Ipek, Serbia, in 1915. Prostitutes were battering on the door for the good professor's attention, but he ignored them:

> The first thing to do was to strip to the skin. Outer clothes were hung on a hook or laid over a chair, away from the washing area. The discarded underwear was loosely packed into my boots, a tablespoonful of chloroform poured into each one, and a string tightly tied around the tips. This executed any vermin that happened to be in the underwear, and made the clothing safer for use the following day. Then came a thorough wash— especially of the hairy parts of the body—with soap and water. After this, I could put on the clean underwear. Before wrapping myself in [my] blanket for sleep on the floor, I would sprinkle it with kerosene.

Though evidence of louse transmission was firm in 1914, the nature of the germ that caused the disease was not. In May of that year, *The New York Times* announced with a splash that young Harry

Eisenberg, seated left, Weigl, seated right, with colleagues in the Austro-Hungarian medical corps, 1914. (Courtesy of National Museum, Przemyśl. Photograph of original by S. Kosiedowski.)

Plotz, barely 24 years old and a recent graduate of Columbia Medical School, had discovered the cause of typhus. Plotz and his vaccine traveled the next year to Serbia accompanied by another brace of headlines, on a mercy mission sponsored by Mt. Sinai Hospital. But the bug Plotz had isolated was not the same as the one killing the Serbs, who refused his offer to immunize their soldiers. It was never exactly clear what Plotz had found—he was unable to maintain his cultures or share them with other scientists—but it wasn't *Rickettsia prowazekii*.

In 1916, Edmund Weil and Arthur Felix, two Czech physicians serving in the Austrian army, developed a diagnostic test for typhus that involved mixing serum from a suspected patient with an organism called *Proteus OX-19*. If the suspension clumped, it indicated the patient had typhus—the clumps representing bonds between typhus antibodies and pieces, or antigens, of OX-19. The test was far from perfect, with frequent false positives, and it seemed to work only when the patient had been sick for several days. It also led to the mistaken theory that typhus was caused by *Proteus OX-19*. (Later, scientists would discover that *OX-19* and *R. prowazekii* each contained proteins that reacted with antibodies in the blood of typhus patients.) Other physicians, including Nicolle, believed that a virus was the causative agent. Both theories were wrong, but understandable.

Consider that before 1930 or so, most scientists believed that bacteria could not live inside cells. To prove that a particular organism caused a disease, the eminent German bacteriologist Robert Koch had stated in 1890, it was necessary to extract it from a sick person, grow it in an artificial medium, and reproduce the disease by injecting it into an experimental animal. Furthermore, by extracting the organism in question from animal blood, one could make a protective vaccine with it through chemical deactivation. Alternatively, broths containing the organism could be injected into a horse, which would produce antibodies that could be harvested and used as a passive immune serum—that is, a serum containing antibodies specific to the disease.

Cultures of the bacteria causing anthrax, typhoid fever, diphtheria, or tetanus met the postulates neatly, or at least seemed to. But no one could figure out how to grow typhus germs in an artificial medium like the bull's blood used for diphtheria and tetanus. Nor could the disease easily be transferred from animal to animal. An ape could get louse-borne typhus, with great experimental difficulties, but the germ at most gave guinea pigs a bit of fever. Typhus-infected blood from the adorable little rodents could not be cultured in a broth.

The 1914 Serbian typhus epidemic burned itself out after a year, but events in Russia soon created a new opportunity for the disease. The world has never seen the equal of the great typhus epidemic that christened the Russian revolution. Circumstances under which it might be repeated are almost too dreadful to imagine. In late 1917, the Bolsheviks declared an armistice with Germany, and Lenin pulled Russia's armies back from the front. They returned home hungry, ragged, and full of typhus. The disease was seeded in the civilian population just as the country plunged into a civil war that drew in Russia's neighbors and enemies. Historical records of the epidemic are sketchy. The Bolshevik regime lacked the resources to track it, and had little interest in revealing the precarious state of its public health to a hostile world. Doctors who treated the disease often died. There were Western witnesses, but back home few believed their stories. Even fewer cared.

The early years of the Russian revolution, a calvary of war, murder, epidemics, and incompetence, were so catastrophic that observers compared the country to Europe in the Middle Ages. The civil war, lasting roughly from 1917 to 1921, was a chaotic clash of armies whose troops often changed sides—the Bolshevik Reds, for example, fought anti-Bolshevik Whites, Ukrainian nationalists, and Poles led by Józef Piłsudski. White armies under various generals fought Communists, Poles, Ukrainians, and ragtag forces of the anarchist Nestor Makhno. Kiev, the Ukrainian capital, was occupied 15 times in three years. Ravaging, unwashed armies and columns of starving, diseased refugees and camp followers spread typhus across the land. Poor military leadership exacerbated the disorder. "A minor setback would precipitate a retreat that snowballed," one historian has written, "as technical breakdown, the devastated terrain, the weather, the local population, disease, desertion and fear of political reprisals all conspired to destroy the fabric of the retreating force."

"I do not suppose that there was a single house or flat in the whole of the south of Russia, from Novorossiysk to Moscow, but had had its case of typhus," wrote a British physician. The implication of this statement, of course, is that all of Russia was lousy. And that was the case, as the writer explained:

> Very well, says the reader, it is easy enough to guard against lice; you only need to wash often, take plenty of baths, change your clothes frequently, and avoid dirty places. But all these

simple precautions were impossible. There was no fuel to thaw water or heat it for a bath, or to wash clothes in; water-pipes had frozen and burst; few people possessed spare shirts or underclothes, and, as for avoiding crowds, you could not move a step without running the risk of infection.

The worst of the epidemic began in the midst of the Polish-Soviet war of 1919–20. Lenin, Trotsky, and the other leading Communists had turned their attention west with the belief that after crushing the new, bourgeois Polish state, the Red Army could continue on to Germany and beyond, inspiring revolutions across Europe. The Polish leader Piłsudski, who trusted neither the Bolsheviks nor the White armies, in mid-1919 made a secret deal with Lenin that allowed the latter to send several divisions to fight the White forces of General Anton Denikin as they approached Moscow from the south. Denikin's army was driven off toward the Black Sea while General Alexander Kolchak, the other major White leader, was routed and fled east over the Urals on the trans-Siberian railway amid a phantasmagoria of terror that covered a vast territory in murder, cannibalism, sickness, and debauchery. The vector of trains aided immensely in the spread of lice and typhus. Every town along the railway was overrun with hungry, freezing people who jammed rail carriages and houses to escape and stay warm. Corpses were packed into warehouses or strewn along roads and railways where they were stripped of all valuables. Every soldier's greatcoat housed visible clusters of the lice, and the insects, dead and living, lay thick as sawdust on the crowded waiting room floors of the stations.

"The sights which I saw . . . and the statistics which I collected were so staggering that, when I afterwards told about them in Europe, my hearers simply shrugged their shoulders and refused to believe me," a British intelligence officer wrote of the White Army's flight. Trains were packed full of dead, dying, and sick typhus patients, often without a soul taking care of them. These so-called death trains were not permitted to stop in stations, and corpses were tossed out the window of moving trains "with as little ceremony as the stoker threw out ashes." Nurses and orderlies robbed the sick and dead. On February 3, 1920, some 20,000 corpses lay unburied in the snow outside the city of Novonikolaevsk.

Not only the Whites suffered. "Comrades," Lenin told the Congress of People's Commissars on December 5, 1919, "it is impossible to imagine the dreadful situation in the typhus regions, where the population is broken, weakened, without material resources, where all public life ceases. To this we say, 'Comrades, we must concentrate everything on this problem. Either the lice will defeat socialism, or socialism will defeat the lice!'" A German Red Cross relief team sent in 1921 gathered unforgettable visions; its members were astonished at the impassivity of the Russians. In the Kazan area, they saw people eating tree bark, acorns and prairie grass, corn stalks, barn sweepings, clay and horse manure. They saw huts full of people, mostly women and children, lying listlessly in unheated rooms awaiting death or muttering and screaming in typhus deliria, towns where a third of the villagers lay on the ground, dead or unconscious, with dogs gnawing at corpses. They collected at least 200 stories of cannibalism and saw graves that "must be guarded because the starving dig the dead up to eat them." Disease spread through Moscow through scavengers returning after scouring the countryside for coal and flour. The winter was very cold, and no one could wash even if he or she wanted to. Mutual delousing was "the favorite indoor and outdoor sport," said an American aid worker.

Conditions were particularly awful among communities of poor Jews. The young American doctor Harry Plotz, who had witnessed epidemic typhus in Serbia in 1915, came to Ukraine in June 1920 on behalf of a Jewish relief organization. At a refugee camp in Kiev, typhus patients lay in the mud, crying for bread. Among the 2,000 refugees were pogrom victims limping about with open saber wounds. "Serbia, during its severe typhus epidemic," wrote Plotz, "never had a sight like this." The director of the Jewish hospital informed Plotz that of 110,000 Jews in the city, 25,000 had died of typhus over a period of six weeks. "The infected lice are transmitted from person to person and so the disease is rapidly propagated. The morale of the people is low, the desire to keep clean is lost," Plotz wrote to the Joint Distribution Committee in New York. At the same time, he said, "Jewish communities are loath to follow orders in regard to bathing and delousing . . . for, under the guise of health propaganda, anti-Semitic literature is distributed, and, in the zeal for cleanliness, beards are violently shaved and pogroms occur."

Typhus would have a transformative effect on Russia. For reasons that may have to do with the immature immune systems of the young, typhus—like viral diseases such as measles and mumps—strikes more severely in older patients; in Russia, it killed more than half of those over 50 whom it sickened, but was only about 1 percent fatal among children. The rural poor, who were more likely to have been exposed as children to typhus, were also less likely to sicken or die. Thus, typhus killed off the aristocratic old guard and the intelligentsia, while sparing, to a greater degree, the peasantry.

This demographic impact of the disease helps explain why Western powers viewed events in Russia less with tender mercy than with fear. Winston Churchill, who had declared that Germany sent Lenin to St. Petersburg in 1917 "the way you might send a vial containing a culture of typhoid or of cholera to be poured into the water supply of a great city," depicted Russia as a land of "armed hordes smiting not only with bayonet and with cannon, but accompanied and preceded by swarms of typhus-bearing vermin which slay the bodies of men, and political doctrines which destroy the health and even the soul of nations." The West focused its support on Poland, attempting to create a cordon sanitaire of guards and delousing stations to keep infected Russians from traveling west. Travelers would be interned, shaved, deloused, and bathed, their clothes exposed to louse-killing chemicals and hot water. Years before communism established the

Iron Curtain, the Western powers constructed a curtain of steam. The hospital laboratory at Przemyśl became part of the weave.

This takes us back to Weigl and Fleck, whose laboratory was quietly advancing on the problem in these terrible epidemic years. Weigl had been working under Filip Eisenberg for three years in the fortress laboratory in Przemyśl when Eisenberg, in late 1917, won a prized professorship at Kraków's Jagiellonian University, Poland's oldest institution of higher learning. On his way out, Eisenberg recommended that Weigl take over leadership of the Przemyśl lab. His method of inoculating lice had drawn the attention of the authorities. In 1917, Emperor Franz Josef, while touring Przemyśl's defenses, was introduced to the young typhus tamer. Weigl gave the monarch a tour of his laboratory, explaining in detail his method of infecting the lice. "That is quite interesting," the emperor kept saying. "Truly it is!" Weigl's aides would chuckle about the visit for years. It was clear that the old emperor had not understood a thing.

Weigl had not been in charge of the laboratory for long when he became ill, an experience that he would use as an important step toward the creation of a typhus vaccine. Accidentally smashing a petri dish, he stuck himself with glass that had been in contact with a container of typhus germs grown in six successive generations of lice. Soon Weigl developed the characteristic rash on his abdomen as well as a high fever, and his blood provided a positive Weil-Felix reaction. His new wife, Zofia Kulikowska Weigl, nursed him through the illness but also conducted experiments on her husband at his request. She placed matchbox-size cages on his body, each containing hundreds of lice, to feed upon his blood in different phases of the illness. One side of each tiny cage had a piece of wire mesh glued over a large oval hole, the mesh sturdy enough to stay in place but fine-grained enough for a louse to feed through. If his blood gave the lice typhus, Weigl reasoned, it would offer new proof that the organism he had been culturing in the lice through anal injections—the same organism with which he had infected himself—was the causative agent of typhus.

From time to time, Weigl emerged from a fitful sleep and jabbered in a psychotic fashion. Zofia had to pretend he was still giving the orders, or he became very angry and could not be calmed down. "His determination to pursue the agent of typhus fever," said a close aide, "was so dominant that it did not leave him even when he was deeply ill." The lice fed heavily upon Weigl and after several days they turned bright red and sluggish, and then died. The accidental experiment had been a success. "The lice set upon me during my feverish period," wrote Weigl, "became thoroughly infected with *Rickettsia prowazekii.*" This was the best evidence he'd collected to date confirming the identity of the causative agent of typhus.

Weigl was cautious about publishing—he was never one to write up an experiment without repeating it many times, and he didn't like to mark each baby step in print. Weigl called such research papers "duck shit." They reminded him, as an outdoorsman, of what the feathered animals left behind while waddling along. In the view of others, Weigl took this publication shyness to extremes. Even as a student, he was always so thrilled to be doing science and excited by his discoveries that he couldn't be bothered to publish anything, until his superiors threatened to withhold his stipends. But having emerged from his own rite of typhus passage, Weigl published the first exposition on his research methods, a 20-pager with graphics in a German medical publication, *Beiträge zur Klinik der Infektionskrankheiten und zur Immunitätsforschung* (Clinical contributions to infectious disease and immunity research).

The paper outlined progress in typhus research to date and then explained the many painstaking steps and small technical details of Weigl's work maintaining *R. prowazekii* in a colony of lice. Its implications were groundbreaking and immediately obvious to the international research community: for the first time, one could study a stable colony of typhus germs in vivo where there was neither a typhus epidemic nor human typhus patients.

World War I ended with the dissolution of the great empires of Europe and the emergence of an independent Polish state for the first time since the 18th century. Polish independence made Weigl's struggle with the disease even more meaningful to him, for something in the happy childhood he experienced with his Polish stepfather had converted Weigl into a strong Polish patriot. He and a friend were discussing the famous scientist Marie Skłodowska-Curie once over drinks, and Weigl criticized Curie for raising her daughters as Frenchwomen, with no Polish identity at all. "Look at me, I'm a full-blooded German," Weigl said, "but I identified with Poland when it wasn't even on the map, and I'll always be Polish."

Health disasters were among the greatest challenges that Poland faced in its first years of independence. The 28 million new citizens of the country underwent terrible hardships between 1914 and 1920 as armies clawed for control of their lands. Cities and towns were occupied, pillaged, and razed repeatedly. Hundreds of thousands starved to death. Millions were homeless. Industry was destroyed, agriculture in chaos. Pogroms ruined hundreds of Jewish towns. As disbanded White and Ukrainian armies and refugees fled into Poland, disease spread. According to the Polish government, the country suffered 673,000 cases of typhus, with 141,500 deaths, in 1918. Many of the victims were Russian POWs. At the armistice of 1918, there were 2 million Russians in German captivity, many of them on Polish territory. When Poland went to war with the Bolsheviks in February 1919, the repatriation of the Russian POWs stopped. American, British, Swedish, and International Red Cross relief teams arrived to try to help the Poles control the epidemic. Herbert Hoover, whom Wilson had appointed as his humanitarian czar for postwar Europe, directed Colonel Harry Gilchrist, a veteran of World War I campaigns in France, to offer his antityphus services to the Polish government. The Americans found appalling conditions in Poland. In teeming POW and refugee camps near Przemyśl, the new public health authorities were unable to provide decent conditions for the sick captives. Men slept on the mud in poorly built huts with broken windows. Prisoners who arrived at one camp after traveling for five days in November 1919 grabbed a dead horse lying by the side of the road and tried to eat its raw carcass. A typhus epidemic that began that month claimed 247 of the 1,100 prisoners there.

An army could forcibly delouse POWs, if it had the facilities, but it was not easy to persuade the "great unwashed" to submit to delousing. In some of the colder, poorer regions of Poland, winter bathing was still viewed with suspicion, though Jewish men and women had regular recourse to the ritual bath or mikveh that traditionally is attached to every Orthodox synagogue. Perhaps because lice were an inevitable part of life throughout most of human history, some traditions held that one's lice protected one from disease; the great 18th-century biologist Linnaeus subscribed to this theory. In eastern Poland, the uneducated—Pole and Jew alike—were said to believe that lice were necessary body armor. But the new health authorities of Poland, and their Western allies, were determined to drive away pests and pestilent ideas. The Americans sent six delousing trains, each capable of cleaning 1,000 refugees per day, to the Polish–Russian border and other areas. The mobile plants consisted of a water tanker with hoses and tents. Children were always the first to volunteer for a bath. "If the older people were as enthusiastic as these children, typhus would no longer be a dread in Poland," Gilchrist wrote. Town officials devised a plan requiring citizens to show a bath ticket in order to buy bread and potatoes. Forged tickets soon appeared. Over time, however, some warmed to the American cleaning teams. In the *Illustrated Daily Courier* of Kraków, an ad appeared on October 30, 1919, describing the appearance of American baths in central Lwów: "on a great square where many institutions are found . . . a passer-by sees an uncommon sight: By one entrance he sees people dirty as Satan; by other doors they come out clean like angels. . . . Oh magic bath! Come quickly to Kraków, for you are more necessary here than anywhere else!"

The Fantastic Laboratory of Dr. Weigl

Western scientists were ready to believe the worst about the hygiene of Eastern European Jews, but came away with mixed opinions. "The Jews were said to be less cleanly than the Christians, and from what I saw of them I should say that this was true," the British epidemiologist E. W. Goodall wrote in 1920. But in the same publication, he attributed the lower mortality rate of Jews in one district to their greater access to medical care. He concluded that although Jews in some places were more likely to get typhus, "it is doubtful, in my opinion, that they so suffered because they were Jews: the more probable reason is because they were more densely crowded together."

Several of the medical teams traveled to Lwów, which was beginning to gain recognition as a center of typhus research. Weigl had started work on his typhus vaccine. By 1921, the year he was appointed full professor in the Department of General Biology at Lwów University, he had something to show for it.

CHAPTER TWO

CITY ON THE EDGE OF TIME

Weigl's appointment was an unusual honor for a 38-year-old in the cramped, graying world of Polish academia. Weigl brought along Fleck and a few other members of his team from Przemyśl, and they settled into the department's headquarters on the basement floor of a former Trinitarian monastery at 4 St. Nicholas Street, near the center of the city. Weigl's team was part of a dynamic group of public health scientists, many of them officers in the Polish military. They put themselves at the service of the state by creating a brand-new health system, which offered universal insurance to its citizens and set about battling the diseases that had plagued the country over the ages. The bacteriologist Ludwik Rajchman was at the forefront of this effort. He led international efforts to fight typhus in Poland and the East, and in 1921 took charge of the new, Geneva-based League of Nations Health Organization, the forerunner of the World Health Organization. Rajchman, an assimilated Jew of left-wing tendencies, persuaded a cousin, the hematologist Ludwik Hirszfeld, to head the Polish National Institute of Hygiene, which the hyperactive Rajchman also had organized. The health agency, known by its Polish initials PZH, established branches throughout the country and set to work rebuilding the country's shattered public health infrastructure—or in some cases, creating it from scratch. The worst typhus epidemics were in the southeast, in the region south of Lwów. During the end of the Habsburg Empire and the beginning of the Polish state, military scientists like Weigl worked closely with PZH epidemiologists to sort out the causes of the disease and crush it. Soon after Weigl moved to Lwów, Hirszfeld invited him to PZH headquarters in Warsaw to demonstrate his louse-inoculation techniques to British, French, German, and American scientists who were studying the disease in Poland.

After returning to Lwów, Weigl began a period of remarkable productivity that corresponded with a golden age of scientific and artistic creativity in the city, a time when Lwów grew rapidly. Between 1921 and the end of World War II, Weigl's lab blossomed, expanded, and finally exploded in size, and then disappeared entirely, much like the population of Lwów itself. Weigl became famous, first in the research world, then in the city, and finally in Poland at large, until he, too, disappeared.

Like many successful Polish academics of this period, Weigl had married a few rungs up the socioeconomic ladder. Zofia Kulikowska, whom Weigl had met when they worked together as students in Nusbaum-Hilarowicz's laboratory, was the daughter of a lawyer who had become wealthy through his own practice after gambling away the family fortune at the craps tables of Monte Carlo. She was beautiful and intelligent and a talented scientist, and they worked side by side while raising their only child, Wiktor, born in 1921.

The couple shared a comforting bourgeois routine that contrasted with the perilous life in the laboratory. The professor and *Pani* (Lady) Weigl walked each morning at nine from their apartment on Wagilewicza Street to the laboratory, a distance of less than a mile, and worked there through the morning. Zofia was the administrator of the laboratory, and also its paymaster. Everyone returned home for lunch, served punctually at two by the Ukrainian maid, with Zofia returning a bit early to help prepare the meal. Weigl would arrive, singing bawdy songs in Czech and German, head into the kitchen, and sniff the pots. At times, he would whisper to his son, "There's nothing good today. Let's go to the pub." At lunch, Weigl would complain about his employees—"so and so is an idiot, I must fire him"—while Zofia diplomatically defended each one. Sometimes the professor napped before returning to the laboratory, where he often stayed deep into the night.

Sunday dinners were more formal. Depending on the season, there was trout cooked different ways, partridges in the autumn, or duck in cream sauce with Czech dumplings. Weigl himself prepared various dishes: crawfish soup, marinated trout, frog legs fried in bread crumbs. He was constantly trying new sauces, developed a finicky way of making tea involving serial filtration, and liked to eat bread smeared with honey mustard. On special occasions, the family dined at the Hotel George, a classy spot for the Lwów bourgeoisie.

Home life featured conversation and jokes and dancing with Zofia's three sisters, all accomplished, intelligent women. Weigl teased his wife about her gilded ancestry, which included a great-grandmother who was an Italian countess. "I keep looking for aristocratic tendencies in you," Weigl would tell his son in a deadpan way. "But so far all I detect is a certain laziness." Some evenings the family watched home movies, powered by a hand crank—birds and animals and comical stick-figure cartoons that Weigl created. At Wiktor's insistence, they took in a Tom Mix film, but Weigl scoffed at the hero's gunfighting skills. "An 1840 Colt revolver didn't have a threaded barrel," he said. "You couldn't shoot accurately with it from more than 20 meters." Weigl was not a great fan of music, but he appreciated a risqué show. Once he traveled to Warsaw to see Josephine Baker perform. He came back disappointed that her outfits were not as skimpy as advertised in Paris, where she wore only ostrich feathers on her head and a gold cord around the hips.

Weigl had many affairs, according to his contemporaries. Eventually, they had significant consequences for Weigl and his family. At home and in the lab, he was absorbed in his own interests, and encouraged his family and lab assistants to find things that fascinated

Weigl, wife, and son in the mountains. (Courtesy of National Museum,
Przemyśl. Photograph of original by S. Kosiedowski.)

them and that they could do without bothering him too much. But he
was an affectionate presence, free of prejudice, brilliant, not pompous
though certainly arrogant.

The family spent holidays at a wooden house in the Carpathian village of Ilemnia, 80 miles south of Lwów. A trout stream ran through
the property, and the opportunities for hiking, hunting, mushroom
collecting, and fishing were endless. Weigl found newts and salaman-
ders that he brought back to the lab—embryology had been the subject of his dissertation. He designed fishing rods and created a trout
fly that was carried for years in the English Hardy catalog as "Weigl's
glory." Said his son, "It was characteristic of father to do everything

perfectly, whether it was his profession, fishing, or dancing. When something didn't interest him, he wouldn't do it." This included finances and administration, which he left to his wife. He hated parlor games and sunbathing, but in 1936 he organized the "Ilemnia Olympics" for Wiktor and his friends. He obtained javelins and disks and, naturally, threw them better than the boys did. Weigl became so fond of Ilemnia that in the mid-1930s he built a laboratory extension on the house. Soon it doubled as a research station for investigations of typhus among the Hutsuls, the mountain people of the area.

In Lwów, the renown of the Weigl laboratory grew steadily at the university through the 1920s and 1930s. Weigl's corner office in the back of the building had a large window that looked out on sycamore, oak, and walnut trees in the university's carefully maintained Botanical Garden, which ran uphill for two city blocks, ending in a row of greenhouses. Leaving the building by the front door and turning to the left, Weigl would pass St. Nicholas Church on his way down the cobblestoned hill to Akademicka Street, the lower end of the Lwów *corso* that ran for a mile and ended at the baroque Opera House. If the weather was fine, he'd often be dressed like a gentleman explorer, in a pith helmet and a wide-collared shirt known as a *słowacka*. On his way home, he would gaily greet students, and often stop at the Café Roma, at the corner of Akademicka below his lab.

Lwów was a city of rolling hills and twisting, undulating streets, with the ruins of the High Castle—built by the city's founding king in 1269 and wrecked repeatedly in the centuries since—towering above everything. The variety of pleasing perspectives, the stock of Habsburg and Italianate buildings, the sheer good bones of the place, have struck visitors even in the city's darkest times. The city had for centuries been a multiethnic crossroads linking the Polish heartland with Russia and the east. Its heterogeneity was symbolized by the cathedral spires of multiple faiths that scraped its skyline—Polish Catholic, Armenian, Ukrainian Uniate, and Eastern Rite, as well as numerous synagogues. In the recollection of those who studied and worked in interwar Lwów, that diversity was a source of both strife and cultural richness. In 1930, Lwów had about 300,000 residents, more than half Polish, a third Jewish. The working class had its own jargon, Bałak, incorporating elements of Yiddish, Ukrainian, and other languages. Fewer than a fifth of the city's residents were Ukrainians, but the countryside was Ukrainian, with some Jewish towns as well, and a few Germans whom the kaiser had enticed to settle in the 18th century.

The Habsburgs had taken control of the region they called Galicia in the partition of Poland in 1772. To a far greater degree than the czar or the Prussians, Austria ruled its subjects with a conniving but relatively soft touch. Lwowites had a great deal of autonomy and self-confidence by the end of the 19th century; many Jews would gratefully remember the reigning Habsburg attitude as lenient bigotry. The crown may not have loved the Jews, but it tolerated them as just another patch in its multiethnic quilt. World war brought Russian occupation, looting, and reoccupation by the Austro-Hungarians, followed in November 1918 by a three-week struggle for the city between Polish and Ukrainian nationalists. When the Poles had seized control of the city for good, their militia fell upon the Jewish quarter, setting off one of the worst pogroms in the city's history.

After independence, one author wrote, the Poles, Ukrainians, and Jews "politically worked against each other, lived daily near one another, and culturally exchanged productively with one another." One might also have said the Poles resented the Jews, the Ukrainians resented the Poles and the Jews, and the Jews, including those who identified with the Polish nation, were optimistic or fearful but generally expected the worst. The interwar era was dominated by the figure of Marshal Józef Piłsudski, the leader of Polish independence and chief of state until 1922, when he stepped down. Piłsudski returned in a 1926 coup d'état and remained Poland's de facto dictator until his death in 1935. Many Jews viewed him as an ersatz, philo-Semitic kaiser who protected them from the worst excesses of Polish nationalism.

Overall, the city was relatively unscathed by the Great War and recovered quickly. The area south of Lwów had one of the world's largest working oil fields, and the rising global consumption of the product put money in many a pocket. New buildings and residential neighborhoods grew steadily until the very start of World War II. For the Polish and Jewish middle class, there were plenty of ominous signs, but city life sparkled with promise. "We were like ants bustling in an anthill over which the heel of a boot is raised," wrote the science fiction fabulist Stanisław Lem, a contemporary of Wiktor Weigl's who recorded the Lwów of his childhood in the memoir *Highcastle*. "Some saw its shadows, or thought they did, but everyone, the uneasy included, ran about their usual business until the very last minute." Poland was a new country, Lwów a growing city, and for Polish youth especially it was a heady time to be alive. "We were proud of our city, and we wanted to make it the best in Poland," said Wacław Szybalski, who like Lem was born in 1921. Szybalski, a brilliant scientist from a noble family, moved to the United States in the 1950s and was a founding member of the postwar genetics community along with his friend James Watson, codiscoverer of the helical form of DNA, and others.

Lwów had a way of assimilating people from outside, whether Armenian and Italian merchants in the 17th century or Jews from Galician villages in the 19th and early 20th. In this it was more like an American city than Kraków or other tradition-bound Polish places. During Poland's partition, academics and cultural figures suppressed by the Prussian and czarist regimes had reinvented themselves in the more easygoing, café-going society of Lwów. Weigl himself, notes Szybalski, was "born 100 percent Austrian and came from a family that knew nothing about Poland. It's characteristic that he became a die-hard Lwówite." Nostalgia for Lwów is quite palpable in those who left. Lem, who grew up in a mixed Polish-Jewish neighborhood near the Opera House, remembered riding to Stryj Park in a two-horse droshky, watching new Disney cartoons and movies at the Marysienka Theater on Jagiellonska Street, and above all Załewski's Confectionary, where "great artists, Leonardos of confection, realized their vocation. . . . I remember pink pigs with chocolate eyes and every variety of fruit, mushroom, meat, plants; and there were fields, too, as if Załewski could reproduce the whole cosmos in sugar and chocolate, using shelled almonds for the sun and icing for the stars . . . Vesuviuses of whipped cream whose volcanic bombs were heavily candied fruit." There was also Piasęcki, which sold the Mideast delicacy halva, and the Yugoslavia, which offered Turkish delight, baklava, and other Balkan treats, as well as kvass, a mild Ukrainian beer brewed from bread.

Akademicka Street was full of elegant stores and cafés, with rows of poplars lining a central promenade. It ended at the Hotel George, an 18th-century pink wedding cake of a building, and beyond the George stood the towering Adam Mickiewicz Column, which honored Poland's great poet-patriot and was a natural meeting place for political rallies. To the north lay curving Legionów, the main shopping street and gathering spot in town. At night, electric signs for soap, chocolates, and electric lights blinked in the darkness on the five-story buildings along the street, where jugglers, fire-eaters, singers and musicians, organ grinders, talking parrots, and traveling family circuses entertained the crowds. At the Marysieńka, near the Opera House, *King Kong, The Mummy*, and *The Werewolf* showed in the early 1930s. The city boasted 21 movie theaters in 1936.

Religious Jews lived mostly in a poorer section of town lying to the north and east of the Opera House, but other, increasingly assimilated Jews lived in mixed districts around the city. A Jewish entrepreneur, Mejer Balaban, brought the Eastern Trade Fair to the hilly green spaces of Stryj Park in 1921. It opened with an alarming bang when a Ukrainian nationalist tried to assassinate Marshal Piłsudski (recognizing the sound of gunfire, the old warrior ducked—two of the bullets wounded Lwów's provincial governor). Despite its inauspicious beginnings, the fair was a much-awaited September custom for the youth, who trawled for free tchochkes and food from Hungarian, Romanian, and Russian stalls, while businesses showed off their new tractors and radios and building materials. By 1928 there were 1,600 exhibitors and 150,000 visitors, and state-owned Radio Lwów began broadcasting from the fair two years later. It became the most popular station in the country, with news, educational programs, and comical sketches by Jewish and Polish comedians. Piłsudski, forever grateful to the city for its defense against the Red Army, would call in to offer his thoughts about the best Lwów sausage stands. The radio personalities Szczepko (a Pole, Kazimierz Wajda) and Tońko (a Jew, Henryk Vogelfänger), known for their racy Lwów slang, starred in movies such as *Włóczęgi* (Tramps), whose theme song "Tylko w Lwowie" (Only in Lwów) became a kind of city anthem. Hundreds of other popular Lwowian songs could be heard in the parks and plazas, which were saturated with music.

Habsburg culture had left its stamp on the city in its classical architecture, in the formal dress of the men in their three-piece suits and canes, in the deferential and differential cap doffings and touchings required of gentlemen greeting acquaintances of varied social status, and, above all, in café culture. Every middle-class Lwowite had a regular café. Some were expensive, some known for their exquisite pastries or regional wines, but all had newspapers bound to wooden sticks. The café was the sine qua non of academic life. "Most of my colleagues slept in their apartments, worked at the university and lived in cafés," one professor wrote of the early 1930s. "Lwów's charm was in its leisurely atmosphere, its superficial quick friendships, its witty and spiteful gossip from which no one was safe and which no one took too seriously. For years the same people met at the same time at the same place in the same cafés, knowing each other's troubles and *affaires*, discussing those of their colleagues but never inviting one another home." On a typical lunch date, the professor sits with a friend "discussing physics, Bolshevism, and the love affairs of our acquaintances, when my companion looks at his watch. 'It is twelve-twenty already. I have a lecture at twelve. I shall come again after the lecture.'" Slowly he gets up to pay his bill. The waiter automatically adds the usual tip.

"Then my colleague shakes hands vigorously with me, we bow deeply and ceremoniously to each other and slowly he goes to his lecture."

Many scientists had moved to Lwów during the partition of Poland because Vienna was kinder to Polish culture and innovation than Moscow or Berlin. In the 1920s, Lwów developed a particularly strong reputation in fine art, philosophy, the sciences, and mathematics. Its mathematicians worked in the cafés on Akademicka. Their favorite was at first the Roma, at Akademicka 26, and later the Szkocka (Scottish Café), across the street, though a few preferred Załewski's, across the tree-covered mall from the Roma, which everyone agreed had the best coffee and pastries.

The Lwów school of mathematics was built initially around the work of logicians such as Jan Lukasiewicz, inventor of Polish notation, on which early computer memory designs such as Hewlett-Packard's reverse Polish were based. In the 1920s, this recondite society included Stanisław Ulam, who later created the H-bomb with Edward Teller; the cone-headed, bottle-shaped Włodzimierz Stożek ("always in good humor and joking incessantly," recalled a colleague, "he loved to consume Frankfurters liberally smeared with horseradish, a dish that he maintained cured melancholy"); the towering, very loud Bronisław Knaster, and Stanisław Mazur, a founder of game theory. Sometimes they were joined by Hugo Steinhaus, a polymath, polylinguist, and one of the only Jews in Poland who achieved a full professorship during the Polish republic without converting to Catholicism. Steinhaus owed this distinction to his international reputation, and to a family that included a brother in parliament and another who died fighting for Polish independence by Piłsudski's side. That was about as Polish as a Jewish family could get.

One day in 1916, while strolling through a Kraków park, Steinhaus heard a young stranger and his friend discussing the "Lebesque integral," a concept known only in the higher spheres of mathematics. Thus began the legend of Stefan Banach, blond, blue-eyed, tall, and heavyset, a self-taught street urchin and chain-smoker of uncertain paternity.

Steinhaus took Banach under his wing and introduced him to influential academics, leading Lwów University to hire him in 1922. Banach shocked the Lwów bourgeoisie with his indifference to convention, his appreciation for beer and soccer matches, and his tendency to walk the streets at all hours in an undershirt. His circle met first at the Roma and then, when the latter stopped allowing him to pay on credit, at the Scottish Café. Some of these discussions, amid the smoke and clatter and laughter of the café, had an intensity, Ulam wrote,

> that I have never seen surpassed, equaled or approximated anywhere, except perhaps at Los Alamos during the war years. I recall a session with Mazur and Banach at the Scottish Café which lasted 17 hours without interruption except for meals. There would be brief spurts of conversation, a few lines would be written on the table, occasional laughter would come from some of the participants, followed by long periods of silence during which we just drank coffee and stared vacantly at each other. The café clients at neighboring tables must have been puzzled by these strange doings.

It was out of such discussions that delirious formulas such as the Banach-Tarski paradox were born. Alfred Tarski was a Warsaw-based mathematician whose Jewish ancestry had cost him a professorship in Lwów that was instead given to the equally famous Leon Chwistek (this failure, indirectly, led to Tarski's escape from Nazism to a safe haven at the University of Calfornia at Berkeley). The paradox, an arcane set geometry theorem, proved that a solid ball in three-dimensional space could be divided into a finite number of pieces that could be put back together in a way that yielded two identical copies of the original ball. In the Scottish Café, an orange could become two oranges.

Frequently, the equations written on the Scottish Café's marble tabletops were erased by unwitting waiters. At his wife's insistence, Banach in 1933 brought in a simple black-and-white composition book,

The Scottish Café (right) and the Roma (left). (Courtesy of the Center for Urban History of East Central Europe.)

which was kept behind the counter. When the table scribbling got intense, the mathematicians called for the notebook to be brought out, and wrote important theorems and problems in it. The Scottish Book, it was called. When the cafés closed, Banach wandered over to the train station, where he could spend the early morning hours over a drink at the all-night cafeteria. In his requirement of music and noise to lubricate mental gears, Banach embodied what was unnatural and noble about city life—the concatenation of clashing smells, languages, accents, flavors, the mixture of rudeness and formality that somehow inspired thoughts both original and humane in what was, after all, a small city. The mathematicians in their cafés, working at their apparently important yet impenetrable problems, added an ethereal element to the life of a city known for its hustlers and beggars, speculators and traders, vodka producers and oilmen (the first refinery in the world had been built near Lwów in 1856).

Café life brought together intellectuals from different milieus, offering an ideal setting for intellectual cross-fertilization. Everyone at the Roma knew Weigl—in fact, he regularly forgot his umbrellas and coats there on his way to and from the office. Sometimes the talk at the Scottish Café focused on science, or the mathematicians gossiped about peers, grumbled and shouted about Nazis or Bolsheviks. Professorial jobs were hard to come by in interwar Poland—especially, but not exclusively, for Jews. The tables at the Szkocka were full of professors, learned unemployables like the Jewish mathematician Juliusz Schauder, and café creatures of all types. The Roma had a character named Ostap Ortwin, a literary critic who was president of the Lwów Literary Club. Ortwin was tall and broad-shouldered, with thick eyebrows and a black Cossack-style mustache—not a typical look for a Jew. He was outspoken and loud, his opinions rattling the Roma's windows, wrote his friend Józef Wittlin, and "the anti-Semitic idiots retreated in reverence" when he strode the streets.

Of course, daily existence was not always as romantic as these café reminiscences suggest. Increasingly, anti-Semitism impinged on public and private life. Despite being an outré bastard, Banach possessed such absurd talent that he could make it in academia, but his Jewish colleagues had few chances. Schauder, who had equations named for him, was forced to work as a private tutor. There was a saying in Polish academia, "talent is passed on from father to son-in-law." Jobs were few, marriage to another professor's daughter was a common ramp to success, and Jewish scholars—with rare exceptions—had to teach high school.

Ludwik Fleck took a number of steps to deal with these disadvantages. He worked from 1921 until 1923 in Weigl's laboratory, where he developed a method of typhus diagnosis involving a weak suspension of typhus antigens injected under the skin, similar to the method doctors around the world still use to test for exposure to tuberculosis. Fleck called it the exanthin reaction. Yet after receiving his doctorate for this work, Fleck found he had no options in academia. There were a few Jewish scientists in Weigl's laboratory—Karolina Reisowa, who had been a colleague of Weigl's in Nusbaum-Hilarowicz's lab, worked on amphibian development; Adam Finkel was a specialist in the blood problems of louse feeders—but both had won their positions under the Habsburgs. Professional advancement in the new Polish republic grew increasingly difficult in the years between 1920 and 1939. Weigl tried hard to help his erstwhile assistant. His best friend was the leading dermatologist in town, Jan Lenartowicz, who hired Fleck in 1923 as a bacteriologist in the Department of Skin and Venereal Diseases at Lwów's General Hospital. In the footnotes of Fleck's scientific papers from this period, one finds frequent expressions of thanks to Weigl for materials and guidance, an indication that the two scientists maintained a connection. In 1923, Fleck married Ernestyna Waldman, a scientific technician and the daughter of a wealthy Stryj merchant. With her dowry, he bought himself a private laboratory that he would use to enhance his earnings from the state jobs he held over the next 12 years. Perhaps Weigl attended the wedding, or at least sent a gift, but all evidence of this sort disappeared in the turbulent decades that followed. Indeed, practically the only memorabilia we have of Fleck's interwar life are the papers he published in scientific journals, mostly in Polish and German.

A few of his contemporaries state that Fleck had a difficult personality in these years—they remark on a degree of sarcasm and bitterness at his exclusion from the mainstream. But bitterness seems to have stimulated rather than discouraged his intellectual curiosity. He assembled a network of friends from various intellectual arenas, and their discussions helped him create a new philosophy of science. The mathematician Steinhaus was one of Fleck's closest friends; they often worked together and published papers using statistical analyses of serological problems—an approach very much ahead of its time. It is amusing to imagine their discussions in the Roma or the Załewski, which was Steinhaus's favorite café. But Fleck was notoriously stingy with his money and was clearly pressed for time, so it's possible that he was the rare Lwów professional who lacked a café *Stammtisch*. Fleck also had regular contact with philosopher Kazimierz Twardowski, the artist-mathematician-philosopher Leon Chwistek, and the psychiatrist

Jakob Frostig, an insightful and amusing conversationalist who knew most of the leaders of psychiatry in Europe, including Freud and Jung. Frostig, who treated schizophrenics with bold but dangerous treatments such as insulin coma and malaria therapy, fled Nazism in 1939 and eventually landed in California, where for several years he worked at the Camarillo State Asylum.

Fleck could get books at the Lwów university library, one of the best in Poland, and his colleagues were available to explain the latest developments in Einsteinian physics, logic, and math.

In 1927, Fleck, then 31, won a six-week fellowship at the State Institute of Serotherapy in Vienna. After completing his work there, he did an intellectual tour d'horizon of Western Europe, attending lectures by Freud in Vienna and Henri Bergson in Paris. According to one source, he visited the Pasteur Institute and the Frankfurt laboratory of the great immunologist Paul Ehrlich. Upon returning to Lwów, he took over the bacteriological lab at the Social Security Hospital, where the pediatrician Dr. Franciszek Groër—another close friend of Weigl's—was his mentor.

Groër, the leading pediatrician in town, was a nutrition expert, organizer of the first pediatric bone marrow transplant in Poland, and an extremely cultivated individual. The son of an attorney and an actress, he also wrote poetry and took beautiful photographs of the city, spoke eight languages fluently, and for a while directed the Lwów opera. The example of his polyglot boss encouraged Fleck's budding absorption in the philosophy of science.

Fleck's early work in this area was inspired by observing how Weigl had maneuvered around what was known and unknown about typhus. One of the key attributes of *R. prowazekii* at the time was its incapacity to grow in artificial broths. Yet, Weigl acknowledged in a 1924 paper, another scientist who worked for a while in his lab had managed to get the bacteria to flourish in a dish. When Weigl injected lice with these cultures, however, they did not become ill with typhus. If *R. prowazekii* was growing in the dish, he said, it probably had adopted a mutated form that no longer caused the disease. Could it still be properly called *R. prowazekii*? At the time, Weigl was one of the only microbiologists of any renown who continued to doubt the fixity of bacterial species. Fleck shared his skepticism. Their confusion stemmed from the fact that mutation is rapid and extensive within bacterial species—an idea whose time had not yet come. In the early decades of bacteriology, the techniques of microbial genetics belonged to the future. Identification of organisms depended on rough postulates and simple observation. Since physical appearance was one of the only ways scientists had to identify a germ, they became frustrated when these organisms eluded definitions by assuming shifting forms.

By the mid-1920s, when Fleck began working on his philosophical examinations of science, Weigl had learned to grow *R. prowazekii* in the intestines of successive generations of lice, to remove the bacteria from the insects and kill the typhus germs. He tested the formulation as a vaccine on animals throughout the 1920s. Occupied as he was with these pragmatic issues, and under increasing pressure from the Polish state to begin vaccinating people, Weigl had no time for philosophical matters related to the morphing of *R. prowazekii*. But they continued to fascinate Fleck, who had been present in Weigl's lab when the science was being born. Fleck's Jewishness excluded him from some circles of academic life in Lwów. But as a hands-on diagnostician he confronted the complexities of bacterial forms on a daily basis, and this led him to new insights into the nature of scientific discoveries and categories. The problems with *R. prowazekii*, Fleck would argue, showed how scientific truths were contextual, depending in part on what society was asking science to do.

Shortly after returning from Vienna late in 1927, Fleck appeared before the Lwów Society for the History of Medicine—a club that was attended by doctors and biologists, but also by geologists, mathematicians, and others of an intellectual turn of mind—to present his first philosophical paper, "On the Specific Characteristics of Medical Thinking." In the paper, Fleck noted that "there is no specific border between

Mugshot of Ludwik Fleck. (Courtesy of
Archiv für Zeitgeschichte, Zurich.)

sickness and health, and a sickness never really presents exactly the same way." Yet the purpose of medicine was to make all the variations of illness fit into a single framework and give it a single name. "How do we find a law for lawless phenomena?" Fleck asked. "This is the basic question of medical thinking. Only statistical observations allow us to create a type out of the many individual cases."

The specificity of disease was a rapidly evolving concept in Fleck's time; in no other field were there so many entities described as "pseudos" (i.e., *typhoid* fever as opposed to typhus), "paras" (e.g., parainfluenza), and other subtypes, which often had nothing to do with each other. Imagine the bearded family house doctor in three-piece suit and watch chain arriving at a Polish bedside in the late 1920s, confronted at once by the habitual terror of serious illness and by the confusing welter of contradictory scientific information arriving in the medical journals—if he bothered to keep up with them. Despite the profusion of new observations in this period of the medical sciences, there were scant new effective disease treatments. In Fleck's learned view, the doctor was probably better off ignoring the literature. Intuition and experience, rather than logic, were the keys to diagnosis, because even

the presence of a particular bug didn't mean anything definitive—
the patient might merely be a carrier. "Only a combination of symptoms and even appearances, *Habitus* (attitude), the entire status of the
patient, decides [the diagnosis]. It is precisely the best diagnosticians
who are most frequently unable to explain why they have given a particular diagnosis, but can only say that the whole picture fits such and
such an illness." Doctors were constantly confronted with "illogical" or
"impossible" medical conditions that could not be effectively broken
down, but only attacked as a total picture, on the basis of the clini-
cian's experience and instincts. Quacks, homeopaths, and psychoana-
lysts were the only practitioners who claimed to have precise, logical
systems of classification, Fleck said: "In medicine we have the rather
unique circumstance that the worse a doctor is, the more 'logical' his
therapy. In medicine you can find evidence of anything, while to date
we've clarified almost nothing."

Fleck's work was "probably the first sociological investigation of
the production of scientific knowledge," according to the sociologist
Thomas Schnelle. And though unheralded, it launched an entirely
new way of looking at the activities of science, viewing them as a collective activity that was just as subject to human foibles as any other
endeavor. Ironically, Fleck launched his ideas shortly after the American writer Paul de Kruif published *Microbe Hunters*, a 1926 bestseller
that put the "great man" squarely at the center of scientific history
and inspired a generation of youthful scientists with its profiles of
heroism. Fleck did not respond directly to this book (which became
very popular in a 1938 Polish edition), but his writing in these years
attacked the legends of heroism that de Kruif and others wove around
new discoveries. Fleck portrayed scientific progress as the work of
thought collectives, not supermen. This had to be so, because the scientist saw only what he was trained to see: "What actually thinks
within a person is not the individual himself but his social community," Fleck wrote. "His mind is structured under the influence of this
ever-present social environment."

Fleck's work anticipated the idea that scientific understandings are shaped by their cultural and historical context. One writer has described him as "a Gregor Mendel of the history and philosophy of science." But his ideas are probably most similar to those of anthropologist contemporaries like Franz Boas. Fleck, like the physicist Thomas Kuhn, was deeply invested in science and tremendously excited by its future. The culturally determined aspect of science was not, for Fleck, a detriment to its advance. What worried him most was the divorce of science and the humanities, for he saw science as the ultimate democratic activity. Unlike religions, in which priests or the "saved" held secrets that gave them power over the masses, science discovered truths that could be shared with everyone. But though society provided scientists with the problems it wanted solved, Fleck wrote, the methods and thoughts of each discipline grew steadily less accessible to the public. Scientists tried to simplify explanations of their activity in order to gain funding, fame, and popular sympathy, yet their work itself was opaque. The ideas popularly understood to be the meat and potatoes of science—"human genome," "brain chemistry," and "global warming," might be good examples in our time—were understood by scientists to be shorthand for infinitely more specific and difficult processes, which required more and more specialized scientific craft and know-how. Wrote Fleck,

> We used to think that science one day would somehow open
> to our understanding in a clear and simple way that secretive
> complex that we call nature. Instead, science itself has become
> a model that is more difficult and complex than nature itself
> and even more difficult to penetrate. It is easier to find yourself
> in the woods than to understand botany. It's easier to heal a
> sick person than to really understand what is wrong with him.

In debunking the view that scientific truths were fixed and eternal, Fleck partook of the avant-garde spirit of his age and place. His

ideas echoed those of the surrealist artist and writer Ignacy Witkiewicz (1885–1939), who was close to Fleck's friend Leon Chwistek. Fleck
and Witkiewicz grasped the essential void of meaning in a universe
in which science was viewed, by the intelligentsia at least, as the new
arbiter of truth, yet an impossibly incomplete (not to say misunderstood) system, and one that lacked an intrinsic morality. Fleck looked
forward with a humanist's optimism to the shades of color and light
that science would gradually reveal. Witkiewicz, on the other hand,
mourned the holes that science punched in holistic versions of the
world. He extolled art over science because it "did not cut the umbili-
cal cord that links it to the whole. [Art] pulsates with the blood of mystery, the vessels float into the surrounding night, and come back filled
with a dark fluid." As the historian of science Ilana Löwy has written,
both Fleck and Witkiewicz "strived to unsettle the existing concept of
reality and to construct a different one, developing new, original con-
ceptual or material tools that could enable this to happen."

Witkiewicz, who had seen the Bolshevik revolution close-up in St.
Petersburg in 1917, committed suicide in response to the 1939 invasion
of Poland, an event predicted in his novel *Insatiability*. Fleck's fate
would be far more difficult and complex.

CHAPTER THREE

THE LOUSE FEEDERS

A s Fleck developed his private laboratory practice in the early 1930s, Rudolf Weigl's work also began to take on a more routinized rhythm. Weigl had assembled a team of talented investigators, among them Zbigniew Stuchly, Jan Starzyk, and Henryk Mosing, a farsighted epidemiologist with spiritual inclinations who organized expeditions to the remotest Carpathian villages. The public health authorities of Poland had taken a growing interest in Weigl's vaccine, but he was in no hurry to test it, let alone push the vaccine into production. He insisted on carrying out hundreds of passages of typhus from louse to louse to various animals and back to lice again. He even tried adapting pigs as lice feeders. Weigl was extremely mindful of past experiences in which pathogens kept alive via serial passage through different animals underwent a genetic shift and a change in virulence—becoming either weaker or more dangerous.

One could say that Weigl dithered on the next step, which was human testing of the vaccine. More charitably, one could say that he was conscious of his lack of a medical degree and metabolically inclined to great deliberation. Whatever the case, Weigl never conducted a clinical trial of his vaccine, and until 1930 did not even vaccinate his staff. Weigl's hesitation on this step is striking and contrasts sharply with the histories of more ambitious or fame-hungry investigators who pushed for human testing in order to establish themselves as scientific leaders. The first human experiment with the Weigl vaccine was published not in Lwów but in Tunisia, where the Pasteur Institute had taken a great interest in the vaccine.

The labs in Lwów and Tunis had developed a strong bond, mediated through the scientist Hélène Sparrow, a Russian-born, half-Polish, half-British scientist who fled to Warsaw in 1920 and spent the next 13 years working on public health and vaccination campaigns under Ludwik Hirszfeld at the National Institute of Hygiene. She also spent time in Paris, in Mexico, and in Weigl's laboratory, before joining the Pasteur Institute in Tunis, where she introduced Charles Nicolle to Weigl's louse-inoculating techniques. In 1928, Nicolle and Sparrow vaccinated four children, ages three to seven, with vaccine that Weigl had provided them during a visit to his institute. Several months to a year later, the children were injected with live typhus germs from an infected guinea pig brain. While certainly unethical by modern standards, this experiment had behind it a kind of logic. Typhus and some other pathogens, particularly viruses, are rarely fatal to children, in whom they produce less serious disease. The trial was a success in that the children remained well. The Pasteur Institute subsequently vaccinated all of its typhus specialists with the Weigl vaccine.

Shortly afterward, Weigl's earliest collaborator, the lab technician Michał Martynowicz, decided to take things into his own hands in Lwów. Weigl had organized the laboratory so that only staff who had previously suffered typhus, and thus were presumably immune, could feed typhus-infected lice or work on other lab problems involving live typhus germs. Martynowicz, who had suffered a bout during World War I in Serbia, fed infected lice, while his wife, Rozalia, fed healthy ones. Without Weigl's permission, Martynowicz vaccinated his wife repeatedly, and she then began feeding cages of typhus lice. "When I learned of this experiment I stopped it immediately," Weigl wrote, "but by that time she had already been bitten hundreds of times." Rozalia, to everyone's satisfaction, did not become ill. She was permitted to

Weigl, Sparrow, and the Nobelist Charles Nicolle, Lwów, 1938.
(Courtesy of National Museum, Przemyśl. Photograph of
original by S. Kosiedowski.)

continue feeding the lice. And gradually, Weigl was pushed to allow
the vaccine to transition from an experimental phase to public use.

By the late 1920s, Weigl's lab had become a mecca for serious typhus
researchers. The endless supply of typhus germs he could offer visiting
scientists was well worth the eight-hour train ride from Warsaw or the
two-day trip from Vienna. And come they did—French researchers
from the Pasteur Institute, Germans from the Koch Institute in Berlin
and the Institute for Naval and Tropical Diseases in Hamburg, Americans from Columbia and Harvard, Russians and Romanians, Britons,
Czechs, and Danes. One of the visitors was Hilda Sikora, a self-taught,
Madagascar-born parasitologist who had been trained by Rocha Lima
in Hamburg. Sikora was a talented artist who drew extremely detailed
anatomical sketches of lice and continued to work with them even after
developing a severe asthmatic reaction. She observed every habit and
preference of the tiny vermin with an attentiveness that tottered per-
versely on the border of love. (She was not alone in her passion: Zinsser

once wrote, "One cannot carry pill boxes full of these little creatures under one's sock for weeks at a time without developing what we may call, without exaggeration, an affectionate sympathy; especially if one has taken advantage of them for scientific purposes and finds each morning a corpse or two, with others obviously suffering—crawling languidly, without appetite, and hardly able to right themselves when placed on their backs.") Sikora's personality was perhaps fitting for this arcane field; she was single and ran a cat shelter in her home and some-times came to the office with a pet snake, which would pop out of her lab coat pocket as she spoke with colleagues, testing the air with its forked tongue. Yet she knew as much about typhus as anyone in the field. The Nazis at the Hamburg institute fired her in 1943 because of her independent attitudes, and she spent the rest of her life as a painter in Vienna.

Weigl's reluctance to test his vaccine on people may have stemmed from the series of terrible accidents that occurred in his laboratory. Over a decade, the lab saw at least 10 typhus outbreaks, including one that claimed the life of Edmund Weil of Prague, co-inventor of the Weil-Felix diagnostic test. Weil had come to Lwów, in search of typhus germs, in May 1922. He dreamed of creating a typhus vaccine and thought he might do this by keeping *R. prowazekii* alive in small mammals. While inoculating a rabbit at Weigl's side, Weil acciden-tally splashed his eye with an emulsion of louse intestines. Disregard-ing the accident, he finished his work and returned home, but fell sick and died two weeks later. Weigl's son Wiktor also got typhus, while playing in the laboratory. Yet rather than keeping researchers away, the risk of typhus seems to have attracted them. "The Weigl laboratory was surrounded with an aura of secrets and anxiety, partly because the work there was dangerous," said Władysław Wolff, who joined the lab in 1928. "A young person was attracted to that—because it was dangerous, and because of the strange things people were doing there. It was romantic, an adventure."

Around this same time, Rajchman and Hirszfeld at the Hygiene

Institute began to press Weigl to release supplies of his vaccine for cleanup efforts against typhus in Poland. Some 300 Polish doctors died fighting typhus between 1915 and 1929, and it was not easy to enroll unprotected medical staff in these campaigns. There is no record of communications between Weigl and the health authorities regarding this matter, but the Weigl lab began to increase production, to about 30 doses per day by the end of 1930, and to more than 100 per day a few years later. In 1931 and 1932, Polish authorities vaccinated a total of 2,794 people, mostly medical staff and others who came into close contact with typhus patients. Only one case of typhus was reported in the vaccinated group, with the exception of a few instances in which typhus had been incubating in patients prior to vaccination. The campaign lacked scientific rigor: vaccines were distributed on the basis of perceived need, and no effort was made to randomize the results or provide placebo to staff in dangerous areas. Yet the anecdotal evidence offered a powerful suggestion that the vaccine worked. And the news of its success began to trickle out of Lwów and into the wider world.

In the summer of 1931, in a clearing near the family's house at Ilemnia, young Wiktor Weigl looked up from his mud pies and saw a curious figure—a tall man in flowing dark robes and a ridiculously wide-brimmed black hat. The visitor, crossing the stream toward the house in the company of two local mountain men, was Josef Rutten, a Belgian priest resident in China. He had been trying to track down Weigl for a year. Rutten led the Scheut missionaries, who worked in some of the poorest villages of Mongolia and northern China, barren areas, freezing cold in the winter, where lice were plentiful and typhus rife. Since 1908, Rutten explained to Weigl, the disease had killed 84 of his priests—nearly half. The mission was spread across vast, desolate areas, and there was no way to avoid lice infestations. Could Weigl help him? Weigl immediately provided 600 doses of the vaccine to Rutten, who returned to Beijing and called together his 200 priests for three rounds of vaccination over a month. During the next several years, the only member of the Scheut order to die of typhus had not been present for the vaccinations. Elated by the vaccine's efficacy, Rutten sent Zhang Hanmin, a student from the microbiology department at Fu Jen Catholic University, to Lwów, where he spent several months learning Weigl's technique before returning to establish a louse-vaccine production facility in China.

Vaccination and delousing campaigns were also organized in various typhus-endemic regions of Poland, in particular south of Lwów. Piotr Radło, a Hygiene Institute officer, Weigl confidante, and district physician in the town of Jaworow, traveled frequently with public health scientists to the isolated mountain towns. In the 1930s, they fought outbreaks of the disease around two small Carpathian towns, to prevent it from spreading to Skole, a prosperous summer resort, and to nearby ski areas. By 1938, about 68,000 Poles had been vaccinated; by March 1940, the number had increased to 160,000. Among the vaccinated there were only 30 recorded cases of typhus, and no deaths. Weigl's vaccine contributed to a dramatic decrease in typhus in Poland, though most of the decline was probably due to other public health measures like louse control. Overall, the number of cases sank from 44,000 in 1919 to 8,500 in 1922 and to 400 in 1929. There were never more than 1,000 per year from 1930 until the beginning of the war.

As Weigl's fame grew, lab administration and the entertainment of visiting dignitaries chewed up more and more of his time, which he did not appreciate. When he got a chance, he'd skip town and head for the Carpathians to join his boys. "When he came to our field lab he became himself again," recalled one of his assistants. "They'd call him from Lwów, saying he had an important visitor, but he preferred to stay with us and look through our microscopes, and in the afternoons we'd go fishing and he'd tell us anecdotes from his life, the happy and jovial professor. When his train left the station in Slawsko, he'd wave out the window a long time." A grainy film that Radło produced in the early 1930s shows the Lwów physicians and technicians driving a Red Cross panel truck over mountain roads to mud-and-thatch dwellings where women washed clothes by beating them on rocks in the river, and families harvested wheat with scythes. The sight of a motor vehicle was rare enough to bring whole villages out to have a look. The public health men set up delousing tents and fumigated houses with hydrogen cyanide while vaccinating peasant leaders and caregivers. Some of the people in the region were religious Jews; many others were Hutsuls—an isolated highland people who spoke their own dialect of Ukrainian. Entire villages surrendered their clothes and entered large white field tents, naked, while their clothes were disinfected in large steam kettles. Young boys happily bathed in cauldrons of hot water provided by the fieldworkers. If there were no roads to the afflicted towns, the doctors brought their gear on horseback over rough and muddy trails.

The fieldwork gave Weigl's team new insights into the survival of typhus in nonepidemic periods. They noted that when a Hutsul man died, his clothes were kept in the family attic. Louse feces in these clothes, it turned out, could still infect a guinea pig several months after their wearer had died. Lice lived comfortably in the folds of the peasants' gaily colored sheepskins, protected by the ill repute in which their wearers held bathing. In many rural parts of Poland, peasants put on their jackets in the fall, fastened them with wire, and took them off in the spring. The hygiene teams found that, vaccination aside, the best way to combat typhus was to encourage village elders to buy a few extra shirts and nightgowns, and to wash them regularly throughout the winter.

As the vaccine passed from an experimental to a manufacturing phase, Weigl's staff in the early 1930s grew to about a dozen scientists with an equal number of technicians and assistants, and more and more louse feeders. The expansion of the Weigl lab and the growing demand for his vaccine required technical innovation. To raise millions of healthy lice, one needed improved systems to breed, infect, and harvest the lice. In the system devised by Weigl and his staff, larvae hatched in temperature-controlled cabinets were put in matchbox-size cages to feed on human blood twice a day for about 10 days. The next

Putting lice into a Weigl clamp. (Courtesy of Emil-von-Behring-
Bibliothek, Philipps-Universität Marburg.)

step was to inject a diluted, typhus-contaminated slurry of louse guts
into the rectums of the healthy lice. Initially, Weigl injected each louse
by hand, placing it on a slide or a paper card and injecting a pipette
attached to a piece of tubing taped over the end of a syringe. Gradually, he mechanized the technique, attaching the pipettes to a hydrau-
lic, foot pedal–controlled pump that squirted a microdroplet of the
emulsion into the louse rectum once the pipette had been moved into
place. A device known as the Weigl clamp held as many as 50 lice at a
time immobile, with their rear ends presented for injection.

After the artificially infected lice had fed on blood again for about
five days, they swelled and turned ruby red. This signified that the
growing bacterial population in the cells lining the louse intestines
had caused them to leak or even burst, which rendered the creatures
incapable of digesting the fresh blood they fed upon. At this point, the
cages were removed and the lice taken to the *preparatorzy* (dissectors),

who used a small lancet to remove the blood-filled intestines, which were crushed and homogenized in a mortar, centrifuged to remove cellular debris, and diluted in saline solution with enough phenol to kill the bacteria. The dead bacteria could no longer infect a person, but the intact proteins in the dead bugs stimulated a person's immune system to protect against typhus.

Vaccination of a large population required mind-boggling amounts of lice nourished on the blood of patient human feeders. Weigl estimated in 1924 that each infected louse intestine contained 10 to 100 million bacteria, and that each individual required the neutralized contents of about 5 billion of these germs to be fully immunized. The first vaccination series Weigl designed contained the ingredients of 350 louse intestines, split into three shots spaced over two- to three-week intervals. The total was reduced to 175 intestines after a few years, and by 1935 Weigl recommended a total of 90 intestines per three doses. The vaccine could be preserved in a refrigerator for three years; immunity lasted at least a year after the third vaccination.

The need for lice feeders was enormous as demand for vaccine grew. By the end of 1933, there were 50 people feeding lice at least once a day in the lab. Many were staff members, others hired to perform this very exotic form of blood donation. It was one of the creepiest jobs one could imagine, but Weigl and his staff were rather matter-of-fact about it. An associate provided the following job description: "Lice feeders must be chosen with care. We recommend the choice of mature men, with calm temperaments and skin that is healthy and smooth. They must have no predisposition to skin conditions such as eczema or uticarias. They must be capable of great patience and self-control—in order to resist the desire to scratch. They must be well behaved and assiduous about cleanliness. Their workplace must have a shower that they make regular use of." Adam Finkel, a hematologist working in the Weigl lab, noted in a 1933 publication that 100 lice—about enough to make a three-dose vaccine series—typically sucked up to 40 milligrams of blood in 15 minutes;

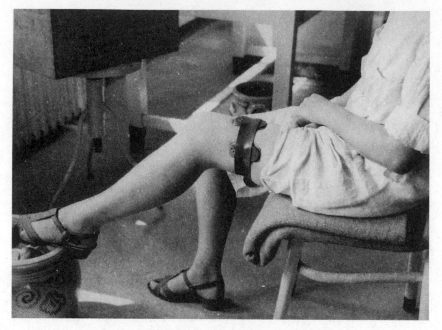

A louse feeder. (Courtesy of National Museum
of Health and Medicine.)

they had to feed twice a day for eight days before they were ready to
harvest. A typical louse feeder nourished 30,000 lice at a time, meaning that the blood of one person feeding lice for a little over a week
could provide vaccine for 300 people. Longtime feeders often developed allergic reactions that forced them to stop feeding. They also
had to be careful about their own nutrition. Feeding 30,000 lice twice
a day resulted in the loss of about 720 grams (a pound and a half) of
blood in one month.

If the work was perilous, the mood was often playful. Weigl was
curious about the private lives of his young employees, and enjoyed
occasionally visiting art studios and bars with them. He allowed his
staff to make amateur films in the institute. One shows a "Louse Theater" production put on by the epidemiologist Piotr Radło, featuring
such titles as "Heroic Expeditions of the Horsemen of Death" and
"Work Is No Dishonor." Weigl was an idiosyncratic boss. Writing was

torture and a waste of time as far as he was concerned. His lack of interest angered assistants, because it reduced the number of publications they could put on their résumés. His style was to allow junior scientists to develop their own questions and experimental designs. He approved of independence, but when unimpressed by a person or idea, did not hide his displeasure.

Whatever Weigl was doing involved a certain degree of obsessive perfectionism. He always had the latest mechanical devices—though he never owned a car—and often made small improvements on them. For instance, he insisted that pots be set on a medium flame for most efficient heating, and that phosphorescent matches be struck at a certain angle in order to have the best chance of lighting. In his laboratory, Weigl designed microscope lens adjustment knobs adopted by the German companies Reichert and Zeiss. He neither requested nor received royalties. Weigl's employees learned not to approach him while he was walking in the Botanical Garden, where he elaborated his thought. He usually addressed them with a familiar "you," or "my child," or *dziecinko*, roughly translatable as "kiddo." If he used the formal *pan* (Mr.), it meant something was wrong, or important.

Deeply immersed in work, Weigl often seemed oblivious to his surroundings. On one occasion, goes a story that circulated in the lab, Weigl was staying at the Bristol Hotel in Warsaw and after a meeting at the health ministry asked the taxi driver to take him to the best restaurant in town, which turned out to be in the Bristol itself. After lunch he forgot where he was staying, but the waiters called around until they found him reserved at the Bristol. By then, however, Weigl had forgotten where he was, so he left the restaurant, got into a taxi, and asked the puzzled driver to take him to the Bristol.

In 1935, Weigl's family had moved to new digs, a spacious five-bedroom house at Poniński 31, with one side looking out over the grounds of the Eastern Trade Fair at Stryj Park, the other on undeveloped hills with orchards and meadows. Weigl took the trolley car the two miles to work each day. Once he boarded without any money and explained to the driver that he was Rudolf Weigl and would pay twice when he returned the next day. "Sure, you're Weigl—and I'm Napoleon," the conductor said. The tabloids presented him as the mad professor of Lwów, keeping lice and feeding them on himself. Once Wiktor and his father were in an outdoor market in the Jewish quarter, and his father selected some items from the stall of an old man, then walked off absent-mindedly without paying. When he returned apologetically, the man said, "Oh, I knew you'd be good for it, Professor." As they walked away, Weigl turned to his son and said, "You see, I can't even steal anything anymore.'"

As vaccine production grew, the institute started to have space problems. Weigl had a certain feline sensitivity to his surroundings, and he didn't want to abandon the basement offices where he worked. So he decided to raise their ceilings by digging, at great cost, huge holes in the ground to incorporate new sewage, gas, and electric lines. Once the new rooms were finished, Weigl went into the studio, sat down on a chair, got up, and sat down again. He told a laboratory assistant to sit in the chair and asked him, "What do you feel?" The assistant looked puzzled, but then another aide came in and said the ceiling was still too low. At Weigl's command, the floor was again broken up, and the entire installation rebuilt. The rooms were painted gold and silver. The money Weigl spent on his finicky feng shui came from an award he'd won, and it would have been enough, a tut-tutting aide noted, to build an entirely new, modern facility with good biosecurity.

That the new Polish state had an anti-Semitism problem became clear to the world in late November 1918, with the worst pogrom in Lwów's history. The slaughter followed a three-week battle for control of the city between Polish and Ukrainian soldiers, a conflict in which Jewish authorities stayed on the sidelines. Armed Poles repaid what they viewed as Jewish disloyalty by allowing the massive destruction of the Jewish quarter. Three days of brutality left 73 dead, 463 injured, and thousands homeless. In 1919, when an American delegation visited Poland to investigate anti-Semitism on behalf of President Woodrow Wilson, none of the Polish newspapers published the statement of goodwill they drew up on arrival. Poles were angry that Wilson had dictated to them the requirement to give minorities equal rights. Both Zionists and Polish nationalists the delegates met described Judaism as a race, not simply a religion. The mixture of optimism and cynicism the delegation detected among Jews, the aggression and grievance of the Poles, were perhaps typical for this time. In Lwów, the delegates found that "the best Poles did not try to excuse the pogrom, but said it was a blot on the name of their city; in other places which we had visited there was always an attempt to deny that anything had taken place, or else it was excused on the ground that the Jews were Bolsheviks."

In the interwar years, there seemed to be as many facets to Jewish-Polish relations as there were Jews and Poles who lived through them. Wacław Szybalski, the son of a wealthy businessman from an old noble family, said that assimilated Jews were an accepted part of his universe. "I personally didn't know whether anyone was Polish or Jewish," he told me during an interview at his lab in Wisconsin in 2010. "We bought our groceries from Friedman. They were Jewish, but my parents never said so, and I didn't know it. Of course, the working-class people, who spoke Yiddish and had beards and so on, were unknown to me." Venturing into the Jewish ghetto, beyond the Opera House, "was like visiting a foreign country."

There were many places in Lwów where Jews, Poles, and Ukrainians assembled together—drinking coffee at the Szkocka and the Załewski, guffawing in the theater, or roaring with laughter by their radios every Sunday over the schlocky slapstick of Tońko and Szczepko. In April 1936, during days of riots sparked by the funeral procession of Ukrainian laborers in which police killed eight protesters, the workers marched 10 abreast with militant slogans painted on banners in Polish, Ukrainian, and Yiddish. The violence of that day in central Lwów made a powerful impact on the young people who witnessed it as a harbinger of things to come. Yet the demonstrations were unified across ethnic lines.

The delicate balance between ethnic conflict and normality is exemplified in a May 1929 outburst that began when a Catholic procession passed by a Jewish school. As the Jewish girls craned their necks to get a view, one fell off a stool and started to cry, causing her companions to laugh. People in the procession took the laughter as a Jewish profaning of their faith, and after it was reported in the anti-Semitic press, thugs supporting the anti-Semitic Endeks (National Democratic Party) began smashing windows of Jewish businesses on the thoroughfares of Legionów and Kopernika. When a crowd raided the school and started beating students, police intervened and made 40 arrests. Piłsudski's interior minister flew into Lwów and quashed the violence, but he refused to meet with the students or their teachers.

Jews and Poles who were polite enough toward each other in public tended not to associate in private—though there were plenty of exceptions to the rule. The causes of this coolness were complex. Frank Stiffel, a Lwowite who would survive both Treblinka and Auschwitz, recalled that as a young man he lived on the same floor as the mathematician Stefan Banach. The two families never greeted each other, which Stiffel attributed to anti-Semitism on Banach's part. But Banach's wife was Jewish and what the Stiffels assumed was prejudice was just as likely the distracted behavior of a man with his head in abstract clouds of thought.

For Jews, the interwar period in Lwów and Poland in general was also a period of thriving cultural expression when many great ideologies and movements were born or came of age. Yiddish theater took off, Zionism and the socialist-motivated Bund expanded, and the mainstream Jewish political movement, Agudat Israel, grew in power. Few Jews joined the Polish Communist Party, but the tiny party's leaders were disproportionately Jewish.

In the aftermath of the Holocaust, anti-Semitism in any form has an equally powerful taint. In the Poland of the 1930s, however, anti-Semitism was usually less hate-filled than it was in Nazified Germany. It was more of a symptom of economic competition between two largely segregated communities that viewed prosperity as a zero-sum game. To a large degree, the new Polish state saw ethnic Poles as its sole constituency. It discriminated against Jews as a backlash against the racial tolerance of the empire, which had not favored Poles over other subjects who lived in the lands that were now Poland. Up until the the start of World War I, some 70 percent of the lawyers and 60 percent of doctors in Lwów were Jews, as were many traders and shop owners. During the economic turmoil of the 1930s, nationalists portrayed Jews as outsiders who hogged Polish resources. Especially in the 1930s, the state encouraged them to emigrate to Palestine. Its other actions against the Jews were relatively mild when compared with those of the Germans.

More alarming were the outbreaks of violence, especially on college campuses. Eleven of 600 Jews who applied to the Lwów medical school in 1930 were accepted; by 1937 the quota had shrunk to zero. Members of anti-Semitic student clubs, who displayed their politics with green boutonnieres, menaced the remaining Jewish students in the streets and the halls of the university, armed with razor blades slotted into wooden sticks. Of the many Jewish students beaten and attacked, at least three died. The Lwów rector dealt with such incidents by closing the university. Between October 1931 and November 1938, the university was closed about a third of the time. When a nationalist student died after attacking a Jewish self-defense group, senior university administrators attended his funeral, as if a "great national hero had fallen for God and country," a witness noted. Yet it is worth pointing out that 12,000 Lwowites, including many non-Jews, showed up in May 1939 for the burial of Markus Landesberg, a murdered Jewish polytechnical student.

The growth of institutional anti-Semitism hurt Ludwik Fleck. Though thoroughly assimilated into Polish culture, Fleck "looked

Jewish." Nationalists occasionally baited him in the streets, and associates felt that he suffered psychologically from such torments. More to the point, the nationalistic policies put a dent in his professional life. In 1935, the Social Security Hospital fired Fleck, under a new law removing Jews from senior public service. Over the first decade and a half of his career, he had been excluded first from the university, then from any and all official positions. His world, like that of all Polish Jews, was shrinking. Fleck joined an antifascist movement in Lwów and his son, Ryszard, then 11 years old, took part in a Jewish self-defense group. Yet despite the ostracism, the late 1930s were fruitful years for Fleck. His three-room laboratory at Ochronek 8, on a shady street near a busy downtown thoroughfare, was thriving. His lectures on biology and philosophy, given to the Lwów historical society and the Jewish Medical Society, were praised and well attended.

In 1933, Fleck sent a manuscript copy of his new book, *The Genesis and Development of a Scientific Fact*, to Moritz Schlick, the leader of the Vienna Circle, a prominent group of philosophers who believed that scientific statements were always verifiable, and in that sense ahistorical. This ran counter to Fleck's thought but he hoped that Schlick would find his book interesting enough to engage with him. Schlick, however, returned the book with the comment that while it was certainly scholarly, the ideas in it were wrong. German publishers had stopped printing books written by Jews around this time. A Swiss publisher released the book in 1935.

As the end of the decade approached, Poland was doing everything wrong for a nation that many could see was on the verge of being plunged into war. The country was in no way prepared to face the might of Nazi Germany or Soviet Russia. Students drilled on the grounds of the High Castle with 19th-century rifles, while mustachioed legionnaires—Piłsudski's men from the previous war—

marched proudly through the streets or rode on old nags. Meanwhile, the government squeezed the Jews, the only allies it could possibly have counted on to form a wall of solidarity against the Nazis. "Poor Poland, you are too weak to try to imitate Hitler," wrote Wiktor Chajes, an assimilated, wealthy Jew who was vice president of Lwów's municipal council.

Weigl may have been absent-minded, but he was by no means oblivious to what was happening. Though he mistrusted politicians and shunned politics, he read the papers, listened to the radio, and predicted long before many others that Hitler would threaten Poland. He hated the bravado of the military, was a radical pacifist, and had no time for the nonsense of racial hatred. In 1937, when the nationalist government passed a law requiring that Jews stand in university classes, Weigl was one of the few professors to reject it. He walked into his lecture hall one day and saw some students standing alone against the wall. "What's going on here? Why don't you sit down?" he asked. One of the nationalists explained that the standing students were Jews. "In that case," Weigl said, "I will stand until they sit."

It was during this period that Weigl became a fanatic of archery. One day he was visiting his favorite hunting shop and noticed a bow. Before long, Weigl had mastered the sport and started a Lwów archery association. He trained his son and several of his friends, including Jan Reutt, Franek Schramm, and Szybalski, who later became mainstays of Weigl's wartime laboratory. They set up their first targets in the Botanical Garden, behind his lab, and eventually began practicing on the grounds of the Eastern Trade Fair.

"Weigl was very good," recalled Szybalski. "He'd shoot from 90 meters away, while I was standing at 30. To shoot 90 meters you have to have a good strong bow. I would be shooting and his arrows would be whistling over my head—'pffft. pffft'—into the target. And he continued to do this until the end of the war." Weigl started buying bows

**Weigl at play. (Courtesy of National Museum, Przemyśl.
Photograph of original by S. Kosiedowski.)**

from all over the world and began designing and producing his own arrows, which he sometimes grooved so that they shot straighter, like bullets from a threaded barrel. He would collect data on how each type of arrow moved and correct his stance to adjust its flight. Soon Weigl's archers were among the best in Poland. As his archery skills improved, Weigl began to lose interest in firearms. On duck-hunting trips with friends he would sit in the blind and admire the sky and water and the bugs in the grass, while his friends blasted away with their shotguns. It was as if he had a premonition of what was coming. Later, he would tell a sympathetic German officer, "When I saw the NKVD and Nazis hunting people, I lost any desire to kill things."

CHAPTER FOUR

THE NAZI DOCTORS AND
THE SHAPE OF THINGS TO COME

The ethnicity of Fleck and Weigl had meant less when they were both scientists in a peaceful country working on related problems. But, if we were thinking like Fleck, we would say that he and Weigl, Jew and Pole, entered different thought collectives when the war began. Both men conducted work under the profound duress of a Nazi system that viewed them as subservient. But there were gradations in the degree of enslavement. Weigl would produce his vaccine in the service of the German army, whose medical division, though certainly not free of anti-Semitism and other corrupting influences, had as its principal objective the protection of the German fighting man. Fleck would be commandeered by doctors of the SS, whose objectives were racial, genocidal, and confused. Weigl at one point described his German overseer as "my younger colleague." Fleck's term for his boss, Erwin Ding, was "dummkopf."

In 1935, the year that Fleck's *Genesis and Development of a Scientific Fact* was published, Dr. Ding was working as a spy for the *Sicherheitsdienst* (Security Service), one of the most fearsome of the many police agencies operating under the SS chief, Heinrich Himmler. Ding carried out his missions in the baroque streets of Leipzig, Germany, filing detailed expense accounts for each one—"Streetcar ride, phone calls, investigation case 2145 (Franz)"; "phone discussion of case 2714 (Richter)." He seems to have been diligent in his work, for he earned marks of *gut* and *sehr gut* (very good) from his superiors. It is peculiar to think of secret police work as a stepping stone to eminence in medical research, which was Ding's dream. But work for the higher police units of the SS represented a bona fide in the Nazi medical thought collective. In a Nazi state that practiced mass murder to cleanse "unhealthy" elements from the body politic, the medic's responsibility was to help cure the *Volk*—the German race—not the individual patient. When Himmler heard in 1941 that German doctors were caring for prisoners slated for experiments at concentration camps, he wrote, enraged, to the senior SS doctor that medicine should "not keep the sick alive but reduce their numbers." The very idea of keeping them alive, "would cause a dog to cry," he added. Thus, Ding's occupation in 1935 was far from unusual for an SS doctor on the rise. *Obersturmbannführer* Joachim Mrugowsky, who was later Ding's boss, also took 1935 off from his medical studies, in order to head the *Sicherheitsdienst* station in the northern German city of Hanover.

Ding was the type of man whom Himmler wanted to form into an elite class of ardent Nazi professionals. He was born in Bielefeld in 1912, the bastard son of a minor noble of Saxony-Anhalt, Baron Karl von Schuler, a doctor and African explorer who left a host of illegitimate children. Illegitimacy was not an impossible hurdle on the path to success as a Nazi—Adolf Hitler, after all, was, among other things, the son of a bastard—but it was a complicating factor, especially if one's paternal bloodline could not be fixed beyond doubt. The Wehrmacht, for example, did not generally accept men born out of wedlock into its officer corps. While the SS higher ranks viewed themselves as the Third Reich's aristocracy, bitterness and social exclusion flung certain ambitious young men, including Ding, into the arms of the SS.

Ding spent the better part of a decade in a passionate attempt to establish his paternity and claim his natural father's name as his own.

The Nazi Doctors and the Shape of Things to Come

The story of his origins was bitter and tawdry. His mother, Else Braun, a secretary in a Dessau clothing factory, had had an eight-year love affair with Schuler, resulting in three sons, of whom Erwin was the youngest. During this long relationship, the charming baron constantly promised Else that it was only a matter of time before he would get his divorce and make their liaison legal. He did obtain a divorce, finally, in 1915. But this only led to a final disgrace for poor Else, because instead of marrying her, Schuler took vows with another woman—a local girl long in the tooth but with a nice dowry, the daughter of a rich coal merchant. At this point, Else, lacking other options, put her youngest boy up for adoption. "He's good child with the best characteristics— attentive, sharp, and extremely intelligent, a lively, healthy little fellow who has already survived measles and whooping cough," she wrote a prospective family in Berlin. Schuler, she told a friend, had promised to pay 1,200 Reichsmarks (roughly $6,000 in 2013 money) to anyone who would take Erwin off her hands. He lived for a while in the Peter-sohn family, then in a second household. A short time later, when Erwin was barely four years old, his mother died. After the funeral, the boy was packed off to live with yet another family, that of the Leipzig salesman Heinrich Ding and his wife.

The Dings adopted Erwin and seem to have treated him well enough, securing him a place in a prestigious Leipzig gymnasium— the German high school for profession-bound children. But they also clashed with Erwin, especially when the elder Ding objected to the teenager's fascination with the Nazi movement. When Heinrich Ding passed away in 1932, Erwin, over the objections of his adoptive mother, immediately joined the *Sturmabteilung*, the storm troopers, and became Nazi party member no. 1,318,211. That year he also graduated with honors in history and foreign languages (French and English), with notes of praise for his skills in swimming and skiing. After a strife-filled year, his adoptive mother kicked him out of the house; their final quarrel concerned his share of the father's inheritance. Ding served a year in the military and then began studying medicine. Under circumstances that are unknown, he met Himmler, who singled him out for advancement. Himmler approved of this bright, malleable young man with no ties to family, church, or antiquated moral codes that would interfere with his placement in the new native aristocracy. And now Ding's future was in the hands of the SS.

Erwin Ding, 23 years old, baby faced and five feet eight inches, with short brown wavy hair, smiles from his 1935 SS personnel file—alert and handsome, in a boyish way, though with eyes a little close together, and an expression that suggests cunning and trouble. In his résumé he writes cheerfully of his future career and the bright prospects of Nazi Germany. But how he hated his name! It was the ridicule-inspiring detritus of an unhappy childhood that he wanted to bury under a glorious career in the service of the master race. In the process of filling out the tiresome questionnaires required of all SS men, Ding launched a legal appeal to change his name to Erwin Schuler. He provided two reasons. In the first place, Ding wrote, he needed to clarify that Schuler was his father in order to show his Aryan genetic background; proof of good blood was far more significant than any lingering bitterness Erwin might have carried for this man who so cruelly used his mother. The Schuler family, according to the numerous genealogical charts Ding filled out for the SS, had an illustrious German ancestry traceable at least to the 16th century.*

The reason closest to his heart for the change, however, was that he was sick of people making fun of him. "From my earliest school days, the name *Ding* has provided my schoolmates and enemies an excuse for ridicule and teasing wordplay," he wrote in an early entreaty. "It's always been, here comes '*Ding an Sich*,' ["the thing in itself"—a reference to Kant's philosophy] or 'There goes Mr. Ding-Dong' 'the Wash-

---

*Ding was sometimes known as Ding, sometimes as Ding-Schuler, which was his preferred name until he was able in September 1944 to change it legally to Schuler; I refer to him generally as Ding, but in quotations he is often called Ding-Schuler.

Erwin Ding, 1935. (Bundesarchiv.)

lady's Ding,' and things of this nature." The name Ding, which means "thing" in German, was an albatross that the ambitious young man could never seem to shake. He obsessed over it nearly to the end of his very busy, criminal existence.

For Ludwik Fleck, 1935 was also an important year. The great hero of Polish independence, Marshal Piłsuldski, died, and the sea of black armbands worn by Piłsudski loyalists in Lwów did nothing to keep politicians of a more anti-Semitic stamp from grabbing the reins of state. "Poland was literally sick with this problem," Ludwik Hirszfeld later wrote, adding, "When I think back about the German atrocities, Polish anti-Semitism seems mild to me. Nationalism was young and, seeking to discharge itself emotionally, fell upon the Jews as the nearest suitable object."

Fleck's main source of income, his private laboratory, was relatively unaffected by the political climate, since doctors, whether Aryan or Jewish, still needed diagnostic help, and his work was held in high regard. The publication of *The Genesis and Development of a Scientific Fact* was a happy achievement, though the book received relatively little attention. Fleck's friend Chwistek, in a newspaper review, praised it as a landmark in philosophy. A few German reviewers, perhaps oblivious to the writer's ethnic origins, speculated about how Fleck's evident scientific relativism fit into the Nazi worldview, which also divided science into different categories—Aryan and non-Aryan. In Lwów, Fleck was asked to give lectures by various learned and medical societies. In 1936, he was elected chairman of the Lwów chapter of the 400-member Jewish Medical Society, and on April 21 he gave a speech at an auditorium on Mariacki Square, the central plaza of Lwów. A year later, he presented an update on new developments in infectious disease at the same locale. Fleck's lectures were advertised in the popular Jewish daily *Chwila* (Moment), published in Polish in morning and evening editions.

Fleck's book was not, ostensibly, aimed at a Jewish audience, though it must have struck a chord among scientifically trained Jews who had learned, through nationalistic exclusion, that the scientific community to which they belonged was just as subject as any other field to cultural tendencies. Fleck's marginality—his enforced independence—clearly liberated his thought. He was a practicing scientist virtually outside the academic stream, a Jew in Catholic Poland, an intellectual on the edge, in some sense, of the enlightened world. All of this may have made it easier to view the structures of the scientific establishment with a critical eye. Fleck was not shy about exposing the pathetic sham of "Jewish versus Aryan" science, but this was not the main thrust of his work. He was looking at something deeper, something constant in the complexion of human behavior.

Science, Fleck wrote, was increasingly dependent on specific techniques, methods of investigation, and instruments. There was no such thing as "pure" scientific truth, because scientists relied utterly, in their inquisitive work, on tools that were artifacts of scientific culture. Specialists no longer believed they were looking into the heart of things; they no longer pretended that any *Ding an sich*, or essence of things, was within their grasp. "When they penetrate ever deeper into objects they find themselves more distant from the 'things' and closer to the 'methods,'" wrote Fleck. "The deeper in the woods, the fewer the trees and the more numerous the woodcutters." No matter how science was practiced, he held, the procedures and concepts behind the work were shared collectively. In modern parlance, Fleck might have said that "thinking outside the box" was a rare phenomenon. In a democratic system, the scientific elite catered not only to each other but also to the interested public, which provided research money and prestige and, perhaps most importantly, validated the collective's work by spreading versions of its successful research findings. Thought collectives consisted of inner, "esoteric circles" of specialists, and what Fleck called "exoteric circles," that is, nonspecialist but interested parties. In fields other than science, the thought collectives were more elitist, keeping their distance from the outer circles through secretiveness and dogmatism. One example, in his view, was the religious organization—Fleck had observed both Jewish and Catholic forms— and another, on a lighter note, the fashion industry, with its arbitrary yet airtight requirements:

> The special mood of the thought collective of fashion is constituted by a readiness immediately to notice that which is fashionable and to consider it of absolute importance, by a feeling of solidarity with other members of the collective, and by an unbounded confidence in the members of the esoteric circle. The most dedicated followers of fashion are found far out in the exoteric circle. They have no immediate contact with the powerful dictators forming the esoteric circle. Specialized "creations" reach them only through what might be called the official channels of intracollective communication, depersonalized and thus all the more compulsive. . . . [T]hey are simply told "ce qu'il vous faut pour cet hiver" [Here's what you must wear] or "à Paris la femme porte". . . . It is coercion of the strongest kind, because it appears in the guise of a self-evident necessity and is thus not even recognized as a coercive force. And woe to the true believer who does not or cannot conform.

Dogmatism was also, of course, the characteristic of scientific thought collectives in the Soviet Union and Nazi Germany. For progress to take place, Fleck believed, the "esoteric circle" needed to interact with the outer circles. Democracy, he said, leads to the development of new ideas and to progress, while isolated elites were characterized by "conservatism and rigidity." Fleck was not a relativist about the democratic requirements of science. Stalinist and Nazi thought styles could not replace a practice that demanded free thought, even if scientific thought was not quite as unencumbered as people assumed.

Although it could rarely offer definitive answers to anything, Fleck wrote, science had to do its best to inform the public—even people with arcane specialties relied on popular versions of science to express their knowledge. To give a sense of how this worked, he provided a hypothetical case in which he was asked to examine a throat swab from a child who might be suffering from diphtheria. After conducting an examination, Fleck tells the family doctor, "The microscopic specimen shows numerous small rods whose shapes and positions correspond to those of diphtheria bacilli. Cultures grown from them produced typical 'Löffler bacilli.'"* If Fleck were communicating his findings to a fellow microbiologist, he would give a much more detailed, nuanced descriptive passage that concluded, "In view of the origin of the examined material, and the morphological and culture characteristics of the bacilli, the diagnosis of Löffler bacilli seems sufficiently well established." The parent, meanwhile, would simply be told, "'Your child has diphtheria."

The fact that the bacteria were found in the throat of a young patient with symptoms of diphtheria was crucial to the diagnosis. You had to know what you were looking for when you looked into a microscope, and your scientific acculturation inevitably shaped what you saw. If Fleck had been ignorant of the surface that had been swabbed,

*Friedrich Löffler (1851–1915) developed staining techniques that allowed him to identify diphtheria bacteria.

it would have been impossible—in 1935, anyway—for him to hazard more than a guess at the identity of these germs, whose forms and shapes were highly variable. Every expert understood this. If Fleck said as much to the family doctor, however, the latter might accuse him of cutting corners, or stating the obvious. As a member of a wider thought collective that also included, broadly, the family doctor and the patient, the scientist had to communicate on different levels to bring about a successful treatment.

> *Every communication and, indeed, all nomenclature tends to make any item of knowledge more exoteric and popular.* Otherwise each word would require a footnote. . . . Each word of the footnote would need in turn a second word pyramid. If continued, this would produce a structure that could be presented only in multidimensional space. Such exhaustive expert knowledge completely lacks clarity and is unsuitable in any practical case. . . . *Certainty, simplicity, vividness originate in popular knowledge.*

Yet the push for clarity had its costs. To get consistent results, scientists needed bacteria to be fixed and stable species. To achieve this uniformity, Fleck noted, they usually injected animals or culture plates with bacteria that had been growing in a given medium for 24 hours or less. This was more likely to provide "fixed" species, but it also meant ignoring any secondary changes that would typically occur in the bacterial cultures after they had sat an additional day or so in the petri dish.

By 1935, strict Kochian logic—the idea that bacteria inevitably cause disease—was out of date. Nicolle and others had shown that some people ("Typhoid Mary," for example) carried and could transmit bacteria without becoming ill. Scientists were starting to notice the abundance of seemingly harmless bacteria in and on the human body. Yet these observations had to reckon with a scientific culture permeated with "primitive images of war" brought down from earlier periods of human thought, Fleck wrote: "The disease demon haunted the birth of modern concepts of infection and forced itself upon research workers irrespective of all rational considerations." This was despite the fact that "man appears as a complex to whose harmonious well-being many bacteria, for instance, are absolutely essential." Imbalance, rather than invasion, was a better analogy for disease, he wrote, but in 1935 this idea was "not yet clear, for it belongs to future rather than present biology. It is found in present-day biology only by implication, and has yet to be sorted out in detail." As Fleck predicted, today we know that people are colonized by trillions of bacteria that play crucial roles in our digestion and other bodily functions. It was not until the 21st century that science began focusing in earnest on these commensal organisms.

Among the procedures Fleck worked on as a bench scientist was the Wassermann reaction. This test's value in establishing a diagnosis of syphilis was the specific "fact" Fleck examined in *Genesis and Development of a Scientific Fact*. The Wassermann test took its name from the German-Jewish scientist August Paul von Wassermann, who with colleagues at the Robert Koch Institute in Berlin announced the creation of the test in 1906. For Fleck, the development of the Wassermann reaction perfectly embodied the culturally conditioned nature of science.

First of all, the test came about because the German health minister, in competition with the French, had offered special funds to scientists to develop a quick test for syphilis. The disease had a major impact on the military and other groups, which gave it a political significance. Culturally, it symbolized the evils of fornication, and thus a blood test was seen not only as crucial to public health but also as necessary to uncovering the tainting of the blood, whose "purity" continued to have deep cultural meaning. "Thus from the very beginning," Fleck wrote, "the rise of the Wassermann reaction was not based upon purely scientific factors alone."

Fleck also found it revealing that the test that Wassermann "discovered" was not really a test for syphilis. Syphilis, an organism known as a treponeme, could not be grown easily in a petri dish. It was like typhus in this way. Since he couldn't grow pure cultures of syphilis, Wassermann used heart tissue from syphilis-infected cows. When he mixed these tissues with the blood of syphilitic patients, it caused a reaction that destroyed the red blood cells—indicating the presence of antibodies to syphilis in the patients' blood. The test had not been out long, however, when other scientists noticed that extracts of non-infected cow hearts produced the same reaction, which was caused not by the treponemes, it turned out, but by cardiolipin, a substance present in beef hearts. The Wassermann reaction, though often inaccurate, quickly became a standard tool in the medical diagnostician's handbasket. If Wassermann had been as clumsy in formulating a test against, say, athlete's foot, his inquiry probably would have ended with the initial failure. But society required action on syphilis.

Fleck was not the only scientist of this period to push against old-school bacteriological notions. The 1930s in Germany saw the growing resurgence of the ideas of Max von Pettenkofer, the Munich hygienist who had lost the environment-versus-germ argument to Robert Koch in the late 19th century. Pettenkofer believed that germs were not fundamental to infectious diseases, which he thought broke out in epidemics where populations lived in filth or had chronically bad health and nutrition. His beliefs were incorporated into an old-new theory called *Geomedizin*, whose leading practitioner was Heinz Zeiss of the Institute for Maritime and Tropical Diseases in Hamburg. Like Pettenkofer, *Geomedizin*'s followers took a holistic view of infectious disease, going beyond the presumed causative agent, the germ. But whereas the social medicine promoted by Pettenkofer's school was aimed at improving the health of individuals by improving community nutrition, water, education, and other factors, *Geomedizin* defined disease in racial and cultural terms. Zeiss and his disciples—the SS doctors Joachim Mrugowsky and Erwin Ding trained with him in Berlin in the late 1930s—amassed great influence under Nazi rule. Zeiss called his field the "science of terrain-related medicine"; a colleague elaborated that "the borders that contain a race [*Volkskörper*] also include a particular disease-causing flora and fauna. The climatic environment of a people, its cultural level, and its customs also fit into its own microworld."

Geomedizin was exactly the kind of quackish, totalizing system of thought that Fleck castigated in his book; it borrowed real scientific findings to prop up a worldview based on culture alone. Fleck viewed such belief systems as deluded claptrap. But they were dangerous beliefs, because the followers of *Geomedizin*, race hygiene, and other dubious Nazi ideas were to become medical authorities in occupied Europe. In a 1944 journal article, for example, Mrugowsky concluded that one could judge a country's level of "culture" by the types of infectious illness that predominated (diseases carried by insects [typhus] and water [typhoid fever] were characteristic of underdeveloped Southern and Eastern European cultures, he wrote; Nordics suffered primarily from respiratory illnesses). It was an entirely pointless article in terms of its scientific content, but it was not without significance, for Mrugowsky, at the time, was one of the leading SS health officers. He was responsible for medical experiments at concentration camps around Europe. He procured the Zyklon B cyanide gas that ended up being used in Auschwitz's gas chambers.

The ideology of *Geomedizin*—that illness was an irrefutable and inevitable result of culture—carried tragic significance for the Jews of Eastern Europe, for it provided an excuse for the doctors who worked with the Nazi invaders to refuse care to the Jews and to quarantine them behind ghetto walls. In Eastern Europe, with its "low cultural level, terrible poverty and lack of cleanliness, typhus is a daily disease in broad swaths of the population, especially the Jews," one *Geomedizin* follower wrote. The louse, carrier of typhus, was the symbol of the Jew in Nazi racial ideology: a filthy, parasitic, blood-sucking disease vector that had penetrated the German nation but was being massively extirpated. "The Jew is a bacillus and a plague," said Julius Streicher, editor of the Nazi newspaper *Der Stürmer*. "He is not a human being, rather an enemy, a criminal, a disease carrier, that in the interests of humanity we must eliminate." The association of lice and Jews was known to Franz Kafka when he opened his 1915 story, *The Metamorphosis*, with Gregor Samsa's waking discovery that he had been transformed into *einem ungeheuren Ungeziefer*—"a monstrous vermin." While some translators prefer "giant bug," Samsa could just as well have been louse as roach.

The belief that certain cultures were inevitable carriers of a given disease embodied what Ludwik Fleck called "proto-ideas" in medicine. An 18th-century example was Cotton Mather's belief that smallpox was caused by "animalcules." It is tempting to view this as a perceptive progenitor of the notion of infectious microorganisms, but Mather's concept was really a proto-idea, a piece of an earlier "thought style" in which the "animalcule" was no indifferent microorganism, but rather an agent of evil. In Mather's time, the invisibility of the microbial world made its denizens impossible to distinguish from the demons and angels whose existence was every bit as real as smallpox to Mather and his compatriots.

Geomedizin's suggestion that Jews were "natural" carriers of typhus stemmed from the "proto-idea" that Jews were plague carriers, parasites, and well-poisoners. This was a convenient linkage for the Nazi physicians ostensibly charged with looking out for the health of Jews. It gave a pseudo-scientific gloss to the notion of Jews as insidious, poisonous contaminants in the body politic of the Aryan race, and provided cover for the most heinous crimes. Exposure to this ideology does not excuse their actions, but even the stupidest and most venal acts flow more easily within the confines of a common thought collective.

The Germans were, of course, correct that diseases like typhus were endemic to the East, including some areas of Poland, among the very poor, Jew and Slav alike. And there were legitimate cultural explanations, many of them poverty-related, like the scarcity of running water for washing and few changes of clothing in towns and

Hermann Eyer in uniform. (Courtesy of Peter Eyer.)

shtetls where winters were hard and people grew accustomed to their lice. But the public health campaigns in Poland in the interwar period, with the contributions of men like Weigl, Rajchman, and Hirszfeld— the latter two, notably, were Jews by birth—had put Poland on the path to elimination of the disease. Typhus wasn't an inevitable consequence of belonging to a less-favored culture as long as that "culture" had the resources with which to combat typhus.

Geomedizin was the dominant philosophical turn of mind in the fields of infectious disease and public health in 1930s Germany; it was Nazi medicine. Although he was not an ideologically reliable Nazi, Dr. Hermann Eyer—who would later oversee Rudolf Weigl's work in a way that paralleled Erwin Ding's relationship to Fleck—also published within the *Geomedizin* world.

Compared with Ding or Mrugowsky, Eyer is a morally complex

figure. He served the Nazi military efficiently, and his scientific ability and organizational skills doubtless did more to strengthen the German war effort than did the clumsy sadism of the SS doctors. Yet Eyer's relationship to power remains somewhat opaque. Though his early publications suggest that anti-Semitism was part of his worldview and approach to disease, his wartime actions would demonstrate an unusual degree of civil courage.

Eyer, like Weigl, was a tinkerer and jack-of-all-trades who took a deep interest in many facets of science and technology. Born in 1906, the son of a Mannheim steel salesman, he had begun studies in machine construction before obtaining PhDs in both chemistry and medicine. Like Weigl, Eyer was skilled at fixing household objects and designing machines. He was also a lifelong practicing Catholic who saw no conflict between his scientific research and his faith. As a faculty member at the University of Erlangen in 1935, Eyer felt pressured to join the Nazi Party and became a candidate member that year, though he abandoned his candidacy after joining the military, where he believed he could pursue an academic career without deeper commitment to the Nazi cause. At this time, the Nazis had forced the well-known Jewish serologist Hans Sachs, who had been Eyer's academic adviser at the University of Heidelberg, to surrender his position; he would eventually emigrate to Ireland. According to his son, Eyer admired and respected Sachs. But the work he published following his adviser's departure suggests that Eyer had decided to seek *Gleichschaltung*, or conformity, laced as it was with the nationalistic, eugenic claptrap of the times. Eyer toured the Ostmark, an impoverished region of Bavaria lying on the Czech border, where he measured villagers' skulls to determine the "Nordic" and "Alpine" attributes of the population, and provided invidious comparisons of Czech and Bavarian "blood." He praised the anti-Semitic *gauleiter* (Nazi district chief) of the Ostmark, Hans Schemm, who had stated, among other things, that "a Jew should dangle from every lamppost." Eyer urged that the health of the area be improved "to build a natural wall on Germany's border out of responsible, duty-conscious citizens."*

In 1937, Eyer studied virology in Berlin under Professor Eugen Haagen, a fanatical Nazi who had worked several years at the Rockefeller Institute in New York. After the annexation of Austria in 1938, Eyer served several months' rotation as a troop doctor in Vienna, while training to become the army's typhus specialist. Although Germany had been a leader in typhus research in the World War I period, its best laboratory, in Hamburg, at the Institute for Maritime and Tropical Diseases, had neglected research on the disease since 1920. By the time war broke out in 1939, Richard Otto, an elderly former student of Koch and Ehrlich at Frankfurt's Institute for Experimental Therapy, was the only senior typhus expert in Germany. The Robert Koch Institute—Germany's leading scientific institution—did not even mention typhus in its official reports until 1940.

Germany profoundly trailed its European enemies in this field. Poland, of course, had the field-tested Weigl vaccine. France, with its colonial presence in North Africa, where typhus was a constant danger, was also pursuing various vaccination procedures. The Pasteur Institute's branch in Casablanca, Morocco, developed a vaccine against epidemic typhus that was made from a weakened strain of a related bacteria, *Rickettsia mooseri*. In 1938–39, physicians there led a mass vaccination campaign to protect Moroccans from the disease. This vaccine was quite toxic, however. At the outbreak of war, Pasteurians in Tunis and Paris were working on another vaccine, one based on the work of the Mexican scientist Maximiliano Ruiz Castañeda, who had demonstrated that it was possible to grow typhus germs in the lungs of immune-compromised mice. Scientists in the United States, meanwhile, had developed an entirely different vaccine production method. Dr. Herald Cox, working at the U.S. Public Health Laboratory

*Eyer's son says that an editor inserted the paean to Schemm without his father's knowledge.

in Montana in the late 1930s, found a way to grow typhus in the yolk sac of chicken eggs, which he then chemically neutralized to make a vaccine. Millions of U.S. troops were inoculated with his shot in the early 1940s. The French and U.S. vaccines would prove of some use by the end of the war, but at its outbreak Weigl's vaccine was the only field-tested prophylactic.

In Germany, the leading scientists with experience of typhus during World War I believed that quarantine and delousing were the best ways to fight the disease. Belatedly, as Germany prepared to invade Poland, a few specialists realized that German troops should have more protection before they invaded the typhus-endemic regions of Poland and the Soviet Union. The health inspectorate of the Wehrmacht was particularly worried. In April 1939, Eyer's boss sent him to Italian-occupied Ethiopia, instructing him to learn as much as possible about typhus and the Weigl vaccination method. Poland and French North Africa, though further along on typhus vaccination measures, were off limits to a Wehrmacht doctor. At the Red Sea port of Massawa (now in Eritrea), an Italian researcher named Giacomo Mariani had created a typhus laboratory that produced a Weigl-type vaccine he had learned to make in Lwów. When Eyer arrived on the Horn of Africa, Mariani greeted him personally with a syringe full of vaccine. Rudolf Weigl, who would mean so much to Eyer's military career, had left Ethiopia only a few weeks before the German doctor's arrival.

In Weigl's life, the visit to occupied Ethiopia would hold a fateful significance. In December 1938, the Italian government had invited him to spend several months there to help Mariani oversee a typhus vaccination campaign aimed at protecting the Italian occupiers and keeping them from bringing the disease home to Italy. Politically this was a difficult decision. Although the countries were not technically at war, Weigl knew that Germany, Italy's ally, intended to invade Poland. The same month that Weigl received the offer, the director of the Pasteur Institute in Morocco, Georges Blanc, had declined to host another Italian scientist who wished to study the French vaccine in Casablanca, citing fascist actions that had "darkened the political horizon."

Typhus was long established in Ethiopia and known as *yehadar hasheta*, meaning "illness of the month of Hedar," presumably because Hedar (November), at the start of the cold dry season, was the time when people began huddling for warmth and sharing lice. As Ethiopia slowly industrialized in the early 20th century, there were frequent outbreaks in up-country mines and towns where people lived in crowded conditions. Following the Italian occupation in 1935, the governor of Eritrea issued a decree requiring the compulsory inoculation of Italian civil servants and solders in contact with the "native population," as well as of all persons, "metropolitan or native," connected with hotels, restaurants, bars, cinemas, brothels, public or private transport. Fear of typhus led to Italian efforts at segregation that are reminiscent of later Nazi ghettoization plans. A September 21, 1938, order prohibited Italians and other Europeans from entering areas reserved for "natives," and Dr. Mariani argued in a 1939 article that control of the disease must be based on the "absolute and constant" separation of Italians and other foreigners from natives. He urged that the Weigl vaccine be made available to Italians and other at-risk whites, while natives got "the easiest vaccine to prepare."

In the 1930s, Weigl's vaccine had been a tool of imperial conquest in the sense that it enabled typhus-naïve missionaries and colonists to penetrate distant interiors, in places such as Manchuria and North Africa, where typhus continued to be endemic and the vaccine provided the only sure protection against death. Now Italy sought the vaccine for a similar purpose. Weigl had always wanted his vaccine to be available to all who needed it. But he could not resist the Italian invitation. In succumbing to it, he displayed characteristic scientific and human curiosity, and political tone-deafness. Weigl's son would later say of the trip, "He opposed fascism, but he welcomed the opportunity to visit an exotic country, gather new strains of *Rickettsia*, and save many lives."

In Lwów, the decision created an uproar in the Weigl household, for Zofia could not decide whether to accompany her husband. They had never been separated for so long, and 17-year-old Wiktor was studying for his *Matura*, the entrance examinations for medical school. In the end, Zofia decided to stay in Lwów to help Wiktor. Weigl brought along his associate and mistress, Dr. Anna Herzig, who was taking an increasingly important administrative and scientific role in the laboratory, as well as his trusted technician Michał Martynowicz.

In January 1939, Weigl traveled to Stockholm to give a series of lectures summarizing his research to the medical society. The possibility of a Nobel Prize seemed to be in the air, and his colleague Charles Nicolle held a Paris news conference at which he stated that Weigl "has saved the lives of thousands of people, and deserves recognition at the highest level as a leader and tireless worker, a fanatic of science." In Lwów, the Weiglovian thought collective was growing. Journalists wrote about him in the newspapers; he gave radio talks about science and evolution. The city fathers presented him with the Lwów Prize, 10,000 zlotys with no strings attached. Zofia wanted to visit the World's Fair in New York, but Weigl spent most of the money refurbishing his lab.

The university authorized a paid vacation for Weigl, Herzig, and Martynowicz from February 1 through April 30, 1939, in order to enable the Ethiopia visit. The three departed in late January from Lwów's glorious central train station, with its leather-cushioned seats and glass chandeliers. It was a bitter moment, not least because everyone knew that war was coming. Zofia wept. The separation gave everyone in the family a taste of estrangement. "I think that in devoting herself to me Mother made a big mistake," Wiktor Weigl would say, "and it would reflect negatively on our family life." Zofia Weigl was ill with cancer, though she did not realize it. For the family, Weigl's departure represented a rupture that would never really heal.

The Fantastic Laboratory of Dr. Weigl

The party went first to Rome, where Pope Pius XII met Weigl in private to award him the Knight Grand Cross of the Order of St. Gregory for his help in protecting the Belgian missionaries in China. They returned from Ethiopia in early May with bows and arrows, rhinoceros skins, and other paraphernalia and gifts, as well as homemade films to show friends and the family. Some 13,500 inoculations had been given by the end of March 1939, but there was some evidence that the Weigl vaccine was not performing well in Ethiopia. The strains that predominated in the African highlands may have been significantly different from those of Eastern Europe. The Italians reported 259 cases of typhus in the colony in 1941–42, roughly the same rate as in the preceding two years of Italian occupation.

Weigl brought back African strains of lice and *Rickettsia* that he would incorporate into his vaccine. After the homecoming celebrations, he returned to work with renewed energy. In fact, he was absent from home more than ever. Incorporating the new lice meant more time in the laboratory, with Anna Herzig, and less time at home. War was coming.

CHAPTER FIVE

WAR AND EPIDEMICS

rwin Ding obtained his medical degree in 1937 and spent his resi-
dency at an SS barracks in Berlin. In November, he married Irene
Wrazidlo, the daughter of a Leipzig venereal disease specialist.
For his state medical examination, Ding wrote and published a dissertation, a slapdash production that could not have fooled anyone as
to the writer's ignorance of the subject, on *pavor nocturnus*—night
terrors in children. In August 1938, he became the main camp doctor at Buchenwald, a place of constant terror. With his pregnant wife,
Ding rented an apartment in Weimar, and bought a motorcycle for the
five-mile ride up the mountain each morning.

Buchenwald had been created in July 1937 by German political
prisoners, mostly Communists, who hacked it out of an old royal hunting ground in the forest of the Ettersberg. Although 56,000 people
would die at Buchenwald, the camp was not established for extermination, unlike the facilities at Sobibor, Treblinka, and Belzec. Like
most of the thousands of other Nazi prison installations, Buchenwald
was designed to punish and control the enemies of the Reich while
extracting their labor until they died. The SS leader Theodor Eicke had
dreamed up this unspeakable system in 1933 at the first Nazi concentration camp, at Dachau. A metal sign reading *"Arbeit macht frei"*—
Freedom through work—hung over the entrance to the Auschwitz

and Dachau camps. A rather more mysterious and belligerent phrase, *"Jedem das Seine"*—To each his own—greeted inmates at Buchenwald.

The first glimpse of the camps has been described in hundreds, perhaps thousands of memoirs of survival—the arrival by boxcar, by truck, or, in the case of Buchenwald, on foot up the steep road from Weimar; sorting by profession, kicks and shouts and beatings administered by SS guards or by camp inmates dressed in striped uniforms with striped cloth hats; the prison uniforms sewn with their peculiar array of colored triangles that one learned, quickly, had slippery meanings—red triangles being political prisoners, though not always ones you could trust, greens common criminals, blacks "asocials" (which could mean alcoholic, or homeless, or vagrant), pinks homosexuals, blues religious dissenters, and yellows, of course, Jews.

The Germans were indifferent to the suffering of the camp inmates, and encouraged death by overwork, beatings, torture, starvation, exposure, dehydration, diarrhea, and other diseases. But there was one illness the Nazis did not want inmates to contract, and that was typhus. They feared that typhus would infect SS men, or Germans outside the camps, and they feared the spread of lice. And so, each incoming load of prisoners passed through disinfection and quarantine. At Buchenwald and other camps, the first rooms seen by new arrivals were the disinfection chambers, where the prisoners stripped and surrendered their clothes, prisoner-barbers shaved every hair from their bodies and heads, and guards chased them into gelatinous baths full of burning chemicals intended to kill any lice remaining upon them. Delousing was a regular occurrence at the camps, especially in periods of typhus epidemic, as described by an Auschwitz inmate:

> You took off your shoes and pants and you were stark naked, standing in front of your barrack. [At the bathhouse] the water was so hot it was almost scalding. . . . And there were some capos, some big shots you know, who took sadistic pride in tripping you when you tried to run out of the shower. If you were

able to get out of the bathhouse, now you had to go back in front
of your barracks, wet, naked, freezing outside, and wait until
your clothing came. And it happened time and time again. . . .
I could hear the sound in my ears when people froze to death
and fell to the ground. . . . Those were our sanitary facilities.

A single louse under some circumstances provided an excuse for
hundreds of prisoners to be stripped naked and bathed in the cold.
The resulting cases of pneumonia and other illnesses dwarfed the
public health threat of the louse, but this had no impact on camp
policy. Prisoners often puzzled at how the SS could allow a starving
prisoner to wander the camp being literally eaten by lice, while insisting that certain rooms in the hospital be kept spotless. The answer
lay in peculiarly Nazi attitudes toward Jews, dirt, and lice—an obsession that it would have taken a Freud to decode. What we can say is
that comparisons of lice and Jews were omnipresent in Nazi literature
and propaganda. Himmler himself stated that Jews were exactly the
same as lice—and by this he meant that like lice on the body, Jews
penetrated the intimate spaces of Europe with their filthy and decadent ideas and practices, that they were disgusting and omnipresent
parasites, and that modern, efficient, science-driven Germany knew
how to get rid of them.

Delousing was so routine in the Nazi realm, in fact, that at Auschwitz it could be used as a pretext to get Jews peacefully to remove their
clothes and enter the gas chambers—which were equipped with fake
shower heads.

There was no gas chamber at Buchenwald, but there was a crematorium to burn the bodies of the prisoners who died in great numbers
every day. Death in the space of several weeks or months claimed
the majority of the inmates, who had neither value to the Nazis nor
friends to look out for them. But fates could vary tremendously. Nearly
every survivor speaks of reaching a breaking point—exhaustion, illness, beating—and then being saved by the intervention of others.

The Fantastic Laboratory of Dr. Weigl

Like all the camps, but more than most, Buchenwald was run by an inmate hierarchy, signaled to a degree by the colors of the triangles on their uniforms. For the most part, the hierarchy represented an insidious system that set prisoner against prisoner while reducing German needs for manpower in the camps. A harsh pecking order offered the prisoner leadership better rations, more space, and the power to do favors for friends. But as a result of this structure, there were people in the camp who had the power to save lives. The *Block-älteste* and the *Stubendienst,* trustees who ruled the living quarters, and the capos who ran the work details, were sometimes gentle, usually brutal, and were always required to enforce the rules. Those who could not carry out the work, and lacked friends, inevitably became *Musulmänner,* "Muslims"—the camp term—no one knows why—for the beaten-down, skin-and-bones inmates who were beyond saving.

Professional status meant little in the camps. Blue-collar skills were useful because they could lead to assignment to indoor work, say, in a workshop or a factory. The SS eagerly shattered the will of professional men and women with back-breaking, calorie-depleting outside work—digging trenches, hauling stones and manure. "A few weeks in Buchenwald made it impossible to judge by anyone's appearance or face what he might have done in civilian life," wrote Walter Poller, a German labor activist brought to the camp a few months after Erwin Ding arrived. "When they stood in rank and file, the scientists beside the laborer, the clergyman beside the habitual criminal, the teacher beside the craftsman, the artist beside the imbecile, the merchant beside the tramp, it would have been hard to distinguish one from another. . . . Life in the camp nearly always destroyed one's own values and sense of dignity. Those who knew how to retain their original personalities despite all they went through were the exception, not the rule."

There were, however, a few professions in the biomedical field that, in the right circumstances, offered an advantage. Some doctors survived as camp physicians, whom the SS and capos required for a variety of reasons. Although the prison hospitals and clinics were often brutal places where mass murder of the weak occurred, at times they could be used to hide threatened prisoners. After a period of numbing work in a rock quarry, political allies placed Poller in the camp hospital. After recovering his strength, he was fortunate enough to be assigned as clerk to the camp doctor, one of the best-protected positions in the camp. Doctor's clerks, who wore white medical frocks, had unusual freedom of movement, and their postwar testimony would be crucial in describing the anatomy of camp life.

The doctor whom Poller served for a year was *Hauptsturmführer* (Captain) Erwin Ding. Poller offers us the first detailed picture of his master:

> A highly intelligent man, who was well-mannered, of an agreeable disposition, friendly and sometimes actually genial. His features were rather pleasant than stern, his eyes lively and observant. Above all, he was exceptionally self-assured, and I was repeatedly surprised at the ease with which he always found a way out of the most complicated situations. Many a time he sat before me at his writing desk, reading the papers I had prepared, and my eyes would rest on his high, nobly-formed forehead, on the fine line of his nose, on the handsome, regular features so full of character, and often I pondered the puzzle such a man set, his high qualifications and abilities contrasting with his abominable crimes.

Ding ably carried out the two major jobs of an SS doctor in a concentration camp. The first was to forge death certificates to conceal the torture and mistreatment of inmates. The second was outright medical murder. During the year he worked for Ding, Poller witnessed a series of horrible crimes. He saw Ding kill an inmate with an injection of atropine to the heart; saw him browbeat a Jewish "race defiler" into agreeing to be castrated; saw Ding murder an apparently autistic inmate; saw him torture a man to death with shots of apomorphine and electrical shocks. When a typhoid fever epidemic broke out in the camp, Ding killed the sickest patients, rather than spend money for medicine. The Reverend Paul Schneider, an anti-Nazi minister, was brought to Ding in the sick ward in July 1939 after being tied to a cross for several days. Ding restored his health for a couple of weeks, then gave him a fatal injection of strophanthin, and falsified the death certificate. When Schneider's widow came to pick up the body, Ding shook her hand and gave his condolences.

While carrying out atrocities, Ding, then 26, was also attempting to pad his résumé with journal publications. At one point, he decided to write a treatise on diabetes, using records compiled by three Jewish doctor slaves. Poller wrote up the report, and Ding added his own details, which he had clearly made up. Ding could present an air of knowledgability, Poller states, but it was "mere façade. The splendid head, intended by nature to carry out valuable work for suffering humanity, had been hollowed and refilled with the stench of Nazi doctrine."

Poller witnessed a particularly revealing episode when a group of Jewish doctors in the camp brought the Austrian radiologist Siegmund Kreuzfuchs before Ding. Kreuzfuchs had invented a method of using X-rays to diagnose ulcers, heart aneurysms, and other ailments. The prisoners hoped that if Ding understood Kreuzfuchs's importance, he might save the life of this "shriveled, emaciated man, already destined to die." Ding spoke with the Jewish doctor for a while and afterwards expressed admiration for his knowledge. A few days later, Kreuzfuchs returned to resume his explanations, but Poller could see that Ding was losing patience. Suddenly, he took a drawing that Kreuzfuchs had made, tore it up, crumpled it, and struck him in the face. As Kreuzfuchs turned helplessly and ran out the door, Ding sneered at him, "'What swine! Such a Jew!'"

"It took me some time," Poller wrote, "to appreciate what had taken place before my eyes."

For Poller, Ding represented something far worse than the typical SS guard who dispensed whippings, kicks, and murder. As a doctor, he belonged to an ancient guild whose first principle was "do no harm." As such, even in his moments of cultured reflection, or during occasional acts of random kindness, he was the embodiment of corruption. The Kreuzfuchs episode revealed something else: Ding's awkward, unspoken, perhaps unconscious awareness of the fraudulence of an existence that gave him the power of life and death over men like Kreuzfuchs, whose accomplishments he could never match.

Meanwhile, Ding pressed on in his pathetic campaign to get a name change. On May 12, 1939, he wrote confidentially to General Karl Genzken, chief of the medical office of the Waffen-SS, seeking his intervention in the process. "As you know, the name 'Ding' inspires everyone to mockery," he wrote. Within days of arriving at Buchenwald, he had been "given the nickname 'Dr. Schniepel.' In the local slang, *Schniepel* was a word for the male sexual organ. He concluded, "In examining my request, I beg you to consider that the stain of an out-of-wedlock birth has clung to me for my entire life . . . a source of conflict throughout my studies and military service, and one that I would like to spare my children."

Three months later, Ding was called back to Berlin. The start of the war found him studying infectious disease under Heinz Zeiss. In May 1940, he was mustered into a frontline Waffen-SS unit and joined the invasion of France.

War began on September 1, 1939, when Germany invaded Poland under the pretext of a phony Polish border attack. Motorized units crushed the Polish cavalry, and within a few days the Nazis had occupied Kraków, the historical center of Polish culture. They had chosen the city to serve as the capital of the newly created *Generalgouvernement*, the conquered parts of central and eastern Poland that were not absorbed into Germany. Hans Frank, Hitler's lawyer, took charge of the government and established his residence in the 14th-century Wawel Castle, home to Polish kings and archbishops.

The Fantastic Laboratory of Dr. Weigl

On November 6, two weeks after the occupation of Kraków, *SS-Obersturmbannführer* (Lieutenant Colonel) Bruno Müller, the Gestapo chief, called all the professors of Poland's most prestigious and oldest institute of higher learning, the Jagiellonian University, to a meeting in the auditorium of the Collegium Novum. Müller was acting under the orders of Reinhard Heydrich, Himmler's deputy, who had declared that Poland's intelligentsia must be "weeded out," as a potential source of rebellion and resistance. After arriving at the hall, Müller sealed the doors with armed guards and informed the 183 professors and instructors who had responded to the invitation (others smelled a rat and stayed away, or arrived too late) that the university would be shut down. Then he had the lot arrested, packed into trucks, and taken to the Gestapo prison on Montelupich Street, and from there to the Wehrmacht barracks. Many of the academics ended up as inmates in the Sachsenhausen and Dachau concentration camps. Over the next several months, however, more than half were released through the intervention of foreign powers, in particular Mussolini, who was angry because some of the professors had ties to Italy. This "special action" against the professors of the Jagiellonian University, which was preparing its 572nd class year, established the treatment that Polish professionals could expect from the Nazis.

Around this same time, Hermann Eyer, then 33 years old, arrived in Kraków and began setting up a mass-production facility for typhus vaccine to be produced by means of the Weigl method. He occupied the microbiology institute of the Jagiellonian University, and seized apartments confiscated from Jewish faculty on Mickiewicz Street to house his German personnel. Eyer himself took over the flat of the biologist Stanislaus Francis Snieszko, who had fled earlier in 1939 to the United States (where he would go on to pioneer modern fish hatchery techniques). Eyer began searching for Polish biologists to work in the lab. Most of them had been rounded up in the raid on the Jagiellonian, but Robert Kudicke, a 63-year-old German microbiologist who had volunteered to lead the fight against typhus in the *Gener-*

algouvernement, alerted Eyer to one of the arrested men, Zdzisław Przybyłkiewicz, a 31-year-old adjunct professor in the microbiology institute. The Polish scientist was located at the Wehrmacht barracks and taken to Eyer on November 9. Przybyłkiewicz went from being a condemned man in a Gestapo prison to deputy director of the Wehrmacht's Institut für Virus und Fleckfieberforschung (Institute for Virus and Typhus Research). Eyer assigned him to lead vaccine production at the Kraków lab.

Years later, there would be speculation about how Przybyłkiewicz had managed to land on his feet in those terrible days. He was not considered a great talent in the scientific realm; he had acquired a reputation as an academic schemer, a womanizer, and a terrible teacher. His expertise on the Weigl method obviously was the salient point, since Eyer was desperately seeking typhus-immune experts. But he was by no means the only typhus expert in Kraków. His former boss and several other Kraków microbiologists were killed at Auschwitz some months later, for plotting to poison German officers by putting typhoid germs in their food.

Eyer had been told, in the days preceding the Polish invasion, that Wehrmacht troops would be occupying Lwów, and that his mission was to take over the Weigl laboratory and expand its production of vaccine for German soldiers. Sent instead to Kraków, he was forced to scramble to set up a typhus vaccine laboratory there on his own. In the first few days in Kraków, Eyer confiscated vaccine from Polish army clinics and used it to immunize 50 German employees. Fifteen of these men, including Eyer, fell ill with typhus over the next six months, but the course of the illnesses was mild. None of the employees died, and only a few suffered petechial rash or hallucinations. The experience, while unpleasant, once again proved the value of the Weigl vaccine. Eyer next needed to enlist louse feeders and other Polish employees; he knew that German lab workers lacked the immunity to handle such jobs. Eyer contacted Friedrich Weigl, Rudolf's older brother and a leading Polish lawyer in Kraków, to assist him in finding employees. The collaboration was successful, and Eyer managed to get vaccine production going in a short time. He delivered his first batch of typhus vaccine to the Wehrmacht health inspectorate in April 1940. In an update to his boss three months later, Eyer reported that the laboratory was raising 300,000 lice, and infecting 2,500 of them with typhus germs every day. Each infector could inject typhus into 1,000 lice a day, Eyer said, and he had designed a sterile filling machine with which two workers could finish 500 portions of vaccine daily. The Gestapo had arrested one of his employees on suspicion of participation in the resistance, but he was released after a week, Eyer wrote.

In an accompanying pamphlet, Eyer said that the institute was making only enough vaccine to protect endangered military personnel such as delousers, caretakers in military clinics, and officers in frequent contact with the "endemically contaminated civilian population." A second brochure, prepared for soldiers, warned that typhus was a very serious disease, and urged German troops to steer clear of Poles and the places they lived and gathered, "since contact with lousy clothing and people brings the danger of becoming lousy yourself. . . . Every soldier who finds even one louse on himself must report it immediately."

Jews, he wrote, had to be isolated in ghettos, because the greatest danger of infection came from "lousy and filthy dwellings of typhus-infected Jews in the Polish interior." Eyer reiterated such sentiments in a journal article published at this time (the journal's Jewish editor had fled the Nazis). It is "the unclean people" who spread typhus, he wrote—be they Abyssinian shepherds or ghetto Jews. The only way to stop its spread was "the complete and pitiless enclosure of all known or suspected endemic carrier populations; in Poland, for example, the isolation of the Jewish ghettos that is currently underway."

In Polish cities, tradition called for students to attend church—or temple, if they were Jews—on the first day of school. On September 1, 1939,

War and Epidemics

Luisa Hornstein was 13 years old and all dressed for synagogue when she heard the sound of airplanes. When the bombing started, she and her family went into the basement, going upstairs only to fetch food and fill pots and tubs with water. They stayed there three weeks.

Hornstein was the youngest of three children in the family of a well-to-do timber merchant in prewar Lwów. The family lived on Bernstein, a leafy street in the Jewish quarter northeast of the Opera House. "I remember hearing Hitler on the radio," she recalled six decades later in Cincinnati, where she was a pediatrician and her son, Frank, was my elementary school chum. "'He was so violent, it was such an awful speech, his voice, and you could hear the masses cheering. My mother was very afraid. 'This is not going to be a good place to live,' she said. 'There is going to be a war.' My father said it would take him five years to liquidate his business. 'Then start now!' my mother said." But now was too late.

The Nazi bombardment destroyed gas, water, and power lines in many parts of town, and this led to hoarding. The Eastern Trade Fair opened on time, but petered out after a week. On September 2, the first refugees streamed in from western Poland, and soon the stream turned into a river—of cars, carts, and wheelbarrows, anything that went on wheels. Thousands of Lwów inhabitants sought safety with friends and relatives in the country. Thousands fled into Hungary and Romania. By the third day of the bombardment, most shops were closed; by the fourth, there was nothing to buy. Trainloads of wounded Polish soldiers started arriving. And in the third week, the German army took up positions on the outskirts of the city and began shelling. Many of the city's defenders were Jews—the Bund enlisted 100 men to build trenches. Three weeks of bombing and shelling killed at least 800 people in Lwów.

And then suddenly, on September 20, the fighting stopped. At first, the Poles thought they had driven the Germans off. Then the Russians arrived. Unbeknownst to the rest of the world, Hitler and Stalin had signed a nonaggression pact with a secret protocol that carved up Poland between them. It called for the invading German forces to withdraw to Przemyśl, 60 miles west of Lwów.

The first days of the Soviet invasion were relatively peaceful. Polish soldiers threw down their arms, took off their uniforms, and walked away, unmolested by the arriving Red Army. Stalin's portrait went up all around town, and Soviet commissars began converting Lwów and the surrounding area into an enclave of the Ukrainian Soviet Socialist Republic.

For many sophisticated Lwowites, the iconic image of the Soviet invasion was the Russian ladies whom they encountered at swimming pools in underwear, or at the theater clad in nightgowns they had purchased from clever shopkeepers who claimed they represented the finest in evening wear. Or perhaps it was the Red Army soldiers with their wrist watches. They bought several at a time, with expressions of joy, and wore all of them at once, whether or not they worked. The Russians were astounded by the abundance of goods in Lwów. A soldier would enter a store to buy a chocolate bar. When he got it, he'd ask if he could buy another. He'd look around to see whether other soldiers were nearby, then in a low voice ask for the whole box. The Russians boasted about how good things were back home. No one believed them. These barbarians blew their noses without handkerchiefs and didn't give their seats on the trolley to women or old people. The humor of the occupation faded when the secret police, the NKVD, began conducting nighttime raids, packing people into railroad cars bound for Siberia, with no explanation. The first to go were the Red Army's political enemies, then the rich, then Jewish refugees from the West. Lwów time was set two hours earlier to Moscow time, which meant you went to work while it was still dark. The occupation confirmed what middle-class Poles had always thought of the Russians. Czarist or Communist, they were ignorant and brutal rubes.

Although the invasion was tragic for everyone, at first it seemed bad for Jews only if they were rich. Businesses were nationalized and thousands of well-to-do Jews were deported. For others, there was a

The Red Army enters Lwów, September 1939. (Bridgeman Art Library.)

nervous waiting game, making do in a new economy. School resumed eventually, but it was completely different. The Soviets decided that at Jewish schools the language would be Yiddish, though most children in the middle-class parts of town, coming from more or less assimilated families, spoke only Polish or German and perhaps a bit of Hebrew. In the Polish schools, the language was now Ukrainian—the "western Ukraine," the area that Austrians and Poles had called Galicia, had been "returned to the motherland." In a kindergarten, the teacher asked the children, "Which of you believes in God, and which in Stalin?" The ones who said Stalin got caramels.

Later, many Poles and Ukrainians would recall that the Jews had done well during the Soviet period, but this was not true, though Jews did become more visible. The majority of the 22,000 Lwów residents sent to the Soviet interior were Jews, often packed 150 at a time into freezing railcars that spent weeks inching to Kazakhstan. Nor were Jews favored in the new government. Of the 1,495 delegates chosen to the Ukrainian national assembly in 1940, for example, only 20 were

Jews. But the Russians ended official discrimination and dispatched high-profile Jewish Communists, commissars, and cultural figures to Lwów. They lifted bans or limits on Jewish admissions to the universities, the militia, and the police. Jews were still a tiny minority in these armed units, but "the presence of any Jewish cops might have seemed outrageous to Ukrainians and Poles precisely because it was unprecedented," as one observer has written.

More than 50,000 Jews were estimated to have fled to Lwów from German-occupied Poland, and close to half a million people now jammed the sidewalks and apartments of the city, hustling to feed themselves. The Soviets nationalized industry, but often allowed former bosses to remain as supervisors. The minimum wage was increased; living standards seesawed between abundance and deprivation. Goods would be put on display to lure peasants into town to sell their crops. A month later the shelves were empty. Lwowites experienced the history of the Soviet economy on fast-forward.

In November, there was a plebiscite for the "western Ukraine" to decide whether to join the Soviet Union. Prior to the vote, lavish amounts of food—caviar, sugar, butter—arrived in town. The result, purchased and rigged, was 97 percent in favor. After the plebiscite, a crackdown on the wealthy, professionals, Polish army officers, and other "enemies" began. An exchange with the Nazis allowed people to choose which tyrant's occupation they preferred. Many Poles and Ukrainians decided to live in Germany. So did a few thousand naïve Jews. The Germans refused to accept the Jews, who were then arrested by Russians as unreliable elements and sent to Siberia or Kazakhstan. Many died there of hardships, but most survived, and on balance the deportations saved Jewish lives, because the deportees were gone when the Nazis arrived in Lwów two years later.

Many young Jews viewed the Soviet occupation as relatively benign—unless their families were marked for deportation. In the schools, Jews, Poles, Ukrainians, and Russians studied together in an idealistic atmosphere. Frank Stiffel, a Jewish medical student, became editor of a literary magazine at the university. He recalled enjoyable bull sessions with his multinational friends, and picnics at which black bread sandwiches and hardboiled eggs were washed down with soft Crimean wine. At home, he argued with his father, a World War I veteran of the kaiser's army, who said he'd gladly exchange the Russians for Germans. Lwów's mathematicians continued their café life, though with less élan and fewer cakes. Banach was much beloved by the Soviet mathematicians, who left a few equations in the Scottish Book—the collection of brain-teasing mathematical problems collected at the Scottish Café—and made him a corresponding member of the Ukrainian Academy of Sciences.

To enter town, the Russian tanks had rumbled down Lyczakowska Street, where Fleck and his family lived at no. 34. There is no record of how he felt upon seeing the Red Army, but one can safely assume there was a measure of relief, and his experience under the Soviets was relatively positive. The Soviets must have considered Fleck a trustworthy scientist; he and his son had participated in anti-Nazi citizens' groups, and his friendship with the philosopher Leon Chwistek, whose Soviet sympathies were well-known, may have added to this reputation. Whatever the case, though Fleck's private laboratory was confiscated, the Soviets named him to lead the microbiology department of the new Ukrainian Medical Institute, which was separated from Lwów's university. He also led the city's Sanitation and Bacteriological Laboratory, which technically made him Weigl's superior, since the latter's laboratory was brought under the aegis of the state. Fleck conducted research as well at the new Mother and Child Hospital, directed by Franciszek Groër.

Fleck's rise in status angered some of his Polish colleagues. After watching their relatives' deportation to Siberia, many Poles felt that to take a job in a Soviet-occupied institution was a form of treason. Some grumbled that Fleck was inappropriately competing with Weigl, his academic mentor.

Weigl, however, held his own within the new order. Just prior to the Nazi invasion, Poland's national health department had established five institutes to expand production of the vaccine, and there had been talk of removing Weigl from immediate responsibility for its manufacture. Much as the Polish health leaders admired Weigl, at times his scientific purity interfered with their intent to produce greater quantities of vaccine. When war broke out, the government ordered Weigl to retreat to Romania with the Polish army, but he refused, telling his staff and friends that he could not abandon Poland when it needed him. During the winter of 1939, the Soviet authorities in Lwów provided 5,000 doses of the Weigl vaccine to the Nazi *Generalgouvernement* in exchange for five German microscopes. Intriguingly, this deal may have been approved by Fleck.

Weigl's colleagues abroad were at least dimly aware of his plight and sought to help. At a November 17, 1939, meeting of the League of Nations Health Committee, Professor Edmond Sergent, director of the Pasteur Institute in Algiers, offered to give Weigl space in one of his laboratories to continue making the antityphus vaccine. It is not clear whether Weigl ever received this offer, but the answer would no doubt have been negative. Weigl would not have wanted to leave, and the Soviets would not have let him go. Like the Germans, they faced an open-ended typhus threat and were eager to vaccinate their troops in preparation for the war against Hitler that they knew would eventually come. In February 1940, no less a figure than Nikita Khrushchev, secretary of the Ukrainian Communist Party, visited Weigl at his laboratory and offered to make him a senior professor at the Soviet Academy of Medicine in Moscow. Weigl declined. As various authorities learned over the years, it was not easy to force Weigl to abandon Lwów.

That said, he was readily tempted by the prospect of meeting other scientists and sharing knowledge. During the 22 months of the Soviet occupation of Lwów, Weigl expanded production of the vaccine and visited Moscow, Leningrad, Kharkov, and Kiev, where he gave lectures and demonstrations on his methods for fighting typhus. Russian professors visited Weigl, too. Lwów was like Vienna to them—a Western paradise. After a few glasses of vodka, the Russian visitors couldn't resist the temptation to share tales of Stalinist horror. One of them gave Weigl the following advice: "Never join the party and do not steal excessively. If you are not a party member, they will court you to join, but once you join and are kicked out, it's curtains. If you steal too much, it will lead to your demise. If you do not steal at all, you will starve. So remember, steal only in moderation, just enough to survive."

Weigl's disinclination to publish accounts of his work had an unintentionally positive effect during the occupation years. In the absence of a "cookbook" on how to mass-produce the Weigl typhus vaccine, the Soviets and the Nazis alike would depend on Weigl himself to continue its production. Both regimes would no doubt have been happy to replace this obstinately independent scientist. But they were obliged to leave management of vaccine production to Weigl and his staff. A certain amount of Weigl's time was taken up in intervening on behalf of workers arrested for one reason or another. He was generally successful, with some notable exceptions. A Ukrainian professor at the typhus institute, Dr. Zajac, was arrested by the NKVD in January 1941 and beaten to death. But Weigl saved several Poles from deportation, or got them returned from the east. Stefania Skwarczyńska, a professor of literature who had been deported to Kazakhstan for having a husband in the Polish army, was sent back and became one of Weigl's louse feeders.

Our most detailed perspective on the Weigl laboratory during the war years comes from Waclaw Szybalski, who has provided his own recollections while gathering those of other witnesses. The Szybalski and Weigl families were close. Szybalski, his brother, and his father worked at the lab during the war and were aware of everything that went on there. Szybalski's father, Stefan, had been president of a hunting club to which Weigl belonged, and Weigl's son, Wiktor, was Wacław Szybalski's best friend. These relationships probably saved their lives. The Soviet scientist who was put in charge of the Weigl institute lived in an apartment confiscated from the Szybalskis in the building they continued to inhabit on St. Mark's Street, across from the Botanical Garden. Stefan Szybalski worked first as a Russian–Polish translator, which enabled him to be present at the meeting with Khrushchev, then as manager of the laboratory's "car pool," such as it was. "We got no compensation for any of the apartments, of course," Szybalski says. "You were glad not to be killed." On two occasions, Weigl saved the Szybalskis from deportation by insisting that they were crucial to his laboratory operations. Like most of the wealthy people in Lwów, the Szybalskis had been issued Soviet passports appended with the dreaded Paragraph 11, which prohibited the holder from living near borders or in cities and was effectively a ticket to Siberia. In the first days of the Soviet invasion, the NKVD had deported about 26,000 Polish reserve officers and murdered them in the Katyn forest and other secret places.

It was certainly a dramatic time to be a young Polish patriot in Lwów. Szybalski, a first-year student of chemistry at the polytechnical, seems to have adjusted easily to the challenges. In the weeks before the Soviet occupation, his chemistry class was 60 percent Polish, 30 percent Jewish, and 10 percent Ukrainian, roughly based on the population breakdown in the city. Under the Russians, the class size was increased from 60 to 120, but 90 percent of the students were Jewish or Ukrainian. The new students included fewer assimilated, well-to-do Jews and more poor Jews from Orthodox families. Szybalski became good friends with some of them and learned a bit of Yiddish. "They had a good sense of humor, making fun of the Russians just like us," he said. "We were all young people. We weren't prejudiced. The Russians were our common enemy."

Szybalski's day during the Soviet occupation typically began with breakfast at eight, followed by a five-minute bike ride to the polytechnical, where he studied part of the time. His major activity at school during this period, however, was the production of TNT for the anti-Soviet resistance. He'd buy the supplies he needed at a hardware store on Akademicka; Professor Edward Sucharda, an organic chemist and rector, instructed Szybalski and three or four other students in the bomb making. The Russians were bringing loads of raw materials and food to Germany, then filling the empty trains with Poles from Lwów and other cities for deportation to Siberia. "Our belief was, 'The fewer train cars they have, the more the confusion, the fewer of us they can deport,'" Szybalski recalled. "We knew it was all temporary because in three months the Americans would win the war and we'd be free. But in the meantime we had to stop the deportations." They built and hid the bombs in the basement of the chemistry lab. Szybalski was not part of the demolition squad, but a few times he was invited to watch. "Once they were transporting live chickens to Germany. All of a sudden, a cloud of feathers and the chickens are running around with the heads off. We melted into the forest."

At the end of June 1940, Stefan Kryński, who had come to Lwów to escape Soviet persecution, landed at the Weigl lab. Weigl told him there were three periods in a man's life. In the first, we think we know everything. In the second, we realize we know nothing. In the third, we start to learn. Unfortunately, most people stay in the first period for so much of their lives that they never manage to generate any new ideas.

He was very sage, Weigl, except, perhaps, when it came to his personal life. Out of loyalty to his wife, he never considered divorcing her, but their relations cooled, especially after the trip to Ethiopia. Most of his life now was in the lab and spent with Anna Herzig. Early in 1940, Zofia sickened and died of cancer. "After the funeral, my father took me for a long walk. It was the first time I had ever seen him crying," recalled Wiktor. As they walked, Weigl told his son that he regretted having gone to Ethiopia. "He could not forgive himself for the fact that he'd spent so little time with her, that he had sacrificed the lives of my mother and our family."

There was little time to grieve, however. With the war and the growth of Jewish ghettos in German-occupied Poland, Weigl's vaccine had never been as important. Production increased, but as typhus spread through the ghettos and other areas where poor Poles were on the move, there was never enough of it. Deliberate Nazi policies caused an explosion of typhus among Polish Jews beginning in the winter of 1940. A November 25, 1939, memorandum to Himmler from lawyers in the Berlin Reich Ministry for the Occupied Eastern Territories expresses the Nazi medical perspective toward these events. It stated, "Medical care from our side must be limited to the prevention of the spreading of epidemics to Reich territory. . . . [W]e are indifferent to the hygienic fate of the Jews. . . . [T]he basic principle holds, that their propagation must be curtailed in every possible way."

The Nazis' ultimate plans for the eradication of Jews from Europe had never been a secret. But genocide could not be carried out overnight, and justification was required to inspire thousands of Germans to take the actions that enabled the Holocaust. The unproven *Geomedizin* notion that typhus was a Jewish disease, one that moreover did no real harm to Jews, since they were the racial and geographi-

German propaganda in Poland: "Jews—Lice—Typhus." (Bundesarchiv.)

cal carriers of it, offered the typical German public health officer in occupied Poland a psychological out. It seemed to justify a policy of keeping Jews locked behind ghetto walls, where typhus could be confined without threatening the vulnerable Aryan population, especially the German occupants. As the historian Christopher Browning writes, "the persistent medieval anti-Semitic stereotype of the Jew as the plague-carrier thus called forth as a modern medical response the revival of a medieval invention—the sealed ghetto."

The medical establishment of the newly occupied territories was a motley collection of opportunistic hacks, misled patriots, and true believers. Jost Walbaum, a longtime Nazi Party member who had befriended *Reichsmarschall* Hermann Göring while treating the latter's morphine addiction, became director of health in the new *Generalgouvernement*. He was directly involved in building the ghettos, the first of which went up in Warsaw in April 1940. As typhus began to spread later in the year, Walbaum and Hans Frank agreed it was of "greatest importance" that all Jews be brought into ghettos as quickly as possible.

To create the ghettos, the Germans took all the Jews deported from other parts of the country or kicked out of their apartments and crammed them into unheated dwellings with no access to money or food. By the time the Nazis sealed the Warsaw ghetto in November 1940, at the start of a terribly cold winter, it contained nearly half a million people—1,100 per hectare, compared with 70 per hectare in the rest of Warsaw. The German occupation doctors, who were constantly warning of the dangers of typhus, had done everything they could to encourage its spread. All around the city, hideous posters went up depicting a frightening caricature of a bearded Jew and a louse, with the words "Jews—Lice—Typhus." In 1941, the German propaganda ministry held a competition inviting Polish playwrights to create scripts depicting the threat of Jews and typhus. The winner, a well-known actress and writer named Helena Rapacka, wrote a play entitled *Quarantine* that depicted the Jews as insidious vermin who should never be protected. The play was performed all over the *Generalgouvernement*, before crowds consisting mainly of *Volksdeutsche*, Poles who identified themselves as ethnic Germans. The authorities threatened actors with death if they did not perform.

The German medical contribution to the atrocities in Poland was advertised for posterity in a collection of reports titled *Kampf den Seuchen: Deutsche Ärzte-Einsatz im Osten* (Fighting epidemics: German Medical Missions in the East), published in Kraków in 1941. The book is a farrago of lies, racism, cheap shots, and cruelty—the opposite of everything scientific medicine stands for. Contributors included the health director Walbaum and the well-known infectious disease and *Geomedizin* specialist Ernst G. Nauck. In a series of essays, the German doctors blamed Poland's growing health problems on the ignorance and cupidity of Jews and Poles, in doing so revealing their own culpability. One writer, Joseph Ruppert, a senior health adviser for the *Generalgouvernement* in Kraków, described Jews as "criminal types, whom one could expect anything, so you unconsciously reach for your pistol to have it ready to shoot at any time." The lack of water in Warsaw in the wake of Luftwaffe bombing of the city's waterworks—"for which the Poles with their criminal defense policies are themselves entirely to blame"—meant that more epidemics would be coming, he wrote. "Since the Jew alone is almost always the carrier of the epidemic, and in the sickening of non-Jews there is always a Jewish infection source to be found, it has been urgent for the protection of the population to limit the movement of the Jewish population." A Dr. Werner Kroll wrote that the Jew was "by nature filthy, has no sense for the aesthetic-hygienic demands of bodily cleanliness. . . . The Jew has absolutely no productive thought and no intellectual interests beyond those required for the practical goal of moneymaking." In Kroll's view, the eradication of the Jew alone would be insufficient to put medicine on the right track. What was needed was a priestly doctor class that opposed the Judeo-Christian worldview of mercy and didn't worry about individuals, but "served the eternal life of the unending bloodline of blood pulsing through the body and soul of the [German] people."

By cramming half a million wretchedly poor people into a few square blocks in the dead of winter, the German doctors created a typhus epidemic. Then they blamed the Jews for it. In the second winter of the German occupation, the self-fulfilling prophecies of the Nazi doctors began to come true. The overcrowded, underfed, and unwashed Warsaw ghetto swarmed with vermin, and the streets were so packed that you could easily pick up lice bumping into someone. The lice "crawled over the pavements, up stairways, and dropped from the ceilings of the public offices," recalled the musician Henryk Szpilman in his memoir, *The Pianist*. "Lice found their way into the folds of your newspaper, your small change. There were even lice on the crust of the loaf you had just bought. And each of these verminous creatures could carry typhus." One saw lice massed like shimmering helmets on the heads of innumerable street urchins, practically eating them alive.

Thousands were dying each month. The Jews of the Warsaw ghetto, despite the urging of their German doctors, preferred to live. If they could not flee, they sought out the only known protection against typhus: Rudolf Weigl's vaccine. By November 1940, it had become the most coveted item on the black market, and Weigl one of the most admired figures in the ghetto. Over the next 18 months, at least 30,000 doses would find their way behind the ghetto walls through a variety of means, some heroic, some the product of simple lucre. Weigl arranged to smuggle the vaccine to the Warsaw ghetto from Lwów through two of his employees, who were ostensibly sent to gather lice for research purposes. Such scientific missions were not unusual— another Polish employee of the institute flew to Stalingrad to recover lice from a sick army officer. Weigl's aides carried large bottles of vaccine, which was said to resemble black coffee. They delivered it to Ludwik Hirszfeld, founding director of the Polish Hygiene Institute, whom the Nazis had sent to the ghetto in 1940. Hirszfeld sold the vaccines to ghetto inhabitants at a low price, using the proceeds to fund desperately needed health care programs for children. The German doctors Robert Kudicke and Rudolf Wohlrab, who had occupied Hirszfeld's office, were trying at the time to produce an egg-based vaccine. Meanwhile, their Polish employees secretly produced their own louse-based vaccine, which they smuggled into the ghetto and to resistance fighters in the forest. Kudicke's private secretary was actually a Home Army activist working with *Action N*, the resistance's sly propaganda arm.

In Lwów, the Jewish survivor Frank Stiffel recalled, two Polish men—"nouveau riche hoodlums"—arrived at his apartment from Warsaw. Stiffel's father managed to obtain about 20 vials of Weigl vaccine each week from hospital workers and nurses in Lwów, and delivered them to the businessmen at a meeting place near the train station. Each dose sold in Warsaw for 1,000 zlotys—in the neighborhood of $200, and a king's ransom at a time when those lucky enough to have a job were glad to earn 100 zlotys a month. "Everyone had to earn a living," said Stiffel. "Once a week these guys would come to buy our supply. This lasted until the Germans occupied Lwów, at which point it was not easy to travel to Warsaw anymore."

In Warsaw, the goal was to obtain the Weigl vaccine by hook or by crook. "The chief subject of conversation among both rich and poor was typhus; the poor simply wondered when they would die of it, while the rich wondered how to get hold of Dr Weigel's [*sic*] vaccine and protect themselves," Szpilman wrote.

> Dr Weigel, an outstanding bacteriologist, became the most popular figure after Hitler: good beside evil, so to speak. People said the Germans had arrested the doctor in Lemberg, but thank God had not murdered him, and indeed they almost recognized him as an honorary German. It was said they had offered him a fine laboratory and a wonderful villa with an equally wonderful car, after placing him under the wonderful supervision of the Gestapo to make sure he did not run

away rather than making as much vaccine as possible for the louse-infested German army in the east. Of course, said the story, Dr Weigel had refused the villa and the car.

I don't know what the facts about him really were. I only know that he lived, thank God, and once he had told the Germans the secret of his vaccine and was no longer useful to them, by some miracle they did not finally consign him to the most wonderful of all gas chambers. In any case, thanks to his invention and German venality many Jews in Warsaw were saved from dying of typhus, if only to die another death later.

Although the ghetto inhabitants were grateful to Weigl, they were not always convinced of the vaccine's value. "I was inoculated yesterday for the second time against typhus," the ghetto leader Adam Czerniaków wrote in his diary in February 1942. "The blood test showed a negative reaction, which indicates that I could still contract the disease. Several months ago the rabbis proposed that a marriage ceremony be performed in a cemetery. This is supposed to bring about the end of the epidemic. The scientists who do the blood testing and at the same time declare that neither a positive nor a negative reaction is conclusive are as helpful as the above-mentioned rabbis." Czerniaków did not contract typhus. He committed suicide in July 1942 rather than participate in the deportation of Warsaw's remaining Jews to Treblinka.

The Nazis, who by then had occupied all of Western Europe save Britain, invaded Yugoslavia in May 1941. As rumors grew of an imminent Nazi drive into the Soviet Union, the Russians tightened security at Weigl's institute in Lwów, prohibiting staff from staying after hours without permission. The NKVD developed a contingency plan, Weigl later told an associate, whereby, in case of war, agents would seize typhus laboratory workers and transport them deep into Russia, where a new vaccine plant would open. Weigl was to go with the first group, but for some reason—probably Soviet disorganization, or surprise at the timing of the Nazi invasion—the plan was never carried out.

Fleck and his friends awaited the next stage of the war with foreboding. On July 20, 1941, the mathematician Hugo Steinhaus visited Fleck's laboratory at the bacteriological institute on Zielona Street and observed clumped cells under a microscope; Fleck was beginning to investigate the phenomenon of leukergy, the agglomeration of white blood cells that he thought might be diagnostic for certain types of illnesses. The two friends discussed the terrifying political situation, which Fleck described as a "permanent sepsis." In the late afternoon, Steinhaus walked into the Wulka hills and lay down in the grass, thinking and worrying.

CHAPTER SIX

PARASITES

The Soviets abandoned Lwów as suddenly as they had entered it. On June 21, 1941, their tanks began rattling past Fleck's apartment on the same route they had taken entering the city 22 months earlier. Operation Barbarossa—the largest invasion in the history of warfare, involving 3.9 million German troops on a 1,800-mile front stretching from the Baltics to the Black Sea—took Stalin by surprise, though he had received plenty of warning from the British and even his own spies. The Soviets had done nothing to prepare the people in the territories they abandoned for war with the Nazis. In Lwów, they left a disoriented city, with many of its best and brightest dead or in exile. The Soviets had rubbed out most of the resistance to Stalin. Thousands of Polish army officers had been murdered or exiled. The Nazis, meanwhile, had had nearly two years to prepare and refine their mechanisms of terror and control in Poland. Ukrainian nationalists lay low under Soviet rule, but the Germans had cultivated and trained these malcontents, holding up promises of an independent Ukrainian state after the Nazi conquest. In the weeks before the invasion, Ukrainian nationalists had begun to whisper that Hitler would be welcomed not with flowers but with the heads of Poles and Jews.

Lwów during the three years of German occupation was a Hobbesian theater, every man for himself under a ruthless occupant. The city was crawling with informants—Ukrainians, Poles, and even a few Jews who would turn in a fellow Jew or a resister for a chance to survive. The Lwów chapter of the the London-based Home Army resistance movement, or AK, was riddled with anti-Semites and thus an unreliable ally. The city was full of Jewish refugees, perhaps as many as 50,000, now trapped in Lwów alongside the 100,000 or so previous Jewish residents. Germany's goal was the annihilation of all these Jews, and it succeeded with surprisingly few exceptions.

The Jews of Lwów had four ways to survive the German occupation. The first was to *pass*—to obtain a non-Jewish identity. The second was to be hidden by friends, or to flee to a small village or into the forest, where if one was lucky one might obtain the protection of a sympathetic villager (especially if the villager received regular payments). The third was to hide in the sewers. None of these avenues was safe or permanent. Nor, in the long run, was the fourth—working in an occupation of value to the German war effort. Thousands of Jews sought such jobs and even paid for them, receiving nothing in return but hard work, starvation rations, and a temporary shelter from the Gestapo that could be exposed at any moment. Eventually, the Gestapo raided nearly all of the allegedly "safe" businesses. But in a few cases, having the right job kept you alive and even allowed you to help others. Simon Wiesenthal, the postwar Nazi hunter, survived the war as a draftsman in the Lwów railroad repair yards, under the jurisdiction of the Wehrmacht. There he used his skills and work tools to create fake identification papers for hundreds of Jews. Others survived for a few years in the oil industry because of their engineering expertise. The odds were grim. More than 130,000 Jews died in Lwów under German occupation. Each of these deaths is a story of misery and terror. Together, they represent a fate that is simply beyond imagining.

The second Nazi invasion of Lwów began with aerial bombing before dawn on June 21, 1941. Later that day, the Soviets started to withdraw from the city, but the German advance briefly stalled a few days later, and Russian NKVD officers returned to complete unfinished business. They had been holding about 3,000 prisoners, many of them at Saint Brigid's, the grim, thick-walled Habsburg dungeon a few blocks from the Opera House. Before abandoning Lwów for good on June 28, the Russians set about killing them. Some were lined up neatly and shot by firing squads. In other cases, hand grenades were tossed into cells, or the prisoners were bayoneted. Some were buried in shallow pits, others left where they'd fallen. A Russian chauffeur who lived in the Szybalskis' building joined in the killing spree before leaving town. "He came back covered in blood and left his bloody things in the apartment," Wacław Szybalski recalled. The Soviets set fire to Saint Brigid's as their final act.

On the last day of June, Szybalski, Wiktor Weigl, and a few other boys accompanied their friend Franek Schramm to look for Schramm's father, a wealthy Jewish lawyer who had been arrested a few days before the Soviet retreat. The Schramms lived on the top floor of the Sprecher-Haus, a graceful seven-story art nouveau structure in the very center of the city, by the Adam Mickiewicz column and the George Hotel. The boys visited the Lącki, Zamarstynowska, and Saint Brigid's prisons. "It was a slaughterhouse. You entered into these cells, and in some the bodies were neatly stacked in six. In others they were lying all around," Szybalski said. "The weather was hot, and we had no gloves. It was a very unpleasant job, and you never knew when the Germans would show up. After three days, I had had enough. After a while, the bodies didn't look so human. We never found his father."

Amid plundering and arson, the first troops of the German 17th Army entered Lwów and hung a giant swastika flag above the town hall at noon on June 29, 1941. Lwów, which under the Russians had become Lviv, was now Lemberg again. Clocks set to Moscow time were now switched to Berlin time, three hours later. The first invaders many residents encountered were members of an Austrian unit—the "Edelweiss"—which some Jews remembered favorably from their service in the kaiser's army. In the wake of the Wehrmacht, more sinister elements slipped into the city: Ukrainian nationalists trained in western Poland, and *Einsatzkommando* units, SS men whose mission was to incite ethnic hatred and murder Jews, Communists, and other perceived enemies. The first posters went up with the notification that anyone resisting German orders would be shot. And the orders would be endless. No Jew could possess a radio. No Jew could possess skis. No Jew could practice medicine on an Aryan. No Jew could be employed. Helping a Jew was forbidden. And on and on, in infinite detail and with ever-refined cruelty, leading to the final, unwritten stipulation: to the Jew it was forbidden to breathe.

On the second day, the Germans put up posters enumerating the alleged atrocities committed by "Jewish Bolshevists" at Saint Brigid's and the two other prisons. This provided the pretext for what occurred a few days later—the worst pogrom in the city's history. The morning of July 3, thousands of Ukrainians, mostly male peasants between the ages of 15 and 30, appeared seemingly out of nowhere and began beating up Jews with staves and metal bars. In plain daylight, in the central streets of the city, they broke bones, tore beards, and forced religious Jews to drink urine or beat each other. They went from house to house stealing and ransacking apartments, shoving valuables into burlap bags. Crowds of men and women lined the streets and applauded the thugs, or simply watched the orgy of violence with amazement. Well-dressed Jews were ordered onto their knees to scrub the pavement in front of the Opera House.

"I heard the howling, the yelling, the giggling of the beasts," recalled a Jewish businessman who worked in downtown Lwów. "They tore our skin and muscles, beat out eyes, broke bones, beat on our heads, shoulders, and arms. . . . The streets were crammed full of onlookers resembling humans."

Staff at Weigl's laboratory saw Ukrainians and SS herding hundreds of Jews through the streets with whips and sticks. There was a strong element of sexual humiliation involved; elegant women were stripped naked and beaten until blood poured from their faces. Dr. Stefan Kryński, who was spending nights in the Weigl lab to avoid

Pogrom in Lwów, July 1, 1941. (Courtesy of the Wiener Library.)

the violence, took in a few of the victims and treated their wounds. "I had no particular sympathy for the Jews, especially after their behavior under Soviet rule," Kryński, then an old man, wrote in 1994, "but I had never imagined that men could be so cruel to fellow human beings simply because of their nation or race. Unfortunately, what we saw in July was only a rehearsal for an enormous spectacle of death."

Rabbi Ezekiel Lewin, leader of the Reform temple in Lwów, had just visited his friend Andrzej Graf Szeptycki, the Greek Catholic archbishop, seeking help in calming the Ukrainians. Szeptycki, who lived in a spacious palace, pleaded with Lewin to stay with him, but the rabbi insisted on returning to his people. He was seized at the doorstep of his house and dragged to Saint Brigid's, where a carnival of violence and horror awaited. Naked Jews, men, women, and children, knelt on the cobblestones washing away blood, or dragged bodies into the courtyard, driven by whips, kicks, and blows from German and Ukrainian rifle butts. The smell of the week-old corpses, rotting in temperatures that soared above 90 degrees, was unbearable. A firing squad shoved Rabbi Lewin into a corner and shot him along with a physician, Dr. Perec Gleich, and Henryk Hescheles, editor of the liberal Polish-language daily *Chwila* (Moment). It was the beginning of the end of assimilated Lwów Jewry.

A Nazi propaganda film made in early July shows Ukrainian children and women, babushkas in head scarves, keening and weeping over hundreds of bodies laid out in a yard. "Nothing stopped these monsters in human form," says the narrator. "With machine guns, knives, axes, and hand grenades these innocent victims of Bolshevik death-lust were cruelly murdered." The next frames show the faces of Jews, swollen from beatings. "The murderous Jewish rabble, who worked hand in hand with the Soviet GPU, were delivered to German troops for punishment by an angry crowd." The Nazis wholly invented the idea that Jews had murdered the Ukrainians, but it was crassly effective propaganda within the brutal circumstances. "We could see them beating Jews in the street from our windows," recalled Alex Redner, whose father, Marek, was a leading internist in Lwów. "My father was going out to bandage people half dead in the street. The wounded came to his office for help. Street mobs were running after Jews. That was the preamble. From that point on we had hardly a day of peace and quiet. From the day the Germans arrived, it was like being a rat trapped at the bottom of a pit."

The number of Jews murdered in the inaugural spate of violence in Lwów has been put at 4,000 to 7,000. On July 25, another blood rite was arranged for the Ukrainians: three days of violence to commemorate a Russian Jew's 1926 murder of the Ukrainian leader Symon Petlura in Paris. An estimated 2,000 Jews died in the "Petlura Days." The Germans unleashed wave upon wave of violence during the following two years, campaigns in which Ukrainians and Nazis, sometimes assisted by Jewish militiamen, descended upon a neighborhood to arrest and kill and deport to the death camps. Each of these *Aktionen,* as they were called, left anywhere from a few thousand to 50,000 dead. From one *Aktion* to another, things calmed down. In these periods of relative inaction, the Jews were subject to daily harassment, beatings, blackmail, and murder, over a background of starvation, terror, depression, and disease.

The first pogroms were followed by an avalanche of Nazi legal orders that left the Jewish community no time to recover or organize. No radios or telephones, no employment of Aryans by Jews, no school for Jewish children, no Jews at food markets or public places of any kind, no Jews on the streetcars or railroads, no Jewish prayer. The last order was accompanied by the burning of most of the city's synagogues, including the 16th-century Golden Rose, with its alabaster Gothic arches. Jews were stripped of everything they owned and ordered to wear blue-on-white Star-of-David armbands.

Hitler had ordered the elimination of the Polish intelligentsia, but more than half the Kraków professors arrested at the Jagiellonian University in 1939 were free within a few months. Some of them even began teaching again, in an underground university that was attended by students such as Karol Wojtyla, the future Pope John Paul II. This made the German leadership unhappy. "The trouble we had with the Kraków professors was terrible," said Hans Frank, the Nazi overlord of Poland, in May 1940. "If we'd been responsible for the thing, it'd have gone differently. If someone is suspicious, we liquidate him immediately."

Things went differently in Lwów. *Überführer* Eberhard Schöngarth, leader of one of the soon-to-be-notorious SS killing squads, arrived in the city on July 2, 1941, three days behind the Wehrmacht. He brought his unit directly to Saint Brigid's prison to view the carnage left by the Soviet occupiers. The SS men were told that some of the victims were German pilots, murdered by Jews. Some of the corpses had been dressed in German uniforms. It seemed that even a death squad needed to gin up some moral indignation in order to murder old men.

The next night, the commando raided two dozen apartments and houses in the nicer quarters of Lwów and kidnapped 26 leading university professors from Jan Kasimir University and the Lwów Polytechnical, along with 26 other people who happened to be present—wives, children, relatives, and unlucky house visitors. They were driven to a former school for orphans on the south side of town, in an area called the Wulka Hills. The old professors were shoved against a wall, questioned, and beaten. The violence was at once methodical and random—a mixture of purposeful torture and pure sadism. After a few hours, gunmen herded the first group of 15 out of the building. Among them were the 69-year-old Stanisław Ruff, chairman of the surgery department at the Lazarus Hospital, on Rappaport Street, and his 55-year-old wife, Anna. They carried the body of their 30-year-old son, Adam, whom the Nazis had gunned down while he suffered an epileptic fit. The SS led the group down the street and into a park. Half an hour later came automatic rifle fire. Soon another group was taken, and then two more, the last as the sun was rising. The killers lined their victims up at the edge of a pit dug a few hours earlier by Ukrainians. They ordered the old men to turn around, and shot them so that they fell facedown in the pit.

The pediatrician Franciszek Groër, Weigl's close friend and Fleck's boss at the time, was among those arrested that night. After ransacking his house for jewelry, artworks, and cash, however, the SS officer in charge discovered that Groër's wife, Cecilia Cumming, was a titled British woman. For some reason, this gave him pause. The Nazis released Groër at daybreak and told him to go home. He was the only survivor of the arrests. Afterwards, the SS looted and seized the apartments of the slain professors. A Dutch businessman who had lived in Lwów before the war and knew its social contours led the SS to plunderable artworks and attractive houses. Few of the valuables were ever recovered. The dead included 18 department chairmen, many of them leading national figures in mathematics, engineering, chemistry, and medicine. Włodzimierz Stożek, the barrel-shaped mathematics chair and regular at the Scottish Café, died with his wife and son. The dapper playwright and feuilletoniste Tadeusz Boy-Żeleński, one of the first prominent Poles to advocate the legalization of abortion, was another victim. Boy-Żeleński was the voice of French literature in Polish, having translated more than 100 French works. He was a celebrated and beloved anticonformist, left-wing democrat, and tweaker of traditional Polish mores. He had the misfortune that night to have been visiting a doctor on Schöngarth's list.

The crime scene was in the middle of a well-to-do neighborhood, and there were witnesses. Dr. Zbigniew Stuchly, microbiologist and member of Weigl's inner circle, awoke to shots that night and watched through his window as the men fell. He could not see their faces, but they made signs of the cross before being shot. The next morning, pale and groggy, he stumbled into his office. "What happened to you?" Weigl asked him. "Are you not sleeping?" When Stuchly began to tell him, Weigl covered his face and begged him to stop. "I can't listen to this!" he said. "Say nothing more!"

Two days later, the Wehrmacht doctor and typhus expert Hermann Eyer arrived in a staff car at the laboratory on St. Nicholas Street. He was taking control of the institute, he said, and he wanted Weigl to continue running it. "Finally you've come, colleague," Weigl responded. "What took you so long?"

By this time, Weigl had decided to cooperate with the Nazi occupation. He knew Eyer through the literature, and they probably had been in contact after 1939. The Wehrmacht was clearly a better partner for Weigl than the SS or the Nazi civilians of the *Generalgouvernement*. The extent to which Weigl knew, in advance, that Eyer was coming isn't clear. But Weigl faced a stark choice: suicide or cooperation. He was a singular man who lived by simple but pragmatic rules. He knew war and hated it, even got angry when marches were played. Weigl became extremely uncomfortable when faced with pain and grief. For this reason, he did not divorce his wife, unable to deal with the conflict, friends say. For the same reason, he offered scientific help to anyone who asked for it, usually without checking references. He decided to cooperate with the Germans, on his own terms. He would continue his work as if nothing had changed.

The assassination of his friends and colleagues came as a powerful shock. At the same time, it was not a surprise. Weigl was 58 years old, a careful observer of the biological world, including his fellow creatures. Having experienced World War I at close proximity, he watched the development of the second catastrophe of his life with terrible foreboding. He knew the Germans well and interpreted Hitler's plans with remarkable clarity. "Anyone who witnesses the atrocities caused by war," he wrote in a notebook at this time,

> must realize that, beyond the terrible destruction, misery and human suffering it causes, war awakens the lowest instincts that lie dormant and slumbering in human beings under the thin coating of civilization and ethical principles consolidated over many generations. During the war [these] instincts awaken in such a hideous form that they would be unrecognizable in the wildest of animals. I can't believe a single man in his soul thinks humanity should settle its disputes through rape and violence, but unfortunately the law of nations has sanctified war, an essentially mindless, mutual mass-murder and a ghastly monument to wild, ancient times.

German officials who visited Lwów during the population exchanges late in 1939 had already approached Weigl and invited him to live in Germany, or in German-occupied Poland. After the murder of the Lwów professors, the Nazis made Weigl an offer they assumed he would not refuse—to put his name on the list of *Volksdeutsche*, ethnic Germans whose "blood" entitled them to the privileges of citizenship, including better rations and living quarters, and freedom from persecution. A group of German officers, among them *SS-Gruppenführer* (Lieutenant General) Fritz Katzmann, Himmler's top henchman in Galicia, invited themselves to Weigl's office. From behind the door, Weigl's assisstants heard Katzmann offer Weigl a university chair in Berlin and German sponsorship for the Nobel Prize. Weigl, always polite to visitors, told Katzmann that while he'd never denied his German ancestry and had even thought about moving to Germany at one time, he could not do so now. He had spent so long setting up his laboratory in Lwów, he said. And it would be disloyal to the Polish people: "One chooses one's nationality only once in life." Appealing to Katzmann with a bit of antiquated chivalry, he added, "Wouldn't it be strange for a German officer to offer honors to a Polish professor, when by accepting the German offer the Pole would have dishonored himself?"

Katzmann, the stereotypical Nazi sort—scar-faced, brutal, short-tempered—could not control himself. He began to threaten Weigl with references to his 25 murdered colleagues. "Don't forget," Katzmann said, "that the German government is capable of breaking the resistance of its opponents." Weigl, stroking his beard, responded, "Herr General, life today has become so sad and disappointing that an old man like me has no hope of living in better times. I often think of ending my life, but this would be a tragedy for my family. However, Herr General, if you should give the order for my liquidation, you would only be doing me a favor, and in the process make me a hero."

When the Nazi invasion began, Weigl had considered abandoning the institute, but the murder of the professors clarified his mind. When he saw that the lab would function under the direction of Eyer, whom he trusted, he decided to stay, though he would never accept Nazi bribes or pretend that he was one of them. "Weigl did not adhere to the principle of 'eye for an eye, tooth for a tooth,'" said Henryk Mosing, his chief epidemiologist. "He felt that even with the enemy you needed to look for some common ground that would lead to the general benefit. He saw that if he left his building the Wehrmacht would make it a barracks and destroy its collections, especially the enormous specimen museum created by the great zoologist Benedykt Dybowski. Moreover he quickly saw that the intelligentsia was out of work and needed a livelihood."

The Fantastic Laboratory of Dr. Weigl

The institute grew quickly in size and personnel. It soon took over most of the four-story building on St. Nicholas Street, as well as the Potocki Street location established by the Soviets. University staff threatened with death, starvation, or deportation as slave laborers to Germany, students and young people, members of the resistance movement were protected by real or fictitious employment in the institute. Anytime a Pole in Lwów was in trouble—for underground activities, helping Jews, or anything else—the institute was there for protection. "Anyone who needed saving became a louse feeder," said Stanisława Woyciechowska, an assistant to Weigl. "They got the *Ausweis*, and they were protected." The orange-paper ID card with the Wehrmacht eagle and the inscriptions *Oberkommando des Heeres* (Army High Command) and *Institut für Fleckfieber und Virus Forschung* (Institute for Typhus and Viral Research) became a ticket to survival for thousands of Poles. Nearly every educated Pole in Lwów sought a job at the institute.

How many Poles worked there has never been firmly established. In the 1980s, some of Weigl's former aides put together an incomplete list of more than 500 people. Some estimates go as high as 5,000; the real figure is probably between 1,200 and 3,000. Among those saved by working in the institute were at least 75 men and women who became full professors in Poland and elsewhere after the war. There were also novelists, high school teachers, and musicians: the poet Zbigniew Herbert, the musician Stanisław Skrowaczewski, the sociologist Józef Chałasiński. "The activities of Rudolf Weigl," wrote Tomasz Cieszyński, whose father, Antoni, was one of the murdered professors, "were key to the biological and spiritual survival of the Polish nation in the face of ethnic, racial, and class extermination."

The Poles working for Weigl would survive because the Nazis feared typhus and lice, and valued the product made from these lice more than they valued human life itself. A simple flash of the *Ausweis* was usually enough to get its holder out of any trouble, especially during the routine stops that often led to murder, enslavement, or deportation. The German guards would hand back the pass with a disgusted shake of the head. "They were human after all, though it was often hard to believe," said Wacław Szybalski. "As the war went on, most of them were very young or very old, because the rest were at the front. The guards liked being in jobs where they weren't being shot at."

The regime created a ghetto in Lwów in October 1941, ordering Jews to live in an impoverished area located mostly to the north of the main railroad line that splits the city, in the districts of Zamarstynowska and Kleparow. The housing was a mixture of lower middle-class apartments and hovels without running water or electricity. The Nazis also set up a forced-labor camp at 134 Janowska Street, on the northwest edge of the ghetto. Janowska would become one of the most wretched torture centers in the Nazi system. It was used as a work camp, a death camp, and a staging area for Jews being shipped from Lwów and other towns to the gas chambers at Belzec and Auschwitz. Janowska was run by spectacularly sadistic officers, each infamous for a particular facet of morbid perversion. An officer named Richard Rokita would walk down a row of saluting inmates on the parade ground and shoot one or two in the nape of the neck. Officer Wepke was known for chopping children in two with an ax. The camp commander, Fritz Gebauer, was generally mild-mannered but occasionally needed to strangle a woman, an action that produced a state of red-faced passion. The worst may have been the deputy commander, Gustav Wilhaus, who enjoyed shooting prisoners from the balcony of his villa. His wife often joined him in demonstrating her marksmanship, firing on Jews standing in a workshop near the house.

For a while, doctors were one of the only Jewish professional groups whom the Nazis provided any special protection. The *General-gouvernement* health department branch, directed by a Westphalian Nazi named Wilhelm Dopheide, issued special armbands for registered doctors that supposedly protected them against random arrest or labor details. As the Jews were kicked out of their homes and squeezed into the crumbling north side district, doctors were given slightly larger space allocations and even rooms for receiving patients. This was probably a tactical move on the part of Dopheide, who had contacts with the T-4 in Berlin, the euthanasia unit that organized the first mass murders of Eastern Jewry. Dopheide showed little interest in the health of Jews. Some 1,200 mentally ill Jews and Poles starved or froze to death in an asylum under his care. When the building had been emptied of patients, the Wehrmacht used it to house injured troops.

The Nazis confiscated the Jewish Lazarus Hospital on Rappaport Street, a large red-brick Moorish building, built in the late 19th century, which had served as a teaching hospital and was equipped with the latest equipment and a fine staff. But Lwów had a prosperous, close-knit medical community, and some of its cohesion remained. As the Nazis murdered, starved, and hunted their coreligionists, the Jewish doctors of Lwów, assisted by refugee doctors from Kraków, Warsaw, and other cities, fought for their patients as best they could. They managed to open three ghetto hospitals, including one in the building of a Polish high school on Kuszewicz Street that many of the doctors had attended as youths. The three-story masonry building lay half a block north of the railroad embankment and offered a bird's-eye view of the Gestapo tortures occurring at the ghetto checkpoints below.

Fleck spent the first year and a half of the Nazi occupation running the bacteriological lab at the Kuszewicz hospital. In September 1941, Ukrainian militiamen threw the Flecks out of their apartment and robbed them of everything except a bundle of bed linen and kitchen utensils. The Flecks paid 10,000 zlotys (about $20,000 at the time) to a Pole to rent his apartment a few blocks from the ghetto hospital, but after taking the money he remained in the apartment with them, and eventually they were forced to leave. Fleck, his wife, Ernestyna, and son, Ryszard, lived for a while in the hospital itself, under the protection of its director, Dr. Maksymilian Kurzrock. Later they found a room nearby at Wybranowski 4, sharing it with two other families. In a January 1942 *Aktion*, Fleck lost his sisters, Antonina Fleck-Silber and Henryka Fleck-Kessler, who had been teachers at the Vocational School for Jewish Girls in Lwów. They were murdered with their husbands at Janowska.

It may have been at this point that Weigl intervened on behalf of his former assistant. There is no written record of an interaction, but sometime later in 1942, the Flecks and his assistants were identified as employees of the Lemberg branch of Eyer's *Institut fur Fleckfieber und Virus Forschung*. Szybalski has reported that Fleck worked at the Weigl institute as a louse feeder, but Fleck's postwar writings say nothing of this, and it seems unlikely. Both of the Weigl institute buildings were more than a two-mile walk from the ghetto, and the Wehrmacht prohibited Jews from working in them. However, Fleck did meet with Weigl at least once during this period, and Weigl provided him with vaccines and lab equipment. Fleck's colleague from his private practice, Olga Elster, joined him in the lab at Kuszewicz Street for a while. Her husband, Edward, ran another ghetto hospital, on Zamarstynowska Street. A while later, another colleague joined them—Anna Seeman, a Vienna-educated scientist-physician who knew Fleck from the Social Security Hospital. Seeman was a gifted microbiologist who walked with a limp as a result of a childhood case of polio. Her husband, Jakob, an engineer and Hebrew scholar, had injured his hand and was given a job as a laboratory technician for protection. Their 10-year-old son, Bronisław, or Bruno, spent months on top of a water heater in the laboratory, hiding from Gestapo raids. Ryszard Fleck, 16, worked at his parents' side as a lab technician.

As the weather turned cold in late 1941, typhus broke out in the unheated dwellings of the beaten-down Jewish ghetto. A disease that Fleck knew from the First World War now added its monotonous terror to the other threats of annihilation. A dozen or more people were stuffed into each ghetto apartment room. The possibilities of bathing or cleaning one's clothes were very limited. Everyone was hungry, and many were starving. "That typhus should quickly spread in these circumstances," wrote Fleck, "was no wonder." The outbreak began in a Soviet POW camp the Nazis had created at the Citadel, a 19th-century Austro-Hungarian barracks. That winter, there were thousands of cases; a year later, Fleck estimated that 70 percent of the ghetto residents had been infected with the disease. The German doctors responded to the epidemic with utter perversity.

The pattern had been established in Warsaw, occupied since September 1939, where German public health officials at first tried to fight the disease by requiring Jews to submit to delousing baths and quarantines. These measures were impractical and punitive. Delousing meant standing naked in the freezing cold while one's apartment was searched and often robbed, and handing over a precious set of clothes likely to be damaged by powerful chemicals. A Warsaw public health official estimated that only a fifth of all typhus cases were being reported to his officers. Frank, the German emperor of Poland, ordered that to prevent spread of the disease, Jews trying to sneak out of the ghetto were to be shot. At a conference of 100 Nazi health officers at a Carpathian spa in October 1941, the issue came to a head with the intervention of Robert Kudicke, who had taken over the Polish Institute of Hygiene from Ludwik Hirszfeld. Speaking "purely academically without making any value judgment," Kudicke said, "the Jewish population simply breaks out of the ghettos because there is nothing to eat. . . . If one wants to prevent that in the future, then one must use the best means for this, namely provide for more sufficient provisioning." Jost Walbaum, the medical chief for occupied Poland, gave the following retort:

> Naturally it would be best and simplest to give the people sufficient provisions, but that cannot be done. This is connected to the food situation and the war situation in general. Thus shooting will be employed when one comes across a Jew outside the ghetto without special permission. One must say it quite openly in this circle, be clear about it. There are only two

ways. We sentence the Jews in the ghetto to death by hunger or we shoot them. Even if the end result is the same, the latter is more intimidating. We cannot do otherwise, even if we want to. We have one and only one responsibility, that the German people are not infected and endangered by these parasites. For that any means must be right.

Here, then, was the German medical community's offer to Polish Jews: die of starvation and typhus in the ghetto, or die by shooting. The loyalty of the German medical profession to authority and its adherence to Nazi ideology seem to have kept any humane solutions from entering their heads. Occasionally the doctors were cruel, and occasionally they were corrupt. But for the most part they were "honorable," on their own terms—hideously impassive in the face of a genocide that they blamed on the victims. Even assuming that most of them did not, at least in the early stages of the war, envision the complete annihilation of the Jews, their membership in the thought collective caused them to tread forward like sleepwalkers. This was groupthink in its most hideous form.

Hirszfeld, who had been ousted from his job by Kudicke and Nauck, was shocked at the stupidity of the German antityphus measures. Posters told everyone who found a louse on himself to report to a physician, and required the reporting of every case of fever. Science had long before abolished such medieval quarantine practices, Hirszfeld said, because in addition to being cruel, they were useless. "But since in this case the point was to liquidate the Jews and not the epidemic as such," he added, "quarantines turned out to be quite useful."

On April 24, 1943, Heinrich Himmler gave a speech to an assembly of SS officers: "Getting rid of lice is not a question of ideology," he told them. "It is a matter of cleanliness. In just the same way, anti-Semitism, for us, has not been a question of ideology, but a matter of cleanliness, which now will soon have been dealt with. We shall soon be deloused.

We have only 20,000 lice left, and then the matter is finished within the whole of Germany."

A few months before the liquidation of the Warsaw ghetto, friends rescued Hirszfeld, and he lived out the war concealed in the country house of Polish aristocrats, where he wrote a memoir. He did not spare the German doctors under whom he had been forced to serve. "If in the institute that I had a part in molding there now works Mr. Nauck and Mr. Kudicke, whereas I—expelled—pine for my workplace: who is the parasite, I or they? And who is profiting from someone else's work?" In the ghetto, there had been little Hirszfeld could do to slow the epidemic. "The wonderful Dr. Weigl," he wrote, secretly sent him large quantities of vaccine. But the shots were available only to a tiny minority. The *Generalgouvernement* had given Kudicke 50 million zlotys to combat the typhus epidemic when it spread beyond the ghetto in 1942; the only part allotted to the Jews was an 8,000-zloty disinfecting sprayer.

Hirszfeld created a makeshift medical school in the ghetto, and one of the topics discussed in his immunology class was the question "Are the Jews really a separate race?" His answer: No. Blood-typing research—Hirszfeld was one of the world's experts—proved that Jews had always mingled with the nations where they dwelt. The idea was controversial among the rabbinate, but the students were fascinated. "After the lecture, several of them came up to me and told me with overflowing emotions: 'We thank you. We feel that you have taken the curse from us. . . . [I]t seemed to me that I was fulfilling the duty of a teacher who was showing new roads to his pupils, roads beset with difficulties but also offering a hope for a better future." At the very edge of civilization, where millions were paying for the world's insane obsession with race, a lonely man shone a lantern of scientific truth. "Unfortunately," Hirszfeld wrote, "I was speaking to human beings sentenced to extermination."

CHAPTER SEVEN

THE FANTASTIC LABORATORY
OF DR. WEIGL

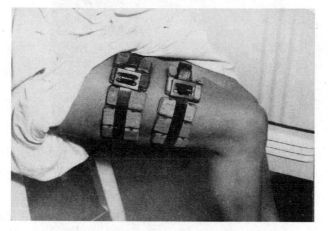

Feeding lice to make vaccine. (Courtesy of
Emil-von-Behring-Bibliothek, Philipps-Universität Marburg.)

The Weigl institute was a mysterious labyrinth of science and deception during the German occupation. Its visible structure was odd enough, organized as it was around the somewhat gruesome production scheme of the vaccine. "Its base was the farmers, who grew the lice from eggs, watched their development and cleaned their cages, for the louse does not tolerate dirt," wrote the novelist and poet Mirosław Żuławski in a memoir. "The feeders built the next part of the pyramid, and they were divided into two categories: the higher aristocracy who fed infected lice and the plebes, like me, who fed the healthy ones." Only those who had suffered through a bout of typhus

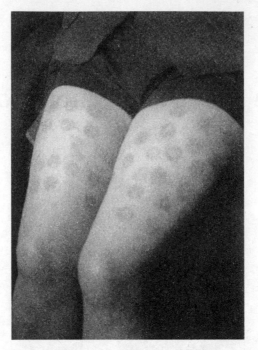

After a feeding. (Courtesy of National Museum, Przemyśl.
Photograph of original by S. Kosiedowski.)

were allowed to feed the typhus-infected lice, and they received double wages. "Next came the injectors, and then the preparers. At the
top of the pyramid stood The Professor—the high priest of typhus
magic."

Weigl had ingeniously brought together several mechanical, chemical, and biological steps in the creation of the vaccine, and its mass
production relied on an intricate set of standards and conditions. The
process was arcane and appeared nightmarish from outside the lab;
inside, however, its peculiarity was cherished, for it created a space of
peace and relative freedom in the hell of occupied Lwów. Under wartime conditions in 1941 the scaling up of the vaccine production was
a remarkable technical feat. The tens of millions of lice used in the
vaccine during the war descended from a cross between lice gathered
from the clothing of Russians in Austrian POW camps during World

War I, and an Ethiopian variety that Weigl had obtained in Addis Ababa. The new creature was designated the "Weigl strain."

Vaccine production began when lice in a petri dish deposited eggs on small squares of cloth, usually cut from Wehrmacht uniforms. Each square was put into a specially designed test tube, where it was held midway down by a partial constriction in the glass and a piece of cotton. After incubation, the lice larvae hatched after three to eight days, fell off the cloth squares, and dropped to the bottom. Each tube yielded some 800 larvae, which formed a pulsating yellowish ball about the size of a hard candy that workers transferred to 4 x 7 x 5 centimeter wooden cages. One wall of the cage consisted of a screen that Weigl had adapted from sifting screens used by Polish flour mills. The sesame seed–sized lice could feed through the screens but not escape. Each cage had a smaller square of woolen fabric on which the lice could deposit the next generation of eggs.

The cages were closed, sealed with paraffin to keep the lice from escaping, and strapped to the legs of the feeder with wide elastic bands. As many as 44 cages could be attached to a single feeder's legs with four separate bands. The lice sucked bood for about 45 minutes every day for 12 days. Men usually attached the cages to their calves, while women placed them on their thighs, where the reddish bite marks could be hidden under a skirt. A person on average fed 25,000 lice a month from hatching until maturity.

Each day the feeder removed his or her cages of lice when the creatures were swollen and shiny with blood, and placed the cages screen down in boxes. The next day, the feeder would retrieve "his" lice for another feeding, until the cycle was over. Lice were periodically transferred to clean, heat-sterilized cages. During the transfers, the technicians collected eggs laid on the fabric and removed dead or sluggish-looking lice, molted skins, body parts, and feces.

When the healthy lice had reached 12 days of age, they were sent to be infected with *Rickettsia*. It was the job of the injectors— the *strzykacze*—to infect each louse manually. Two injectors worked

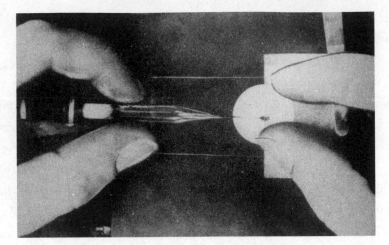

Injecting typhus culture into the louse by hand. (Courtesy of National Museum, Przemyśl. Photograph of original by S. Kosiedowski.)

together—one, using a small forceps, placed each louse in a slot in the clamp with its rear in the air. His partner, while viewing the rear of the louse under a 32X binocular microscope, inserted a glass pipette into the anus and used a foot pedal to release a valve that pumped a microdroplet of rickettsial solution into the louse. Each injection cycle required about a second. Two highly skilled operators could inject up to 2,000 lice in an hour. The infected lice were then loaded into cages and fed five more days on the blood of the injectors themselves.

When the population of *Rickettsia prowazekii* reached 10 million per louse gut cell, the cells burst. Undigested human blood leaked into the abdomen, and the lice turned deep ruby red. At this point, the lice were shaken out of the cages into jars filled with 0.5 percent phenol. Thus killed, they were transferred to the dissectors— *preparatorzy*—who harvested the louse guts to make the vaccine. This was also a highly meticulous activity. The dissector used a scalpel to make an incision between the thorax and abdomen under a binocular microscope at 16X power, where everything appeared backwards and upside down. She pulled the infected gut out with the needle and tip of a scalpel, taking care not to damage the gut so that the entire rickettsial harvest could be transferred into a jar. The apprenticeship for the dissector lasted two weeks and was unpaid. A supervisor with a stopwatch monitored the trainees as they gradually increased their speed. A good dissector could harvest 300 louse midguts per hour, or one louse every twelve seconds. It was the kind of activity that would cause blindness in short order, and shifts were limited to six hours. The infected midguts were ground in a special mortar with a phenol solution that killed the *Rickettsia*. This mixture, the vaccine, was taken to a filling room and prepared at three different strengths. At the height of production, the Lwów and Kraków labs each produced thousands of doses every day.

Much of what we know about the wartime structure of the Weigl lab comes from Wacław Szybalski, whose career in genetics—an interest spurred by Weigl—later took him to Cold Spring Harbor Laboratory, Rutgers University, and the University of Wisconsin. Though only 19 years old in 1941, Szybalski was a remarkably self-possessed and determined young scientist. As a young teenager, he attended the lectures of famous Lwów professors, and while studying chemistry at Lwów Polytechnical, from 1939 to 1941 (when not making bombs in the basement), he attended the mathematics lectures of Banach,

A louse dissected for removal of its typhus-rich intestines. (Courtesy of National Museum, Przemyśl. Photograph of original by S. Kosiedowski.)

Antoni Łomnicki, Stożek, and Kazimierz Bartel. The latter had been prime minister of Poland on three occasions in the late 1920s, and Szybalski was the star pupil in his class, "Descriptive Geometry and Perspective." The Nazis arrested Bartel shortly after the invasion. When he refused to head a puppet government, they murdered him, on July 26, 1941.

In the first days of the Nazi occupation, Weigl asked Szybalski to gather a group of men and women, including as many senior professors as possible, and to supervise them as lice feeders. His "breeding unit" was one of scores or perhaps hundreds of teams at the institute, each consisting of a leader and 12–15 feeders, or *karmiciele*. Szybalski's group included the famous mathematicians of the Lwów school who had not been murdered or driven into exile: Banach, Jerzy Albrycht,

Weigl at work during the war. (Courtesy of National Museum, Przemyśl. Photograph of original by S. Kosiedowski.)

Feliks Baranski, Bronisław Knaster, Władysław Orlicz. Their Scottish Book had been buried under a soccer field, where it was retrieved after the war. Szybalski's group also included the chemist Tadeusz Baranowski; the former university rector Seweryn Krzemieniewski and his wife, Helena, both biologists; and the composer Stanisław Skrowaczewski, who would later conduct the Minneapolis Symphony Orchestra. Szybalski selected the mathematicians, particularly Banach, partly for selfish reasons. "I thought I would learn from being in their company and listening to their discussions every day. As a former Boy Scout and diehard Lwów patriot, I imagined I could somehow protect them from the dangers of war." The German invasion caught Banach in Kiev. Rather than retreat with the Red Army, he took the last train back to Lwów to return to his child and wife, who was Jewish. The Gestapo arrested Banach, but he was released after a few weeks; his family fled to Kraków, where they lived out the war in hiding.

Szybalski's routine changed following the occupation. Weigl had given his family a radio, and he awoke each morning at six to listen to the BBC. After breakfast, he pushed his bicycle up St. Mark's Street, past the cast iron fence of the Botanical Garden, and coasted to the heavy wooden doors of the Weigl institute, which even by then was humming with activity. For two hours, he would prepare the lice for the day's feeding. The louse cages, cleared of molted skins and feces, went into a high-pressure sterilizer, and Szybalski put the healthy lice into new, clean cages. "It was easy," he recalled. "The lice didn't run fast." His feeders would come in before noon. This was the hour the Lwów's professoriat had traditionally gathered in the city's cafés, but only Nazis, spies, and *Volksdeutsche* visited cafés now. The Weigl institute had become the center of intellectual life. And nearly the entire university of Lwów was in attendance, broken into seminar-sized groups. "There was a huge table in the center of the room, and people sat around it," Szybalski recalled. "They brought in books, sometimes, or something to eat. And they talked."

The Fantastic Laboratory of Dr. Weigl

The caged lice made the feeders itch, but scratching was forbidden, because it could lead to infections that hurt the lice. Conversation was the best distraction. "When you put on the lice cages," Szybalski explained, "the first feeling is like a hot iron, as 500 or 1,000 of them pierce your skin. You don't want that to be repeated, so you try not to move the cages, because then the lice lose their place and have to bite again." Marek Zakrzewski was one of the youngest members of Szybalski's group. His career as a feeder started on a rough note: he got blisters from the bites. The condition resolved, fortunately, and Zakrzewski returned to feeding, and found himself looking forward to the daily discussions. He especially liked listening to Mieczysław Kreutz, a chatty psychologist. One winter day, Kreutz turned to Banach and Knaster and asked them the following question: "Gentlemen," he said, "when my wife used to make ice cream, she would pour some liquid and ice into the container, then pour in salt and turn the crank. I asked her, why do you use salt? She says it makes the ice cream freeze. Coming over here today, I see the tram conductor throwing something on the tracks. What is it? Salt. Why? So the rails don't freeze. So how is it? One throws salt to cause freezing, the other to prevent it." A passionate, uninformed debate followed. Zakrzewski, an engineering student, knew the answer, but traditional Polish academic protocol called for students to speak only when spoken to. So the problem remained unsolved. (Answer: in both instances, salt lowers the freezing point. This melts ice on roadways; the ice cream is mixed while surrounded by colder-than-freezing water.)

Banach usually sat quietly chain-smoking while Knaster yakked on, whether mathematics or politics was the subject. The Krzemieniewskis explained the life habits of the creatures they were feeding. Aleksander Kosiba, a meteorologist, regaled them with tales from his polar exhibitions. Sushi being known only to the Japanese at this time, the feeders were thrilled by his descriptions of eating raw fish and whale meat. Even in this lugubrious atmosphere, their legs clasped with cages of hungry insects in a room reeking of wood alcohol, smoke, and their own blood, the feeders wrinkled their noses at these exotic flavors. It was intellectually stimulating but also surrealistic to listen to the long discussions about the frontiers of mathematics, topology and the theory of numbers. But Szybalski had to make sure that in the fervor of discussion they did not overfeed the lice. The mathematicians, especially, were generally too distracted to know when to stop, and the Weigl laboratory lice had lost their natural instinct to stop feeding. This could have disastrous consequences. Overfed lice were hard to handle. They would burst and create a sticky mess.

As for the feeders, "they never complained," said Szybalski. "They were happy to be able to survive, or to hope they would survive—it wasn't guaranteed. Every day you said goodbye you never knew if you'd see them again. Your life was unprotected. It depended upon the whims of soldiers and policemen and militia." Szybalski and his friends

Lice feeders during the war. (Courtesy of the Emil-Behring-Bibliothek, Philipps-Universität Marburg.)

kept their wits by imagining that the war would end. It would be only another month or two, they said, over and over again. They were young and unafraid because death happened to other people, not them.

Szybalski was particularly fond of Banach, who told him that mathematics was the most magnificent expression of the human soul. They shared a passion for learning and for Lwów, and they called each other "brother," which was strictly against academic tradition. Banach was like that. He liked nothing better than to thumb his nose at hauteur. He also appreciated Szybalski because every day the young man related to him all the latest, forbidden radio news from around the world. Banach's love for Lwów was epitomized in the possibly apocryphal story told about Banach and his Hungarian-born friend John von Neumann. In the late 1930s, as the walls closed in on Poland, von Neumann came to Lwów on three occasions to transmit a message from Norbert Wiener of MIT. The university would pay Banach generously to emigrate to the United States and teach in Cambridge. "How much?" Banach asked, finally. Von Neumann wrote a 1 and told him, "as many zeros as you want after that." Banach looked at the paper for a moment and then said, "It isn't enough."

During the war, von Neumann and Stan Ulam would help design the atomic bomb at Los Alamos. While his friends harnessed the curve of binding energy in the New Mexico desert, Banach smoked and strapped lice boxes to his legs in Lwów.

Throughout the war, his cough grew worse; he lost weight and often looked pale. "To help him, I cheated a little with the number of lice in his cage whenever he seemed tired," Szybalski recalled. "I did not want him to lose too much blood. I considered it legitimate for the good of Polish mathematics." In 1944, Banach was arrested for currency violations—he made deals on the black market to manage a chronic shortness of cash. Weigl called on Hermann Eyer to fish him out of prison after a few days. Eyer also rescued lab workers from Gestapo prisons and even concentration camps.

Szybalski's father, Stefan, who had begun the war as a prosperous aristocrat and businessman, kept falling lower on the social scale. During the Soviet occupation, he'd been a translator and driver. Now he had to become a louse feeder. Wacław's brother, Stanisław, had a slightly higher status: he was a louse dissector. Their mother continued to be the center of the family. Every afternoon at two, they met for the important meal. Occasionally there was nothing but soup and bread, but usually the women managed to scrounge meat and vegetables, and dessert. Wacław wired the apartment's electrical meter to run backwards and installed a suction pump to increase the gas pressure. He brewed bathtub vodka to make a few extra dollars. Family and patriotism kept them strong. There was a little poem that circulated in Lwów about the *Volksdeutsche*, Poles who had exchanged their birthright for better diets and Nazi protection.

What is your motto, little *Volksdeutscher*? White bread!
What made you? The war.
How will you die? Hanged from a dry branch.
What will your grave monument be? A pile of shit.

In 1943, the Germans partially reopened the Lwów Polytechnical University. The German war effort required more Polish technicians in industry, even if they were *Untermenschen*. Now Szybalski spent half the day at school. "They didn't know what to do," he said. "On the one hand, they felt they had to kill everyone. But if they killed us all it would interfere with the war effort." When it came to the Jews, however, elimination came first, exploitation next. At the Weigl institute, everyone knew about the slave camp at Janowska, about Belzec, and about the mass shootings that regularly occurred on the outskirts of town. But the Jews were walled off in the ghetto, and so was the scale of their suffering. Jews, the Germans made perfectly clear, were not to be employed at the institute. Szybalski had a crush on a Jewish girl from his chemistry class, named Roza, and offered to hide her in the family's apartment during the winter of 1942. The penalty for protecting a Jew was death. Roza would not leave her own family behind, however. Szybalski never heard from her again.

The Nazis were proving wretchedly incompetent at preventing typhus from spreading out of the ghetto. This problem grew from the contradictory impulses of the SS state. It was policy to eradicate the Jews, but the war required every drop of labor extracted from the Reich's enemies before they died. Public hygiene experts urged the confining of Jews to the ghetto. But the military and other authorities needed the Jews to show up for work. So they trudged through town to factories and other public places, seeding them with infected lice in the process. Each Jew in Lwów had an ID book, and the authorities devised a continually shifting set of stamps that identified workers as crucial to the economy—A for *Arbeiter* (worker), R for *Rüstung* (defense). Without a stamp, one faced death as a "useless eater." The sick dragged themselves out of bed to work.

Wherever Jews went, the murderers hounded them. Early in 1942, the Lwów health chief Dopheide ordered all typhus patients brought to the hospital on Kuszewicz Street. After the hospital had filled with about 500 patients, heavy trucks pulled up outside it. Gestapo and black-clad Ukrainian militiamen raided the building, defenestrated some of the patients, hauled out the rest, and flung them into the trucks. In broad daylight and in plain view of the city's residents, the trucks drove to a sandy hill on the edge of town, where the patients were machine-gunned and buried in pits. "The brutality of these actions is difficult to describe," Fleck recalled immediately after the war. "Hunting human beings with dogs was part of it. Dragging seriously ill patients out of their homes or hospitals, where they often lay after operations with open wounds or broken limbs, was another. Wrenching out the arms and legs of small children, who were tossed like bundles up on to the transport wagons."

In the hospital, where Fleck and his colleagues attempted to tend to the sick, the Gestapo swept through with such "cleansings" every few weeks. When relatives got wind that an *Aktion* was in the offing, they would come to the hospital to evacuate their loved one. Eventually, the wholesale murder of their patients discouraged doctors from bringing them to hospitals for treatment. The ghetto itself became a secret hospital, with patients hidden in attics and cellars, under blankets and pillows, behind dressers and false walls. Dr. Marek Redner recalled being called to a quiet, immaculate apartment where he was told, after the family decided it could trust him, that four typhus-infected members were concealed in the beds. Sometimes "the typhus patients were hidden in places I could only reach crawling into narrow places, literally on my stomach. Two or three times daily I had to provide care in the most incredible positions, sometimes climbing a ladder or standing on stacked furniture." One day, while administering a cardiac stimulant to a sick man, Redner heard a commotion behind him and saw a huge wall mirror being pushed aside. From behind it appeared the corpse of a beautiful young woman being dragged out by the legs, long black hair sweeping the floor behind her.

Patients with psychotic reactions to typhus posed a particularly frightening challenge to their families and doctors. Their screams and unpredictable actions could attract the attention of the Gestapo or neighborhood spies. Other patients showed extraordinary stamina. "Frequently it was necessary to visit a patient hiding in an attic where the winter temperature was 20 below zero," said Redner. "Strangely, these patients were recovering well even though they lacked suitable bedding or blankets. I concluded that the low temperature had a beneficial effect, lowering the fever like a permanent compress and stimulating the circulation." That was true only for the young, who even in normal circumstances are more likely to survive typhus. Most of the patients over the age of 50 died.

Samuel Drix, a medical student when the war broke out, contracted typhus at the Janowska camp and had a fever of 108 degrees, temporary deafness, and an inability to read—alexia. "I could not read a letter smuggled from my parents—I saw characters but could not understand their meaning. And then came apraxia—I wanted to write a letter to my parents, but I could not write. . . . I also lost appetite, which—with our starvation diet—was simply unheard of." After recovering, Drix treated hundreds of typhus patients and developed an ability to diagnose the disease with a quick glance. He, too, observed an unheard-of resistance in many patients. "Inmates went through this terrible sickness, walking around with a constant fever of more than 40 degrees Celsius [104 Fahrenheit] lasting for more than two weeks. . . . I really cannot explain it, but it seems that the human mind and body have unexpected inner strength that comes out at such times of struggle for existence."

Most of the survivors would die anyway, murdered in the streets or the camps. In his memoir, Ludwik Hirszfeld asked whether his and his colleagues' achievements had been worth it. All the patients and the doctors he'd known in the ghetto were dead. "What does it matter now how the murdered ones intended to combat tuberculosis or venereal diseases? Yet perhaps there will be a few who will be touched by knowing how those condemned to death tried to live in dignity and to reassemble the norms of life."

After the war, Fleck and Hirszfeld shared their experiences in medical hope and futility. During the war, they fought typhus separately in the ghettos of Lwów and Warsaw. Both struggled with the meager tools at hand to manage the catastrophe that engulfed their community. As typhus spread freely through the Lwów ghetto, Fleck made a bold, desperate attempt to turn his knowledge into a practical prophylactic. It is surely one of the most remarkable episodes of medical innovation accomplished under the crushing oppression of Nazism.

Studying the urine of patients who responded to the exanthin reaction, Fleck determined that during a period of several days around the appearance of the first symptoms of typhus, the patient's urine contained typhus antigens that were recognizable to the immune system. Similar findings had been described in certain pneumonia patients. Fleck hoped these particles might be useful, and in early 1942 he began research on the urine of typhus patients in the ghetto hospital in Lwów. Initially, he hoped to devise a diagnostic method that gave results more quickly than the Weil-Felix reaction. Eventually, he hoped to make a vaccine. Within a few months, his success at creating an early diagnostic was clear enough for Fleck to bring the results to the attention of other hospital doctors, to Hirszfeld in Warsaw, and to Professor Groër, who had returned to the Mother and Child Hospital. The ghetto newspaper published an announcement of his work on May 23, 1942.

Fleck and his colleagues needed to find a way to concentrate the antigen if they hoped to make a vaccine from the urine. They did this by putting urine samples in a vacuum at 40 degrees Celsius, concentrating them ten times, then filtering the concentrate. "In a normal lab this is an easy technique, in an improvised ghetto lab it was in no way easy," Fleck wrote later. They found an oil pump to run the filter, but the apparatus had to be improvised by making a water-driven mill wheel fashioned with a jigsaw. While Fleck worked on the vaccine, the Germans raided the hospital and the apartments and streets around it. Patients were carried off and liquidated. Co-workers disappeared, sometimes for days, sometimes for good. "The work suffered as a result," Fleck wrote. "But the results were good."

To get more precise information on when, in the course of an illness, the patient began to excrete antigen in urine, Fleck and his team began gathering liters of the liquid from patients and their family contacts. They were able to find antigen in patients who were not yet ill, especially in the first two days of incubation of the sickness, sometimes even four days before the appearance of fever. At this point, they began testing to see whether it was possible to protect guinea pigs against infection by injecting them with the antigen. Guinea pigs evince a subtle but defined reaction when infected with typhus; they show no obvious symptoms except an increase in body temperature. Here again, Fleck succeeded. "Guinea pigs immunized with urine preparations did not react to the injections of blood from the sick, while the unimmunized controls showed the typical fever curve," he wrote.

Now Fleck felt he had a basis to make a vaccine. The difficulties were immense. He and his co-workers were collecting up to 100 liters of urine every day in the hospital, but the hospital lacked equipment to process it. One of Fleck's colleagues, Dr. Bernard Umschweif, had worked before the war in the Laokoon chemical factory, which was owned by a Jewish businessman. The factory had been confiscated and was now in the hands of a German, a Dr. Schwanenberg. Fleck decided to take a calculated risk by making contact with the German. He and Umschweif walked to Laokoon, about a mile away, and offered Schwanenberg a patent for production of the vaccine if he would allow them to produce it in his factory. Schwanenberg agreed, and also said he would seek permission from the Gestapo to hire them as Jewish employees.

News of Fleck's vaccine spread quickly through the medical community of Lwów. A non-Jewish colleague who dared to visit the Jewish hospital on Kuszewicz Street in 1942 was astonished at the discipline and seriousness of the Jewish doctors. "I talked to Fleck and other friends there, and I found that they were still full of medical ambitions, and trying not to anticipate their fate," said the physician. "They worked very efficiently in less than modest circumstances, and they even had scientific aspirations. Fleck's discovery, which allowed the early diagnosis of typhus, was a very valuable one, theoretically and clinically, and it soon became known throughout town. It gave rise to a joke: instead of the German term *Fleckfieber*, the disease should now be called 'Fleck's typhus.'"

At the Weigl institute, vestiges of normality blended into moments of horror. People sold homemade vodka and soap, cakes and bean soup, in the locker room. Once a new lady came in to work with them but seemed very nervous and left after a few days. They heard later that she was a Jew, and had hanged herself from her radiator.

For the young Poles, life could be tolerable and occasionally pleasant. Feeders of healthy lice got 100 zlotys per month, about enough to buy 10 pounds of butter or 20 pounds of sugar on the black market. In addition to wages, they obtained artificial butter, ersatz honey, and sugar beet marmalade, with the occasional piece of sausage. The wages were not much, but the Nazis were not hounding them through the streets. And the institute was a source of fascination.

Decades later, men and women would describe the empty rooms and crumbling walls of its mysterious basement. One room, which according to legend was haunted by the spirit of "the bishop" (the building had, after all, once been a convent) resembled a "torture chamber" with hooks, chains, and brackets mysteriously embedded in the walls. The window of Weigl's corner, underground office looked out on the Botanical Garden. The adjoining rooms had been converted into an animal house full of squeaking mice and snuffling guinea pigs that sang for their breakfast in the morning. The groundskeeper was a one-eyed, one-legged World War I veteran named Bakowski. He was notorious among the employees' children for chasing them out of the garden. He was intensely loyal to Weigl. When the weather was good, the dissectors and feeders headed to the garden during breaks. Sometimes they played soccer. Romances began; people gossiped about them. On the weekend, there were occasionally outings to the country. Wacław Szybalski's brother, Stan, recalled that two friendly German guards accompanied them on one lakeside excursion, to make sure they encountered no problems with Ukrainian militia.

"We were one big family," the novelist Mirosław Żuławski wrote. "Although we were paid a pittance, and the additional allocations weren't enough to replace the blood we lost, to be a Weigl employee was a mark of nobility." It was good manners to make sure the louse boxes were sealed firmly. If they were loose, people in the tram would begin to move away as a louse peacefully wandered around a collar or sleeve. A year after the war ended, when asked, "What did you do?," Żuławski would raise a leg and show faded red patches on his calves. Everyone from Lwów would understand.

Disease was a permanent hazard at the institute, but one with unexpected benefits at times. The employees spoke of three common occupational illnesses. *Weiglowka* referred to the malaise suffered post vaccination. *Quintana* was caused by a second form of *Rickettsia, R. quintana,* and was a nonfatal disease known in the West as trench fever. The institute workers, though vaccinated, often got sick with typhus. But the doctors preferred to call it *zakładowka*, "institute disease," perhaps to draw attention away from the vaccine's imperfections. Some cases were serious, but no one died. Alfred Jahn, a good-looking geography graduate student with working-class Lwów roots, was part of Szybalski's lice-feeding group for a while, but after suffering terrible louse rashes became a dissector. Soon, however, he came down with a 104-degree fever. Dr. Mosing visited him and stated calmly, "It's not typhus. It's *zakladowka*." Jahn now qualified to feed infected lice. Millions of typhus bacteria could enter his body without threat of harm (people only rarely got typhus twice), and he received double wages and more food. Jahn decided to see how many insects he could raise in a month. His record was 32,000. "Nobody knew if that was bad for our health, if there were long-term effects to being exposed to so much venom month after month," Jahn wrote in a memoir. "We were experimental rabbits, but we didn't care."

For others, illness meant the end of a job. Żuławski awoke with a fever one night and thought he'd eaten too many onion and potato fritters. Soon it got worse. Dr. Mosing came, took blood and urine samples, and diagnosed acute glomerulonephritis, caused by a reaction to lice proteins. No more feeding sessions for Żuławski. "All good things must come to an end," he wrote. Stan Szybalski contracted an infection caused by *Rickettsia quintana*. He had a high fever and the shakes, a splitting headache, and terrible vomiting, and his sense of balance was permanently weakened. Exactly 50 years later, living in

Florida, Szybalski had another attack of *quintana*. Luckily, his doctor was a German immigrant familiar with the disease.

Weigl's senior staff probably worried more about sick lice than about sick people. Some feeders were particularly dangerous to the lice—a severely undernourished man developed terrible oozing blisters and memory problems, and the lice he was feeding died, which led to fears of a zoonotic epidemic in the louse population. Eventually the man recovered, and the louse deaths were isolated. Precautions had to be taken to keep cages from being overfilled, because this hindered ventilation and made the insects wet, leading to staph infections that could be fatal to the lice. The quality of the vaccine was lower during the summer when the feeders sweated and the lice tended to get sick. Terrible epidemics of a bacterium called *Rickettsia rochalima*, which spread from louse to louse through feces without human intermediaries, could ruin the colony and did so in 1939 and again in 1941. The pathogen did not affect humans, but *R. prowazekii* would not grow in lice infected with *R. rochalima*. The only way to stop the outbreaks was to destroy the infected colony, followed by thorough disinfection of the laboratory, and rebuilding from a stock of clean lice held in reserve. Weigl was less worried by *quintana*: it was easier to isolate and didn't require destruction of the colony, since *quintana*-infected lice could simultaneously be infected with *R. prowazekii* without lowering the quality of the vaccine. As for the feeders infected with *quintana*—well, they would survive.

The Lwów institute teemed with underground activity hidden behind the façade of vaccine production and invisible to those who didn't need to know. The details usually did not go through Weigl, who, though involved in shipping vaccine illegally to the ghettos, spent much of his time pursuing scientific experiments—on the infectivity of feces, on possible egg cultures of typhus, on epidemiology—and his archery. All the hiring went through Anna Herzig, his tough assistant, girlfriend, and future wife, and she was abreast of all conspiracies. Just after the German occupation, an aristocratic Catholic intellectual named Stanisława Grabska arrived from Warsaw. She had grown up in Lwów, on an estate that had been confiscated and converted to Wehrmacht housing. London had sent her back to Lwów to unify the Warsaw and Galician commands of the Home Army. Some in the institute knew about her mission, but there were no leaks, and she fulfilled it safely. At the institute, her job was to dissect infected lice.

Louse feeding was an effective cover for an underground activist. It justified at least two departures from the house during the day and provided free time for underground activities. The many Home Army louse feeders included the district chief, Army Major Karol Borkowiec, the university docent Stefania Skwarczyńska, who managed underground publications, and a leading conspirator named Tadeusz Galiński. About half the dissectors were resistance members, led by the veterinarian Lesław Ogielski. "Almost the entire leadership of the conspiracy was there," Żuławski recalled of his days in the institute. "The [London] government-in-exile delegate for the region fed every morning with me. His closest colleague, Wanda, often fed lice for me when I could not come, because she was a healthy, pretty girl and not afraid to get anemia. I am convinced that the professor was informed about the underground, but despite the fact that the Gestapo and Wehrmacht guarded the entrance, he never lost his cool. We often saw him relaxing in the garden, shooting his bow. Archery was his passion."

Jerzy Sokolowski, who had been a military officer based in Lwów and who joined the resistance after Poland's defeat, was parachuted into Poland by the British in March 1942 to conduct sabotage behind German lines. Sokolowski met Weigl in Lwów and arranged for vaccines to be shipped to him under a German officer's name in Smolensk, Russia, where typhus was killing members of the Home Army.

Wacław Szybalski also sometimes carried out missions for the resistance. In 1943, the Home Army ordered him to draw up a map of the railroad station at Belzec, the final destination for hundreds of thousands of Polish Jews, so that Allies could bomb the station. Szybalski and a friend rode their bicycles to the death camp, a distance of about 60 miles through the countryside. He remembered coming over a hill on a beautiful day. "Just as we were approaching Belzec, we encountered this sickening smell, really strong." A smell of burning human bodies. The friend had contacts in the area who helped them map it so that American or English bombers could destroy the station and prevent transports from reaching the camp. Szybalski drew up a map, and later saw black marketeers trading in gold recovered from murdered Jews' fillings. Their report went to Jan Karski, the famous courier, and from him to Churchill and Roosevelt. "Unfortunately none of them was really interested in helping Polish Jews and nobody acted on it," said Szybalski. "Our mission was a total waste."

Bitter as such experiences were, they did not discourage all of the young Poles. Some mornings, as he sat with his legs stretched out on a bench, Mirosław Żuławski would imagine that the boxes on his calves were "like little life jackets that were keeping the resistance movement out of deep waters." Work at the institute provided an unheard-of security for people like him. From time to time, German officials came to Żuławski's house with the intention of seizing furniture. "I always greeted them politely, and asked whether they'd been vaccinated against typhus, because unfortunately, typhus-infected lice crawled over me every day. I never saw one of those Germans again."

The junior Weigl institute employees were cautious around their German supervisors, but the older ones felt a degree of trust in Hermann Eyer, although, as one stated, "you never knew if this was because of his heart, or because he realized the Third Reich wouldn't last forever." German officers who worked for Eyer stated that none of the vaccine was ever sabotaged—evidence, they said, of the goodwill the Polish workers had toward their humanitarian boss. But while it is true that Eyer and the Germans were viewed as a generally civilized bunch, the Poles did conduct sabotage. A low-key sort took place in the rooms of the dissectors. Their daily production norm was 1,600 lice in six hours. Working longer than that was impossible because of the intense concentration required. But it turned out that if you dissected 1,200 or 1,300 lice, then warmed the bowl of louse guts with your hands, it would increase its size, so that it looked like 1,600 guts and was viewed as such by those who ground up and neutralized the emulsion. "This trick was used only for the vaccine that went to the German Wehrmacht," one dissector wrote. "The containers we prepared for Professor Weigl—for the Polish or Jewish underground—had to contain the correct amount."

Eyer permitted Weigl a private supply of 200 doses of vaccine each month to vaccinate his employees and their families, or anyone else he chose. A total of 8,000 doses more were used for "vaccine trials," whose "volunteers" included orphans, underground combatants, and the faculty of the Roman Catholic seminary in Lwów. Larger amounts, like the 30,000 doses that went to the Warsaw ghetto, were off the books.

Woman and typhus-afflicted child in the Warsaw ghetto, 1942.
(Courtesy United States Holocaust Memorial Museum.)

The Fantastic Laboratory of Dr. Weigl

Clever bookkeeping allowed extensive pilferage great and small. Once a *Volksdeutscher* employed in the warehouse surprised the Weigl aide Jan Starzyk by telling him, "Will you please ask them to steal only one dose at a time instead of the whole set? Otherwise someone is going to notice." Starzyk added, "I didn't know who 'they' were. I didn't have to know." Others falsified bills of lading in order to save vaccine for the Home Army or the ghetto. Employees entered the lab over the weekend to gather up louse feces from the cages to make vaccine. It contained high concentrations of typhus germs, but the Germans didn't include the waste in their account books. Sometimes, the louse feces were used in a form of sabotage—smeared on the headrests of the German-only passenger railroad cars with the hope of infecting and debilitating Nazi officers.

Eyer's deputy in Lwów, Josef Daniels, once came by a vaccine filling room and noticed that the number of intestines in each lot was fewer than noted in the records. He said to Zbigniew Stuchly, "Thank God the Wehrmacht runs this place. If this were discovered by the SS there would be terrible consequences." This warning was often repeated by the Wehrmacht officers. The German in charge of the Potocki Street facility told Starzyk, "Don't do anything to attract the Gestapo. Once they get in, we're all lost."

Some of the dissector units were made up entirely of women, and in a gradually warming atmosphere of trust and friendship, they would talk, listen to music on a gramophone, and even dance in the hall. A German walked by one day and joked that the "Typhus Institute" had become the "Typhus Cabaret." Not all the Germans thought that was funny. But Eyer had a hands-off attitude toward the Weigl lab, and some of the men he put in place to oversee it were happy to have a laugh. Eyer was a regular churchgoer, which was frowned upon among the Nazi brass. Six of his lab assistants and guards were priests, and other openly religious Catholics served on his staff. The Gestapo in Kraków referred to the institute as "the parson's seminary." But Eyer's success in producing vaccine buffered him from the menacing SS. In 1941, Eyer was relaxed enough to bring his wife from Berlin to Kraków, where she spent a month working as a feeder of healthy lice. They vacationed in the mountain resort of Zakopane, where Peter, their first child, was conceived. Eyer treated the Kraków and Lwów louse feeders as blood donors and provided them increased food rations. They received the highest wage allowed in the *General-gouvernement*, with various bonuses. The institute's doctors provided free medical care.

For all that, Eyer could be punitive. Odo Bujwid, a renowned Polish microbiologist who many years earlier had founded the Kraków institute Eyer now occupied, ran a private vaccine laboratory with his daughter, Sofia. As the risk of typhus increased in 1941, they decided to create a vaccine for use by Poles. Sofia Bujwid personally collected lice off a group of alcoholics outside a church to start the project, and hired louse feeders to produce a Weigl-style vaccine. When the lab was ready, in May 1941, she sent her teenage son to Eyer's assistant, Zdzisław Przybyłkiewicz, to purchase two Wehrmacht vaccines to use in quality checks. Eyer had the boy arrested, then visited Bujwid and told her he had had no choice, because the vaccine was only for the German army. Furthermore, Eyer forbade the Bujwids, under threat of arrest, to have future contact with Przybyłkiewicz. Sofia Bujwid's son ended up in Auschwitz, but was later released, and the Bujwids resumed making their own vaccine.

The Jews of Kraków suffered the same terrible fate as Jews elsewhere in Poland; Eyer said after the war that he simply did not believe the reports he heard about deportations and mass murder. The 70,000 Jews crammed into the Kraków ghetto, in dwellings built for a quarter that number, endured terrible typhus outbreaks with no help from the Wehrmacht, which maintained strict control of their movements. In early 1944, the Gestapo liquidated the Jewish medical service in Kraków, murdering the remaining doctors and shooting patients in their beds. Of the 190 Jewish doctors who had lived in the city when war broke out in 1939, 142 died in the ghetto or in concentration camps.

The Fantastic Laboratory of Dr. Weigl

. . .

After showing the factory owner Schwanenberg his vaccine, Fleck was ordered to report to Gestapo headquarters on Pełczyńska Street—the most feared building in Lwów. "The way there was more dangerous than typhus," Fleck said. "A Jew seldom returned living from that address." Fleck, accompanied by the Jewish hospital director Maksymilian Kurzrock, brought experimental designs, diagrams, and samples. Some uniformed medical specialists questioned them in the presence of the Gestapo. The specialists wrote things down, repeated questions, Fleck said, and "shouted at us and threatened us. Some of the questions were not very intelligent. For example, they asked if the vaccine would work for Aryans. I replied, 'Of course, but it must be made from Aryan and not Jewish urine.'" The specialists did not respond to Fleck's sarcasm, if indeed they understood that it was sarcasm, but decided to send the samples to Professor Richard Otto, the leading German typhus expert, in Frankfurt. "We left the room and weren't sure if we'd get out of the building alive, since they had the samples and the protocols," Fleck wrote. "They didn't need us anymore even if the vaccine interested them. However, they let us go, and outside there was only the usual daily risk."

A week later, a German commission led by Professor Kudicke came to inspect the ghetto laboratory. The German military was in a growing panic over the lack of vaccines for its troops, who were beginning to contract the disease on the eastern front in large numbers. Kudicke treated Fleck rudely, sitting at a desk while the Jewish doctor stood in front of him describing his methods. The Nazi doctors watched Fleck's team making antigen and then went away. Later the Gestapo sent an official to watch over them. He promised that sick patients who brought in urine would be described as "urine donors" and not threatened with liquidation. The lab workers got a special ID card that said, "involved in the production of typhus vaccine," which gave them a feeling of security.

Production moved to the Laokoon factory. Sterilized, refrigerated urine from hospitalized typhus patients was poured into 50-liter metal flasks sent to Laokoon every day. The factory had an excellent apparatus to concentrate and filter the antigen, which was combined with aluminum hydroxide, a protein stabilizer and immune system stimulator that is still used in many vaccines, including the DTP shot that prevents whooping cough, tetanus, and diphtheria. A number of Polish and Jewish scientists worked at the plant. The chemist Janina Opieńska-Blauth had been ordered to find ways to remove the bitterness of horse chestnuts so that they could be used as food. Others were devising hormonal preparations from animal organ extracts. According to Opieńska-Blauth's account, Fleck and his team were somehow known to be on Professor Weigl's staff. The Germans were so worried by typhus, she said, that they were even protecting and feeding Jews with expertise on the subject. Schwanenberg was not particularly friendly, but wanted to keep his Jewish employees from being swept up in raids, so he ordered them to live on the factory grounds. This edict offered welcome protection. Out on the streets, each day the occupation grew more dangerous. The SS wanted to finish off the business of killing the Jews, and the Gestapo were less and less likely to respect a Jew's work papers.

Finally, after about eight months of work, the vaccine was ready for human testing. On August 28, 1942, Fleck injected himself. "Aug. 29," he wrote in his notebook, "large area of local edema and redness; August 30, the reaction vanishes." Fleck also vaccinated his wife, child, and two other people, and a week later Dr. Edward Elster injected 32 volunteers with the vaccine at the Zamarstynowska hospital. "The local reaction was slightly painful, no general reaction was observed," Fleck wrote. Afterward Fleck vaccinated about 500 inmates at Janowska under the supervision of Dr. Kurzrock, who had a protector in the Gestapo, an officer whose wife he had treated.

The "vaccine trial" came at one of the most dramatic moments in the history of Lwów. The Jewish population, somewhere between

150,000 and 200,000 before the German invasion, was now roughly half that size as a result of killings and deportations, starvation, typhus, and other diseases. On August 1, Hans Frank said, "With insect powder and other necessary articles, we're going to make this a place where a German man can live again, after we get rid of the rest of the Jews." A few days later, the Nazis began their largest murder campaign in Lwów. Raids intensified on the Jewish hospitals. Unlike previous actions, these saw the Nazis kill the patients and also most of the doctors, including Olga Elster and her husband, Edward.

In all, about 50,000 Jews were slaughtered in the August action. Dr. Dopheide, the district medical chief, arrived at the Zamarstynowska hospital while it was being raided. After the SS had taken out the doctors, Dopheide and his aides entered the building and stole its equipment. Dopheide never paid any consequences for his actions. In postwar testimony, he said he was "ordered to take part in such actions in which people were driven together and forcibly deloused. Whether such people, especially Jews, were then taken away, I cannot say. The Jewish measures were not disclosed to us." On September 1, the final day of the action, a Gestapo spy was found dead near the ghetto. The Gestapo concluded he had been killed by the Jews and in revenge dragged 12 members of the Jewish council from their offices. They were hanged from the balconies of houses along Łokietka Street. The ropes were thin and most of the men fell, while still alive, and broke limbs. One of them had to be hanged three times before he died.

Again, Fleck clung to life. Kurzrock's Gestapo connection provided a few dozen doctors with new stamps for their passports. Some chose to join their families in death at Janowska. Fleck survived and continued his trial vaccinations on the doomed inmates at the camp, hoping they would be protected from typhus. The shot's value was never evaluated, however, because the vaccinated inmates were murdered in the following weeks. Kurzrock survived for a while longer. The following summer, the SS officer who had always promised to protect him invited Kurzrock to his villa and shot him in the head.

The Fantastic Laboratory of Dr. Weigl

On September 7, the ghetto was sealed, but a small clinic continued to operate where typhus patients were treated and some were vaccinated. In late 1944, the first description of Nazi-occupied Lwów appeared in an account by Adolf Folkmann, an escapee who told his story to a Swedish political scientist. Folkmann's account, entitled *The Promise Hitler Kept*, included a brief account of Fleck's vaccine. "Dr. Fleck produced his serum at the risk of his life and injected as many Jews as possible. When the German authorities learned of this, they arrested Dr. Fleck and his assistants. They forced those arrested to instruct several German doctors in the production of the new serum, at which point the discoverers of the serum disappeared from the city." According to Folkmann, Fleck and his assistants had all been murdered. Dr. Franciszek Groër, Fleck's boss, also believed Fleck had died, for in early 1945 he published a brief research note by his former employee, with an asterisk noting that Fleck had passed away in 1942.

One afternoon in 1942, a young lab worker named Tomasz Cieszyński knocked on the door of Weigl's office and entered. Weigl had been pacing the room and talking, but stopped when he saw the young man. Anna Herzig, sitting at the opposite end of the room, lost her temper and shouted, "Go away at once!" Weigl came over to Cieszyński and said, "Sit down and don't disturb us." Then he resumed the conversation. Stacked in the corner was a pile of boxes full of vaccine, headed for the Warsaw ghetto. The discussion Cieszyński overheard concerned how the institute would smuggle them in to Hirszfeld. When it was over, Weigl turned to Cieszyński: "Go home," he said, "and keep this a secret."

Smuggling vaccine to Jews was punishable by death. So was employing Jews. Despite this, Weigl made a concerted effort to protect close Jewish colleagues, sending an aide, Zbigniew Stuchly, to Kraków with an offer to find a place at the institute for Filip Eisenberg, who had been Weigl's boss at Przemyśl during the Great War. Eisenberg demurred, saying he would remain in his home. He was put on a train to Belzec and gassed with thousands of others. Stuchly also offered protection to Adam Finkel, the hematologist who'd been on Weigl's PhD committee and studied the immunological profile of lice feeders. Perhaps Finkel was disinclined to leave his relatives. Despite repeated discussions with Stuchly, he decided to remain in the Lwów ghetto and perished. "We couldn't save anyone but Henryk Meisel," Stuchly later recalled.

Meisel and his wife, Paula, are the only Jews known for certain to have worked for any length of time at Weigl's institute during the war. They were well-known bacteriologists, assimilated Jews who had worked for the Polish National Institute of Hygiene since its inception in 1920, and Henryk Meisel was one of Weigl's oldest colleagues. After the Nazi invasion, Meisel was put to work producing rabies vaccine and examining the sterility of typhus vaccines at the St. Nicholas Street laboratory. For their safety, the Meisels were moved out of the ghetto to Grabszczyzna, the Wehrmacht-occupied villa where the resistance leader Stefania Grabska had grown up. Eyer told his superiors that Meisel's expertise was vital to the war effort, since the *Clostridia* bacteria he studied often caused wound infections. Every day, an Austrian soldier named Moser accompanied the Meisels to the institute and back. They wore armbands with the Jewish star under the word *Arzt* (doctor, in German). Moser later recalled, "I was often asked by the SS men, 'Where are you going with those Jews?' I would always answer, 'Not on a sightseeing trip, and if you want to know more details you can get them from my boss.'" After a while, the Meisels moved into the institute, to gain more certain protection from the Gestapo. Halina Ogrodzińska, an activist in Żegota, an underground resistance group that aided Jews, worked with Meisel in the Weigl laboratory and sometimes gave Polish literature lessons to his daughter, Felicja. Early in the war, each time she visited their home Dr. Meisel's mother would make scrambled eggs or an omelet, always urging Ogrodzińska to "eat, eat." As pressure grew, Meisel sent his sister to Warsaw, where she survived, and Felicja entered a Catholic orphanage. Meisel had a long discussion with his mother, and "they decided that because she was so old, the best solution would be for her to take poison," Ogrodzińska said later. "They never spoke about this with the rest of the family, and one day she was dead—like that. I was still very young, but Dr. Meisel liked to talk to me, and he badly needed to speak with someone. He told me he had a very heavy heart, but I already knew that."

Felicja ended up hiding in 18 places during the war, including the Botanical Garden, behind the institute. Sometimes, when her parents missed her terribly, she would be brought in for a visit for a few hours. Just before New Year's Day, 1943, Meisel and his wife were deported to Auschwitz. Felicja, who was 14, remained in hiding. One night she slept in the institute basement. "I spent the night with the animals. I heard the guinea pigs singing in the morning. It was beautiful, like bird song." Several months later, she had to flee the city and was told to meet her contact at the main train station, where Ukrainian, Polish, and German thugs made a living as Jew chasers. To conceal herself, she fell in with a group of Hitler Youth, but she entered the wrong platform and found herself crossing the tracks, with her train about to depart. As she said later, "Someone took me by the scruff of the neck like a dog and said, 'Not this way!' And thanks to that, running, I got on my train at the last minute."

Hermann Eyer walked a tightrope for the years of the war. First and foremost, he was producing a vaccine to protect the Wehrmacht, a job he took with the utmost seriousness. Like other German officers of the time who were less than enthusiastic about Nazism, Eyer saw no contradiction between disdain for the government and support for its agents of global conquest. "Every physician was faced with this question," says his son, Peter Eyer. "Should I help the wounded soldier survive, knowing that if he's put back together he'll use his rifle to kill people? Should I help him? The answer is not simple." After the war, Eyer stood firmly behind his work. "I estimate quite conservatively that my efforts and those of my associates saved at least 10,000 people from certain death by typhus. From a moral perspective that's a contribution few could equal," he wrote to a colleague. But since the 10,000 were mostly German soldiers, "those in the East saw what we did as worthy of condemnation, because it helped prolong the war."

The historical record shows that Eyer demonstrated loyalty to his Polish employees, intervening repeatedly to save men and women who'd been arrested by the Gestapo. Himmler's agents were not pleased about this. They were under orders not to disturb his enterprise or arrest his employees—there were exceptions, of course—and those facts rankled. The Gestapo, many of whom had been working-class cops in civilian life, had only the vaguest idea of what went on at the institute. They understood that its Polish employees were guinea pigs of some sort. But the guinea pigs were happy to volunteer, as a former Kraków Gestapo commander stated after the war, "first, because they got better rations; second, because they were safe from arrest, and third, because the Home Army knew the institute was a safe harbor for its people." After the war, these same Gestapo agents turned their enmity on Eyer, accusing him of conducting unethical medical experiments, a charge that had no evidence behind it but led to Eyer's being brought in for questioning as late as the 1970s.

Eyer may have been anti-Semitic, but he showed courage in protecting his Polish workers and in tolerating their subversive activities. Such behavior was rare among the German medical corps. This, perhaps, was the worst crime of the Nazi doctors: while it is unfair to assign collective guilt, it is striking how few of them did anything at all to help. Indeed, Ludwik Hirszfeld, whose work on blood types was twisted into hateful nonsense by Nazi scientists, found the doctors' betrayal harder to take than any other aspect of Nazism. "When the Germans decided to kill everyone in the [ghetto], none of the German scientists and physicians who were in Warsaw, not even those who knew exactly who I was, warned me or offered me the slightest help. Men like Kudicke and [Kudicke's assistant Rudolf] Wohlrab visited me in the district hospital and talked with me about science," he wrote from hiding in 1944. "I see blood on the hands of German scientists, on those who wrote about race hygiene, the Nordic soul, living space, a mission in the East, and in whatever other ways violence was anticipated and motivated. I see blood also on those even more numerous scientists who knew that this was nonsense but kept silent and on the street did not even greet their colleagues who had fallen into disfavor. There are moments in the life of a nation when a man must not keep quiet lest he become an accomplice."

Of all the German physicians he dealt with as a ghetto physician, Hirszfeld singled one out for praise: Hermann Eyer. In an interview some years after the war, he said that Eyer had helped fight the typhus epidemic in the Warsaw ghetto by sending precious vaccines. This was an example, he said, "of a German doctor's great courage and humanist engagement."

The Nazis tolerated Weigl because they needed him, but their mistrust grew. For the first year of the German occupation, the official Polish-language newspaper, *Lwowska Gazeta*, ran many articles about typhus. It discussed the symptoms and methods of prevention, the most effective, according to the paper, being the avoidance of contact with Jews. In 1942, it carried the happy news that a new, "superior" German institute was being built to run and perhaps eventually replace the Weigl institute. By this time, German attitudes toward Weigl had soured. When in April 1943 a Marburg newspaper mistakenly hailed Weigl's vaccine as "a victory of German science," Joseph Goebbels's propaganda office put out word that Weigl was a Pole, and possibly a Jew, who should never be mentioned in the press.

In December 1942, after much ceremony and a great scientific "conference" in the Lwów Opera House, the "Lemberg" branch of the Behringwerke was inaugurated, with plans at the top levels of the German government for it to become a great center of vaccine production. *Reichsmarschall* Hermann Göring had ordered manufactur-

Richard Haas, chief of the Behring vaccine plant in Lwów, speaks with Nazi officers attending its ceremonial opening in December 1942. Hans Frank, the Nazi leader of Poland, stands with hands hanging loose. (Emil-von-Behring-Bibliothek, Philipps-Universität Marburg.)

ers to make a priority of supplying the company with everything it needed for the typhus vaccine laboratory. In anticipation of the opening, IG Farben arranged for a new biography to clean up the image of the institute's namesake, Emil von Behring. This required some work: Behring had earlier been denounced by Nazi publications because his wife was Jewish. Many Nazi publications, following the Führer's lead, were dubious about vaccines, considering them Jewish science that poisoned Aryan blood. Many of the bigwigs of German typhus research were present at the Behringwerke ceremony: Heinz Zeiss; Joachim Mrugowsky and Erwin Ding from the SS Hygiene Institute; Eugen Gildemeister from Berlin; Rudolf Wohlrab and Robert Kudicke from the *Generalgouvernement*; Albert Demnitz, Rudolf Gönnert, and Richard Haas from IG Farben; and, of course, Hermann Eyer. Zeiss set the tone of the meeting with his lecture, "*Geomedizin* in the Eastern Territories." Eyer and Mrugowsky gave speeches, as did Haas, who would direct the new laboratory and in doing so, they said, create a sparkling new center for German science in the East. The *Generalgouvernement* leader Hans Frank, the Galicia SS chief Fritz Katzmann, and a murderer's row of their accomplices politely applauded.

Weigl was invited to the ceremony, but declined. The idea of sitting with Frank nauseated him. "I will not shake the hand of a man who has murdered my friends," he told Gildemeister, who had come to his office to urge him to attend. Gildemeister, who was testing vaccines on prisoners at the Buchenwald concentration camp at the time, nodded sympathetically. Weigl did, however, give Behringwerke assistance in producing his vaccine. Under a September 1942 agreement, the Weigl institute began training Behringwerke louse feeders by adding one box of lice after another, up to six at one session, to desensitize their skin to louse bites. After training, the feeders began work in the new Behringwerke lab, which occupied the same Zielona (Ukrainian: Zelena) Street building that had been Ludwik Fleck's workplace during the Soviet occupation. A large piece of land was purchased to create an egg farm and grow food for the institution and its animals. The plan was for the institute to produce 20,000 vaccines with the Weigl method and 20,000 egg yolk sac vaccines each month.

Much as the Germans despised Weigl, they continued to depend upon him, especially to recruit lice feeders and other employees. A contract that survives in the files of the Behringwerke states that Weigl was to be paid 900 zlotys a month in return for his cooperation. The less experienced German staff of the Behringwerke arrogantly viewed Weigl's methods as obstacles to be overcome. But when problems arose, the only solution was to ask for his help. At one point, the Behringwerke decided to replace the wooden lice cages, which sometimes warped, with metal ones. Most of the lice escaped, and the institute scientists had to come begging to Weigl for a new seed colony. He agreed. Weigl never refused help to a scientific colleague. When the first several batches of vaccine had little efficacy, Weigl sent over a deputy to straighten out the production process. Though the work was similar, social conditions at the Behringwerke lab were different from those at the Weigl institute. Some Polish employees had tried to sabotage the vaccine work, the Berhringwerke chief Haas wrote to his colleagues in Marburg in 1943, but "when the SS shot a worker who had stolen material from the plant, it had a good result."

Across town, in the ghetto, the terror was reaching a climax.

On February 4, 1943, Gestapo cars pulled up in front of the Laokoon factory, where Fleck was working. The officers ordered Fleck and Bernard Umschweif, along with Ernestyna and Ryszard Fleck, Umschweif's wife, Natalia, and five-year-old son, Karol, to get in. From the factory, they headed west along the park lying below the High Castle and skirting the railroad tracks that separated the ghetto from central Lwów. This road led to Janowska and certain death. But at a crucial moment, the truck crossed under the railroad embankment and pulled up at the Jewish hospital on Kuszewicz Street, amid streets that smoked and smelled of burning flesh during yet another *Aktion*. An SS officer entered the bacteriological laboratory, where the remainder of Fleck's staff were still working, and ordered everyone out onto the street. Perhaps acting with Dr. Fleck's assistance, the SS instructed Dr. Owsiej Abramowicz, one of Fleck's assistants, to board the truck, along with Jakob Seeman. And then there was Anna Seeman, limping toward the truck. The SS officer told her to stay put, but Fleck, who had been told the scientists were being taken to work somewhere, spoke up. He sensed that anyone left off the truck was doomed.

"Eine Tänzerin brauchen Sie im Labor nicht," he told the SS man. *A laboratory doesn't need ballerinas.*

The SS man shrugged, and Anna Seeman climbed aboard the truck, grasping her husband's outstretched arm. Their son, Bruno, was still inside the lab bathroom. Two and a half years later, at the age of 13, he was interviewed in Warsaw by a committee of Jewish remembrance. His mother, Seeman said, hadn't been sure whether the truck represented death or life. Initially, he said, "mom asked the SS men if she could leave me behind, and they agreed. But an hour later she came back to the laboratory and took me with her. She told me that we were all going to the Reich, where we would work in a chemical factory."

Thus Fleck saved not only Anna Seeman but her son as well. "Few people would have had the courage to behave the way he did in those evil circumstances," she told an interviewer later. "Fleck refused to be dehumanized." For three days, Fleck and the 10 other members of his entourage were held at Łącki Street prison. Most of the time, the prevailing view of the group was that they would all be killed. But on February 7, a horse-drawn cart took them to the Lwów railway station. They were given bread and marmalade for a journey, and put in two closed compartments—"railroad cars for humans," as Bruno Seeman testified. "Not like the other prisoners in the animal wagons. But there we learned, because they told us, that we were not going to the Reich, but to the camp in Auschwitz."

CHAPTER EIGHT

ARMIES OF WINTER

German soldiers at the Battle of Stalingrad. (Superstock.)

I n the ghetto in Lwów, Poland, in February 1943, there was only one reason the Gestapo would spare the life of a little Jewish doctor and his underfed, crippled assistant, let alone their children. The German war effort needed them. The specialized knowledge Fleck and his colleagues possessed took on growing value in light of the abysmal news from the eastern front. The month that Fleck was sent to Auschwitz, the German Sixth Army surrendered at Stalingrad, marking a key turning point in the war. After that, the Nazis were in more or less permanent retreat.

Even by the end of 1941, Operation Barbarossa was shaping up not to be the heroic cakewalk Hitler had expected. Stalin's troops were overrun, slaughtered, and captured by the millions in the first months of the operation, as the Germans pushed deep into Ukraine and Russia. But the Soviets regrouped; by September, Red Army resistance and the fall rains had combined to slow the advance of the Germans, who suffered terrible casualties and the loss of much of their armor. Hitler's war plan required the fall of Moscow before the start of winter. In early December, after the Wehrmacht advanced to as close as ten miles from the Kremlin, a Soviet counterattack drove back the Germans. Operation Barbarossa was not designed for retreat. As the Germans lost their strategic initiative and began moving from trench to trench, the diseases of earlier wars found them.

Much has been written concerning the arrogance and hubris of Hitler and his generals. Having whipped the formidable French army in a six-week blitzkrieg, they assumed that the demoralized, less-than-human soldiers of the Red Army would quickly abandon the fight. Convinced that the German boys could "live off the land" by confiscating what they needed from the Russians, military quartermasters had failed to assure good supply lines to the quick-moving front. The lack of winter clothing in the troop packs was one of the most obvious signs of German miscalculation. German propaganda had made much of the typhus threat in the Soviet lands, but the army's provisioners had failed to take heed, perhaps assuming that German troops would have little contact with their racial inferiors. This was a grievous mistake. The winter of 1941 was one of the coldest on record, with temperatures in western Russia dropping to minus 42 degrees Fahrenheit. Within a few months of the start of Barbarossa, German troops became lousy and were ordered to boil their clothes instead of washing them, which was entirely impractical. Delousing stations had served Germany well during World War I, but in this war, engineering battalions were not provisioned with adequate equipment to begin with, and most of what they had was lost during the first retreat. This might not have been quite as critical if Germany had vaccinated its troops against typhus, but it had not. By late 1941, only a small percentage of Wehrmacht doctors, let alone other medical staff, had received the three shots of Weigl vaccine required for a year of protection. Common soldiers had not been vaccinated at all. Hitler had not only failed to provide warm clothing for his men. Their protection against disease was frankly inadequate.

To be sure, Germany was not the only country that lacked typhus vaccine. Britain had decided early in the war to forgo vaccination in favor of delousing measures; the British army paid for this decision with outbreaks in North Africa, although according to one published report, only 11 British service members died in 1943–44. By the time the United States entered the war, Herald Cox's egg-grown vaccine was available, and medics vaccinated millions of American troops headed for the European and North African theaters. But the typhus threat U.S. and British troops faced in sun-drenched North Africa, or even, later, in Italy, did not compare with that of the frozen steppes of the eastern front. The Soviet army also lacked vaccine. But there was one thing Soviet soldiers had that their German enemies lacked: warm winter coats. These quickly became a primary means for the spread of typhus to the Wehrmacht, for shivering German troops routinely robbed the lousy Soviet POWs of their clothes. With those men, typhus must have seemed like a distant threat.

By November 1941, the Wehrmacht had seized 3.8 million Soviet POWs, and held them in vast encampments across half of Europe. German labor officials, who had been told to make free use of the POWs as forced laborers in the Reich, were discovering that this figure was something of an illusion. The number of *living* Soviet prisoners by November was about 1.58 million, according to labor officials, and an additional 15,000 were dying of typhus every day. Thousands more died daily of starvation and cold. By the time the war ended,

5.7 million Soviet soldiers had fallen into German hands, and 3.3 million died. If cold, chaotic retreat, and lousiness were the dry tinder for typhus, the POW camps provided the spark, for the Soviet troops brought the disease with them. Like German soldiers, Russian recruits were given baths in caustic chemicals and shaved before putting on their first uniforms, but they quickly became lousy again. In their propaganda, the Soviets countered Nazi claims of Slavic slovenliness with their own attacks on the tendency of "Aryan culture" to "spread epidemics." In reality, the Red Army couldn't kill all the lice in Russia, and too many soldiers from godforsaken villages brought the germs with them when they enlisted.

German military doctors began reporting typhus outbreaks in the POW camps in October. At three camps clustered near the Baltic in northwest Poland, 90 German guards also fell ill that month. "The number of sick Russians is assumed to be high," the physician on the scene reported, "but it can't be known precisely, because diagnosis is impossible in their dark crowded quarters. Of course not all the deaths are caused by typhus—many Russians die of hunger edema." Germany in general did not feed Soviet POWs. At a POW camp on the Elbe River in northeast Germany in January 1942, the death rate was 2 percent per day. A Wehrmacht health inspector there, a Dr. Büttner, witnessed cannibalism. "A man who [Büttner's] translator said was Azerbaijani ate the raw flesh of a dead prisoner right out in public without causing a stir," he wrote. Büttner refused to accept the explanation that German-imposed starvation had caused this behavior. He had been told the Russian men got warm meals twice a day. No, he said, "it must be some kind of cultish custom." Only someone infused with Nazi racial prejudice could have believed this. Soviet prisoners often resorted to cannibalism. Even more frequently, witnesses came upon ravenous Soviet work details, the prisoners ripping open dead animals with their fingernails or stuffing themselves with raw potatoes, grass, or dung.

In the southern and central sectors of the front, the first epidemic wave swept the Wehrmacht in December 1941, shortly after the first Russian counteroffensives. On a single day in January, the 6th, 17th, and 11th Armies and the 1st Armored Division reported a total of 560 cases. Vaccines would have been helpful, but even if they'd been available, there was no way to vaccinate with the troops in constant movement. Delousing would also be tough. "The local difficulties can't be resolved through memos from above, and if you don't improvise and aren't resourceful, you'll get nothing done," said a unit physician. Some units tried to delouse by leaving their clothing out in the cold for 24 hours. But most of the soldiers, even those holding static positions, lacked a change of clothing. German doctors struggled to understand the epidemic. One wrote that it was "well known" that the Soviet POWs "throw lice at German soldiers, especially officers, in order to cause them to become lousy." But such accounts of clumsy biological warfare—which were also reported on the Soviet side, implicating German troops— were essentially war propaganda.

Typhus seemed to catch hold most easily when the troops were on the move, because they brushed up against the civilian population and had no way to keep clean. An adviser with Army Group North noted that during the winter of 1941–42 there were 660 cases and 60 deaths in one division, but 4,900 cases with 700 deaths in another that had fought in the same region. The explanation, he believed, was that the second unit had been forced into retreat and shared dwellings (and perhaps beds) with the civilian population. "Where parts of the army more or less remain in their fixed positions, despite the tense fighting conditions the number of infections have remained relatively low," agreed Dr. Kurt Lydtin, another physician on the northern front. "Epidemics have occurred only where, as a result of Russian attacks, the fighting has broken out in areas newly occupied by our troops."

On January 12, 1942, typhus was diagnosed in the 18th Motorized Division, whose units had taken part in the capture of Tikhvin, south of Leningrad, in November but were driven out in mid-December and found themselves creeping through snowdrifts near the town of Staraya Russa. "Enormous masses of troops passed through this thickly populated area, traveling in powerful columns on narrow streets bordered by heavy snow," Lydtin reported. "The troops were forced to seek shelter from the cold, and it was impossible to evacuate the civilian population." The typhus outbreak a few weeks later fit with the expected incubation time, he said. The troops were becoming increasingly lousy. "The majority of the sick I see are in an unbelievable state of filth," he reported. "Many louse-infected soldiers, in the field with no break for months, have scratched themselves until their leathery skin resembles that of a beggar. It will be difficult to control epidemics in these conditions. Soldiers in a land where there is typhus can't afford to let their guard down like this. The hygiene situation was better in 1914/15."

These alarming reports, filed by the military's consulting hygienists, landed on the desk of the senior military doctor, at the time General Siegfried Handloser. Like the typhus vaccine expert Hermann Eyer, the consulting hygienists were part of the Army Medical Inspectorate. The urgency of the reporting was intensified by the alarming fact that their medical colleagues were among the most vulnerable to typhus. "A doctor who was generally very calm suddenly became mistrustful," wrote one physician. "Only after intense pressure from his fellows did he go to the hospital, where he demanded an X-ray for his intense headache. Afterward he became very sad and sobbed, worried that he could have infected someone else." Many German doctors had not seen typhus before and were astonished by the profound symptoms of the disease. "The faces of the soldiers had lost their characteristics, and were limp and swollen. Sometimes they were reddish, often pale," a physician wrote. "The eyelids were thick, with bags under the eyes, the face was dazed and sometimes shiny." The symptoms reminded them of *Russlandmüde*, "Russia exhaustion," the German version of the "1,000-yard stare" that afflicted soldiers who had seen too much battle for too long. In recovery, the patients did not behave with the stoicism and sense of duty expected of a German soldier.

They ignored demands to write letters home, or wrote them but forgot what they'd said. They could not read and complained of powerful pain and thirst. They lost their hair or it turned gray; they became depressed or manic. With uncanny regularity, a soldier in the midst of a raging fever would seek to rise from his bed claiming that the Führer had awarded him the Knight's Cross, or that he had invented a terrible new weapon that would quickly end the war.

To cope with the symptoms of the disease, German doctors used strophanthin to stimulate the heart, phenobarbital and scopolamine to control psychosis. Nothing worked very well. The Weil-Felix reaction, a crucial but weak diagnostic tool, bedeviled the hygienists as it had confounded typhus experts for decades. The test was reliable only when the patient had been sick for four days, and even then there were false positives. Not knowing whether their patients had typhus or not, hygienists ordered unnecessary quarantines, or sent sick soldiers to the rear on freezing truck rides when they would have been more comfortable and more likely to survive if left in place. The Czech Jews Weil and Felix, the former in the hereafter, the latter in British exile, might have chuckled to see the trouble their imperfect tool was giving the doctors of the master race. Even Fleck, in his ghetto laboratory, had developed a better diagnostic.

Many Wehrmacht doctors experimented with convalescent serum, the blood of cured typhus patients. They injected the material into the sick men with the hope that some antibodies would be transferred in the process. The procedure had been tried and had failed many times in past decades, but the watchword of desperate physicians was "Something has to be done." At some prison camps, the physicians ran trials to test the efficacy of serum, using Russian POWs, who would be artificially infected with typhus, then injected with sera. In general it had no effect. The Russians died of typhus under medical observation.

The German soldiers' letters home that told about the typhus epidemic, describing gruesome deaths and comrades gone out of their heads, began to have an unnerving effect, which spurred Nazi propaganda leaders to suppress them. On January 23, 1942, Joseph Goebbels's office asked the army to prohibit its soldiers from mentioning typhus in their letters. "The civilian population is already worried enough about the situation in the East and the terrible cold, and it is not necessary to feed these anxieties with reports of this sort from the soldiers," reads a memo from his office. "Senior officers must be aware that we have only partial remedies for this epidemic, because the [vaccine] is not available in the necessary quantities." A memo 12 days later reported that 235 Germans, 858 foreign workers, and 2,705 Jews had fallen ill of typhus within the Reich. It forbade all reporting on typhus and restricted any information on the disease to doctors specifically requesting it.

To combat typhus at the front, army troops took harsh measures against civilians. When the Second Army, retreating from the siege of Moscow, came across 32,000 "old and sick civilians" in March 1942, it packed them onto a train that was sent to a no-man's-land near the front, where they were "given food and abandoned," according to a doctor's account. Typhus cases in the army declined, he said, and so his unit had adopted the policy of "deporting superfluous eaters and hygienically inaccessible elements in the direction of the enemy bandits." This kind of typhus control became one of the brutal scorched-earth policies in Wehrmacht-held territory.

Germany's failure to employ effective insecticide powders against the louse is somewhat baffling, though characteristic of Nazi infighting. The government ordered 10,000 tons of DDT powder from the Swiss chemical concern JR Geigy AG in 1942, and IG Farben, without obtaining a license, began producing a powder called Lauseto, which contained 15 percent DDT. But Hitler's pet doctor, Theodor Morell, touted an insecticide called Russla and told Hitler that DDT might harm Germany's youth and should be avoided. Because of Morell's influence on the Führer and IG Farben's conflicts with business competitors, DDT was little used on the eastern front, though it was eventually sprayed against malarial mosquitoes in Greece. Russla, meanwhile, was not as effective as DDT; and moreover, it stank, which led soldiers to avoid it. In the winter of 1942, desperate troop physicians pursued a folk legend that ants could be employed to eat lice and their nits. Experiments showed this was so, but that was of little consolation, since ants hibernate during the winter. Formic acid, originally derived from ants, proved ineffective at killing lice.

The more the Germans retreated, the lousier they got. By August 1942, nearly 40,000 typhus cases had been reported on the eastern front, with about 4,500 deaths. Good statistics for the remainder of the war are unavailable, with estimates for the entire conflict ranging from 70,000 to 90,000 cases. During three years at the eastern front in the First World War, German military hospitals had treated 6,000 cases of typhus, 1,400 of them fatal. Typhus was only one of the illnesses—others included tuberculosis and diarrhea—that plagued the trenches. But the disease meant something more to the Nazis than just the casualties it caused. By January 1942, the German medical services were in a typhus panic. Germany's soldiers were sickening and dying of the disease. The ghettos were full of Jews with it. And the economy relied upon the labor of millions of slave workers from the East, any of whom could be carrying it.

Despite Nazi Germany's angst about lice and typhus, or perhaps precisely because of the obsessive and therefore impractical handling of the disease, neither the government nor IG Farben had done much in the interwar period to study typhus or prepare a vaccine. The louse- and typhus-infused rhetoric of medical Nazism was aimed at the Jew and Slav, but the disease had been reported only rarely in Germany during the first four decades of the 20th century. The country's research focus reflected the latter fact, rather than the dreams of *lebensraum* occupation of the East. At the outbreak of war, no German laboratory even possessed a strain of epidemic typhus that could be used in vaccine research. This changed after Eyer set up his laboratory in Kraków. But as the health authorities awoke to the threat of the disease, they addressed it from competing power centers, as was characteristic of institutions in Nazi Germany. The army health inspector Waldmann, and his successor Handloser, entrusted their entire vaccine policy to Eyer in Kraków. Researchers from the German research centers with some knowledge of typhus—in Frankfurt, Hamburg, and Berlin—sent their leading men to Warsaw, where the *Generalgouvernement* funded research. The scientists Eugen Gildemeister and Eugen Haagen of the Koch Institute began trying to create a vaccine that used a related bacteria, known as murine typhus. Gildemeister would work in Berlin during the war, while Haagen set up a laboratory at the University of Strasbourg, France, where he experimented on prisoners from the Auschwitz and Natzweiler concentration camps. Meanwhile, IG Farben cranked up its own long-neglected typhus vaccine research arm at the Behringwerke laboratories in Marburg, Germany, and later in Lwów.

The leading scientists mistrusted and deceived one another, and made free use of the Nazi bureaucracy to jockey for influence. Though they had worked side by side for years, Gildemeister and Haagen hated each other. Gerhard Rose, vice president of the Koch Institute and a consultant to the Luftwaffe, constantly fought with Gildemeister, whom he described as "a fearsome bureaucrat, and terribly formal." All three resented the much younger Eyer, who was virtually the only typhus scientist to whom the army listened. They also mistrusted IG Farben when it became evident that the company, to cut financial corners, was making a vaccine that was too weak to be effective. The differences were partly scientific. Eyer was a steadfast defendant of Weigl's louse intestine vaccine, the only tested product: "When you have the immense responsibility of producing a reliable vaccine in the quickest possible time to protect not some strange people but rather the German soldier, from a dastardly enemy, the complexity of the method is beside the point," he said. "What is required is the unconditional guarantee that it be effective." The louse was the natural growth medium for typhus, he said. When typhus grew in such "alien cultures" as guinea pig, mouse, rabbit, and eggs, it was subject to unpredictable mutations, and thus less stable and reliable. This was substantially correct, but some of the other scientists felt that Eyer had raised the point to a dogma.

Although Gildemeister, Haagen, IG Farben, and Wohlrab (in Warsaw) were all working on versions of an egg-based vaccine by 1941, none could persuade the army to use any vaccine other than the Weigl type. This infuriated the other scientists; the Koch Institute forbade its employees to talk to Eyer, although Haagen and Gildemeister had originally trained him. "Eyer was a very capable man, especially in the areas of organization and laboratory technique—but he had blinkers on," Rose claimed in postwar interrogations. "He'd completely convinced himself of the louse process and didn't want to let anything else on the table. He wanted the monopoly, in the scientific sense." Gildemeister, Rose, and Otto saw—correctly—that Eyer could never cover the military's needs with louse vaccines. (Eyer's name, which sounds exactly like the German word for eggs—*Eier*—was also a source of confusion.) The army medical chief Handloser, who comes across as rather dim-witted in his postwar interviews, placed his trust in Eyer and refused to accept entreaties from the egg men. Rose, on the other hand, declared, "The Army wouldn't take [the egg vaccines], so, more for me." Rose's trust in those vaccines was never tested: Luftwaffe troops, being mostly airborne, did not spend much time in trenches where the lice were.

By the end of 1941, as typhus began to plague the Wehrmacht, Eyer's labs in Kraków and Lwów were delivering to the army about 20,000 doses of vaccine per month—enough to vaccinate some 6,500 troops. Eyer produced a small amount of additional vaccine, grown in mouse lungs and lice, in the Polish town of Rabka. More than 5 million troops were by then involved in the eastern campaign. Desperate military, SS, business, and civilian leaders showered Eyer and his military supervisors with requests for vaccine they could not spare. The military suggested that private industry take up the slack. But Behringwerke, IG Farben's main vaccine-producing component, did not produce a typhus preventive until April 1941, and, like all the egg-based vaccines produced by the Germans, it had serious problems. The American Cox vaccine relied on a series of inexplicable but vital techniques to work properly. The vaccine had to be stored in particular solvents at particular temperatures for set time periods during different growth stages. Why? No one knew. This period was called the "empirical phase" of vaccine development. The finer production details were not included in the journal articles Cox had published on his vaccine. Unable to spend time with Herald Cox, the Germans lacked access to the true egg vaccine thought collective—the vaccine as made by flesh-and-blood scientists, rather than as described in books. Their vaccines didn't work.

The Weigl vaccine, on the other hand, seemed to be working. It usually protected those lucky enough to have been vaccinated from death, psychosis, and disability. There were failures, however. Army Group Center in early 1942 reported many severe cases and deaths in a division of vaccinated tank troops—although perhaps the report should be taken with a grain of salt, since the reporting physician was a Behringwerke director allied with Eyer's scientific foes.

Finally, the shortage of vaccine forced matters to a head. The German doctors decided upon a notorious course of medical experimentation that would echo through medical practice around the world for years to come. These developments would also bring Weigl and Fleck back together, indirectly, when the enemies of Weigl's wartime chief persuaded the SS to create a rival vaccine—which Fleck would help produce.

At the urging of Gildemeister, senior Nazi government, academic, and pharmaceutical officials met in Berlin on December 29, 1941, to discuss measures to counter typhus. The top Nazi health officers were represented along with senior IG Farben officers. Eyer was absent, but a Dr. Scholz represented the views of Eyer and his boss, Siegfried Handloser. Scholz began the meeting, held at the interior ministry, with the statement that the army would use only vaccine produced with

Weigl's technique, which "offered a fairly certain protection against a fatal course."

While restricting the vaccine options meant that no more than a small percentage of army troops could be vaccinated, at least for the time being, Scholz explained that this fit with Hitler's views. The Führer, he said, was not interested in vaccinating the whole army with a prophylactic that was only partially efficacious. If the men were too sick to fight, they were of no battlefield use to the Reich. "When it was confirmed to him that a complete protection against the disease could not be effected, although certainly some deaths could be prevented by the inoculation, the Führer decided that for the time being there was no question of vaccinating the German Army," Scholz said. The army's policy would therefore be to vaccinate only medics and others who treated typhus or otherwise were at constant risk of illness. Hitler's inhumane judgment on his own soldiers thus vindicated the Wehrmacht's refusal to accept vaccines that were not made by means of the Weigl method.

However, other German officials had already decided to ignore the supreme leader's views. An interior ministry official concluded the conference by stressing the urgent need to increase production everywhere. Although the egg-based vaccine was inferior to Weigl's, he said, this should be kept quiet so as not to create "bad publicity" for the former. Leaving open the possibility that the army might use egg-based vaccines in the future, he also urged the Behringwerke vaccines to be further tested. *Standartenführer* (Colonel) Joachim Mrugowsky, chief of the Waffen-SS Hygiene Institute, would be asked to take care of testing the vaccine, the assembled officials agreed. Why a group of senior pharmaceutical and public health experts would ask an SS officer to test a vaccine remains unsaid in the minutes from these meetings. It was a hotly discussed topic at the Nuremberg Doctors' Trial. But the explanation is clear: the vaccines were to be tested in the concentration camps, where the usual rules of medical ethics did not apply.

Mrugowsky, who was Erwin Ding's superior and one of a handful of top Nazi medical decision makers, was the son of a well-off doctor whose death in World War I plunged the family into poverty. Mrugowsky, who had joined the SS in 1930, was a specialist in public health, which under Nazidom was more about eugenics than public welfare. One could say that Ludwik Fleck and Mrugowsky represented opposing critiques of the bacteriological tradition. Whereas Fleck saw the complex workings of immunity and organism as key elements of the epidemiology of infectious disease, Mrugowsky viewed patterns of infection in terms of race and blood. The only member of the "public" whose health counted was the non-Jewish "Aryan" German. The individual mattered, Mrugowsky wrote in his PhD dissertation, only if he was German and then only in that he was "a small member of his clan and his *Volk*." As for the Slav and the Jew, they were worthy of notice only as "illness carriers," "parasites," or "vermin," that is to say, something to be avoided at best, or eradicated. After being named in 1938 to head the new SS Hygiene Institute, whose purpose was to assure the "hygienic conditions" of the eastern lands occupied by Germany, Mrugowsky pushed aside the theosophist Karl Genzken to become chief hygienist on the staff of *Reichsarzt* SS Ernst-Robert Grawitz. This made him the no. 2 health official in the SS.

Mrugowsky's staff of 200 included Kurt Gerstein, an engineer who had been jailed for opposing the Nazi regime in the 1930s and seems to have joined the SS in order to spy on its activities. He won Mrugowsky's confidence by designing water filters and arranging the purchase and installation of delousing machinery for Waffen-SS troops. Gerstein would become a peculiar sort of witness (the "spy of God," as a French author put it) to the Holocaust and the SS death machinery. As an aide to Mrugowsky, Gerstein provisioned the gas chambers at Auschwitz and Majdanek. Bacteriological laboratories in Kiev and Riga and at Auschwitz and Buchenwald formed another facet of Mrugowsky's expansive domain. He was responsible for a series of medical experiments that occurred throughout the concentration camp system.

Armies of Winter

As the scholar Paul Weindling has aptly noted, "preventive medicine and genocide were inextricably linked" at the SS Hygiene Institute. In October 1941, Gerhard Peters, general manager of the chemical firm Degesch, wrote to the army inspectorate, touting a new disinfectant called Zyklon B. Already, the chemical had been used to delouse the clothes and housing of 5 million soldiers and prisoners, and special chambers were available to delouse another 5 million. The problem with Zyklon B was that while killing lice very effectively, it was also extremely toxic to humans. In January 1942, Himmler responded through an aide that he was very interested indeed in Peters's product. His response came the week of the Wannsee Conference, the gathering of senior Nazi officials outside Berlin at which the final solution of European Jewry was sealed. That month, Mrugowsky arranged for Degesch to deliver 1,200–1,500 kilograms of Zyklon B to Auschwitz every three or four months. Ostensibly, the Zyklon B was for delousing, but camp Commandant Rudolf Höss had decided to use it to kill Jews. Gerstein would spend the war carrying out deliveries of Zyklon, while secretly reporting on the Nazi extermination methods to unbelieving or indifferent pastors, diplomats, and others.

IG Farben and the Wehrmacht's supply office also contacted scientists and health officials in Romania, Denmark, and France in attempts to procure additional typhus vaccine. The overtures to France's Pasteur Institute were the most important. The Pasteur scientists Paul Durand and Hélène Sparrow in Tunis had developed a promising vaccine based on Ruiz Castañeda's demonstration that *Rickettsia* would grow in mice whose immune systems had been weakened by X-rays. Instead of radiation, Durand and Sparrow exposed the animals to extreme cold and paratyphoid bacteria, then injected *Rickettsia* into their windpipes. The cultures grew quickly in the mouse lungs and, after being harvested, purified, and exposed to formalin, provided a killed-typhus vaccine. Durand brought the vaccine to Pasteur's typhus lab chief, Paul Giroud, in Paris, where the two of them expanded its use to rabbits. Many tricks were involved in the production of this vaccine. Giroud once wrote that it was necessary to vary the technique for each rabbit, depending on its size and health status. But the rickettsial cultures derived from the rabbit's lungs—when the technique worked—were rich and offered a promising alternative to chicken eggs or lice.

For Germany, the only question was how to get hold of the Pasteurian vaccine. In January 1942, a potential avenue opened up. In the first week of that month, French officials from the Pasteur Institute and the French health ministry paid calls upon German health and interior ministry officials on behalf of French POWs. The French had learned that approximately 400 of their POWs had fallen ill of typhus, with 90 deaths, after Soviet POWs arrived at Stalag IV-B, a large camp east of the Elbe River in Brandenburg. The disease had spread to the French after their medics treated desperately ill Russians. During the visit to Berlin, the French officials received permission to visit French POW camps regularly over the coming months to administer Giroud's vaccine. Gildemeister and other German officials pointedly expressed Germany's interest in gaining access to the vaccine. In effect, a swap was arranged—French know-how and vaccine in exchange for the right to protect French nationals held by the Third Reich.

The Pasteur Institute, rife with resistance members, would play a cat-and-mouse game with the Wehrmacht and IG Farben throughout the war. German policies toward the French were far more lenient than those in Poland, and this extended to the relationship with vaccine providers. Weigl was, in principle, directly under Nazi command; Giroud and the Pasteurians were independent and could negotiate effectively with the Germans. While they never outright refused a German request, the French seem to have manipulated the Germans' effort at politesse, offering innumerable excuses and delays in a way that kept vaccine deliveries to a minimum. Meanwhile, the institute established a secret typhus vaccine production laboratory in Laroche-Beaulieu, in Vichy France, which was not occupied by German troops until the end of the war.

To give a flavor of this relationship: on February 2, 1942, the Wehrmacht supply office contacted the French health ministry with a request to purchase 50,000 doses of Giroud's vaccine. After consulting with the Pasteur Institute director Jacques Trefouel, the ministry replied that the vaccine was still being tested. In fact, there was plenty of vaccine, but Trefouel had told the ministry he needed it to fight typhus outbreaks in North Africa and among French POWs. The French aim was to vaccinate 1.2 million French POWs and thus prevent them from returning to France with typhus.

By war's end, Giroud and his aides had produced about 2.2 million doses—enough to vaccinate roughly 750,000 people. About a tenth of the production had been sold to Germany. While the typhus vaccine trade with Germany was small, the Pasteurians did share the technology. Numerous German scientists were invited, or rather invited themselves, to the Pasteur Institute for training. In the words of the writer Céline, who was associated with the Pasteur during the war, the institute "had to concede to periodic visits by one or another 'Professor Fritz' in response to German demands for access to technical know-how." One of the first, in the fall of 1942, was Erwin Ding. He spent three months trying to learn Giroud's difficult method, and returned in December to Buchenwald.

CHAPTER NINE

THE TERRIFYING CLINIC
OF DR. DING

Roll call at Buchenwald, 1938. (American Jewish Joint
Distribution Committee, courtesy of USHMM.)

There were really two Buchenwalds, an upper camp and a lower camp, separated by barbed wire, and within the upper camp there were more divisions. Where some men fought like rats for a piece of bread, it was a constant struggle to maintain a degree of solidarity rather than descend into the primitive state that Himmler and his lieutenants had designed for the prisoners. As the chemist

The Terrifying Clinic of Dr. Ding

Albert Kirrmann of the University of Strasbourg wrote after the war, "The abyss between the corner tramp and the elegant party-goer who passes by on a Paris night is far less profound than that between the *Lagerälteste* [the senior inmate trustee], strolling through the parade ground in his sumptuous boots, beautiful St. Bernard at his side, and the piteous skeleton of the Little Camp, dressed in rags and staggering with weakness." The lower camp was a warren of tents and poorly constructed barracks, lying at the bottom of the hill where Buchenwald stood. It was here that the most miserable camp inmates lived—the recent arrivals, mostly Jews, who had been transported in sealed boxcars from other camps and awaited assignment to hard-labor details where most died of overwork, starvation, exposure, and disease.

Conditions improved at the upper camp of Buchenwald after 1942, when the political prisoners, the "Reds," emerged triumphant from a fierce conflict with the common criminals, the "Greens." As in all the concentration camps, day-to-day power in Buchenwald was wielded by the inmates themselves. The worst capos and block leaders used the system to exploit and torture those beneath them, but the Communists and other Reds (most but not all "Reds" were leftists; a minority were Christian or conservative opponents of the Nazis) brought a degree of humanitarian purpose when they took over key positions. The Greens, being violent, irrational, and opportunistic, were a good temperamental fit with the Nazis and the camp motto, "To each his own." But though brutal and pitiless, the Greens were generally incapable of organizing factory work. As Himmler began to demand more production from the camps, midlevel SS found the Reds to be better partners. They may have been the Reich's mortal enemies, but they offered a solid cadre of bright, well-organized workers and tradesmen. Inmates of Buchenwald and its subsidiary camps built machine guns, V-1 and V-2 rockets, and their guidance systems. The work required skill and discipline. By the end of the war, the cream of European communism was confined at Buchenwald. German leftists had been in the camps for 12 years; solidarity, street fighting, and a tough working-class upbringing had equipped them better than most for camp life. When the Reds kept things running smoothly—with a minimum of obvious sabotage—camp SS officers were less likely to be reprimanded for shoddy performances that might have ended their sinecures. A degree of symbiosis developed between the Reds and the SS, and that benefited the camp inmates in general.

At times, it went beyond mere coexistence. After Ding left Buchenwald for the first time in 1939, he was replaced as camp doctor by Waldemar Hoven, a 36-year-old SS man from a well-off farming family in the Black Forest. Hoven had quit high school and wandered the world for 14 years, spending three of them on a Minnesota farm. Given his erratic behavior, Hoven may have had a dissociative disorder of some kind. After graduating from medical school in 1939, he caught Himmler's eye by sending the SS supremo an original Friedrich Schiller letter purchased in Paris. Not long afterwards, the new sycophant was put in charge of the Buchenwald hospital. Dedicated Communists staffed some of the top inmate medical positions, and soon Hoven was a regular part of their intrigues.

Hoven was a rakish, impetuous fellow, a would-be Rudolf Valentino known for theft, drinking, womanizing, and homosexual rape. Among his conquests was the camp commandant's wife, Ilse Koch, who would enter history as an axiomatic figure of female perversity— "the Bitch of Buchenwald." Inmates would sometimes look up from their shovels to see Frau Koch standing above them, riding whip in hand, in a skirt with no underwear. She periodically ordered the murder of prisoners she had tired of looking at. Others were poisoned and their skins harvested. At the camp pathology laboratory, a Communist capo and his assistants surgically removed Ilse Koch's favored tattoos and converted them into book covers, lampshades, wallets, and other keepsakes. She had shrunken heads made as toys for her children. None of this seemed to bother her husband, the commandant Karl-Otto

Koch, who stole thousands of marks budgeted for feeding prisoners and stocked his villa with cured meats and champagne. When he got wind of his wife's affair with Hoven, though, he demanded a share of the latter's loot.

Hoven was also known for his characteristic style of murder—via injections of sodium evipan or phenol. He'd give death shots to a whole row of prisoners, then stroll from the operating room, cigarette in hand, merrily whistling "A Perfect Day." He admitted at Nuremberg to having killed 150 patients this way, but they were "traitors," he said, who had to be done away with to protect the camp prisoner government for which he was working. Such statements were obviously self-serving, but there was an element of uncomfortable truth to them, for Hoven employed his wickedness effectively in the struggle against the Greens. Ernst Busse, a top German Communist in the camp, once even stated, "Waldemar is crazy, you would almost think he were one of our men." Through his control of the hospital, Hoven could protect Red inmates in danger and kill unfriendly Greens, and thus was key to the breaking of Green power in the camp. "And what supremacy of the professional criminals in the Buchenwald camp would have meant," one inmate later testified, "can only be appreciated by someone who has anything to do with professional criminals."

As the Reds consolidated their control over the hospitals, medical training became a prized asset, as is evident in the preponderance of doctors in the Buchenwald survival literature. But placement in a medical job was not always an unmitigated plus, because some positions were morally compromised. Arthur Dietzsch, the German inmate chosen in January 1942 to head the new block for medical experiments, is a case in point. Dietzsch was an unexceptional man with exceptionally bad luck, even by the sorrowful standards of Germany in the first half of the past century. The Kafkaesque turns of his life led the nationalist writer Ernst von Salomon to portray Dietzsch as the ur-German everyman in a 1960 metabiography, *Das Schicksal des A.D.* (translated as *The Captive*). Born in 1901, Dietzsch was good-looking in a somewhat frightening way, with sharp, triangular features, piercing blue eyes, and a square jaw. He possessed many of the "secondary virtues" of the good Prussian citizen—diligence and truthfulness and cleanliness and discipline—and beautiful handwriting. From the time he joined the army in 1920, each of his steps led to trouble. Convicted of espionage after being drawn into a web of military intrigue, he was thrown into prison in 1924 and remained there for all but one of the next 27 years. Dietzsch came to Buchenwald in 1938 and was made an assistant to Walter Krämer, a Communist carpenter and former member of the German parliament who had learned some medicine during his lengthy sojourn through the camps.

In November 1941, Koch, the Buchenwald commandant, had the Gestapo seize Dietzsch, Krämer, and two other medical aides in an effort to conceal the fact that Krämer had treated Koch for syphilis. Dietzsch survived six weeks of torture and starvation, but upon his release from the Gestapo bunker, found himself in an exposed place— "on the wire," in the camp lingo—because he had learned unwholesome secrets about a Nazi commander. Another medical secretary suggested that Dietzsch go to work in a new facility—the typhus station of the Waffen-SS Hygiene Institute, headed by Erwin Ding, who was returning to Buchenwald.

Ding had studiously courted higher-ups in the SS medical hierarchy, and he was known among colleagues in Berlin as a consummate office politician. He'd spent several months as a doctor at the Dachau concentration camp, then joined the invasion of France as adjutant to a division physician. From France, Ding sent home boastful letters to his wife in Berlin, claiming feats he had never achieved. His bosses watched their backs, while colleagues were often disgusted by his braggadocio. "He had an extraordinary need for recognition," was how one officer put it. The typhus station at Buchenwald, with its ostensible importance to the German war effort, seemed to Ding like an excellent place to get it.

Ding had left Buchenwald as a camp doctor. He returned as a "scientist" in charge of a "research station." While still responsible for aspects of camp hygiene, Ding's main mission was to conduct human experiments testing the efficacy of antibiotics and vaccines that might protect the Wehrmacht from typhus on the eastern front. He opened an isolation unit for typhus research in January 1942, and moved it to its permanent home in Block 46 the following June. The nature of Block 46 had been established in the protocol of the December 29, 1941, meeting in Berlin, where Nazi health authorities had hurriedly sought a way to combat the eastern typhus epidemics: "Since animal experiments cannot provide adequate evaluation [of typhus vaccine]," it read, "experiments must be conducted on people."

Shortly after Block 46 opened, Ding gathered Dietzsch and the other inmates and warned them that they were subject to a special military law and would be killed if they disclosed anything they saw. As the nature of the job began to dawn on Dietzsch, he pleaded with the inmate big shots to get him out of it, but Ding insisted that he required a political prisoner, not a Green, in the position, and the Communists didn't want one of their own to work in such a morally compromised location. They insisted that Dietzsch, a fellow traveler but not a cadre, remain there.

Ding opened Block 46 with no clear sense of how to proceed scientifically. The indicated way to test the efficacy and safety of a vaccine against a typhus was to vaccinate patients entering an epidemic area, and to measure their rates of disease and death against an unvaccinated control group. An ethical experimental design would have provided the control group a "standard-of-care" prophylactic, in this case the Weigl vaccine. Theoretically, the SS could have tested the vaccine on a group of Jews in any of the vast, typhus-ridden ghettos it controlled. But that seems never to have crossed anyone's mind. Ding would test the typhus vaccines on inmates, who would then be intentionally exposed to the disease. Not only was this approach horribly wrong; it was physically impractical. Typhus was not a regular visitor at Buchenwald, because both the SS and the internal camp leadership worked hard to keep it out. Every inmate at the camp had his or her story of the brutal initiatory body shave and bath in caustic soap, the waits in freezing cold for deloused clothing to dry, the deaths by exposure and pneumonia. The sight of a single louse in a barracks was enough to send everyone to quarantine for a week. In fact, the men sometimes purchased lice from others in order to get a few days off a work detail. "The Germans could care less if we were sick but they were very afraid of epidemics, and above all they feared typhus," recalled a French inmate.

Since there was no typhus in the camp, Ding sought out the Robert Koch Institute, whose director, Gildemeister, brought down a container of *Rickettsia* cultures grown in egg yolk sac. On March 3, 1942, Gildemeister and Ding injected the material into 145 patients. Most of them became sick, and so did Ding, who mistakenly jabbed himself with a needle. His illness was severe, and it derailed him and the typhus vaccine project for several months. After recovering, Ding spent his three months of training at the Pasteur Institute in Paris. In November 1942, perhaps in some vestigial hope of obtaining meaningful data from Buchenwald, Mrugowsky arranged for the Behringwerke in Lwów to send typhus-infected lice to Ding. The idea was that infection by lice, even if intentional, would provide a more "natural" experimental basis to judge the value of the vaccines that were being tested. Richard Haas, Behring's man in Lwów, had his own reasons for sending the lice. Chronically short of feeders, he hoped that Buchenwald inmates might become a new lice farm for vaccine production. Neither Mrugowsky nor Haas would get his wish, however.

On November 30, 1942, Haas shipped to the camp 200 boxes, each containing 150 lice infected with typhus. Ding was not in Buchenwald when the lice arrived, and Hoven, who was nominally in charge of the typhus station in Ding's absence, was leery of introducing lice to the camp. "Now they've really gone crazy," Hoven said; he and Dietzsch burned all 30,000 lice in their boxes. To conceal the real reason for their action, Hoven wrote to Haas that the paraffin wax used to seal the boxes had melted during transport, that the lids were insecure and some lice had escaped. This was all nonsense. In their primitive wisdom, Dietzsch and Hoven recoiled at the idea of bringing contaminated vermin into the camp, after so much time and human suffering had gone to keeping them out.

Haas, sensing that something was amiss, sent a second consignment a few days later. This time, the lice were accompanied by a Behring biologist, Dr. Rudolf Gönnert, who had instructions to unpack the lice boxes and supervise their application to patients. But the Behring men could not compete with the scheming minds of an SS doctor and a capo. After learning that the visitor needed to get home on a particular train, Hoven and Dietzsch delayed preparations as long as they could. The 19 homosexual prisoners chosen for the experiment were stripped naked, buckled to hospital chairs, and covered with white sheets. But just after the lice boxes were strapped to their legs, an SS man arrived at the laboratory door to inform the visitor that a car was waiting for him. He had to hurry, the messenger said, or he would miss his train in Weimar. As soon as Gönnert was gone, Hoven and Dietzsch removed the lice boxes and again burned them all. None of the men fell ill, and the report was falsified.

While convalescing at home in Berlin, Ding hit upon his own crazy idea for how to maintain a steady supply of typhus germs. In 1916, a Turkish doctor had injected prisoners with the blood of feverish patients. This seemed to Ding like an outstanding way to conduct his experiments with a minimum of uncertainty. While a real typhus epidemic could not be arranged, it would be easy enough to keep a few sick patients in Block 46, their blood available to infect test subjects whenever needed. Lice were inconvenient, but human beings were a dime a dozen. Decades earlier, Rudolf Weigl had figured out how to use laboratory lice as a reservoir of typhus. Ding's idea was to use human beings for the same purpose.

It would take some "tinkering" before this strategy produced any results. In the first set of experiments, the injections produced such

massive infections that nearly all the patients died, whether vaccinated or not. Later subjects were injected with a smaller amount, 0.5 to
1 cubic centimeters of blood drawn from a "passage person," a typhus
carrier usually in the fifth or sixth day of infection. When the test
subjects were infected with this quantity of typhus, prior vaccination
seemed to offer them some degree of protection. Ding and Dietzsch
injected some inmates with the blood of patients suffering naturally
occurring typhus, usually brought in from Buchenwald-dependent
subcamps, miserable slave labor enclosures where typhus abounded.
Each new "wild" strain was injected into at least two patients. If new
strains weren't available, the disease was transmitted by injection from
carrier to carrier. The many vaccines tested at Buchenwald included
yolk sac–based vaccines from Berlin, Frankfurt, Marburg, and Lwów,
dog-lung vaccines from Romania, and mouse- and rabbit-lung vaccines from the Pasteur Institute. Mrugowsky wanted the human test
subjects to resemble the German fighting man, which ruled out Eastern Europeans who might already be immune to typhus as a result
of childhood or other exposure. Starting in December 1943, Himmler
ordered police in Berlin to send test subjects culled from prisons holding common criminals. In practice, though, many of the subjects
continued to be Buchenwald inmates, including Russians, Poles, and
Frenchmen who were selected to undergo the meaningless torment
for reasons related to internal camp politics, or because they had, in
fact, volunteered.

To get the Block 46 inmates into a state of health resembling that
of the German soldier, Dietzsch and his nurses fattened the prisoners on mugs full of milk, white bread with butter, eggs and honey,
soup with oats, pasta and flour, tea and real coffee with sugar. None
of these foods were available in the camp, where the typical daily
ration was a chunk of dark bread and a quart of thin rutabaga soup.
Hungry inmates sometimes took the calculated risk of enduring
typhus in exchange for three months in the experimental block with
good nourishment. "They chose a means of suicide that had a cer-

tain chance of survival," a French physician said. The prisoners were "stuffed like turkeys in preparation for their utilization," as one witness put it. Said a prisoner who survived the tests, "They made us pretty sick, but they fed us well." Less than 15 percent of the test subjects died of typhus, though others were executed after leaving the typhus hospital.

Having already stuck himself once to bad effect, Ding seldom performed the injections, leaving Dietzsch in control of the experimental block. Waldemar Hoven occasionally came by, but only to supervise the tailor, shoemaker, and tanner who were working for him illegally in a couple of attic rooms of Block 46. Stranded in the building without any friends, Arthur Dietzsch found himself with hellish responsibilities. The criminal patients whom he had to nourish and sacrifice posed an immense challenge. Some were stool pigeons, some smugglers, thugs, or murderers. They hated the politicals like Dietzsch, whom they blamed for putting them in the experimental block in the first place. These patients or their Green allies tried to kill him at least four times, Dietzsch claimed after the war. He could more than defend himself, and in doing so used care-giving techniques that resembled those of a medieval madhouse. He yelled at patients and beat them for trifling offenses, such as urinating on a toilet seat or noisily closing a door. He withheld food from disruptive inmates and sometimes ordered the seriously ill to be chained to their beds with a urine flask taped to their thighs to keep them from wetting sheets.

But he also nursed the inmates, in his fashion, for the experimental block was well-stocked with strophanthin, caffeine, glucose, and the other state-of-the-art typhus treatments, whose therapeutic effect was to strengthen the patient and his heart. Some prisoners testified later that Dietzsch took a sadistic pleasure inflicting pain on the test subjects. On the other hand, it cannot have been easy to maintain order in a 90-bed infirmary filled with criminals and other patients in the throes of feverish hysteria. Dietzsch would claim that he tied down patients only to keep them from committing suicide, attacking others, or smashing everything in sight. Given what we know about the behavior of typhus patients, this may have been true.

Dietzsch became a big shot—well fed and well dressed, with enough extra rations to keep an enormous Newfoundland dog. And before long, everyone in the camp—SS and inmates alike—had heard enough about Block 46 to dread the place. Survivors, when they talked, brought forth gruesome images. One day in the fall of 1943, a Czech political prisoner named Willy Bahner got a white slip of paper from his block master telling him to report to the prisoners' hospital, where he found about 65 other prisoners. "We didn't know what it was all about, since we hadn't reported sick." Dietzsch escorted them on the short walk over to Block 46, where they were given baths and clean clothes and taken to a dormitory on the second floor. On the third day, Dietzsch called them down and gave each an injection. Two weeks

Dietzsch at the Buchenwald trial. (National Archives.)

later, with prisoners moaning and yelling all around him, Bahner began to run a fever. He saw at least eight men die.

By the time the camp was liberated, Ding had supervised 24 test series, involving around 1,000 patients. If the 150–200 "passage people" are included, between 300 and 400 people died there of intentional infection with typhus. Survivors suffered lifelong disabilities, including memory loss, epileptic fits, impotence, and chronic headaches. Ding knew the work was immoral, and kept his paperwork in order to show any future judges that he was not ultimately responsible for it. This strategy was useful, for in May 1943, an SS judge named Konrad Morgen arrived at Buchenwald and remained for six months while conducting an investigation on Himmler's orders. The Morgen episode was surely one of the weirdest at Buchenwald. The judge's mission was to winkle out corruption and abuse, but in a highly selective way that reflected his status as an SS cat's-paw. He had already been sent to the eastern front once for conducting an overly vigorous investigation at Auschwitz. Morgen appears to have been taken in by Ding, who posed as a real typhus expert conducting humane, scientific experiments.

Nothing could have been further from the truth. As Eugen Kogon wrote in his masterful account of Buchenwald, *The Theory and Practice of Hell*, "The scientific value of these tests was either nil or else of but insignificant proportions." Despite this, the German military luminaries who knew about the tests made no effort to stop them— with one exception. Gerhard Rose, a tropical medicine expert, protested acerbically at a May 1943 conference of military surgeons after Ding presented some data there. But later he had a change of heart and sent a Danish-made typhus vaccine to be tested at Buchenwald. Ding gloated over this to Kogon. "See," he said, "Rose has come along as well."

The vaccine tests were inconclusive, but Ding's career was advancing. In early November 1942, he wrote to one of his former guardians that he had been promoted to *Oberstabsarzt*—a senior military rank—and to *SS Sturmbannführer* (major). "I was stunned and over-joyed about it, because to be *Oberstabsarzt* at the age of 30 is already a nice career!" He was attending the Behringwerke inauguration in Lwów and just back from a big conference in Berlin, where scientists from the government, the Robert Koch Institute, and IG Farben were lining up to work with him, Ding said. He attached a copy of his "latest major work," an article about typhus serodiagnosis published in 1943. Like each of Ding's six wartime typhus papers, it had been written by slave doctors on his staff.

Typhus was not the only test subject at Block 46. In one exper-imental series, apparently conducted to determine the value of dif-ferent treatments for typhoid—the food- and water-borne bacterial illness—60 inmates were brought into the block, fed amply on por-ridge, oatmeal, and fruit for two days, then forced to fast for 24 hours. When Dietzsch produced bowls of potato salad, the young inmates fell upon them like hungry wolves. They were unaware that the salad had been liberally spiked with typhoid cultures. "Within two hours I stroked my hair and it hurt, and we started to get fever. Then we real-ized that there was a little more to it than a late supper," said Henry Mikols, a Pole who had been brought to Buchenwald as a "red triangle" a few weeks earlier.

> Everyone got angry and someone hit the capo, and he gave that man a shot and he stiffened. . . . Other people screamed, had diarrhea, high temperature. I heard music playing in my ears, didn't know where it was coming from unless they were playing Strauss to keep us happy. . . . When the doctor came I said I wanted to write a letter to my mother and father. He took a pencil and piece of paper. I said, "Dear mother and father, I don't feel good, but since I am Catholic, I have turned to my God for help." He looked at me, "*Nein, nein, du stirbst nicht* [No, you're not going to die]." Then I see two other white jackets and they give me two injections in my chest. I felt a burning

sensation and when they woke me up an hour or two later, my health was coming back.

Out of 60 people who entered the block, Mikols said, "only eight of us left through the gate." The nurses took samples of his feces to send for testing in Berlin. "I said to my friend, 'I hope they serve this to Adolf on a platter.'"

For some of the prisoners, Block 46 was an even more humiliating experience. The Dutchman Peter Schenk, who was only 17 when he came to Buchenwald, got a job as a tailor in Block 46, but found that in exchange for the job he was sexually assaulted. According to Schenk, he was "chosen a couple times a month" to be tied up and raped in a room next to the crematorium. In taped testimony given in 1996, Schenk accused Ding of being the rapist, but circumstancial evidence suggests he was more likely referring to the camp physician Hoven, who was accused of homosexual rapes by other inmates, and in whose tailor shop Schenk worked.

Ding also tested drugs for IG Farben. Its conglomerate subsidiary Hoechst had an antibiotic candidate, acridine, that it had shelved in 1938 when the drug failed animal tests. The war gave Hoechst a chance to try to resuscitate it as a typhus treatment; company executives' hearts quickened when they thought of potential sales to the Wehrmacht. The company began communications with Mrugowsky about testing the drug in 1941, and in November 1942, 1,000 tablets were sent to *SS-Obersturmführer* [First Lieutenant] Helmuth Vetter, a contract researcher with IG Farben and doctor at Auschwitz associated with its Hygiene Institute station. Vetter wrote a few months later that patients tolerated the drug very poorly; almost all suffered terrible vomiting and diarrhea and unrelenting burning sensations in the mouth. It was "worthless" as typhus treatment, Vetter said, but Hoechst refused to be dissuaded so easily. Sure they vomited, Hoechst officer Rudolf Fussgänger wrote back, but the mortality of typhus patients who took the pills was 30 percent, compared with 34 percent of the controls, which he considered significant. Hoechst then sent batches of the drug to Buchenwald. In April, Ding paid a visit to Hoechst's Leverkusen headquarters, and 10 days later began testing the drug, with the company's approval. Fifty percent of the patients in his experiment died, with no significant difference between those who received acridine and the controls—except that those who got the drug vomited an average of seven times a day. As the Block 46 capo Dietzsch noted after the war, "You could only have tested such an unacceptable preparation in a concentration camp, where you didn't have to ask permission, where there was no free will."

CHAPTER TEN

"Paradise" at Auschwitz

The main Auschwitz gate with the sign "Arbeit macht frei." (USHMM.)

To be sent to Auschwitz could, in extremely rare instances, be almost a stroke of good luck. In the case of Ludwik Fleck, his family, and associates, it provided what would turn out to be their best chance at survival. The deportation of the Fleck scientific team in February 1943 was a tiny piece of the sweeping bureaucratic response to Germany's failures on the eastern front, which heightened the need to put the Reich's economic and technological resources to good use.

As part of this shift, Himmler decided to employ captive scientists and instructed *Obergruppenführer* (General) Oswald Pohl, chief of the new SS Main Economic and Administrative Office, to set up a research station at a suitable concentration camp. Pohl chose Auschwitz—plenty of "research" was already going on there—and delegated the task to Mrugowsky, head of the Waffen-SS Hygiene Institute.

Mrugowsky, in turn, selected *Hauptsturmführer* (Captain) Bruno Weber, a 28-year-old Rhinelander, to lead a bacteriological institute at Auschwitz. Weber had spent a semester at the University of Chicago in 1937 and was working as an SS hygienist in Munich. In November or December 1942, he visited several Jewish ghettos and concentration camps, interviewing bacteriologists, pathologists, chemists, and other prospective staff. As job searches go, it was a relatively painless process for Weber. As he wrote to Mrugowsky, "I am undertaking the arrest by the Gestapo of the most eminent specialists of all the European faculties. Many of them are already assembled at the Institute of Hygiene."

Weber may have learned about Fleck's urine-extract vaccine through Kudicke or other *Generalgouvernement* officials. In the weeks before the SS began the final destruction of the Lwów ghetto, Weber paid a visit to the Jewish hospital on Kuszewicz Street. According to one account, by an Auschwitz inmate who knew Fleck, a negotiation process followed in which Weber offered Fleck a "position"—the alternative being death in the ghetto. Fleck accepted on the condition that his son, wife, and close associates be included. The ten members of Fleck's party—his family, the Umschweifs and Seemans and their children, and Abramowicz—were registered at Auschwitz on the night of February 7 after arriving in regular passenger cars guarded by two German soldiers.

At this point, however, the SS plans for the scientists seem to have grown muddled. After going to the trouble of bringing them to Auschwitz in their own train compartment, camp officials allowed Fleck and his team members to be abused and exposed to typhus, so that they barely survived long enough to report to the research station. Perhaps Weber wanted to give the Jews a taste of camp life, or some other Nazi officer was annoyed at Weber's interesting assignment and decided to take it out on "Weber's Jews"—a common occurrence in SS circles. Or, since Nazis typically considered Fleck and his colleagues to be tools more than human beings, Weber was simply neglectful of them at a time when he was busy equipping his research institute with looted equipment. The institute was not ready when the Lwów team arrived, nor were the scientists' "quarters" prepared. Weber had to park them somewhere. Auschwitz was a concentration camp and not a pharmaceutical company or a university, and they got the usual treatment.

Fleck's group was initially housed in a large bathroom in "Canada," the warehouse in the main camp where mountains of clothing, jewelry, and other items confiscated from the murdered Jews of Europe were sorted, stolen, or sent back to Germany. Children were routinely gassed and murdered on arrival at Auschwitz, and there was nowhere else where families could live together. On February 11, the camp assigned numbers 100965–100969 to five male "employees of the Weigl institute": Abramowicz, Ryszard Fleck, Ludwik Fleck, Jakob Seeman, and Bernhard Umschweif. The wives, Anna Seeman, Natalia Umschweif, and Ernestyna Fleck received numbers 34965–34967. The children did not get their numbers immediately, which was worrisome. Everyone knew that a tattoo meant at least a short-term reprieve from the gas chambers. According to the Auschwitz logbook, it was not until February 20 that Bronisław ("Bruno") Seeman, who was 10 years old, and Karol Umschweif, 5, got their tattoos. In an interview in 1997, Bruno Seeman recalled the nine-day period as going on for two or three months.

The women and children were taken to a building at Birkenau, the section of Auschwitz that had women's barracks as well as the large gas chambers and crematoria. They were not physically mistreated there, but got little food and were exposed to the brutal Silesian winter. "There was roll call every morning," Bruno Seeman remembered.

"You had to stand in the cold for what seemed like forever. If you collapsed they took you to the terminal block."

The men entered the domain of a notorious capo, the Polish political prisoner Mieczysław Pańszczyk of Kraków. He had been at Auschwitz since June 1940 and bragged that he had killed more than 10,000 prisoners "with my own hands," usually with a hypodermic full of poison. In March, Fleck and Ryszard, then 19 years old, worked as corpse haulers. Decades later Ryszard Fleck still remembered the special instructions he got on the procedure: "The first time I wanted to grab the dead person by the arms to carefully remove him from the bed. Friends taught me to pull him out by his legs and throw him on the floor. Then you'd strip him from his gown and spit on his chest to write his number on his chest with a carbon pencil. We put the corpses in a corner of the hall and arranged them with one head facing the right and the other facing the left, so the pile didn't come apart. I was startled the first time I saw a patient sitting on the pile of corpses, drinking tea."

Ludwik and Ryszard Fleck both came down with typhus. Their cases were relatively minor, which Fleck attributed to the protective effects of his vaccine, although it is also conceivable that his exposures during years of work with typhus germs provided him a measure of immunity. "Since the concentration camp administration liquidated any prisoner who got sick with typhus, I concealed my illness with the help of other prisoners, including doctors who secretly treated me," Fleck wrote. "My son spent only one day in bed." However, Ryszard was so weak that he narrowly escaped being selected for the gas, the routine treatment for prisoners too sick to work. Meanwhile, the capo Pańszczyk broke two of Fleck's ribs by stomping on him, which led to a pleural infusion, a weakened heart, and an inflammation of the gall bladder. Fleck entered the camp hospital semi-conscious; in addition to his other injuries, he had an ugly skin infection and limbs swollen from hunger. Fleck's prewar reputation may have been what saved him at the Auschwitz infirmary, where inmate doctors from the Polish underground were in control. A Pole who had studied under Hirszfeld, and the hospital director, Władysław Fejkel, a Kraków bacteriologist at Auschwitz since 1940, looked after him.

On April 8, two months after Fleck's team arrived at Auschwitz, Weber opened his research station, the *Hygienische-Bakteriologische Untersuchungsstelle der Waffen-SS und Polizei Süd-Ost, Auschwitz, Oberschlesien*. Informally, it was known as the Hygiene Institute, and it was initially based in a three-story brick building, Block 10, next to the execution block. The scientists were housed in Block 20, nearby, and worked near their wives, who lived in Block 10 itself. Fleck took over the serology laboratory. The Lwów scientists' arrival at Block 10 coincided with some of the most notorious Nazi medical experiments, gruesome events that displayed the decadent depths to which German professionals could fall under Nazism. On April 1, Camp Commandant Rudolf Höss placed Block 10 under the command of SS Brigadier General Professor Carl Clauberg, who set up an experimental station to continue the sterilization experiments he had begun in the women's camp in Birkenau in December 1942. About 20 women of different nationalities were brought to Block 10 to work as slave doctors and medical orderlies in Clauberg's service. The doctors performed sterilizations in a suite of rooms separated by thin wooden walls from Fleck's lab. Without antiseptics or anesthesia, Clauberg injected a chemical irritant into the women's wombs, causing inflammation that blocked the fallopian tubes. If the woman did not die of infection, she was usually murdered in order to be autopsied. At least 400 died this way. In June 1943, Clauberg wrote to Himmler, "The non-surgical method of sterilizing women that I have invented is now almost perfected." He promised that a single physician with 10 assistants "will be able to carry out in the course of a single day the sterilization of hundreds, or even 1,000 women."

The women—French, Belgian, Greek, Dutch, and Slovak—were crammed into a windowless room. No one explained the procedures to them, and some of the women came to the horrified conclusion that they were undergoing artificial insemination. "What kind of monsters will we give birth to?" they wondered. One of the Nazi physicians, Horst Schumann, sterilized with X-rays, while Bruno Weber, Fleck's boss, injected the women with nonmatching blood types, which caused terrible pain, shock, kidney failure, and death. Even had such wretched experiments been morally justified, they had no scientific value, since it was impossible to know whether sterility was due to the interventions or the terrible nutrition and stress of the camp.

Fleck witnessed these terrible occurrences from his laboratory next door, where he and other scientists conducted experiments with the women's blood aimed at improving immunoglobulin for front-line troops. The blood draws killed many of the more undernourished prisoners. A German-Jewish physician named Maximilian Samuel, supposedly a genetics expert—"a crazy old man," Fleck called him—conducted experiments side by side with the SS doctors until they tired of him and sent him to the gas chambers. During this time, Fleck befriended Adelaide Hautval, a non-Jewish French resistance member. Clauberg had brought her into Block 10 as a physician, but she bravely refused his requests to assist in experimental surgeries on the other women prisoners. Hautval survived, apparently, only because the chief camp doctor, Eduard Wirths, felt sympathy for her.

"It was strictly forbidden to have meetings in this lab," Hautval recalled after the war:

> Naturally, I ignored the orders and frequently visited my friends. There was a nice, warm atmosphere provided by Dr. Fleck and Dr. Anna Seeman. It was a somewhat calming atmosphere, with a lot of human understanding. Fleck was a calm but spiritual man, didn't speak much and yet there was much feeling in his presence. His sense of humor was colored with deep pessimism. Once he told us that he saw our names written in the sky with smoke from the crematoria chimneys. But he had a sense of humor too. One day I noticed there were two

**Nazi SS doctors and other officers at Auschwitz, 1944.
(Anonymous donor to the USHMM.)**

mirrors in the room and joked that they must be for Jews and Aryans. I said, "Come on, let's commit *Rassenschande*" [illegal race mixing] and pulled him in front of the two mirrors where we could see each other together.

From time to time, Dr. Hautval brought experimental samples to Fleck. Whenever a patient's sample came up positive for typhus or diphtheria, Fleck would equivocate in his report. "His team was always helpful to us. They were always ready to examine my patients, and they knew to falsify the results in the official documents, since the real results could lead to death."

The windows of Block 10 were closed with boards, but the inmates could peek into the courtyard next door through the cracks. Every day or two, the Gestapo brought in groups of up to 50 prisoners, lined them against the wall and shot them. Sometimes blood ran under the door of Block 10. The victims were political prisoners. Jews, by then, were mostly killed by gas. One day, Fleck saw two SS men kill dozens of prisoners with 8-cc shots of carbolic acid to the heart. "The victims stood naked on the floor without understanding what awaited them. They were told they would be vaccinated and get showers and were led one by one into the bathroom. Later, other prisoners hauled a mountain of corpses to the crematorium."

At night, Block 10 was locked, which gave the children a feeling of relief, said Seeman: "It meant we'd live until the morning."

To understand the bizarre, terrifying world Fleck and his group had entered, it may be helpful to take a step back. During the winter of 1941–42, the Nazis were forced to reckon with the shortage of economic and military resources for the eastern campaign. In March 1942, Himmler reorganized the concentration camps and made Pohl, the top SS economic official, their boss. At the same time, the Wannsee Conference in January 1942 had crystallized plans for the total extermination of European Jewry. The use of gas to murder Jews had begun at Chelmno in late 1941, and industrial-scale murder began at Belzec in March, followed by Sobibor and Treblinka. The capacity of these death camps wasn't sufficient, so Himmler ordered the construction of an enormous complex of gas chambers and crematories at Auschwitz.

Yet even as the gassings intensified, the hundreds of other camps built since 1933, large and small, were being modified to make better use of able-bodied Jews and other prisoners. Among other things, the concentration camps were useful locations at which to conceal factories to replace the production lost in Allied bombing of Germany's cities and industrial areas. Though "death through exhaustion," as Himmler called it, marked no change of heart from the main Nazi goal, the focus on labor sometimes improved daily life for the prisoners who were not immediately killed. In December 1942 and again the following month, Pohl ordered all camp commandants to lower the mortality rates in the camps. This order opened a small wedge between the Gestapo and the camp doctors, whose job, theoretically, was to preserve health. Hermann Langbein, a German political prisoner who was secretary to Edward Wirths, the main camp doctor at Auschwitz, described the situation this way: "Since the instructions to lower the mortality rate were primarily directed at the SS doctors, some of whom could, on the basis of their profession, more easily be persuaded at least to limit the mass murders, the resistance movement of the prisoners in several camps attempted to influence physicians on duty there."

Langbein, a former Spanish Civil War revolutionary and political prisoner, developed a close relationship with Wirths, a Bavarian country doctor. Though Wirths played his part in the murder of Jews and experiments on prisoners, he had a genuinely troubled conscience, Langbein said, and "was capable of being influenced." The camp commander Höss stated after the war, "Wirths frequently complained to me that he could not reconcile the killings demanded of him with his medical conscience and that this caused him suffering." Wirths was especially soft on imprisoned doctors, Höss wrote. "I often gained the impression that he treated them as colleagues."

The experience of Louis J. Micheels, a Dutch Jewish medical student, indicates how some prisoner physicians could benefit from Wirths' humane side. Arriving at the ramp at Auschwitz in 1943, Micheels saw a "tall, impressive looking SS man" with a Hippocratic insignia on his coat." I stepped up to him, clicked my heels and said, something like, 'Herr *Oberarzt*, I have to report to you 20 patients, elderly, seriously ill, who came with me in this transport here.'" That day, Wirths was "working a shift" as an angel of death. That is, he was deciding which arrivals were assigned work and which went straight to their deaths. He told Micheels to stand by a chest with a red cross on it, where he watched the Nazis drag elderly people from the cars and toss them into a truck. "I saw a woman with two little children—she had loaned me a copy of *Candide* that I read with great pleasure. The image is still very much with me, seeing her run toward her place in lineup," Micheels said. "I didn't know at the time but it was a lineup for the gas chamber."

Micheels ended up in the camp hospital, where nurses and other doctors "addressed you with your name. You were almost a person again." Langbein's influence on Wirths had vastly improved conditions there. Whereas Wirths's predecessor had "fought typhus by having the lice gassed together with the patients," Wirths relieved the SS men and the capo at the hospital who routinely beat to death patients seeking treatment. Langbein was working closely with Władysław Fejkel, the Polish doctor—"cultivated and humane, [who] had succeeded," in the words of another inmate, "at the tour de force of being on good terms at the same time with both the prisoners and the SS."

Wirths wrote detailed and frank reports about conditions at the camp to Pohl and to Grawitz, the chief SS medical officer. The reports may have contributed to a change in leadership at the camp that occurred after Himmler sent Judge Konrad Morgen to investigate thefts of the valuables of slain Jews. A few SS were executed. Arthur Liebehenschel replaced Rudolf Höss as camp commandant in November 1943.

Toward the end of 1942, a fifth of the Jews who were not gassed on arrival at Auschwitz died each month. By July and August 1943, the monthly death rate among those who received a tattoo declined to 3.5 percent. The number of inmates working at Auschwitz swelled from 88,000 in December 1942 to 224,000 in August 1943. Overcrowding increased disease, but it also heightened the chaos and gave the resistance more room in which to operate. As defeats at the front increased the demand for German manpower to serve there, many of the most sadistic camp guards shipped out, and were replaced by less zealous, older men and ethnic Germans from the Slavic lands. This also improved conditions.

On May 5, 1943, Weber's research institute moved from Block 10 to the Auschwitz subcamp Rajsko, built in a confiscated Polish village of the same name. Inmates were already growing fruits and vegetables for the SS and raising farm animals at Rajsko, where in 1942, the SS scientist Joachim Caesar had established an agricultural research station. The focus of his research was dandelions—special Ukrainian dandelions, *Taraxacum kok-saghyz*, whose roots were used by the Soviets as a source of latex to make rubber. Himmler had become obsessed with *kok-saghyz* and thought he could improve German self-sufficiency in rubber by cultivating the plant massively in Ukraine, France, and Romania. He visited Caesar's operations twice.

The United States was also interested in *kok-saghyz*. In exchange for U.S. jeeps, aircraft, food, and other support, the Soviets sent the U.S. Agriculture Department seeds from the plant, portraying it as having revolutionary potential for wartime rubber production. About 200 American and Canadian scientists worked on the *kok-saghyz* project, trying different soils and fertilizers to improve the latex yield. About two years and millions of dollars later, having shown the Soviet hype to be overblown, they gave up. Himmler and Caesar, however, persevered. At its height, the Auschwitz-Rajsko dandelion battalion had 150 inmates, but it never produced enough rubber to put tires on a single car. "The soil in Auschwitz is, after all, terrible, nothing but clay," one prisoner noted.

At Monowitz, another Auschwitz subcamp, the Italian chemist Primo Levi and thousands of other inmates slaved for more than a year to erect an enormous artificial rubber plant for IG Farben. Like Rajsko, Monowitz produced nothing tangible. But while the human toll at Monowitz was ghastly, Rajsko was one of the most pleasant workplaces in the camp system. The word Rajsko, as it happens, means "heavenly" in Polish. Compared with the main camp, it was heaven. Food rations were technically the same in both places, but the German SS woman in charge of the food at Rajsko, while anti-Semitic and rude, insisted on strict adherence to the distribution rules. In most of the camp, SS stole the rations or gave them to favored prisoners. Rajsko prisoners could supplement their rations with vegetables stolen from the gardens and the flesh of guinea pigs and rabbits from the experimental station. There were no selections for the gas chambers at Rajsko, and the morning roll call was only five or ten minutes long—in the main camp, it could go on for hours. Many of the inmates at Rajsko worked in warmed greenhouses. They ate at tables, slept in their own beds, and could take showers—an unheard-of luxury in a concentration camp. The only showers they had experienced at Auschwitz were part of the terrifying delousing process, or the false showers where their friends, mothers, and brothers had been suffocated with Zyklon gas.

The women in the Rajsko *kok-saghyz* commando lived at first in the women's camp at Birkenau, which was frequently plagued by typhus. In October 1942, Caesar and his wife fell ill with the disease, and she died. When the widowed commander returned from his convalescence, he decided that, to keep Rajsko free of lice and typhus, his women would have to live in a dormitory at the outcamp. The inmates were thrilled. Now they had their own beds and could bathe when they wanted. Soon all the women at Birkenau dreamed of coming to Rajsko. At Birkenau, there was no water. Women drank off the eaves when it rained. The toilets were far from the barracks, the rooms covered in human waste.

The leaders of the *kok-saghyz* detail were French and Polish Communists, and they were past masters in sabotage. Orders called for the women to grow the dandelions and cut their flowers, delicately collecting each seed and gathering the roots, which were cooked down and tested for latex production. "Those dandelion seeds, gee, they certainly do tend to float away," recalled Simone Alizon, a French resistance fighter who ended up at Rajsko. "And when we blew on them—well they flew away even faster. So the data from the seed collection were false. In the lab, different cooking methods gave contradictory or random results [on the latex weight]. The calculations based on these inexact data were also false. And each of us played his part with utter gravity. I doubt that our experiments would ever have allowed our executioners to develop a rubber industry, but the dandelions saved my life!"

She concluded, "It's not a good idea to depend on the work of slaves."

"Paradise" at Auschwitz

Fleck and the other Hygiene Institute workers walked to Rajsko every day from Block 20 in the main Auschwitz camp. Weber had moved the Hygiene Institute into a large building, across the road from Caesar's greenhouses on a triangular block of land surrounded by barbed wire and watchtowers. SS men with machine guns manned the towers and accompanied the scientists to and from work each day. The scientists carried a patch with a black diamond sewn into it on their left arm, with the initials HKB (Häftlings Krankenbau—prisoner hospital) painted on it. The capos and other leaders had yellow armbands with the lettering "Laboratorium Rajsko." The walk took about an hour, and if the weather was not too bad it could be almost pleasant. After waking at 4:30 a.m. for roll call, the captive scientists' column followed the banks of the Sola River past the agricultural station, where women inmates looked up from their fieldwork to wave at them. They passed a row of colorful peasant farmhouses. "In the morning the sky was sometimes a beautiful red, setting aglow the fields to the left across the river," Micheels, the Dutch student, wrote later. "In the distance, on the right, we could see the chimneys of the crematoria in Birkenau." The Rajsko inmates often remarked on this contrast. It was difficult to describe the emotions it stirred in them—sorrow, terror, hope, guilt.

The prisoner scientists were a cosmopolitan mixture of Jews and non-Jews from Poland, Germany, the Czech Republic, Romania, Slovakia, Holland, and France. Weber and the other SS doctors who ran these institutions put on dumb shows of the international scientific style. But the establishments were all form and no substance. They had spotless, well-equipped laboratories where specialists in different fields were instructed to carry out the mechanical actions characteristic of scientific technique. But their actions did not really constitute science, since freedom of inquiry was restricted to matters that were out of date, senseless, unethical, or impractical. It was as if a drunken squad of football players had locked the university's tenured staff in a laboratory and ordered them to *do some science.*

The Fantastic Laboratory of Dr. Weigl

Arriving at the institute, the scientists passed through a gate and entered the three-story building. The ground floor had a large bacteriological laboratory, with incubators, driers, refrigerators, centrifuges, and microscopes stolen from laboratories in France and Poland. In a smaller lab across the hall, a Polish scientist did entomological and water research, while a technician prepared culture media for the bacteriological and serological labs. On the next floor was a chemical lab that spanned the length of the building. Although it had a fabulous microscope and a tomograph for making fine-grained microscopic sections, the lab's primary purpose was to distill alcohol for the SS. After Josef Mengele arrived at Auschwitz and became the chief doctor of the Gypsy camp in mid-1943, he began sending samples from his infamous twin experiments to the lab for analysis. Mengele treated twin children brought to Auschwitz as if they were a collection of living dolls, performing hundreds of surgeries to conjoin twins, change eye color, amputate limbs, and remove kidneys, always without anesthesia. The heads of two of Mengele's Gypsy children, who had suffered from a malnutrition-related disease causing terrible ulcerations on their small faces, were encased inside jars there. The open eyes of the children stared out through the formalin and glass at the prisoners working in the lab.

On the same floor, Fleck and his team conducted serological examinations. The work, Fleck said, was similar to what he'd done at his private lab in Lwów—examinations of samples for syphilis, typhus, typhoid, and other diseases. "If the patients in the hospital had not been ceaselessly selected for extermination," Fleck wrote, "one might have thought that these blood, urine, and stool tests served the purpose of healing the sick. That was just another facet of the demonic nonsense that made up life in the Auschwitz camp." After the war, several witnesses would say that Fleck was working on his typhus vaccine while at Auschwitz. Bruno Seeman recalled that Fleck obtained "great volumes of urine" from the prisoner hospital, although "nothing ever came of it." The dandelion scientist Caesar stated that Weber had asked him to provide eggs for a typhus vaccine. Yet though Fleck seems to have been selected by Weber because of his vaccine work, there is no other evidence that Fleck was involved in making a vaccine at Auschwitz.

A general state of befuddlement surrounded the purpose of the Hygiene Institute. Weber showed no particular interest in the results of the serological research. Yet at its peak, in 1944, the scientists conducted more than 110,000 separate analyses. Most were performed on inmates who were going to die no matter the results, though there were also samples from SS men with tuberculosis or syphilis.

In a little room between Fleck's lab and the chemistry room, Bruno Weber and his assistant sat writing up the "research," when they were not carrying out their duties at the "ramp," sorting out the arriving Jews. In an attic workshop, two Warsaw tailors made sure the SS uniforms were always crisp. A shoemaker and a barber tidied up the SS men and their gear; a mechanic looked over Weber's Peugeot in the garage. On the building's top floor, two French researchers, Jakub Lewin of Paris and Marc Klein of Strasbourg University, created dried sera for identifying blood groups. They also often did blood alcohol tests for SS men who had committed some offense or were accused of being drunk on the job. One day, Weber walked into the laboratory and asked a member of Fleck's group what he was doing. When he responded that he was titrating blood group sera, Weber responded, "Yeah, we have no more group B sera. Those knuckleheads gassed all the gypsies." (Gypsies have disproportionately high rates of B-group blood types.)

Fleck and his team were something of a mystery to the other inmates. Although everyone knew there were no children at Auschwitz, they had children. Their wives had been saved, too, and they had resources of which most of the inmates could only dream. Frank Stiffel, an inmate from Lwów, was at the point of death in the hospital when one of Dr. Fleck's assistants, Bernhard Umschweif, suddenly appeared, saying that a mutual friend had sent him. Umschweif spoonfed Stiffel lemonade made from citric acid and sugar, and gave him milk. "My wife is working in the garden near the laboratory, and we have a son, for whom we receive milk," he said. Stiffel was stunned. "Wife? Son? Milk?" Later Umschweif returned with a carrot and a small grater, with which he prepared Stiffel carrot juice. When Stiffel was better, Umschweif brought him blutwurst and bread.

Despite their celebrity status among the inmates, the children lived in a state of utter and constant terror. Their mothers went to their work during the day, and the children were on their own—Bruno, Karol, and a third boy, Peter. In the autumn, they joined a unit that gathered blueberries and wild strawberries, growing in the ash-enriched soil behind the Birkenau crematoria. For a while, there were some older children in the main camp who served as messengers, but one day toward the end of 1943 they all went away. After that, Bruno See-man became very worried. "There was no assurance whatsoever what might happen," he testified. "The three of us were the only kids there. It wouldn't have taken much for them to decide they didn't want kids."

As a Nazi boss, Bruno Weber was "not the worst and not the best," as one inmate said. He ran the labs at a frantic pace, demanding the scientists work from sunup to sundown processing hundreds or even thousands of samples every day. One inmate described Weber as "elegant, cold and haughty, but 'correct.'" Micheels said he was "probably the most arrogant, suspicious, and occasionally vicious man I have ever met." He had neatly combed dark hair and bright blue eyes and "strutted like a peacock in his spotless uniform and shiny boots," a German shepherd by his side. He was equally nasty to Jews and non-Jews. The scientists spent an inordinate amount of time—about an hour each day—cleaning their laboratories for daily inspection. If Weber or the other SS found a speck of dirt, they would make the doctors do the "toad dance," bending at the knees and jumping around the laboratory. Weber was needlessly cruel in other ways. The installation had five sheep, whose blood was used to make the Wassermann tests for diagnosing syphilis. Sheep's blood could also be used to cultivate pathogens such as *Streptococcus pyogenes* (Group A strep), but Weber insisted it be used only for the syphilis tests. For the other cultures, he told Fleck and the other doctors, they should use their own blood. Despite their meager diets, each of the researchers had to surrender 10–15 cubic centimeters of blood every week.

One irksome task required of the scientists was the regular autopsies on barnyard animals and rabbits. The doctors conducted dozens of cultures every day—sometimes using their own blood as a culture medium—to determine the cause of death of the little rabbits. Often the cause was coccidiosis, a disease triggered by intestinal parasites that were of no relevance to human health. Thanks to the animal research, "we remained alive because like all our comrades, we ate the cadavers to nourish ourselves," the French scientist André Lettich wrote after the war. "But we were indignant that we were being obliged to conduct these autopsies and cultures knowing that the men who ordered our work were gassing and burning thousands of innocent men, women and children at the same time." In July 1944, in the midst of the wholesale destruction of the Hungarian Jews, Wirths brought Lettich a tiny dead rabbit, about five days old, in an envelope. A letter explained that the camp commandant wanted to know the cause of death.

Weber enjoyed walking around the grounds with his rifle and shooting any bird he found in his path. If he hit but only wounded a bird, he would bring it to the French-Polish scientist Léon Landau to take care of. One day, he brought Landau a pigeon with a wing three-quarters blown off and said, "Do everything you can to keep this bird alive." Landau amputated the bird's wing, but in the process nicked an artery. Weber went into a crazy rage, called him assassin and threatened him with disciplinary action, which is to say, death, unless he saved the bird's life. Weber returned some time later, and Landau showed him that the bird was still living. "I don't care," Weber said. "You can kill it."

Fleck's son, Ryszard, witnessed one of the more ghastly episodes at the Rajsko laboratory. Every few days, an SS man brought a big piece of cow or horse flesh to the lab technician, a young Slovak Jew named Imre Gönczi. His job was to trim the fat, pulverize the meat, cook it in glassware, then filter and sterilize the liquid protein broth, which was used by Fleck and other scientists to grow bacterial cultures. One day, the SS man brought Gönczi a big tub containing small pieces of bloody flesh that looked different from the others. Gönczi brought it to a Czech scientist, who confirmed his suspicions. But they couldn't let on that they knew. "'Til then, I had always shared the leftover boiled horse or beef meat with the other members of the commando," Gönczi said. Apparently, the SS had noticed that the prisoners were eating the boiled meat. They wanted it for themselves, so they confiscated the meat and replaced it with the body parts of prisoners executed by the Gestapo. "Now, when the guard would ask me, 'So, how was the meat?' I had to find some excuse for explaining that we hadn't eaten it," Gönczi said. The deliveries from the crematorium continued every week for half a year. Ryszard Fleck had to wash the pots. A man in his group collected the flesh and wrapped it in paper. When no one was watching, he'd bury the remains outside, saying a prayer for the dead.

The most important experiment being conducted in these laboratories, one could say, was the one that showed how easy it was to conduct bad science with a straight face. The scientists conducted exams exactly the way they had done back at their universities. But the results were fungible, and the scientists learned to twist the delicate training of a lifetime in order to fit with the thought style of an alien collective. If an SS man became enraged when a test showed his girlfriend had diphtheria, there was always an alternative analysis that could show a negative result. "Our relations with the SS were sensitive," wrote Klein, the French scientist. "We were at times required to falsify a diagnostic in order to save a sick comrade or protect a medical friend. Luckily, the SS never verified the tests, although they always signed them as if they were their work." He often asked himself what purpose the Rajsko institute served. The answer was plain, though. "The SS found relatively easy, stable positions in these laboratories, totally protected from the dangers of a war whose fronts were active and deadly. It was in their interest to have a well-operated lab with overinflated results on a variety of exams. These allowed them to project an image of indispensability to the central SS authorities."

As for the inmates, they enjoyed protection from the more dangerous or difficult commandos by wearing the doctor's blouse. And they hoped it would be enough to survive.

In the spring of 1944, 437,000 Hungarian Jews were gassed and burned at Auschwitz in the space of three months. The chimneys smoked constantly, belching bright fire into the sky at night. "Before that time I always said that May was the most beautiful month of the year," wrote Wanda Blankenheim of Lwów, who survived Rajsko. "For me it is now always the most horrible month of the year. All May we watched and smelled burning bones, burning people. We saw it with our own eyes." Another doctor wrote,

When we woke from our sleep at night—we who witnessed all of this and yet continued to eat and sleep like normal people— the inside walls of our block were lit up with the reflection of the blaze. And when I got up and crept out the back doors of the block that faced the crematorium opposite and looked toward the second one, I saw the flames of the open fire next to it and watched as they tossed the dead (and sometimes not quite dead) bodies of the children onto it. I heard their screams, saw how the fire lapped at their tender bodies. No metamorphosis of my being, regardless of whether in this life or the next, will ever expunge this horror from my soul.

Ludwik Fleck was fortunate to miss this particular agony. In December 1943, the Hygiene Institute's laboratory at Buchenwald, run by *Sturmbannführer* Ding, was having trouble producing a typhus vaccine. Ding and Mrugowsky were casting about for help, and they decided to requisition Fleck. Near the end of the month, he left Auschwitz in a private car, headed for the concentration camp on the out-skirts of Weimar, Germany. He left behind his son and wife. If they survived, he said, they would all meet again at Professor Groër's clinic in Lwów.

In Lwów, as the war went on, Weigl's employees at the typhus insti-tute began to have intense disagreements about the morality of their work. An editor from the famous Ossolineum publishing house, Jadwiga Lekczyńska, whose job was to prepare the louse intestines, refused ever to use less than the prescribed amount, although many of her colleagues faked it in order to make a weaker vaccine for the Germans. "The building we are working in has a Red Cross on the roof," she said. So she followed the norm that, as one writer put it, "assured the effectiveness of the vaccine for a thug murdering people in Belarus or Ukrainian villages, the butcher in uniform who mas-sacred ghetto residents." Knaster, the loud mathematician, disagreed. Sabotage was the holy duty of every Pole, he later told the journalist Ryszard Wójcik. "I have heard the abstract disputes about what means are morally acceptable in the fight against the enemy," he said. "A phy-sician's duty is to help a sick person; I as a Pole feel indifferent if a Ger-man soldier dies because he was killed by a piece of lead or a typhus germ. The loss of each Nazi increases by a certain percent the chance of survival for the occupied population, decreases the number of the gassed, shot, hanged people."

The dilemma of Weigl's workers was presented in the 1971 film *The Third Part of the Night*, by Mirosław Żuławski's son, the avant-garde filmmaker Andrzej Żuławski. The film has elements of surrealism, yet the depiction of life in Lwów and the laboratory is utterly real-istic, though hardly comprehensible as such to the typical Western viewer. Toward the close of the grim film, a louse feeder expresses his anguish and frustration at the Nazi atrocities: "The lab assistants should sabotage the vaccine. The vaccines should be made less effective," he says. "The whole situation should be brought to a conclusion and a breaking point, so that not a trace of submission and baseness is left in us, even if this leads to mass arrests and torture! Perhaps this occupation is like a plague, sent to make people realize the meaning of their lives."

In practice, the Poles compromised. They were human beings and wanted to survive. The heroic and well-intentioned among them protected a few Jews, but it was a struggle just to save their own skins. "It was understood that the vaccine was barely adequate for the Germans, but good enough," Szybalski said. "That was the price you had to pay. You had to be careful, because if the Germans didn't like the vaccine, they'd kill. Every few days I'd be walking down Akademicka Street and see people hanging from the streetlights with signs around their necks. We didn't want to end up like that. So you compromised to survive. You seldom get 100 percent in life, especially during a Nazi occupation."

As for Weigl, he continued to focus on his science during the war, with the goal of improving his vaccine. Stuchly worked on the biology and metabolism of lice, Kryński focused on the toxicity of *R. prowazekii*, and Mosing did epidemiological studies. Little of this work was ever published, and it is clear from postwar memoirs that Weigl's assistants understood better than he that vaccine, per se, was not their top priority during the war.

Weigl was a bit like the Alec Guinness character in *The Bridge on the River Kwai*, the imprisoned British officer in the Japanese POW camp who only belatedly understands the need to blow up the bridge he had so lovingly constructed. Weigl regarded his vaccine the same way he shot a bow and arrow: no compromise in quality, it had to be a bull's-eye. As Wacław Szybalski reported ruefully, "Weigl was a perfectionist and absolutely in love with his vaccine. He believed that it was his legacy. And this is the sad story."

CHAPTER ELEVEN

BUCHENWALD: RABBIT STEW AND FAKE VACCINE

I f Fleck had passed through a brutal gauntlet to arrive at his lab bench at Auschwitz, the welcome to Buchenwald was more civilized. By the time he arrived at his destination, the SS Hygiene Institute's Department of Virus and Typhus Research had been operating for six months in Block 50, a three-story masonry building on the edge of the main camp. The work at Block 50 was complex, but the risk of death was more remote than almost anywhere else in the camp, and daily life was relatively comfortable. Unlike the majority of the Buchenwald inmates, who rose from tangled, stinking piles on wooden barrack shelves at 4:30 a.m. to stand for hours in the *Appellplatz* to be counted each morning, Block 50's inmates slept in their own beds with sheets and blankets and had no morning or evening roll call. They did not have to fight for their rations, which included a bit of sugar, fat, and extra bread each week, and the tone in their laboratories was usually conversational rather than guttural.

Many of the doctors and scientists in Block 50 were political prisoners, but Erwin Ding, who ran the institute, was not entirely off the mark with his tasteless description of the place. He called it the *ultima refugia judaeorum*, "last refuge of the Jews." Ding addressed the inmates with the formal *Sie*, a rare bit of politesse in the camps. Apart from Ding and Doctor Hoven, SS men steered clear of Block 50.

Buchenwald: Rabbit Stew and Fake Vaccine

They respected the big black-and-white sign reading *Eintritt verboten* (Stay out) because they were scientific illiterates who had been warned to avoid anything to do with lice or typhus.

Physically and strategically, Block 50 was squarely at the center of the ghoulish surrealism of Buchenwald in the final years of the Third Reich. At the typhus research station, humanity reached its depraved depths, but some individuals achieved the heights of bravery as well. Block 50 stood half a mile down the mud road from the camp entrance in the last row of buildings within the central grounds. From the windows of Block 50, the inmates could peer across a triple line of barbed wire into the notorious Little Camp.

Mrugowsky from the beginning had been interested in having the Hygiene Institute produce typhus vaccine for Waffen-SS units at the front, but his plans kept being delayed. When British bombers destroyed the institute's headquarters in Berlin in 1942, he decided to produce the vaccine at Buchenwald. But what kind of vaccine? A large louse farm was out of the question, more so after Behringwerke's failed experiment at the camp. The Wehrmacht, with Eyer in the lead, was dubious about egg production; besides, where would the chickens for such a laboratory be housed? German civilians, let alone concentration camp inmates, could not be trusted around chickens or their eggs. The Giroud vaccine, made from rabbit lungs, had been tested at Buchenwald and seemed to be roughly as effective as Weigl's. The SS medical chief Grawitz was impatient for vaccine—as was Himmler. On December 11, 1942, Mrugowsky chose production of the Pasteur rabbit-lung vaccine for Buchenwald. "This vaccine has been tested among concentration camp inmates with excellent results," he wrote in a memo. Ding made two more visits to the Pasteur Institute in early 1943, and began assembling scientists to produce the vaccine with the help of his new clerk, an imprisoned German intellectual named Eugen Kogon. Ding and Kogon moved themselves and the vaccine production wing of the typhus institute into Block 50 on August 10, 1943.

Even before Ludwik Fleck arrived at Block 50, staffing the vaccine

Eugen Kogon testifying in April 1947 at the Buchenwald trial.
(National Archive.)

laboratory seemed to be quite easy. There were plenty of doctors in the camp, and others who'd doubled as doctors to save their skins or follow the directives of the camp leadership. ("I had a foot injury and was operated on by a mechanic and a butcher," one inmate remarked.) Willy Jellinek, a bright young Austrian pastry chef known as Jumbo, was in charge of the tubercular ward for a while, and helped write Hoven's dissertation on lung disease for the University of Heidelberg. Jellinek came to Block 50 to prepare culture broths for the vaccine; August Cohn, a charismatic former Communist labor leader, was rescued from a death sentence and put in charge of the rabbits. No vaccine experts were imprisoned in Buchenwald at the time, but Ding found an infectious disease specialist, the 36-year-old Marian Ciepielowski, to lead the vaccine production team, though Ciepielowski ended up there more by chance than design. A socialist from the Carpathians near Lwów, he had worked in a Kraków hospital before being arrested for an anti-Nazi conspiracy in April 1941. Ciepielowski spent his first year at Buchenwald working with pick and shovel on a road detail. "Every day, dozens of people around me were suffocated, clubbed, stomped, and shot to death, and we were all mistreated sadistically," Ciepielowski wrote his sister later. He survived, with a crippled right hand, but was arrested in one of the periodic political bloodlettings in the camp. At this point, friends smuggled Ciepielowski into Block 50. Within the space of a week, he went from the threshold of the gallows to one of the more comfortable positions at Buchenwald. Ciepielowski, handsome and blue-eyed with a well-defined widow's peak, was extremely crafty when it came to sabotage. Other inmates remarked upon his sangfroid. He was also a dedicated physician and treated many of the experimental typhus patients in Block 46.

Perhaps the most important prisoner in Block 50, however, was neither a scientist nor a doctor. Eugen Kogon, born in 1903, was a resolute Catholic humanist and journalist whom the Nazis had persecuted since the mid-1930s and imprisoned at Buchenwald in 1939. Kogon's steadfast loyalty and intelligence had enabled him to maneuver past three attempts to send him to death at Auschwitz. He shrewdly sized up Erwin Ding and made himself indispensable to the man, gaining a degree of confidence and independence practically unique in the annals of camp life. His relationship with Ding was most comparable, though, to that of Auschwitz's chief doctor, Eduard Wirths, and his secretary Hermann Langbein. Like Langbein, Kogon was a non-Communist who had learned to work with the camp Communists while remaining outside their command structure, in itself a remarkable feat. Like Langbein, too, he was a great humanitarian who would become an influential postwar interpreter of the concentration camp system, and a defender of its inmates. Kogon, however, had much more difficult material to work with, for Ding was a darker soul. It was up to Kogon to convert this nearly unscrupulous opportunist into a useful collaborator who committed acts of treason against the SS system. He did this by appealing to the vestiges of Ding's better nature—and to Ding's will to save his own skin.

They had long conversations lasting deep into the night in which Kogon told Ding of "our world of the spirit, of morality, of humanitarianism and human grandeur," Kogon wrote in *The Theory and Practice of Hell*. "If there is anything of which I am proud during the time of my concentration camp detention it is the fact that I succeeded in this very difficult task which no one else had dared to undertake." Before long, Kogon had convinced Ding that the Nazis would lose the war, and that his behavior would matter when it ended. Ding grew to trust Kogon so much that Nazi officers visiting him were puzzled by the relationship. They seemed so close that even prisoners working in Kogon's ward suspected him of being in cahoots with Ding; his network of conspiracy was so compartmentalized that he even appeared on an early UN War Crimes Commission list of Nazi criminals. Kogon maneuvered Ding into allowing Block 50 to become a refuge for persecuted prisoners and a center of conspiracies, though Ding was not aware of the most important ones. He wrote up petitions to the Reich Main Security Office and had Ding sign them, enabling the crew "to enjoy protection from threatening death shipments and other forms of imminent action." Under Ding's signature, he also asked SS officers in Berlin to allow specific prisoners to receive letters or packages from home. The vaccine detail swelled to 65 men, including 12 Russians as well as Czechs, Poles, Germans, Austrians, Frenchmen, and one Luxembourgeois. Sometimes, after their discussions, Ding would be full of admiration for Kogon and his idealistic worldview. "Other times," Kogon wrote, "he'd say, 'Yes, but you've got to admit that the Thousand-Year Reich is a great accomplishment,' then roar off on his motorcycle."

Konrad Morgen, the SS judge sent to cleanse Buchenwald of corruption, didn't know what to make of Kogon. On one visit to Block 50, he noted that whenever Ding needed some fact or documents, at exactly the right moment the door of his office opened "as though by magic, and a man in a white physician's coat entered and asked in a military-deferential tone, yet with a certain undertone of intimacy,

Buchenwald: Rabbit Stew and Fake Vaccine

'Your orders, *Sturmbannführer*!' After several repetitions of this performance which never failed to have a flabbergasting effect on me, I
asked Dr. Ding-Schuler whether he was employing a crystal ball gazer
as an assistant." Ding revealed that he had an electric buzzer to sum-
mon Kogon from the room next door. Ding told Morgen, "Eugen even
answers my love letters."

Another political prisoner with remarkable privileges was Walter
Hummelsheim, a former German diplomat and Princeton University student who had been arrested for plotting against Hitler. Hummelsheim, like Kogon a clerk in Block 50, spoke flawless French and
made a powerful impression on French resistance fighters who began
arriving in the camp in 1943. While most of the prisoners had shaved
heads and stumbled along in filthy clothing, Hummelsheim wore his
hair long and combed, with sharply creased trousers and a jacket tai-
lored from the striped camp material. One day, a French prisoner was
sick and happened past the Institute of Hygiene as Hummelsheim
was leaving. Ding was away from camp that day, and Hummelsheim
invited him in to rest. He gave him aspirin and a few mouthfuls of
a steaming yellow liquid—rabbit soup. "Typhus rabbit to be exact.
Don't make such a face. It's been sterilized," he said. Hummelsheim
explained that after the rabbit's lungs were removed to make vaccine,
the rest of the animal was boiled to make soup and meat.

Block 50 had a well-cared-for aspect outside and in, with a balcony
and a little garden enclosed in a mesh fence and men in white jackets circulating around it. A door had been cut into the barbed-wire
fence behind the block, and pressing an electric button summoned a
Russian deportee in an immaculate striped uniform. The staff wore
white jackets and pants, rubber gloves, booties, and face masks. They
showered every day. In the basement were rabbit cages and dissec-
tion rooms, upstairs sterilization, bacteriology and serology depart-
ments, a pharmacy, and a well-furnished library. The building was
startlingly spotless; the scientists spent an hour or two every morning
cleaning it. "Ruining an experiment was less serious than leaving a

grain of dust on a door jamb for the Germans," said the French chemist Albert Kirrmann. "The best way to please the boss was to align all the reagent bottles in a row on the shelf with carefully handwritten labels. He loved showing his house to important visitors, as if he were a museum director."

As for the vaccine itself, Ding from the beginning was wrestling with problems well beyond his understanding. Leading microbiologists had found it terribly difficult to produce the vaccine at the Pasteur Institute in Paris. If they had been familiar with the philosophical work of Ludwik Fleck, the SS men might have begun to understand the absurdity of expecting slave doctors to create such a vaccine in a concentration camp. Making a vaccine was not a mechanical task like producing pencils or aspirin or even rockets to fire upon London. Vaccines were made from constantly evolving live organisms. The vaccine-making business was a most arcane thought collective, in the sense that Fleck described scientific groups with highly specialized knowledge and technique. To learn how to make the Giroud vaccine would normally require years of hand-to-hand training.

As Fleck wrote, "sciences do not grow as crystals, by apposition, but rather as living organisms, by developing every, or amost every, detail in harmony with the whole." When one produces a vaccine, each step of the process might need to be altered at the same time in order to accommodate a particular change in the production method. For example, the Rockefeller Institute scientists who developed the yellow fever vaccine in the 1930s found that after a certain number of passages—that is, after the virus had grown in a particular sequence of animal-flesh cultures—for some reason it became weakened enough to be injected into people in a way that provided immunity but not disease. The Nazi medical bureaucracy, of course, had not considered such challenges. Ding pressed the prisoners as soon as they set up Block 50 to produce something. He wanted tangible results. But the prisoners were intelligent enough to realize that this wouldn't be as easy as Ding hoped. The complexities of *Rickettsia prowazekii* "allowed us to take the route we wanted to take," Kogon said after the war.

The route was sabotage—although the team initially hit upon it by accident.

The Block 50 crew worked from a 70-page German instruction manual, apparently translated and modified by Ding or one of his assistants, from Pasteur Institute papers. It described each step of the Giroud vaccine production process. The recipe was not for the faint of heart, and certainly not for the antivivisectionist. It involved transmitting the typhus bacteria through four different species. First, blood from feverish Block 46 "passage people" was injected into guinea pigs. When the animals were successfully infected, technicians ground up their brains or testes—where for some reason the bacteria grew well. After removing most of the host tissue, the remaining liquid was injected into mice. After they sickened, the mice were killed and their lungs ground up and diluted into solutions used to infect the rabbits. These creatures, pure-blood Angoras and mixed chinchilla breeds, were infected at five months of age by stabbing a thick needle through their necks into the tracheal tube. But rabbits were not normally susceptible to typhus. The germ grew in their lungs only after their immune systems had been weakened. To do this, the inmates experimented with ways of making life unpleasant for the rabbits to the point that it ruined their immune systems. The irony of doing this in a concentration camp cannot have escaped them. They settled on a method that involved shaving the rabbits' chests and exposing them to freezing temperatures in winter, or dunking them in ice baths in warm weather. For good measure, they injected the rabbits with paratyphoid bacteria or toxins. Then came the tricky part: killing the rabbit when rickettsial growth in the lungs was at its height, but before secondary infections—*bactéries banales*, Giroud called them—set in. If the process was successful, a single rabbit could provide enough rickettsial bacteria to make vaccine sufficient to immunize 100 people.

The Fantastic Laboratory of Dr. Weigl

The procedure was inexact and subject to multiple misunderstanding and falsification. It took ten different culture preparations to test the bacteria. Microscopic inspections and pH buffering were required, and the *Rickettsia* took many forms, depending on how the rabbit had been prepared, how severely infected, and other factors. Tests of the vaccine's efficacy were done on-site, with further examination at the Pasteur Institute. The first samples of the vaccine were not ready until just before Christmas 1943. Ding selected a group of prisoners for the experiment. "If it doesn't work," he told Kogon, "I'll commit suicide." It did not work, but Ding, instead of killing himself, faked the results.

It was at this moment that Ludwik Fleck arrived in Block 50. Kogon remembered Fleck as a "somewhat dreamy scholar, always friendly." Slightly stooped, gaunt, bespectacled, calm, and reserved, Kogon said later, "an oddly lovable, friendly person." Kogon knew nothing of Fleck's philosophical work, and their discussions concerned only matters of the laboratory and vaccine. Kogon was involved in many conspiracies and didn't want to complicate his life by bringing new colleagues into them. "Fleck never initiated such discussions; he wasn't the conspiratorial type and didn't have lots of contacts with the camp organization," Kogon said. "But without him, the fake vaccine couldn't have been made."

Fleck befriended Willy Jellinek, the young Austrian pastry cook, who came to regard Fleck as a second father. Jellinek remembered Fleck as a thoughtful, intelligent older man shuffling quietly but deliberately through the war. They discussed Fleck's life in Lwów and his trips to Vienna, his experiences in Auschwitz. Both were relieved that the bacterial cultures prepared for the Buchenwald laboratory involved sheep and other animals, rather than human flesh. From the beginning, Jellinek said, Fleck walked a thin line with Ding. He considered the SS man a "little swindler" who knew that the work they were doing was pointless, but hoped that people like Fleck would give him something with which to impress his bosses. Ding employed Fleck in writing journal articles: also on each assignment, Fleck dragged out the task as long as possible, assuring Ding that the work was almost complete but had to be "just so" in order for Ding to win his *Habilitation*. In fact, Fleck worried that if he ever finished the work Ding needed, he'd be killed.

In 1939, Mrugowsky had been appointed to a full professorship in Berlin on the basis of a half-serious *Habilitationsschrift*, the post-doctoral publication that German universities require of their senior faculty members. Ding, who was scheming to take Mrugowsky's position, wanted his own *Habilitation* and hoped to earn it with a series of publications on the experiments at Buchenwald. He ordered Fleck, Ciepielowski, and Kogon to help him write scientific publications and prepare for his examinations on bacteriology. Fleck managed to teach Ding quite a bit but did so diplomatically, careful not to humiliate him, Jellinek said. Ding was not a good student. For example, in order to help him classify Gram-positive and Gram-negative bacteria, a fairly basic delineation in microbiology, Fleck had to use different-colored inks for the names of bacteria belonging to the two types.

Fleck's authority on medical issues was recognized in the block. Kogon often spoke with the vaccine chef Ciepielowski—they slept in the same cell—and when they were discussing science, Ciepielowski would frequently say, "I'll ask Fleck." Kogon claimed that Fleck was in possession of a special protective letter issued and signed by Himmler himself. Kogon had never seen anything like it, he said, and he believed the letter had enabled Fleck to protect his wife and son. No one else in Block 50 mentions the letter, nor does Fleck. Possibly, Kogon was referring to the protective letter provided to Fleck by the Lwów Gestapo to do his work at the Laokoon factory.

Fleck described the moment of his arrival at Block 50 in his first postwar publication, in 1946, an essay titled "Problems of the Science of Science." In a sense, the experience at Block 50 confirmed for Fleck his philosophy of how science worked. He structured the essay as a debate between Simplicius, who believes that science is equivalent to progress, and Sympatius, who sees the cultural construct. The debate is modeled, a bit grandiloquently, on Galileo's *Dialogue*, in which

The Fantastic Laboratory of Dr. Weigl

Simplicius represents the perspective of those who believe the sun revolves around the earth.

The wise Sympatius states that science is not just a system of thoughts but a complex phenomenon that includes many institutions and events. It is expressed in writing, in unwritten customs involving a variety of methods and traditions, in specific mental preparation and manual dexterity. It has its various structures and hierarchies, means of communication and cooperation, within scientific groups and with the public. "I had a very rare opportunity," he continues, "of watching, for nearly two years, the scientific work of a collective composed of laymen only. . . . The collective worked on complex problems from the field of typhus; they had at their disposal fully equipped laboratories, plenty of experimental animals and an extensive specialist literature. This was in the Buchenwald concentration camp. . . ."

The collective, he writes, consisted of eight members, some trained in sciences, but none in the special field of vaccinology. The identities of the team members cannot be deciphered definitively, but they include a "young Polish physician, without any specialist preparation"—Ciepielowski; an "eminent Austrian political figure," who may be Kogon; a young Czech physician, with rudiments of bacteriological preparation" (Karl Makovicka); a Dutch biology student; a Viennese confectioner (Jellinek); a rubber factory worker; and two others. The workers were looking for *Rickettsia* in the lungs of mice and rabbits; despite Giroud's painstaking description of the many forms these bacteria could take, the nonspecialists didn't know what they were looking at. As Fleck had written in *Genesis*, "you have to be taught how to see." To identify bacteria and cellular structures on the basis of written descriptions and illustrations, he said, was "to pass, so to say, backwards along the path normally chosen for knowledge." Using descriptions and illustrations provided by Giroud and the German scientist Hilda Sikora, the Buchenwald team looked into their microscopes and continuously misunderstood what they saw. That is, they "found" all the stages of *Rickettsia* that the two masters described, although there were, in fact, no germs at all in the cultures. Perhaps the rabbits had withstood their tortures too well. Fleck writes,

> From the dyestuff precipitates, fat globules, various bacteria and cellular remnants they managed to [see] the entire developmental cycle [of the typhus bacteria.] . . . This construction grew slowly, in the atmosphere of a mutual stimulation and strengthening of opinions. The collective mood, which became the motor of this fantastic synthesis, was composed of a tense expectation of the effect, of the desire to be the first to establish something, not to be too late with the confirmation that something had been established, and to satisfy the boss who had been urging them along all the time.

Fleck reports the following conversation among the boss (Ding), the Dutch biology student, and his assistant:

Biologist: What can be these shining, uniformly pink bodies? We have not seen them thus far. Is it possible?
Assistant: I have noticed them, too; their presence struck me at once. Perhaps these are those *corps homogènes rouges* according to Giroud?
Biologist: This is what I was thinking.
Boss: Yes, they might be that.
Assistant: Of course, what else could they be?
Biologist: At last, we've got them.
Boss: And it's high time, too. At last something positive.

"There was no individual author of the error," Fleck wrote. "The error grew out of the collective atmosphere." He called this "the harmony of self-delusion," it might also be described as groupthink. Despite what the group believed, the *corps homogènes rouges* it found were not typhus germs but rabbit white blood cells. Yet the collective "was thirsting for a positive result," and so the good news was passed along—"at long last, *Rickettsia* has been found in the preparations obtained from rabbits' lungs. When the joyful tidings spread among the collective, the certainty of the result became doubtless. . . . The confectioner and the rubber-factory worker, who represented 'common sense,' popularized the discovery. . . ."

> The records of experiments, the summaries of results, the suggested modifications of methods were sent to the world outside the camp to genuine German specialists, men well-known in the world of science, and returned with words of praise. The German boss got a high decoration. So great is the persuasive power of a harmonious system, and so limited is the value of testing the inner harmony of the system.
>
> An interesting shock occurred only when rabbits' lungs with typhus germs arrived from a genuine scientific institute. . . . But he would err who believed that a single direct contact with scientific reality would bring about the downfall of the entire edifice. . . . The collective failed even to admit in private that its entire construction was faulty; quite on the contrary, it created a synthesis of the old theory with the new facts. . . .
>
> . . . [There arrives] a characteristic moment at which the worker or the collective body assume that no further verification is required. The opinion becomes rounded, systematized, limited; in short it becomes mature. . . .

Here, Fleck referred to an episode in which Dr. Combiescu, a Romanian typhus expert, challenged the lab's method of making the vaccine, saying there was no way it could work. Ciepielowski—who by then had been informed by Fleck that there were no *Rickettsia* in the rabbit lungs—was able to convince Ding that Combiescu was wrong, however, and even wrote up a paper that Ding intended to publish in the *Zeitschrift für Hygiene und Infektionskrankheiten.*

Buchenwald: Rabbit Stew and Fake Vaccine

It is not that there is no difference between truth and illusion, says
Sympatius:

> What I want to do is to say that scientific results and views
> are basically determined exclusively as single historical events
> at successive development stages of the scientific thought-style.
> . . . Neither a Robinson Crusoe, nor a group of Robinsons, even
> if equipped with technical means, will glide automatically onto
> the tracks of science, if they are isolated from the scientific com-
> munity. . . . Every thought-collective considers that the people
> who do not belong to it are incompetent. Practical applicability
> is not a touchstone, for due to the harmony of illusions even
> a false view is applicable. The alchemists' gold allegedly did
> enrich many people, and even the cost of wars was paid for by
> alchemists' gold.

In his lyrical riff on the functioning of a concentration camp
thought collective, Fleck of course omits the fact that the duress of the
surroundings played its own implacable part in shaping the collective's
capacity for credulity and mutual conviction. The thought collective in
Block 50 may in fact not have been convinced it had found *Rickettsia*
in the lungs of rabbits—but it needed to convince Ding and his bosses
that this was so. Their lives hung in the balance; it was produce or per-
ish. In another publication, Fleck wrote explicitly that when he arrived
at Block 50, "none of the other prisoners had experience in culturing
microorganisms and it was from me that they learned they were making a fully valueless anti-typhus vaccine." This is also the authoritative
version of Eugen Kogon:

> When Ludwig Fleck came to Block 50 in Buchenwald, he told
> us, after seeing the typhus germs, that what we had produced
> in the rabbit lungs was not *Rickettsia*, but some other type of
> bacteria. We asked him not to say anything about what he'd

seen to Ding-Schuler, but to experiment with us, to try to allow us to find a good way out of the difficulty. He worked with us, and he kept the secret. It was only after the Kraków Institute [Eyer's operation] furnished us with mouse lungs and infected material from mouse intestine that we could be sure our animal material contained the *Rickettsia*. After that we could produce a vaccine that was, without a doubt, very efficacious, but it could only be produced in small quantities. . . .

Since Ding-Schuler demanded large quantities of vaccine, we produced two types: one that had no value and was perfectly harmless, and went to the front; and a second type, in very small quantities, that was very efficacious and used in special cases like for comrades who worked in difficult places in the camp. Ding-Schuler never heard about these arrangements. Since he was entirely lacking in bacteriological knowledge, he never penetrated the production secret. He depended entirely on the reports that the experts of Block 50 provided him. When he was able to send thirty or forty liters of vaccine to Berlin, he was happy. . . . The inefficacy of our vaccine could have been revealed, and there were outside experts that the SS had at its disposition who could have investigated and discovered that it wasn't real. Nothing like that happened. The adventure continued until March 1945.

Ding, in short, was "a dummkopf who earned a dissertation only on the basis of his services for the party," as Fleck testified later. "The scientists and doctors who were conducting work at Buchenwald could employ his cluelessness and scientific illiteracy for our own purposes. . . . *We made a vaccine that did not work.* For controls we sent a sample that did work. Ding-Schuler, the illiterate, didn't realize what was going on [italics added]."

Block 50 produced a total of 600 liters of fake vaccine, enough to fully vaccinate about 200,000 people. It was used by SS men in the camps and also German fighting units. About six liters of good, "red-dot" vaccine (the labels got secret markings) were produced and administered to people in the camp, or used to pull the wool over the eyes of the SS health authorities. On a few occasions, fake-vaccinated troops fell ill, and the SS suspiciously requested control vaccine from the Buchenwald group. "We of course sent it to them," Fleck said. "The control vaccine was naturally a completely valid vaccine." The SS had no other way to test whether the typhus patients had been vaccinated with an ostensibly effective product. No vaccine was expected to be 100 percent effective.

The secret was held close to the vest. Most of the scientists in Block 50 did not know what was going on. The French chemist Kirrmann, for example, who worked in the same building, gave no indication in his postwar memoirs that the vaccine was fake. Even Fleck's son, who arrived at the camp in 1945 on a transport from Auschwitz, seems to have gotten an inexact version of events. According to Ryszard Fleck's testimony at Yad Vashem in 1971, sabotage was already going on when his father arrived. "On the first day of work at the institute two prisoners with knives in their hands approached my father, stuck knives up to his chest and let him in on the secret that this vaccine didn't work, meaning the *Rickettsia* were not growing in the rabbit lungs and that in general the vaccine was fake. The Germans, they said, didn't know anything about it, and Father was not allowed to tell them about it. Father obeyed, of course." While the brandishing of knives is certainly plausible, it may have occurred *after* Fleck informed the other inmates that they were producing a worthless vaccine. Ryszard Fleck arrived at Buchenwald more than a year after this event would have occurred.

The bold act of vaccine sabotage gave heart—and palpitations—to the inmates who were in on it. Most of the inmates at Buchenwald, however, cared little about the vaccine. For them, the crucial product of Block 50 was not the vaccine but the broth and flesh of the rabbits cooked after they were used to make it. Once the lungs of the animals had been removed to harvest the (real or nonexistent) *Rickettsia*, protocol called for the remainder of the animal to be burned in a small crematorium inside Block 50. But concentration camp inmates, of course, did not destroy something as precious as rabbit flesh. Every week, the inmates brought 70 dead rabbits to Hans Baermann, the young German Jew who prepared the precious nutrient by boiling the hares for three hours over a coal fire. The men in the block ate some of the rabbit, divvied up the rest, and smuggled it to needier parts of the camp. August Cohn, a German-Jewish inmate who went into Weimar to buy rabbits every week with a benevolent SS guard, distributed the cooked flesh to Jewish inmates in the Little Camp and to a group of British POWs. Hummelsheim, the bilingual German resistance member, took rabbit to French inmates.

After the war, British and French inmates would seize the narrative of what happened in both typhus blocks. Thanks to their nationalities, links to British and French intelligence agencies and prestigious institutions like the Pasteur, their voices established the world's understanding of events. But not everything they said was exactly true. The Jews and Slavs who had been there were mostly living in displaced-person camps, or struggling with the new realities of Cold War life and thus unable to speak out. One central figure in the history of Block 50 was Alfred Balachowsky, who led a British spy network in France during the war and worked at the Pasteur Institute afterward. Following the liberation of Buchenwald, France's information minister—the writer André Malraux—sent Balachowsky on a tour of the United States to give a French account of life the camps. His testimony was featured in the International Military Tribunal, the first trial held at Nuremberg. Balachowsky was audacious and brilliant in his way, but he was a chronic exaggerator, and for some reason he despised Fleck.

Born in Russia and brought to France as a child, Balachowsky was an entomologist of prodigious talent and work habits; at the age of 32, he copublished a 2,000-page monograph on the harmful insects of the world, and was a pioneer in the field of biological pest control. During the war, he led a unit of the British Special Operations Executive, or SOE, arranging secret landings of spies and matériel. The Gestapo rolled up the network in July 1943 and sent Balachowsky to Buchenwald the following February. From there, he was transported to Dora, the notorious and secretive underground prison factory where Werner von Braun oversaw the building of the V-1 and V-2 rockets that terrorized Britain. After learning of Balachowsky's fate, Hummelsheim got Ding to rescue the Frenchman. Balachowsky was skeletal and sick upon arrival at Buchenwald in April—"like one of the tragic caricatures of Goya," a friend said, but after a few weeks of rabbit soup he had recovered. Balachowsky's diaries from Buchenwald, which begin April 11, 1944, and end April 3, 1945, are among the few written documents remaining from Block 50. They suggest that he lived reasonably well after being saved from Dora. Frenchmen at Buchenwald could receive packages, and Balachowsky got a generous measure—about two parcels every week. The Red Cross, his mother, and his wife sent him dozens of books, milk, sugar, and oranges. In his spare time, he read, strolled around the camp, and took tea with French and British spies. For Christmas, a horse was slaughtered for dinner.

After the war, Balachowsky assumed great moral authority because of his stature as a resistance leader, a Pasteurian, and ultimately, a rescuer of British spies. Balachowsky's version was the existential heroic account of Buchenwald, the kind of narrative that Malraux, author of *Man's Hope* and *Man's Fate*, could celebrate without hesitation. Fleck, on the other hand, was an outsider, a downtrodden Jew trying not to attract attention. Polish Jews received no packages from the Red Cross and no letters from home, because home no longer existed. It was probably easier to be a conspirator on a full stomach. Fleck and Balachowsky had political differences—Fleck was grateful to the Communists, who had protected him, while Balachowsky, he said, had "fascistic views." They often fought.

The Fantastic Laboratory of Dr. Weigl

In Block 50, where Ciepielowski managed vaccine production, Balachowsky was put in charge of infecting the rabbits, and also filled vaccine ampules with the final product. Fleck conducted bacteriological examinations to determine the concentration of *Rickettsia* in the vaccine (and falsified the result, unless it was a "good" batch destined for camp inmates) and searched for contamination that could sicken the vaccinated troops. On one occasion, Balachowsky and Fleck got into a furious argument when Fleck returned a 10-liter flask of vaccine that was not sterile. Balachowsky, he said, did not understand that it was one thing to give the Germans a useless vaccine, another to poison them. If some vaccinated German soldiers got typhus, the authorities wouldn't assume the vaccine had been sabotaged. If they died of bacterial contamination, on the other hand, the investigation of the disaster could easily get everyone in Block 50 killed.

The mistrust would spill over after the war, when Balachowsky denounced Fleck in testimony submitted to Nuremberg, accusing him of having informed Ding about immunological reactions to vaccine in a way that led the Nazi doctor to order a new, fatal experiment. Fleck did not become aware of this accusation until 1958. He responded angrily, pointing out that Balachowsky spoke no German, misunderstood the vaccine production problems, and had no understanding of how Fleck and other "initiated" prisoners had to maneuver around Ding and other German officers.

Kogon, who admired Balachowsky, nonetheless said on several occasions after the war that his friend had spoken of things he knew nothing about, and exaggerated the part he'd played in the conspiracy. Bizarrely, Balachowsky's scurrilous accusations against Fleck were rehashed by a Swedish scholar in 2006.

By the summer of 1944, the war was taking a dramatic turn. When the camp loudspeakers announced the Normandy invasion in June, the French scientists immediately jumped up and started singing the "Marseillaise," and Fleck enthusiastically joined in. August Cohn, the German Communist, said, "Now we can begin to rebuild our Fatherland." Fleck said, "I'm a Pole and want to go home." Paris was liberated on August 24; the same day, the massive Allied bombing raid hit the outskirts of the camp, destroying two enormous munitions factories and setting fire to many camp buildings. The washroom, the storage warehouses, and the SS barracks were severely damaged, and dozens of SS men, their wives, and children were crushed to death. The bombs slightly damaged Block 50, which was adjacent to the burning storage warehouse, and put the vaccine enterprise out of commission for several days. A bomb struck Ding's rooms and destroyed everything he owned (his wife and children were in Weimar).

As night fell, the inmates of Block 50 and their neighbors were mustered into a bucket brigade to try to save the laundry building. They watched as the Goethe oak burned. By then, the tree was long dead—a solid gray silhouette that bore no leaves in the summer and was never visited by birds. On the night of the raid, though, it came alive once more, like a gigantic torch with thousands of candles, the carbonized branches tumbling to the ground one by one. Little by little, the fire advanced toward the center of the tree, and as it consumed it, the drums of defeat beat at Germany's doors. "Even today when I close my eyes," Fleck wrote, "I can still see the roof of the washroom burning, the naked skeleton of the oak with its crest in flames. I hear the crackling of the fire, I see the sparks rising, the burning limbs falling like pieces of asphalt, tattered and rolled. I smell the smoke, and I see the prisoners forming a large chain, passing the buckets of water from the tank to the fire. They save the washroom, but they don't extinguish the flames on the oak. And in their faces there is a secret happiness, a silent triumph: Legend has become reality!"

That night, despite the deaths of hundreds of inmates, a huge celebration was held in Block 50. There was typhus rabbit for everyone.

In Kraków, Eyer's production of the army's typhus vaccine had expanded throughout 1943 and early 1944, coming to employ 1,500 Polish lice feeders and other workers. Most of Eyer's waking hours were dedicated to producing protective vaccines for the Wehrmacht, but he spent a smaller share of it protecting his Polish workers and their families from Nazi repression. Eyer found himself frequently seeking assistance from unsavory men like Fritz Katzmann, the Lwów-based SS commander for Galicia. "I knew him all too well," Eyer recalled later, "for I was so often in that lion's den trying to help one or another poor soul." Weigl's older brother, Friedrich, a federal prosecutor and member of the resistance in Kraków, was arrested and taken to Auschwitz in March 1944. Friedrich's daughter Olga, who worked as a louse feeder in the Kraków institute, recalled in a postwar letter to Eyer, "It was a rainy day, and you came to me from the city, wet as a frog. You asked me if I had any news of my father. I said that if we had a friend among the Germans, perhaps we could help him. You said, 'Dear child, you have one.' And you proved it to us." Friedrich Weigl was freed a few weeks later.

After the Warsaw Uprising broke out in August 1944, the Gestapo began to fear that a similar insurrection would occur in Kraków, and on a Sunday afternoon it preventively rounded up thousands of Poles, including 30 of Eyer's employees. They were all taken south of the city to Plaszów, the Auschwitz satellite camp run by the infamous Amon Goeth. After bitter negotiations with the SS, Eyer was able to win the release of his employees, and 5 others besides. Three days later, trucks picked them up at the camp and returned them to the institute. As they walked into the building, the workers exploded with cheers and sobs of relief.

The war was not easy for Eyer's family. His apartment in Berlin was destroyed by bombing in 1942, and his wife, Gertrud, and son, Peter, moved to Munich. A year later, the carpet bombing of Munich forced them to relocate to Freiburg, where they lived with Eyer's sister and her two children. After they'd been in Freiburg for about a year, Eyer suddenly got a bad feeling about the place. It wasn't strategically located and had no major heavy industry, but for some reason he felt it was going to be bombed. In November 1944, Gertrud and Peter returned to Munich on a train that was repeatedly attacked, forcing them to run into the bushes twice. But Hermann Eyer's gut had been correct. On November 20, 1944, American bombers attacked Freiburg for the first time, destroying the house where the family had been living. Eyer's sister and her children died.

Just before the bombing raid at Buchenwald in August 1944, 43 members of the French resistance arrived in the camp and, after delousing, entered Block 17, a mostly French ward. The group was led by a British citizen named Forest Frederick Edward Yeo-Thomas, a legendary escape artist known to the Germans as "the White Rabbit." Yeo-Thomas, a senior commander of the British Special Operations Executive, or SOE, had fought with the Poles against the Soviet Union in 1920, then retired to Paris to run a fashion house. The SOE called him up at the beginning of the war, and he parachuted three times behind enemy lines in France before being captured in February 1944.

On September 9, 16 of Yeo-Thomas's men were called to the Buchenwald gate and did not return. Their colleagues learned a short time later that they had been hanged in the Gestapo bunker. Balachowsky sought help from Kogon, Ding's inmate confidant, and a plot was hatched. Kogon figured that the best way to save the SOE men was to arrange for their identities to be switched with dead inmates. Earlier that week, 15 French slave laborers suffering from typhus had arrived from Cologne and entered Block 46 for treatment. Several of them appeared to be hopeless cases. The scheme, as Dietzsch and Kogon developed it in consultation with the SOE agents, was to wait until the French laborers died, then switch their identities with the SOE agents.

The secrecy surrounding Block 46, the horror of typhus, and the awful way it was spread and treated there, had earned Dietzsch a fearsome reputation, even among the SS. That reputation could sometimes be put to good use.

To start the plan rolling, Dietzsch gave Yeo-Thomas a shot that produced fever but no lasting illness, and ordered him to report next morning to his block leader with complaints of violent headache and heaviness of limbs—the typical first stage of typhus. As planned, Yeo-Thomas's block leader sent him to the infirmary, where the inmate doctor, suspecting typhus, called Dietzsch to come pick him up. Dietzsch pretended not to know Yeo-Thomas but took him to Block 46 for treatment. While Yeo-Thomas waited for his body double to die, Dietzsch gave him a job as a temperature plotter on the upper floor of the typhus ward. Next, Yeo-Thomas inveigled Dietzsch into admitting two of his comrades, an English pilot, Harry Peulevé, and the German-French agent Stéphane Hessel, a member of De Gaulle's personal staff. They entered the ward by means of the same scheme employed for Yeo-Thomas. As the charade proceeded, Dietzsch worried constantly that his nurses, who were criminal Greens, would catch wind of what was happening and turn him in to the Gestapo.

On October 5, the Gestapo called out the names of 21 more members of the group; 20 were taken to the Gestapo bunker and shot. The 21st was Peulevé, a supposed typhus case in Block 46. Ding, whom Kogon had let in on the secret, came by and met Yeo-Thomas at this point; the Englishman recalled later that Ding spoke French perfectly. "Knowing that Dr. Ding-Schuler was a gentleman, like a good many of these SS types, who was a bit afraid of his skin, we played on his feelings for his wife and children," Yeo-Thomas said. "I told him when the time came for him to be tried I would at least be able to say one good word for him before he was strung up." Ding agreed to save as many of the SOE men as possible, and promised to save his laboratory records for the Allied forces to examine. Then he left the block in Dietzsch's hands.

The Gestapo telephoned Dietzsch soon thereafter, demanding that

Peuleve be sent up the hill, but Dietzsch said the patient was too sick to be executed. Two men with a car came to pick him up, but Dietzsch, knowing the Gestapo's fear of the typhus ward, menacingly invited them in to retrieve Peulevé themselves. Dietzsch had given Peulevé an injection of milk that made him sick; the terrified Gestapo agents took one look at him and excused themselves on the grounds that they lacked a stretcher. A few hours later, the infirmary chief sent over an alcoholic SS corporal to give Peulevé a death shot in the heart, but the corporal asked Dietzsch to take care of it. Dietzsch took the hypodermic needle into the ward and pretended to inject Peulevé. Ding, meanwhile, called the camp commander, saying it made no sense to execute a dying man.

At this point, according to Yeo-Thomas, Dietzsch and the spies decided to hasten the death of Marcel Seigneur, one of the genuinely sick French laborers, "knowing that he was going to die whatever happened." They were spared the implementation of that morally fraught decision when Seigneur died a natural death at the last minute. Dietzsch rushed the corpse to the crematorium with Peulevé's name written on the inside thigh. From this point, Peulevé lived under the name of Marcel Seigneur.

The other two cases took even longer to resolve. As a memento of the experience, Yeo-Thomas kept a medical report, signed by Ding, that detailed his fictional typhus agony, with each imaginary rash, headache, hallucination, and serum reaction. All the fakery that characterized the typhus institute was put to use protecting him. On October 14, Ding entered the ward to congratulate Yeo-Thomas on his "death" the day before, informing him that the order for his execution had just arrived. One of the painful things Yeo-Thomas had to do when the war ended was to visit the widow and two children of the sick Frenchman, police officer Maurice Chouquet, whose body had entered the crematorium with Yeo-Thomas's name written on it. Yeo-Thomas had to sign various forms and affidavits in order for Mme. Chouquet to receive a pension.

That left Hessel, waiting anxiously in his room on the top floor of Block 46. He spoke as much as he could with his double, Michel Boitel, trying to learn the details of his life before Boitel passed away. It was a terrible circumstance under which to get to know someone. On October 20, Boitel died, leaving Hessel with heavy guilt—over Boitel, and the *resistants* who died while he lived. "Why me?" he wrote. "Because Yeo-Thomas wanted to keep a French officer alive? Because I speak German? Who knows?" Hessel became a French UN official after the war and helped write the 1948 Universal Declaration of Human Rights. At age 93, in 2010, he published an internationally best-selling call to activism entitled *Indignez-vous!* (Time for outrage).

Yeo-Thomas remained in Block 46 until November 9. Typhus experiments were going on all the while, and Yeo-Thomas busied himself with making charts, his new camp job. "Being dead, I thought I might as well occupy myself." By the time he left, only Hessel, Peulevé, and three of the other original SOE agents remained alive. Yeo-Thomas was sent to a Jewish work detail where about 15 men were beaten to death every day, from which he again escaped. For all his ingenuity and cunning, though, Yeo-Thomas never caught on to the fact that the men in Block 50 were making a fake vaccine.

On January 17, 1945, the SS began evacuating Auschwitz, forcing 30,000 inmates to march west on foot through the snow in. The temperature was 16 degrees below zero Fahrenheit. Rajsko was evacuated along with the rest of the camp. Among the survivors still working there were Fleck's wife, Ernestyna, his son, Ryszard, and the other members of the Lwów microbiology team who had entered Auschwitz two years earlier. They were joined by Henryk and Paula Meisel, who had worked, protected, in Weigl's laboratory, before being shipped to the camp.

In the beginning, they walked on foot in groups of several hundred. An SS man stood at the gate of the camp and systematically gave everyone a kick in the ass as they passed by. They walked on side roads because the Germans feared Russian patrols, and sometimes the Germans fired into the forests on the side of the road, spooked by the fear of partisans, who never materialized. Those who could not walk anymore were shot. The Rajsko inmates were luckier than most: their nutrition had been better than that of other prisoners at Auschwitz, which gave them more stamina.

When the snow grew deep, Anna Seeman, being lame, was put on a cart, and her son, Bruno, got on with her, but it was so cold that he got out and started walking. After more than 40 kilometers, they were put on an open railcar with no water and no food and taken to Frankfurt an der Oder. The dead were tossed out of the car. Early March found them in at Malchow, a camp attached to an underground weapons factory that no longer operated. There was little to eat, and it was here that the first member of Fleck's group, Nusia Umschweif, succumbed to disease and hunger. When the Russians approached Malchow, the prisoners were forced to return to the road, and Bruno had to abandon his mother, Anna, in an empty hut. On May 2, they encountered Russians, who fed and helped them. A few days later, Bruno was reunited with his mother.

The men, separated from the women and children, suffered on on their own. Bernard Umschweif and another medical colleague, Stefan Blankenheim, died after eating grass. Henryk Meisel had to carry Ryszard Fleck on his shoulders, until they were put on a transport to Buchenwald in open cars. At Buchenwald, Jews arrived from Auschwitz by the thousands, and there was nowhere to house them. They died by the hundreds every day in the Little Camp, their suffering met mostly with scorn in the established barracks. "I hesitate to write this: the atrocious misery of the Jews of Auschwitz did not elicit feelings of pity in the camp," wrote one Frenchman.

Alfred Balachowsky's diary from this period, with its nasty anti-Semitism, bears this out. In a January 20, 1945, entry, he wrote, "Large convoy of Jews (5,000) arrive from Auschwitz . . . small degenerate beings with filmy sore eyes, a completely dazed race character-ized by its minuscule size." A few days later, he speaks of another convoy of "dirty, half-witted, repellent Jews, physically ugly, small degenerates with abnormal eyes, thin and bony, huge ears, prominent noses, awful."

The French, sustained by food packages from home, wondered why the Jews had not fled during the trip to Buchenwald. They were lightly guarded, and the Russians were close behind. The apparent pas-sivity of the Jews in the Little Camp, and the epidemics they brought with them, unleashed a wave of anti-Semitic feeling. About 2,000 men died at the camp in January, another 5,600 in February, and 5,000 in March. Fat rats feasted on huge piles of corpses as the crematorium ran out of coal to burn them.

Again, Fleck was lucky. Somehow he managed to learn of Ryszard's arrival in the Little Camp, and persuaded Ding to have him brought to Block 50. Ryszard arrived at Buchenwald in terrible shape—a sickly, undernourished 20-year-old with damaged lungs and severe frostbite on his feet and hands. Fleck did what he could to nurse him back to health, giving him most of his food.

On February 9, Erwin Ding was in Weimar with his family when a bomb destroyed an orphanage nearby, killing 30 children. Leaping into the ruins to rescue survivors, Ding tore a ligament in his left knee, and spent the rest of the war on crutches or limping. Increasingly he was plotting with Kogon, attempting to hasten the end of the Buchen-wald camp in a way that would enable him to survive. He burned all his papers and demanded that Kogon burn the diary of experiments in Block 46. But the tables were turned now, and the inmates knew it. "The next day I told Ding-Schuler I hadn't burned the journal," Kogon said. "He was surprised and demanded to know whether it was not a terrible weapon against him. I responded that if he could show before a court that he had saved the journal, this would show that his inten-tions were honest."

In the final days, the SS ordered the 8,000 Jews in the camp to assemble in the parade ground, but thankfully the Communists created a disturbance that distracted the guards, and the Nazis were able to collect only about 2,000 of them. Those Jews, among the last people transported out of Buchenwald, starved to death on a rail siding outside the Dachau concentration camp.

As the Americans approached Buchenwald in early April, Ding sent Kogon out of the camp to communicate with the Allied troops and offer the camp's capitulation. To do this, he had Kogon nailed into a vaccine crate and loaded on a truck that carried him to Ding's house in Weimar, where the Nazi's family uncrated him. Then he wrote a letter, with the forged signature of an American officer, warning the Buchenwald commandant not to ship any more prisoners out of the camp. His action helped keep the 21,000 remaining inmates of Buchenwald from being sent on death marches.

On April 11, a crowd of prisoners trotted through the potholed streets of the camp to Block 50, where they entered the basement and cleared away the pile of coal used to cook the vaccine rabbits. Underneath it were more than 100 rifles and a machine gun, with boxes of bullets and grenades, homemade Molotov cocktails, knives, and 20 pistols. Many of the weapons had been recovered from the rubble of the Gustloff works and secretly hidden there. SS men were fleeing into the woods. Some were captured and shot or beaten to death. Ryszard Fleck remembered it as a happy moment. "A prisoner showed up on the balcony of the Hygiene Institute holding a picture of Hitler that he took from Ding's office, in a glass frame, and he threw it down. The sound of the breaking glass was accompanied by the cheers of the prisoners who were gathered downstairs. He did the same with pictures of Goering and Goebbels."

A few hours later, a column of the U.S. Third Army entered the camp. The young soldiers couldn't believe what they saw.

"When I walked into that gate I saw before me the walking dead," said Leon Bass, an African-American GI from Philadelphia who was 19 years old that day. "I saw human beings that had been beaten, starved, tortured. They had been denied everything that would make anyone's life liveable. They had skeletal faces and deepset eyes. Their skulls had been shaven and they were holding onto one another just to keep from falling." He entered a barracks and was hit by the stench of death and human waste, the smell of burning flesh from fires outside, and felt the stares of dying inmates. He began giving his food out as fast as he could, though later he was told that many inmates died of overeating in those first few days. "In ignorance," he said, "you do the wrong thing."

The Communists put up banners and held a huge parade of freedom. But in the Little Camp people were still dying, and a few of the more perspicacious observers, such as the writer Meyer Levin, realized quickly that "there were two Buchenwalds, the upper and the lower, separated by a high barbed wire fence; and the upper camp meant possible life, and the lower camp was death. In the upper area . . . the prisoners bore a human resemblance, they had strength enough to walk around. The lower camp received the transports from Auschwitz, and sent out transports to places like Ohrdruf; it was from this well of uttermost misery that the about-to-die tottered forth to replace the dead." Here, wrote Levin, were survivors who had "passed through sieve after sieve of death." Some six million had fallen through. The survivors "were like a bit of cinder adhering to the mesh."

CHAPTER TWELVE

IMPERFECT JUSTICE

About a week after the U.S. military liberated Buchenwald, after Eisenhower and Patton and Edward R. Murrow and many Jeeps full of journalists had toured the camp, had seen the piles of corpses and Ilse Koch's collection of shrunken heads and lampshades, had walked the yards and barracks full of skeletal survivors, watched prisoners die after eating too much of the rich food shoved at them by horrified GIs, had toured the gruesome typhus station, Erwin Schuler turned himself in to American intelligence officers at his home in Weimar, where he had returned to the side of his pregnant wife and two young children.

Only a few months earlier, he'd gotten the long-awaited news: a municipal judge in Leipzig had officially changed his name. "My oldest daughter is just getting ready to enter school," he wrote a friend, "and I am so happy to spare her, especially as a young girl, the burden of the name 'Ding.'" He was no longer Ding or Ding-Schuler, except in the miles of evidence and testimony that echoed with his name for years to come.

Just as he won his new name, though, Schuler developed a hyphenated personality. On the one hand, he was a senior representative of the master race, a doctor with powers of life and death over thousands. On the other, he was intermittently aware that the war was lost.

Dr. Ding, in white coat, and colleagues, in front of Block 50.
(Courtesy of Gedekstätte Buchenwald. Copyright Dienst
voor de Oorlogsslachtoffers, Brussels.)

There were ways to pretend, to Kogon and some of the other inmates, and perhaps to himself, that he was playing a double game, that his true allegiance was with the good, the causes of science and progress represented by the inmates whose lives he controlled, inmates whom he treated respectfully most of the time, but occasionally threatened to kill. In his correspondence with Mrugowsky and other SS officers in 1945, we see efforts, in writing at least, to improve conditions at the camp—to provide drinkable water and reasonable sewage disposal and even a tubercular ward.

Ding-Schuler had made a Faustian bargain to become an SS doctor, and there, under the missing shade of the burned-out Goethe oak, he watched the deal go up in smoke. "He had joined the SS to make a rapid career, though his medical knowledge was weak," said Kogon. "He wanted to become known within the medical world, to be attached to a university, to aggrandize his personal reputation, yet at the same time he would sacrifice anyone if his career was in play." In Block 50, he felt as if he were in his playroom with grown-up toys, talking to real scientists in the refuge he had built for them in a concentration camp. When he tired of that, he would stroll down the barbed wire to see Dietzsch in Block 46, and "they would converse like a couple of criminals."

Ding-Schuler had believed, or hoped, that his title would bring him fame, wealth, success, and power that he would never have achieved as a clever but impatient bastard child from a small town; and there were days sitting with gleaming boots upon his desk and authoritative volumes on the shelf, when he could pretend he had achieved something, pretend, at least, that he was a Roman overlord with Greek intellectuals at his beck and call. He wanted what the scientists had, but there was no longer any way to get it. The experience with the radiologist Kreuzfuchs had not been the only time when his own ignorance sparked a fit of rage. He was not a free man. At a whim, he could extinguish their lives the way a smoker squashes a cigarette butt. Perhaps he recognized that, despite this, the scientists were free men, free souls in pursuit of truth.

If citizen Schuler was expecting clemency from the Americans, he would be quickly disappointed. Schuler had repented by saving Yeo-Thomas and helping Kogon prevent the liquidation of Buchenwald, he thought. But this meant next to nothing to his captors, who were interested in his crimes, not the extenuating circumstances or his internal struggle. Two months after his arrest, Schuler tried to commit suicide at the Freising internment camp north of Munich. At 2 a.m. on a Saturday in June he took sleeping pills, morphine, and codeine and tried to slit his wrists with a razor blade. The blade was blunt, so he resorted to a pair of scissors, but in the meantime the drugs made him drowsy, and he passed out. Ding-Schuler told interrogators he no longer wanted to live, "because of what happened in the course of recent years, and the unbearable nature of my situation." It may have been coincidental, but Ding-Schler's erstwhile associate Dr. Waldemar Hoven had been brought in chains to Freising that day. Ding-Schuler thought Hoven was dead; instead, he would testify against him. Ding-Schuler felt anguish over his family, who were in Russian-held territory. "My wife is alone with my two children, with no support since the loss of all my property," he told interrogators. "A third should have been born in May, but I don't know what my wife's situation is."

After the war, the British spy Yeo-Thomas returned to Germany with a U.S. intelligence officer to track down the Nazis who'd killed and tormented his men. He also tried to find Schuler, writing to his superior officers that he was confident the latter would be an excellent witness in the war crimes trials. But he was too late. In August, Schuler succeeded in hanging himself from the window bars of his cell. In a suicide note, he asked the interrogators to tell his wife he died of a heart attack, and to let Yeo-Thomas and Kogon know they were released from their responsibilities to him, "but to take care of my wife." He hoped she would remarry. But Irene Ding-Schuler failed to escape from under her husband's dark shadow. She died in 1948 in a Leipzig hospital—of typhus.

There were many Nazi suicides—the good, the evil, the indifferently bad. One of Schuler's colleagues in the Hygiene Institute, the decontamination engineer Karl Gerstein—the "spy for God" to whom no one listened—committed suicide in French custody. Eduard Wirths, the Auschwitz doctor who, despite sending thousands to their deaths at least had a guilty conscience and saved a few souls, killed himself while in the hands of the British. Ernst-Robert Grawitz, the senior SS doctor and Mrugowsky's boss, used a tank grenade to blow himself up with his wife at their home in Berlin.

Many more tried to escape judgment in life, and they often succeeded. Bruno Weber, Fleck's boss at Auschwitz, went underground after the war. Following a lengthy cops-and-robbers routine, British agents captured him in 1946 at the house of a friend who'd stored his medical books, and brought him to a prison camp for war criminals at Minden, but after questioning by Polish investigators he was released.

The SS commander of Galicia, Fritz Katzmann, who had the blood of 430,000 Jews on his hands, changed his identity and lived undisturbed until his death of natural causes in 1957, in Darmstadt. Several hundred Nazi war criminals were hanged in the West, and the Soviet Union and its allies executed as many as 40,000 Nazis. As the United States buckled to West German pressure during the early Cold War years, most of the others went free, and the search for the fugitives largely stopped. A series of amnesties freed nearly 800,000 former Nazis convicted of a range of crimes. By 1952, only about 1,200 were still incarcerated in Allied jails or camps.

In their declaration at Yalta on November 1, 1943, Roosevelt, Churchill, and Stalin had warned Germans who took part in atrocities that "they will be brought back to the scene of the crimes and judged on the spot by the peoples whom they have outraged." Yet there often seemed to be an element of chance in the selection of suspects for war crimes trials. The International Military Tribunal tried a cross section of 24 top Nazi officials, sentencing 12 to death by hanging on October 1, 1946. As relations grew strained with the Soviet Union, the international tribunal broke up. The United States held 12 subsequent trials of German war criminals at Nuremberg. The first, *U.S.A. v. Karl Brandt et al.*, dealt with the crimes of Ding-Schuler and other medical men. It was known as the Doctors' Trial, and it led to the so-called Nuremberg Code.

The origins of the code, standards that refined existing ideas about ethical medicine, were obscure until recently. But files from the London War Office show that it grew out of a complex network of motives, including American medical authorities' concern about onerous restrictions on clinical trials. The medical war crimes investigation began as the convergence of two efforts. One was the industrial espionage programs known as FIAT (Field Information Agency, Technical) and CIOS (Combined Intelligence Objectives Subcommittee), whose technical experts accompanied occupying troops, gathering intelligence to exploit German science for any economic, technical, or scientific value it might bring the Western Allies. This wing of the investigation would lead to Operation Paperclip, which brought brilliant but ethically dubious scientists like Wernher von Braun to the United States in a smooth, unwholesome transition to Cold War. But as these investigations progressed, British, Canadian, and U.S. intelligence agents realized that much of the material on their hands was of scientific value only to demonstrate the depravity to which scientific men could descend.

At a May 15, 1946, meeting at IG Farben headquarters in Germany, FIAT officials offered to share their materials with war crime investigators. They had detailed information on the typhus experiments at Buchenwald, as well as experiments with freezing, poison gas, phosphorus burns, removal of ligaments and limbs from living subjects, cancer and healthy tissue transplants, artificial insemination, sterilization, and abortion. Everyone at the meeting agreed that a medical crimes trial should be held as soon as possible. The French, whose prisoners had been cruelly abused in the concentration camps, were particularly keen to prosecute Nazi doctors. In a July 31, 1946, consultation at the Pasteur Institute, Allied scientists and lawyers laid out the guidelines for prosecution. British and American scientists, who had conducted many experiments in prisons and mental asylums (though nothing approaching the scale of the Nazi crimes), worried that the trial could turn the public's stomach against human experimentation in general. Some, such as the British entomologist Kenneth Mellanby, who had attempted to "volunteer" conscientious objectors to test vaccines by having them injected with typhus germs in 1942 (his uncle Edward Mellanby, who headed Britain's Medical Research Council, rejected the idea as "crazy"), even argued that Schuler's experiments had been beneficial. Andrew C. Ivy, an American gastroenterologist who represented the American Medical Association and the U.S. War Department, warned that "unless appropriate care is taken, the publicity associated with the trial of the experimenters in question . . . may so stir public opinion against the use of humans in any experimental manner whatsoever that a hindrance will thereby result to the progress of science."

Ivy proposed that certain broad principles be set out on the use of humans as subjects in experimental work. The "Principles and Rules of Experimentation on Human Subjects" that he proffered at the meeting are, in their essentials, the Nuremberg Code:

1. Consent of the subject is required; i.e. only volunteers should be used.
    (a) The volunteers before giving their consent, should be told of the hazards, if any.
    (b) Insurance against an accident should be provided, if it is possible to secure it.
2. The experiment to be performed should be so designed and based on the results of animal experimentation, that the anticipated results will justify the performance of the experiment; that is, the experiment must be useful and be as such to yield results for the good of society.
3. The experiment should be conducted
    (a) So as to avoid unnecessary physical and mental suffering and injury, and
    (b) by scientifically qualified persons.
    (c) The experiment should not be conducted if there is a prior reason to believe that death or disabling injury will occur.

The Doctors' Trial, U.S. Military Tribunal no. 1, began with an indictment of 22 men and 1 woman on October 25, 1946. The charge was "war crimes and crimes against humanity." As the British scholar Paul Weindling has pointed out, the American prosecutors were less concerned with criticizing scientific practices than with demonstrating how the depravity of the Nazi system had penetrated even the medical profession. "It is incumbent upon us to set forth with conspicuous clarity the ideas and motives which moved these defendants to treat their fellow men as less than beasts," the prosecutor Telford Taylor stated. "I do not think the German people have as yet any conception of how deeply the criminal folly that was Nazism bit into every phase of German life, or of how utterly ravaging the consequences were." The defendants in the Doctors' Trial were a grab bag of senior and low-ranking Nazis who sometimes had little to do with one another. The chief accused, Karl Brandt, had been Hitler's personal physician and designed the euthanasia program, the mass murder of German "mental defectives" that established systems for murdering millions of Jews and others. Others on the dock included Karl Genzken, chief of the Waffen-SS medical service; Joachim Mrugowsky; the army medical chief Siegfried Handloser; and the Buchenwald physician Waldemar Hoven. Gerhard Rose, vice president of the Robert Koch Institute, was on the stand representing academic medicine.

For all the defendants, the impulse and strategy was to blame the dead. Himmler, the master deviant, was dead, as were Grawitz and Ding-Schuler. The midlevel officers Mrugowsky and Genzken testified at first that they knew nothing. Yes, there were experiments, but the details were left to Ding-Schuler and Grawitz, who were ambitious and sneaky and concealed information to consolidate their powers, they said. Mrugowsky and Genzken, *par contre*, were upstanding men, and had been deceived, their witnesses said. Hoven—at one point the Americans declared him insane—also blamed Ding-Schuler, though he admitted murdering 150 people. Eugen Kogon, who recognized the services he had performed for the camp underground, pleaded for Hoven's pardon on the grounds that Germany could not exorcise its demons by laying the blame on a few individuals. Many of Fleck's colleagues from Block 50 gave powerful testimony on the cruel events at Block 46. Fleck himself did not appear, though he was called to provide testimony at a later Nuremberg trial.

Doctor colleagues of the accused helped gather evidence for them and testified on their behalf. Gerhard Rose was in fact a rather random choice for prosecution, since his sins were dwarfed by those of

Waldemar Hoven at Nuremberg. (National Archives.)

colleagues who worked at Auschwitz or in the Warsaw ghetto. Georg Nauck of the Institute for Maritime and Tropical Diseases supplied documents and publications for Rose's defense. The latter defended the Buchenwald vaccine experiments by stating that the Pasteur Institute's live typhus vaccine, which the French administered 3.5 million times to combat an Algerian typhus epidemic, led to five or six cases of typhus per thousand vaccinated, and thus had caused 20,000 cases of the disease. If the French could justify using the vaccine on the assumption that the ends justified the risk, Rose testified, then Germans were within their rights to test vaccines in the camps.

When that line of challenge failed, Mrugowsky brought out another. He argued that the experimenters at Buchenwald were not bound by the Hippocratic oath, because they were not practicing medicine but rather preparing a defensive weapon. The people experimented upon were not patients, he said—they were prisoners of war. "The experiments were research," Mrugowsky argued in his final defense, "required by an extraordinarily pressing state emergency, and ordered by the highest competent government authorities. . . . Millions of soldiers had to give up their lives because they were called upon to fight by the state . . . in the same way the state ordered the medical men to make experiments with new weapons against dangerous diseases. These weapons were the vaccines."

Furthermore, Mrugowsky argued, what was the significance of 142 deaths over three years of experiments (a number based on the typhus charts in possession of the prosecution) at Buchenwald, when in the winter of 1942, 15,000 Russian soldiers died of typhus *every day* in German POW camps? He compared the experiments to Emil von Behring's work at Berlin's Charité Hospital in the 1890s, which established the value of diphtheria serum. The control subjects in that group died, he said—240 children. But "their sacrifice allowed us to recognize the value of the serum." Pointing to the unethical practices of non-Nazi medicine might have been an effective argument had the entire enterprise of Nazi medicine not been infused with utter contempt for life and health. In a broader historical perspective, however, Mrugowsky had a point—not one that could be made in his own defense, but an argument in favor of stricter medical ethics worldwide.

In a crowning irony to the typhus story, it surfaced during the trial that American medics had vaccinated all the Nazi defendants with the Buchenwald rabbit-lung vaccine. At the trial, Mrugowsky, Handloser, and the others learned for the first time that Fleck, Ciepielowski, and Kogon had suckered them for 18 months with a false vaccine. Indeed, it was not clear whether the Americans knew of the deception, and whether they had administered the Doctor's Trial defendants with good vaccine or the worthless solution that the inmates had prepared for Germany's troops. Early in his testimony, Mrugowsky boasted that the vaccine produced at Buchenwald "was the best vaccine we had in Germany. The American occupation troops used it at their camps, after the defeat," he said.

After Kogon and Ciepielowski testified that the vaccine had been bogus, Mrugowsky appeared stunned. He accused them of violating medical ethics. "These are some of the most curious remarks I have heard here," he said. "Their attitude has nothing in common with the concepts of humanity expressed by the *Herren* here today."

This was met by laughter in the gallery.

On August 20, 1947, Mrugowsky, Hoven, and five others were sentenced to death by hanging. Seven others were acquitted, while Handloser, Rose, Genzken, and the others received lesser charges and were freed within several years.

Fleck came to Nuremberg several months later as an expert witness in the sixth U.S. trial, *U.S. v. Carl Krauch*, which involved senior executives of IG Farben. He was given access to prosecution documents, and made a powerful case that IG Farben officials were fully aware that Ding's vaccine was being tested on artificially infected prisoners in a concentration camp. No scientist of any skill or understanding could have been fooled by the wording of Ding's typhus papers—which Fleck had helped write—into believing the infections he described were not artificially induced, Fleck testified. One could not determine how long someone had been sick with typhus unless the infection was intentional, because the timing of an infection depended on a number of factors, including the patient's immune defenses. Yet in Ding-Schuler's papers, blood draws were described as occurring "one day after infection," or "three days after infection," he said. In addition, "there was never a typhus epidemic at Buchenwald." Rudolf Weigl began experimenting with his vaccine in 1919, Fleck noted. Over 30 years, he vaccinated more than 50,000 people and covered whole typhus-endemic regions. Weigl would never have dreamed of employing the methods used by the SS on behalf of IG Farben, he said. Before the Buchenwald experiments began, Robert Kudicke and Eugen Gildemeister had vaccinated about 6,000 people in Warsaw. Yet Behring had delivered vaccine for testing to Waldemar Hoven. Why? "No specialist would think that Hoven in Buchenwald was better situated than Kudicke in the Warsaw ghetto to test a typhus vaccine," Fleck said. "It was obvious to all that these were artificial vaccinations."

Fleck was devastated by what he'd been shown at Nuremberg, which he described to Ludwik Hirszfeld, in a letter, as a "ghostly theater." He was stunned that scientists such as Kudicke and Gildemeister had taken part in planning meetings for the Buchenwald experiments without raising objections. "Now they squirm about in a cowardly and miserable way. [The IG Farben doctor Richard] Bieling tries to wash their sins away, and the young doctors who worked at Behring try to make the truth disappear by shamelessly lying," he wrote. "It was all so nauseating that I was impatient to get out of there."

Of the 24 indicted IG Farben officials, half were convicted, and most of these were free within a few years. Many implicated company officials were not even charged.

Many other scientists were troubled by the postwar state of German medicine. The Rockefeller Foundation's medical chief, Alan Gregg, during a visit in 1947, found the destruction appalling, German physicians' failure to recognize the enormity of Nazi crimes even worse. "They still seem to me to be strangers to self-reproach and the responsibilities that attend freedom," he wrote. He felt a huge sense of relief leaving the country. "It isn't that you can vomit what you have already had to eat—you can't—but at least you don't have to sit smilingly and eat more and more."

Hirszfeld's prediction, that the German ghetto doctors would pay a price for looking the other way while their patients were murdered, did not come true. Most went back to their old lives after a few months or years of Allied investigation. Nauck, who helped create the Polish ghettos, was hired by FIAT to write reports on wartime science. Kudicke returned from Warsaw to the University of Frankfurt, while Richard Haas, head of the Behringwerke in Lwów, landed a post at the University of Freiburg. The *Generalgouvernement* public health chief, Jost Walbaum, became a homeopathic doctor in Lower Saxony; Wilhelm Dopheide, Walbaum's man in Lwów, lay low as a state medical consultant in the town of Hagen. Hermann Eyer was friendly with several of these men and wrote their obituaries in the medical press in later years. His assessments tended to avoid the "difficult period" of the war. None of the men were ever punished for their wartime activities.

On January 17, 1945, with the Red Army on the doorstep, Eyer's staff abandoned the Kraków institute. In the closing weeks of the war, he moved what was left of the typhus station from Kraków to Częstochowa, Poland, and finally to Roth, Germany, where he surrendered to the U.S. Army in April 1945. A three-member scientific intelligence team led by the virologist Joseph Smadel inspected the station in Roth and interrogated Eyer and 54 members of his staff. Although he was somewhat mystified by aspects of Eyer's technique, Smadel seemed to take a shine to him. He noted that Eyer's technicians "denied that Eyer had any Nazi affiliations; in fact they maintained that the Wehrmacht was as non political as is the American Army. In agreement with their expressed statements regarding Eyer it may be noted that his own correspondence that was examined never ended with 'Heil Hitler' but that many letters he received from others did."

The U.S. Army held Eyer at a military prison in Augsburg and Mannheim until November, when he was released and immediately became chief of the microbiology department at the University of Bonn. A year later, he was arrested again, this time by British officials at the request of the Poles, who accused Eyer of having mistreated Polish employees and stolen or wrecked Polish equipment. The Brits held Eyer in four different military prisons for nearly a year while his case was investigated. His wife collected positive affidavits from 20 people, mostly former German subalterns but also a few Poles and Ukrainians who had worked under him in Kraków. In late 1947, the British allowed him to return to Bonn. His wartime work had been clean, it seems, in every sense except that it had supported history's most genocidal force. Unlike too many of his colleagues, Eyer had stood up for Polish colleagues, had stuck out his neck to do the right thing. Would he have performed differently if he had overseen wretched ghettos, like Walbaum and Kudicke, rather than directing what was essentially a pharmaceutical laboratory? Perhaps. The German federal chancellor Helmut Kohl once acknowledged the moral failure of Germany when he spoke of his own gratitude for "the mercy of a late birth"— the fact that his generation was too young to have been called upon to kill unjustly. Eyer's fortunate record must have owed something to the mercy of a less freighted military assignment. "My father was proud," Peter Eyer stated during a long interview in 2011, "that during the Nazi years he did not have to commit any injustice." Eyer felt intense remorse for the fate of the Jews after the war. But it would be his good deeds that made trouble for him. The friendship he showed Poles, Rudolf Weigl in particular, would be turned against both men, in a shabby story of Cold War politics.

Poland is a country cursed by a difficult past in which historical figures tend to be tarred with the brush of treason or, if they die, gilded in overly bright halos. As a flawed, flesh-and-blood man of science, Weigl found no place in the romantic narrative of sacrifice that dominated postwar Polish culture. Ryszard Wójcik, a journalist who has done much to bring Weigl posthumous acclaim, explains this in his book *Pact with the Devil*. Here, he quotes a former louse feeder who, having become an important postwar scientist, spoke in the late 1970s on condition of anonymity:

> You ask about how far a compromise can be stretched. I'll tell you frankly. In this country, in which for the last two hundred years its citizens have been doomed to have their dignity violated and where there is a permanent divide between fruitless steadfastness and rational collaboration in the name of survival, there has been for a long time a place for those in the steadfast category: The sweet and cozy sands of the cemetery.

Imperfect Justice

All the steadfast, flawless people lie in the cemeteries. They were executed, shot, freed by suicide.

Weigl had lent his assistance to the Germans in a concrete way during the three years of the occupation. He oversaw the production of millions of vaccines designed to protect an army bent on the mass murder and subjection of Poles among others. By Hermann Eyer's postwar estimate, the production of the Weigl vaccine in Kraków and Lwów during World War II saved the lives of 10,000 Wehrmacht soldiers. The vaccine did not keep the soldiers entirely well, but it kept them from dying. And thus it bolstered, to a small extent, the fighting capacity of Germany, thereby extending the war, the killing, and the misery of the Jews and other subject peoples behind German lines. Weigl saw a way for his life's work to provide two kinds of protection—to those who took the vaccine, and those who made it. We do not know whether he questioned the ethics of producing a vaccine that protected those who killed his friends. We do know that the thousands of people saved by his vaccine included the scientific and artistic intelligentsia of Lwów, and that his laboratory smuggled thousands of vaccines to the desperate ghettos of Poland, while providing a haven for the Polish resistance movement. The Weigl lab was a force for good. It could not achieve moral perfection.

The postwar years were difficult for Weigl, politically and professionally. As the Soviets approached Lwów in April 1944, he packed some of his equipment and retreated to the mountain town of Krościenko, while the Germans took the rest and headed west. Several months later, a squad of Soviet soldiers accompanied by an NKVD officer arrived at his house in Krościenko and took him to Kraków. In 1945, he was offered a position as a professor at the Jagiellonian University in Kraków, but was required to teach at least five hours of lectures and two hours of laboratory courses each week—a heavy load for any professor, especially a famous one who preferred to teach as little as possible. Weigl lacked the energy and disposition to engage in the kind of politicking that would have been required to maintain his status. During the first four years after the war, an NKVD colonel lived on the same floor of his apartment building and kept constant watch on his comings and goings. The colonel was amazed, a friend of the Weigls named Henryk Gaertner said, that the professor kept refusing Soviet offers to make his vaccine in Moscow. "He'd say, "You could have your own apartment, your own driver, a good salary,'" recalled Gaertner. Weigl, as always, refused the offers. Meanwhile, his position worsened as he lost a power play with a younger scientist who wanted his place.

Weigl found himself tangling with Zdzisław Przybyłkiewicz, a microbiologist whom he had trained in the late 1930s and who went on to become Eyer's top Polish assistant in Kraków during the war. Weigl did not think much of Przybyłkiewicz's work, and in 1946 refused to approve the latter's *Habilitationsschrift*, calling it second-rate. Przybyłkiewicz managed to win *Habilitation* anyway because the second committee member who might have vetoed it (Ludwik Hirszfeld, as it happened) excused himself on the grounds of unfamiliarity with the subject. Having received his *Habilitation*, Przybyłkiewicz became a full professor, and he had powerful allies in Kraków. The influx of Lwów professors into the city had led to feelings of insecurity and resentment among academics at the Jagiellonian University. In this atmosphere, it was easier for Przybyłkiewicz to rally support to his side of the conflict.

Colleagues over the years would accuse Przybyłkiewicz of requesting bribes to treat patients, of fathering children out of wedlock, of sleeping with students and driving away competent scientists— including Jan Starzyk, Weigl's former assistant—if he saw them as competition. He was a mediocre scientist and a terrible teacher, they said, and by the early 1960s he'd become a police informer, according to his secret police file. Sofia Bujdwid, who had protected Przybyłkiewicz in the final months of the war by giving him a job at her father's lab, claimed that he later orchestrated the confiscation of her lab, house, and other property. In a letter she left for posterity, Bujdwid described Przybyłkiewicz as a callow, scheming ignoramus loaded with hatred for his betters—"a louse," she called him.

But a louse, if that's what he was, with influence. Przybyłkiewicz became director of the Department of Public Hygiene at the Jagiellonian University medical school in 1946, and a short time later the government sent him to Munich to retrieve Polish lab equipment. Among the materials, he found a signed portrait of Weigl, with the caption, "to my young friend Hermann Eyer." Przybyłkiewicz accused Eyer of stealing Polish property—it was this accusation that lay behind Eyer's arrest in the British sector. Przybyłkiewicz used the photograph to stigmatize Weigl as a collaborator, though he himself had worked more closely with Eyer than had any other Polish scientist.* He also claimed (falsely) that Weigl had met Eyer in Ethiopia in 1939, and had at that point begun cooperating with the Germans.

Weigl's name started to fall into ill repute. Most of his old associates made themselves scarce and stopped using his name as a reference. In late 1940s Poland, it was poisonous to be associated with the career of a collaborator. It did not help that many members of the Lwów circle, including Weigl's son, Wiktor, were increasingly antagonistic toward Weigl's second wife, Anna Herzig who, some claimed, jealously guarded access to him.

Most of Weigl's students were searching for their own places in postwar Poland. Perhaps the most loyal among them, the epidemiologist Henryk Mosing, remained in Lwów and led rickettsial research that helped end typhus's reign in the Soviet Union. Mosing did much to keep his mentor's work from slipping into obscurity. He studied the mechanisms by which typhus persisted in nonepidemic periods, and used a test designed by Weigl to diagnose unsymptomatic carriers. In the immediate postwar years, a certain moral ambiguity colored

*Przybyłkiewicz was the only scientist affiliated with Weigl's institute who published with Eyer during the occupation, coauthoring an article about typhus.

Weigl with his second wife, Anna Herzig, daughter-in-law, and grandchildren, in Kraków, 1950s. (Courtesy of National Museum, Przemyśl. Photograph of original by S. Kosiedowski.)

many survivors' memories of the Weigl laboratory. The Soviet line on Polish "collaborators" muddied the distinction between those who had shown great bravery in difficult circumstances and those fortunate enough to have avoided imperfect choices. Andrzej Żuławski's powerful 1971 film, *The Third Part of the Night*, presented a somewhat jaded version of life at the institute. The mood of the young lab workers and louse feeders living reluctantly in Weigl's safekeeping is somber, morbid, and full of self-loathing.

In March 1948, Weigl was transferred to the medical university in Poznań, but he rarely showed up for his lectures and soon retired. Next, he set up a small research center in Kraków, but it was subject to state control, and the vaccine made there was labeled as if it had been produced by the National Institute of Hygiene. Each autumn, Weigl and his staff worried that the health ministry would cut their contract. His nephew, Fryderyk Weigl, summed up Weigl's treatment in the postwar era thus: "The Germans had offered him a chair in Berlin, the Russians an institute in Moscow. The Poles gave my uncle a small appartment on Sebastian Street and a lot of political headaches. This is a difficult thing. Very sad."

Eyer felt disappointment rather than anger toward Przybyłkiewicz, who he suspected was simply a weak man trying to make a career for himself in a difficult situation. Eyer wrote to a friend, "The world is bad. It was bad what the Germans did during the war, and bad what the Poles are doing now to me and my Polish colleagues. Why is the world so bad?"

Despite all he had done to hold his family together during the war, history had one final trick to play on Ludwik Fleck. As a 20-year-old citizen of a city that Stalin had declared capital of western Soviet Ukraine, Ryszard Fleck in April 1945 was immediately drafted into the Red Army and trucked from Buchenwald to a mustering site in Chemnitz, Germany. He found himself the only Jew in a group of Russian and Ukrainain farmers who'd been sent to Germany as slave laborers. A Soviet general harangued them for "cooperating" with the Germans and said they would need to be rehabilitated before they could return home. Since by then it was harvest time, they would redeem themselves by bringing in the German wheat, after which they would be drafted into the army. Everyone enthusiastically cheered, "Long live Stalin!"

After several months, Ryszard fell ill—he had developed tuberculosis in the camps—and was mustered out of the Red Army. In early 1946, he finally arrived in Lwów to find the city nearly empty of friends and acquaintances. His old house was occupied by Russian soldiers; his parents had come and gone and were living in Lublin, a city in central Poland. Ernestyna had arrived first in Lwów, after surviving the Auschwitz death march and Ravensbruck concentration camp. Ludwik, after spending a month in the infirmary at Buchenwald and several more weeks in a hospital halfway home, had gone immediately to see his old mentor Groër. He found Ernestyna waiting for him in the doctor's anteroom. In the statement he gave years later at Yad Vashem, the Holocaust memorial in Israel, Ryszard spoke little of being reunited with his parents. Certainly there were strains—Ryszard had never been a good student, and had nothing of his father's charm or intellect. Enduring the misery and terror of the war years had not brightened his prospects. After receiving a high school diploma in Lublin, Ryszard registered for a kibbutz and left for Germany, where he was held in a displaced persons (DP) camp for a year before being smuggled to Sète, France. There, in early July 1947, he and 4,500 other Holocaust survivors boarded the American steamer *President Warfield.* Halfway through its famous voyage, the ship was rechristened *Exodus.* Two Jews died fighting British troops who boarded the *Exodus* near Palestine, and global news coverage of the combat, between British riot troops and miserable refugees, ignited a wave of sympathy for the Jews and their desire for a homeland. (In 1960, *Exodus* became a film epic directed by Otto Preminger, with Paul Newman and Eva Marie Saint, and a famous score by Ernest Gold.) At Haifa, the British removed the refugees and returned them to Germany. When he finally got to Israel, Ryszard lived on a kibbutz and then worked in a lab at a hospital in Petach Tikva. Once his father had said to him, "Never have children, because it will break your heart trying to protect them." Ryszard obeyed.

The fate of Fleck's Lwów team was mixed and at times heartbreaking. Bruno and Anna Seeman were separated from her husband, Jakob, and assumed for many months that he was dead. Finally he found them, in Kraków. The Umschweifs had perished. "Dad always said, he didn't eat the grass and that's why he survived," Bruno Seeman recalled. The Seemans ended up in France, where Bruno would become an engineer, with many patents to his name, for the multinational oil field company Schlumberger. He moved frequently, from France to Texas to the Mideast and elsewhere. His friends in the company called him "the Wandering Jew."

Imperfect Justice

Ciepielowski, the chief of the vaccine-making crew at Buchenwald's Block 50, made the best of a difficult life. For two years, he worked as a doctor for refugees in the American zone in Germany. At one point, a large German pharmaceutical company approached him about production of the rabbit-lung vaccine, asking for his help. The laboratory was following the instructions Ding had published in 1944, the company official said, but the lungs yielded no *Rickettsia*. Ciepielowski explained, with a laugh, that the vaccine had never been meant to protect anyone. He would marry a beautiful Polish woman and emigrate to New Jersey, where he was a doctor at Roosevelt Hospital in Metuchen. He died in 1972 of a lung disease contracted at Buchenwald.

Another Block 50 inmate, the former Communist activist August Cohn, also emigrated to the United States, but had a rougher time of it. After working with U.S. occupation forces to hunt Nazis in the Kassel area, Cohn despaired of European communism and moved to New York in late 1946, at age 36. Two years later, while working as a cabinetmaker, he was arrested for allegedly failing to identify himself as a former Communist in his immigration papers. This was untrue; Cohn had never hidden his past from U.S. officials. But it was the height of the McCarthy era, and some of those diplomats did not want to admit what they had known. After a long and expensive legal battle, Cohn was permitted to remain in the United States.

Eugen Kogon helped found the Christian Democratic Union, Germany's most influential postwar political party, but left it in the early 1950s because of his opposition to the stationing of U.S. nuclear weapons on German soil. His portrait of camp life, *The Theory and Practice of Hell*, sold 300,000 copies in Germany and was translated into 11 languages. He was a well-known figure on German talk shows and newspaper feuilletons. In later years, Kogon grew bitter over the country's rush to forget the past. He was "an angry old man" who couldn't stomach the moral levity of consumerist Germany.

Unlikely friendships sprang up in the scorched soil of Germany.

In November 1950, the Block 46 capo Arthur Dietzsch was released from an American prison where he'd been sentenced for his part in the typhus experiments. He wrote to his former conspirator at Buchenwald, the British "White Rabbit," Wing Commander Yeo-Thomas. The old spy was an immensely loyal individual and provided great help to Dietzsch, a man whom he viewed, whatever his faults, as his personal savior. Yeo-Thomas and his wife visited Dietzsch and his wife, Lilly, in Germany, found him jobs, and sent him gifts and hundreds of deutschmarks in financial help over the years. Dietzsch's wife wrote to Yeo-Thomas that her husband frequently woke up screaming with nightmares. "The SS is torturing me again," he told her. But the friendship with Yeo-Thomas was a rock of comfort. "Tommy," wrote Dietzsch in a 1957 letter, "I must confess that I never met a man like you. You have always helped me at the right moment. For my part, this means a bond for lifetime." Many of the Buchenwald inmates who had considered Dietzsch a brute reconsidered later. In the 1960s, he was invited to attend inmate reunions in West Germany—a prematurely aged man with a pot belly, a crew cut, a small dog, and a hearing aid. "Of all my saviors, it is to Dietzsch to whom I have been most unjust in my consideration," the SOE agent Stéphane Hessel wrote in a 2007 memoir. His early assessment of Dietzsch, no doubt influenced by Balachowsky, was "deformed by the Manicheism of the camps. What would we have done without his courage and loyalty?"

On April 17, 1945, at Buchenwald, Ludwik Fleck declared on an American military questionnaire that he intended to "emigrate to one of the overseas democratic countries," and gave the address of a distant relative in New York and two other American references. But his destination plan was at some point crossed out and replaced with a handwritten word: "Moskau." Perhaps Fleck did this to assure that he would be able to reconnect with Ryszard and Ernestyna in now-Soviet Lwów. More likely, a Soviet representative, jealously enforcing control of some sort, made the change. Fleck's vision of life after the war was probably fluid. Some acquaintances—and correspondence in his secret police files—say he wanted to emigrate to Israel immediately. But despite his experiences, including postwar Polish anti-Semitism, Fleck never stopped "feeling" Polish. And he always pined for Lwów.

The new Soviet rulers of Lwów estimated that half the city's 300,000 prewar residents had died of murder, illness, or hunger. Poland, the Big Three had agreed at Yalta, was a republic on wheels whose borders would now roll west. Poland surrendered the lands east of the 1921 Curzon line to the Soviet Union—an area that included the cities of Lwów and Vilnius (in Soviet Lithuania)—and gained much of Silesia, including the former German cities of Breslau (now Wrocław) and Gleiwitz (Gliwice). At a huge rally at the Lwów Opera House on July 30, 1944, the Ukrainian Communist leader Khrushchev announced that Lwów was a Ukrainian city. He did not mention Jewish or Polish suffering there. About 800 Jews came out of the sewers and other hiding places, but they only spooked the people of Lwów, who offered little help. Meeting with Polish intellectuals on December 6, 1944, Communist officials said the city's schools would hencefore teach in Ukrainian. Those who wanted their children to speak Polish should take them to Poland. By March 12, 1945, only 30,000 of the estimated 87,000 Poles who were present at war's end had departed voluntarily. Having failed to persuade the rest to leave their homes, the Soviets began massive deportations. Eventually, 1.5–2 million Poles would move west from Ukraine, while 500,000 Ukrainians would move east. Banach, the mathematician, remained behind; he died of lung cancer in 1945.

Where the Lwowites settled was often a matter of chance. If the train stopped long enough for a family to locate an empty apartment, they'd stay. The trail of deportees ended up distributed along the rail line that ran through southern Poland—in cities like Przemyśl, Gliwice, Kraków, and Katowice. Many went to Wrocław, although the city had been leveled in the final days of the war. The Poles had suffered, proportionately, more than any other nation during World War

II, losing 6 million of their 30 million citizens, 3 million of them Jews. They received scant justice. Their Allies permitted Stalin to take half their territory, the hundreds of thousands of partisans who'd fought the Nazis were murdered, jailed, or forced to keep quiet. There was even less justice for the former residents of Lwów. As Polish citizens of a city that was no longer Polish, and which furthermore had been "reclaimed" for Ukraine after centuries of "occupation," the Poles of Lwów were an inconvenient people. There could be no justice for the loss of life and property. The Germans who killed the Lwów professors, for example, were never prosecuted; Poland was not permitted to prosecute Nazi crimes that occurred east of the Soviet–Nazi demarcation line of September 1939.

"They did everything possible to erase Polish Lwów from history, to pretend that it didn't exist," says Wacław Szybalski. "That really hurt me. I loved my city."

The way forward for Lwowites in socialist Poland was to renounce the past, but it was extremely painful. The poet Adam Zagajewski, born in Lwów in 1945, grew up hearing the Lwów dialect and recollections of his parents and their friends. He wrote,

> There was too much
> of Lvov, it brimmed the container,
> it burst glasses, overflowed
> each pond, lake, smoked through every
> chimney, turned into fire, storm,
> laughed with lightning, grew meek,
> returned home, read the New Testament,
> slept on a sofa beside the Carpathian rug,
> there was too much of Lvov, and now
> there isn't any. . . .

Fleck, after stopping briefly in Kraków, ended up in bleak Lublin, wrecked during the war, its Jews gassed at Majdanek. Ludwik

Hirszfeld, who had been named to head the Department of Medical Microbiology at the new Marie-Curie University there, instead took a position in Wrocław. After helping Fleck obtain his *Habilitation*, Hirszfeld handed off the job to him. Lublin was a postwar desert, poor and culturally barren, Fleck wrote to his friend Hugo Steinhaus in November 1946. Cold winds whistled through the broken windows of the immunology laboratory and classrooms. There were no cafés, and students came to early lectures hungry and stayed that way all day. Intact apartments were hard to find, and Fleck lived in a converted room in the medical faculty. The building had been the Chachmei Lublin Yeshiva, the biggest Talmudic school in the world when it opened in 1930. The Nazis burned the books and torahs of its remarkable library in the town square in 1939, then painted the building in camouflage and used it as a military police barracks. "Lublin is a true Ultima Thule," Fleck wrote Steinhaus; "it is inhabited by anthropods whose reaction time is so slow that you can speak with three of them at the same time. Before the first answers, you can listen to the second and ask the third a question. In addition, people here are very pious, and priests take part in all parts of daily life."

Despite the poor contrast Lublin made with Lwów, Fleck took up his work with enthusiasm and was popular with students. To save money on clothes, he wore his red-striped shirt from Buchenwald around his apartment. A friend pointed out that the government provided money for people who'd been held in the camps, but Fleck shrugged. "I used to be rich, and I know the taste of being so," he said. "Now I am passionately interested in other things." In the laboratory, he improvised ways of getting the university to stretch its budget. For example, there was no money for a typewriter until Fleck described it as an "Anthropodattelgraphen." Once Fleck saw a line of people waiting for something at a store. After discovering it was toilet paper, which was in extremely short supply, Fleck got in line himself. He appeared at his office with several rolls hanging around his neck on a string. In his first lecture, to clear up any ambiguity, he introduced imself with characteristic straightforwardness and defiance: "My name is Ludwik Fleck. I am a Jew, and a bacteriologist." Those who knew him during this period say that he was a warm, quick-witted presence, a demanding boss but kindly and appreciative of a good joke. Although there are no records of Fleck's reflection on how concentration camp life had changed him, perhaps he felt something like the German-Jewish Dr. Lucie Adelsberger, whom he had met at Auschwitz:

> Once you learn by painful, personal experience how everything vanishes—money and possessions, honor and reputation—and that the only thing that remains is a person's inner attitude, you acquire a profound disregard for the superficialities of life. . . . We who had to watch 990 out of every 1000 people die are no longer able—and this is a real defect—to take our own personal lives and our own future seriously. On the other hand, we take increased enjoyment in the little things of everyday life. After all that deprivation we consciously enjoy every slice of bread and every piece of cake. We treasure the warm coat that protects us against the cold; every single little amenity of life seems like a gift from heaven. We lap up the kindness of others the way a dry sponge absorbs water. . . . It's a miracle and a gift of God that we survived Auschwitz; it's also an obligation. The legacy of the dead rests in our hands.

Fleck remained in Lublin until 1952. He worked primarily on leukergy, the meaningful clumping of white blood cells during infections that he had noted first in the Jewish hospital on Kuszewicz Street during the war. He had lots of visitors, friends, and acquaintances; there were no cafés, so they talked to him in the lab while he tracked his leukocytes. The chemist Janina Opieńska-Blauth, who had worked with Fleck at the Laokoon factory in Lwów and now shared a wall with him, remembered that he had a philosophical attitude toward irritating problems. "He was friendly and helpful to colleagues and to assistants, whom he addressed as 'my children,'" she said.

Fleck traveled on scientific business to Austria, Czechoslovakia, Germany, the USSR, France, Denmark, and even Boston in 1954, where he attended a hematology conference and was invited by the Harvard pathologist Sidney Farber (founder of the Dana-Farber Cancer Institute) to address his lab staff about his research on leukergy. The Polish secret police jealously guarded foreign travel, so Fleck must have enjoyed the support of Communist-linked academics. A 1954 letter in his secret police file says Fleck sought to emigrate to Palestine in the first two years after the war, but after being refused "showed a positive relationship to the present reality." According to that letter, written to assist Fleck's election to the Polish Academy of Sciences, he opposed U.S. imperialism at a conference organized to protest alleged U.S. biological warfare in Korea, and favorably contrasted conditions for science under communism to late 1930s Poland.

On the streets of Lublin, children would pass him by and say, "There's a Jew the Germans didn't kill. Why not?"

Most of Fleck's assistants were women, who appreciated his learning and chivalry. "The professor was not really handsome, but that's the point," said Ewa Pleszczyńska, one of Fleck's assistants in Lublin. "Someone once said he was ugly, and I got angry: How could you say that Professor Fleck is ugly? His inner beauty radiated so intensely that it completely erased his looks." Students were spellbound by his lectures on the history of medicine. He emphasized the importance of clear writing. "A scientific paper is well-written," he said, "only when it can be understood by a layman." Said another, "He didn't speak about himself. He never boasted. The professor was uncomfortable playing the hero, but he was one. Because even in these terrible conditions, he could still help people." Fleck's assistants felt that his bravery had saved him during the war, perhaps by showing the Nazis that they were dealing with a formidable person. "You know," Pleszczyńska told an interviewer, "the dog doesn't chase the cat until the cat runs away."

After returning from Nuremberg, Fleck defended the principles of the Nuremberg Code and went a step further. Scientists should not conduct experiments on the insane unless the medicines being tested could provide health benefits to the subjects, he wrote in a Polish medical journal. When testing drugs or vaccine in prisons, doctors should experiment only on true volunteers, whose sacrifice to advance science should be acknowledged with rewards such as shorter sentences. Any time a risky experiment was to be carried out, Fleck added, it should be explained by the doctor in plain language—"the way a person talks to a person." That was an idea ahead of its time. A quick scan of research published in *Science* magazine, Fleck wrote, showed that U.S. clinicians routinely violated these principles.

Fleck was an ideal person to put medical experimentation in context. Alas, he was also working in an impoverished country behind the rapidly descending Iron Curtain. And context, as Fleck understood, was vital—as was public relations, or what Fleck called the exchange of ideas within a thought community that included "esoteric" (expert) and "exoteric" (wider public) audiences for science. Polish scientists did not communicate well with the world. They were poor and frightened, and it was hard to travel to the West, for political and financial reasons. Many scientists emigrated. Those who stayed struggled with poverty and obscurity. Ah, to be a Frenchman like Balachowsky, at the gilded Pasteur Institute. Bestowed with medals, lavished with laboratory equipment and funds, Balachowsky toured the United States and Mexico in 1946, visiting friends, hiking in the mountains, preaching on the horrors of the concentration camps. His testimony at Nuremberg was fraught with errors, but nobody questioned him.

Rudolf Weigl, meanwhile, was coming to the end of his road. The Polish Ministry of Health had decided to entrust manufacture of the louse vaccine to his former aide Kryński, who had taken a position in Lublin, and to Przybyłkiewicz in Kraków. This decision broke Weigl's heart. He made no effort to ingratiate himself with the new order. He refrained from putting his name to petitions of socialist solidarity that scientists were expected to sign; he did not go along to get along. The authorities tolerated him because of his scientific reputation, but did nothing to acknowledge his contributions or the merit of his ideas. The government withdrew its long-standing nomination for the Nobel Prize, and he was never named to the Polish National Academy, a cruel omission. Polish science students did not learn about his work. "Young Polish intellectuals know who Schindler was, but have no idea who Weigl was," a co-worker wrote in 1994. Like the rest of Polish Lwów, Weigl was shunted aside. How could one defend what had never existed?

He died of a heart attack on August 11, 1957, while resting in Zakopane, in the Carpathians. At Weigl's memorial service in Kraków, Henryk Mosing, who had obtained special permission to come to Kraków from Lviv, gave a powerful eulogy, drawing together the strands of Weigl's personality, his bravery and brilliant scientific and technological mind. Mosing was a deeply religious man: he was secretly ordained in Poland by Cardinal Stefan Wyszyński, at a ceremony attended by the future Pope John Paul II. He appeared suddenly at the grave site— delays at the Russian–Polish border had kept Mosing from arriving at the service—and gave an emotional, impromptu speech that tremendously moved those who were there. At first, many of them didn't recognize Mosing at all—he was an apparition from Lwów, their past, a city that no longer existed for them. "Rudolf Stefan Weigl transformed the louse, a symbol of dirt, misery, and aversion," Mosing concluded, "into a useful object of scientific research and a lifesaving tool."

As the service ended and relatives returned to Weigl's house, they discovered that Anna Herzig had already packed up most of his possessions. In the postwar era, housing was at a premium, and another tenant was ready to move into the house and kept asking when it would be empty. Relatives and friends were told to go in and grab what they could before the rest disappeared. "People pounced on that apartment like a flock of vultures," said his nephew Fryderyk Weigl. "I have this image of people taking typewriters, refrigerators, with his papers on the floor and people stepping on them. It was chaotic." While a few of Weigl's lab implements were preserved and eventually put into museums, most of his life and laboratory were dispersed to the four winds.

Thus it was left to Hermann Eyer to write the most touching obituary to Weigl—in German. "Many doctors from all parts of the world have been able to address the problems of typhus thanks to his friendly readiness to help," Eyer wrote. "He was one of the greats of his generation of biologists, possessed of an unequaled depth of knowledge and abilities."

The whispering campaign continued after Weigl's death. Even in 1983, Przybyłkiewicz continued to denounce Weigl as a traitor, and it was not until the post-Communist 1990s that Weigl's associates began to rehabilitate him. Eventually—in 2000—a bust of Weigl was erected at Wrocław University's medical faculty, and a street was named after him there. In 2002, Wacław Szybalski and others began organizing a biannual Polish-Ukrainian scientific conference in his honor. As of this writing, Lviv has not recognized him with so much as a plaque.

Hermann Eyer, who was ingenious, hardworking, and levelheaded, did well after his first, rough postwar years. In the Germany of the 1950s, the keys to academic success were to keep one's head down, build a career and strong institutions, and ignore the ugly past. In 1956, after leading the creation of the University of Bonn's school of public health, Eyer won an invitation to do the same at the University of Munich, where his successful career continued.

In 1956, the year before Weigl's death, Eyer received an unexpected letter. He had assumed that Henryk and Paula Meisel, the Jewish couple he had helped shield at the typhus institute in Lwów, had been murdered at Auschwitz. But here, on the stationery of an Italian hotel, was proof this was not so: "I obtained your address here at a conference in Rome and fulfill what for years has been the need of my heart," Meisel wrote to him. "If only in a letter, I can send you a few words of thanks. . . . I was always aware that your situation was not easy. And I also appreciated that in this terrible time of darkness you didn't suffer the common psychosis and managed to maintain your humanity." In this and subsequent letters, Meisel described the terrible illnesses and starvation he and his wife had suffered in the camps and the early postwar period. They were physically battered, but life was on the mend; they had returned to work at the state health institute; their daughter had married a well-known scientist, and they had two beautiful grandchildren.

Eyer's response was heartfelt, if a bit awkward. "It would be hard for you to understand how much happiness I have experienced in hearing a sign of life from you," he wrote back. "All the difficulties and sorrow I had on your account again came into my mind. How great the happiness now, after so many years, to realize that it was not all for nothing. It seems to me that both of us have had burdens to carry. Those evil times left their mark on me, also, and I, too, was not spared the realization that evil too often triumphs in this world." Later, he wrote, "Understand, when I write you, how thankful I and my wife are that despite the horrible things you and your wife had to pass through, you maintain that generous feeling that allows you to consider me a friend. . . . It is only too easy for me to imagine the terrible suffering you have felt and had to endure, and thus your modest acceptance and happiness with that which remains to you is truly moving."

Their correspondence, which continued for many years, was warm. Meisel always stressed that the Nazi years were not really over for him. "They often are discussed, and the pain goes on. But you can be sure that in my house and my laboratory, your name is always mentioned with great respect." In 1972, Meisel asked Eyer to help him get payments from the German state, which provided small sums of money to victims of Nazi oppression if they could offer proof. Describing the hard times his family had experienced, he added, "My friend, do you think we want payment for that? No, such things can never be made good. But our lives are not easy now. We want our daughter to have an easier life than we did."

Three years later, Eyer wrote Meisel a sad letter. He was glad to hear that Meisel's daughter was doing well, that his grandchildren were now studying science. Eyer had two sons who both turned to science, the younger becoming a mechanical engineering whiz. But in the summer of 1975, the boy, then 19, had accidentally poisoned himself while doing an experiment in their basement.

Fleck spent seven years in Lublin until being called to Warsaw by his old mentor Groër, who made him director of the bacteriology laboratory at the Mother and Child Hospital. During his Lublin years, Fleck developed a following of loyal female assistants. One of his closest aides was Barbara Narbutowicz, who like Fleck had been in concentration camps. He brought her to Warsaw, where they worked on bacteriophages—viruses that infect bacteria. After Fleck left Poland, Narbutowicz became a lab chief. She was an aristocratic woman who spoke beautiful French but was modest and hardworking. She and Fleck "understood each other very well," said another aide, Danuta Borecka. "I would say that they were in love."

Fleck was a wonderful talker and was always very well-groomed and close-shaven, with pressed shirts and pants—well cared for, in a word. He was terribly nearsighted and wore spectacles that wandered up his nose to his forehead and back. The caustic poverty and untruth of Stalin-era Poland did not seem to wear him down, and others found a refuge in Fleck's inner freedom. One assistant remembered a dinner at his Warsaw apartment, in a new block on Nowolipie Street. They ate rice with ham, jam, and black coffee with cookies. Ernestyna was an expert shopper—a treasured skill under communism—and had the gift of imparting charm to a very modest, simply furnished apartment.

Also, the Flecks had beautiful silver. Had it been saved, somehow, from the fires of Lwów, an heirloom preserved? No one knew, but it was evident that before the war they had lived in an elegant way.

At work, Fleck ignored the rules that could be ignored, never raised his voice, and never humiliated students or assistants. He sometimes allowed poor students to pass examinations because he could tell they were going to excel in other fields and didn't want to hold them back. Once he had a pregnant student in this category, and an aide said, "How could you pass that girl?" Fleck responded, "What, I should keep her here until she has the baby?"

While they were living in Warsaw, Fleck and his aide Danuta Borecka boarded a tram after a long wait, and the driver apologized, saying, "We don't have enough employees." Fleck responded jokingly, "Why don't you hire me?" The conductor sneered, "With that face? With a nose like that?" Fleck didn't say anything, but Borecka could tell he was offended. Fleck did not generally complain of anti-Semitism. Yet

Ludwik and Ernestyna Fleck (seated, right) with his lab members
in Warsaw before leaving for Israel, 1957.
(Courtesy of Archiv für Zeitgeschichte, Zurich.)

it was clearly a factor in postwar life. Certain colleagues—especially those who had survived long years of Soviet penal colonies in Siberia, and might have been anti-Semitic to begin with—were suspicious of Fleck because of his wartime work for Soviet-run institutions in Lwów. At a gathering of medical historians in Wrocław in the 1980s, the former Weigl assistant Zbigniew Stuchly said Fleck should never have worked in the camps with the Nazis—it would have been better to commit suicide instead. During the late 1950s, Fleck's theory of leukergy was attacked, apparently because it had received such a good reception from Polish scientists who were now out of favor, having been ousted in the de-Stalinization campaign of 1956.

When Balachowsky's accusations regarding Fleck's behavior at Buchenwald came to light in Poland, people began to claim that Fleck had been a Nazi collaborator. It was a terribly painful accusation for Fleck, naturally. Barbara Narbutowicz gathered testimony from his friends and brought this and other material to the health ministry, which took no action against Fleck.

By the time Fleck left Warsaw for Israel in 1957, a campaign against the remaining Jews in Poland was in full swing, tied to a backlash against the worst Stalin-era Polish leaders, some of whom happened to be Jewish. Fleck had long thought about moving to Israel; after suffering a heart attack while traveling in Brazil in 1956, Fleck told friends he would not live long and needed to bring his son and wife together. The anti-Semitic drive provided a context for Fleck's departure, but doesn't seem to have provoked it. Israeli embassy officials in Warsaw, who were trying to get as many Jews out as possible, told Fleck there was a job waiting for him at Hebrew University. When he arrived, it turned out to have been a false promise, but the Lwów "mafia" in Israel quickly found him another position, at the new state bacteriological laboratory at Ness Ziona.

From Israel, Fleck sent his friends in Poland oranges and fresh herbs, and told them the climate was wonderful. But he never learned to say a single phrase correctly in Hebrew, and could only write his last name—pei, lamed, khaf (פ, ל, ך). "Please do not think that we live here in paradise," he wrote a friend. "This country has many problems, both internal and external . . . porous, hostile, dangerous borders. A mixed, multilingual, heterogenous population, permanent arrival of new immigrants, often very poor, in need of being settled in somehow. Great idealism on the one hand, extremely selfish, demoralized bums on the other. Young people born in this country haven't a clue as to what all these foreign, incomprehensible newcomers want. In spite of all this we feel good. Just a pity I'm not younger. I might have been more useful."

Although Ness Ziona was and remains Israel's secret biological weapons lab, more routine microbiological research also went on there, and most, if not all, of Fleck's limited research work there seems to have fallen into this category, though he published a *Nature* paper concerning brucellosis that might have been related to biodefense. Israeli colleagues were impressed by Fleck's commitment to fighting disease. He helped lead a campaign against outbreaks of leptospirosis, a rare but severe bacterial disease, on poultry farms. "He introduced the idea that epidemiology could help anyone in the country who needed it," said David Ben-Nathan, a retired scientist who knew Fleck slightly. "He had suffered typhus, he knew what it was like. He had seen incredible suffering and helped people. And that was the main idea he brought to the institute, that we should be helping people, and it continued after he left."

One of Fleck's best friends in Israel was Aleksander Kohn, a Lwów-born virologist who came to Israel before the war and in 1955 founded a science parody magazine, the *Journal of Irreproducible Results*. Fleck and Kohn had many discussions about microbiology, the history of science, experimental technique, and Fleck's wartime life. "He looked upon the activities of the SS and the camp authorities as human weakness. Retrospectively, he felt that as an adult he'd become the victim of naughty children," Kohn said of his friend. As for Fleck's scientific ideas, the phenomenon of leukergy is discussed in more than 120 journal articles, but his disrupted work never developed enough to make a major impact.

In interviews he gave in the 1950s, Fleck spoke of a sequel to his monograph *Genesis and Development of a Scientific Fact*, but no manuscript was found in his papers. In the early 1960s, the physicist-philosopher Thomas Kuhn took Fleck's ideas a few steps forward. He absorbed the notion of the thought collective into what Kuhn called "normal science," and added the idea of the "paradigm shift"—the process by which facts once inconvenient to the thought collective suddenly break through and remold it. Social constructivists consider Fleck one of the fathers of their discipline, but—to use a Fleckian term—his ideas were more like a "proto idea" of social constructivism, a precursor with a different significance. The practitioners of this field belong to a different thought collective, one transformed by the loosening respect for all types of authority that began in the 1960s. While pointing out its social malleability, Fleck never relativized the value of science. He probably would have been drawn to some of the more cutting-edge biomedical disciplines such as epigenetics, which are acknowledged by the mainstream but less developed partly because of the lack of broad public awareness. He would glory in the free scientific exchanges of the Internet era. He was never a man of extremes.

Many documents from Ludwik Fleck's life disappeared in the upheavals of the 20th century. Letters and documents were lost during the war. Correspondence with the Lublin biochemist Józef Parnas was confiscated by the Polish secret police when Parnas got into trouble in 1968. When Fleck died, he left his papers in the care of his best friend in Israel, Markus Klingberg, deputy director of Ness Ziona. But Klingberg, a Pole who had been an epidemiologist in the Soviet Union during the war, was arrested by Israel's Shin Beth intelligence service in 1983 as a spy for the Soviet Union. Fleck's papers were seized and, Klingberg says, destroyed. Luckily, a German sociology student who had visited Klingberg a few years earlier had photocopied many of them.

Klingberg recruited at least two spies during his quarter-century espionage career in Israel, and some Fleck scholars have speculated that he might have recruited Fleck as well. After all, Fleck never concealed his gratitude toward the Communist inmates who saved his life at Buchenwald. But Klingberg denies such a thing occurred. "Fleck was at Auschwitz! After all he had been through, I didn't want to complicate his life," Klingberg told me in an interview in Paris, where he was allowed to join his daughter in 2003 after 20 years in Israeli prisons. It seems doubtful Fleck would have been a willing Soviet spy. He was a man of the left, but no great adept of Marxian versions of the truth. In any case, he did not live long in Israel.

In 1961, less than four years after his arrival, Fleck suffered a second heart attack, while undergoing treatment for malignant lymphoma, and died a few days later in hospital. Just before his death, he and Ernestyna had received a letter from the West German government announcing the approval of their *Wiedergutmachung*, a payment of several thousand dollars in compensation for their suffering at the hands of the Nazis. They cried with relief, for life was hard, and Fleck worried about Ernestyna's future.

His body was brought from their apartment to the institute, and the funeral cortege left from there to the cemetery nearby. Today, the institute's epidemiology building bears his name.

AFTERWORD

When the Germans abandoned Naples in October 1943 under American attack, they dynamited the water supply; a short time later, typhus broke out among the lice-ridden residents who had sought shelter from Allied bombing raids in the subterranean maze of old tunnels beneath the city. The invaders offered typhus vaccine to priests, medical workers, and a few others; the GIs themselves had all been vaccinated with the Cox vaccine, and not a single GI died of typhus. But the vaccine was employed sparsely in combating the Naples typhus epidemic. Most of the work was done with portable metal pesticide sprayers, the kind that suburban dads used to kill garden bugs. GIs sprayed three million lousy Neapolitans with DDT. The U.S. Typhus Commission had tested the powder against typhus in North Africa, where the sprayers came in handy to get at vermin in the robes of modest Muslim women, and they worked just as well in Italy. In the first typhus epidemic encountered by the U.S. Army in World War II, DDT, not vaccine, defeated the disease. The epidemic burned out in February.

The Allies came too late to stop typhus at Dachau, where the disease killed hundreds in April 1945, or at Bergen-Belsen. Anne Frank and her sister, Margot, were among 17,000 inmates of that camp who died of typhus in the final weeks of the war. Typhus killed hundreds of thousands of Jews and other inmates in hundreds of other concentration camps spread across Europe. These were the last major typhus epidemics in Europe. Everywhere the Allied troops went, they liberally dusted friend and foe with DDT. The miracle powder killed the vector and thus eliminated the spread of typhus, and practically eliminated the disease as a threat to mankind. The Cox vaccine surely had some efficacy, but it was never studied well enough for anyone to know how much. Giroud's vaccine protected thousands of French POWs, and, according to Weigl, 5–6 million individuals were vaccinated with his vaccine, including 1 million civilians. The figure is certainly exaggerated. How many of those who received his vaccine survived because of it? Did the vaccine change the course of history? Perhaps only in small ways. Some hundreds or thousands of concentration camp and ghetto inhabitants, having passed through a thousand deadly threats, may have never known whether it was vaccine or something else that ultimately saved them.

Weigl's lice live on. For 40 years, Henryk Mosing continued his master's research on rickettsial diseases, working for the Ukrainian health ministry at the building on Zelena (formerly Zielona) Street in Lwów, now Lviv, where Fleck had been the boss under the Soviets, IG Farben during the Nazi occupation. He used Weigl's methodology, but improved diagnostic tests and conducted research on the pathophysiology of louse-carried typhus. About 10,000 descendants of the Weigl lice first created in 1939 are kept alive, fed each day by lab workers for a small stipend. These lice are quite different from "wild" lice. Like the scientists who feed them, they have been entirely shaped by the culture of the laboratory.

Advances in knowledge on lice and typhus have come elsewhere in recent decades. In 1975, U.S. scientists discovered that in addition to humans and lice, the disease is carried by flying squirrels. About 40 percent of the flying squirrels in the southeastern United States are estimated to carry antibodies to *Rickettsia prowazekii*. The germ does not sicken the squirrels or their lice, however, and transmission to people is extremely rare—only a handful of squirrel-to-person transmissions have been documented over the past 35 years. Yet the easy carriage of the causative germ suggests that sometime in the past, the squirrel, or its lice or fleas, may have brought the disease into human circulation. This suggests that typhus was part of the Columbian exchange, traveling back to Europe with Spanish *conquistadores*.

Nowadays fewer people are lousy, and typhus, when it appears, can be controlled with a single dose of a common antibiotic like doxycycline. Typhus outbreaks still occur in a few cold, impoverished pockets of the world—in the Peruvian Andes, in the Atlas Mountains of North Africa, in Ethiopia, and even in Russia. In 1997, a deadly febrile disease broke out in Rwandan refugee camps in the highlands of Burundi, with 100,000 cases and 15,000 deaths. Its cause was mysterious until one of the victims, a Swiss nurse, was flown home sick and died of a hemorrhagic fever. An autopsy revealed she had typhus. A year later, typhus broke out in a Russian psychiatric hospital where the patients and nurses had not removed their clothes for months on account of freezing temperatures caused by a broken generator. Other rickettsial diseases continue to circulate more abundantly. About a million Asians each year sicken of chigger-borne scrub typhus, which is fatal in roughly 10 percent of diagnosed cases. Flea-carried murine typhus—*Rickettsia typhi*—strikes from time to time in the Americas; an outbreak hospitalized 23 people in 2008 in Austin, Texas. Tick-borne rickettsial diseases like Rocky Mountain spotted fever are still around.

Overall, classical typhus is so unusual that many of the world's top experts on *Rickettsia* have never seen it. David Walker, a leading rickettsial expert who works at the University of Texas at Galveston, arrived in an Andean village in Peru at the tail end of an epidemic once, and found families where both parents had died. "But I've never seen an actual case of the disease," he says. There are certainly many very poor people in cold places who still carry the typhus germ. The disease is much easier to control than it ever was. Yet in some remote corners of the globe, no doubt, it is only a single catastrophe away from returning.

Walker's department in Texas was established by Ludwik Anigstein, a Polish émigré whom Fleck visited during a trip to the United States in 1954. Looking through Anigstein's papers many years ago, Walker found the story of Fleck's urine-based typhus vaccine and decided to investigate. He looked for *Rickettsia prowazekii* antigens in the urine of guinea pigs and other animals infected with the disease, but never found any. "Maybe I was incompetent," he told me. "Or maybe it wasn't there."

Fleck's scientific discoveries have not held up in a significant way, but his ideas about how to think remain very relevant. In the wake of the Nazi intellectual disaster, which festered in a pseudo-Darwinian mishmash of Nietzsche, Spencer, and Galton, scientists like Fleck and Hirszfeld were looking for new scientific metaphors, different ways of interpreting science and sharing its culture with the public. Fleck understood that the vast complexity of biology left room for new concepts and approaches. He wanted scientific thought collectives to be open, democratic communities that allowed in different streams of interpretation.

I visited Lwów recently and wondered at the vitality of a place with so many shattered and buried dreams. I watched smartly dressed Ukrainian men and women—ambling, strolling, trotting purposefully through the streets. Tourist shops sold posters and T-shirts celebrating anti-Semitic Ukrainian nationalists, and the street that once was Sapiehy, a major thoroughfare in a mixed Polish-Jewish part of town, has been renamed for the Ukrainian nationalist (and anti-Semite) Stepan Bandera. These things were troubling, but it struck me there was no denying the continuity of urban life, each and every inhabitant focused on his or her own worries and plans. All cities, even the most peaceful, are built upon the bones of the dead. The lack of memorials to Lwów's Jewish and Polish forefathers is appalling, yet the dead are, in some sense, always forgotten. From time to time, we stop to share their stories and perhaps allow them to live through us on the streets they once walked. New thought collectives are born continually.

Everything passes, including greatness. "In my career," the geneticist Wacław Szybalski told me, "many things I did were great at the time, but now they are passé. I think that if Weigl had lived much longer he'd have been unhappy to be honored for things that no longer had value, things of the past." Yet the story of Weigl's lab, for the filmmaker Andrzej Żuławski, was just as important as the story of the great battles of the war. "Maybe Hiroshima beats it," he said. "But I'm alive because of those lice. I always say that the blood of those contaminated lice fills my veins, which accounts for part of my mad character." He keeps a small wooden louse cage that his father used in Weigl's laboratory. "All his life, my father carried this with him, and it was on his desk," Żuławski says. "It was very, very important to him. Now I have it on my desk."

There was no return to Lwów, but the exiles carried Lwów with them.

> . . . people bade goodbye
> without handkerchiefs, no tears, such a dry
> mouth, I won't see you anymore, so much death
> awaits you, why must every city
> become Jerusalem and every man a Jew,
> and now in a hurry just
> pack, always, each day,
> and go breathless, go to Lvov, after all
> it exists, quiet and pure as
> a peach. It is everywhere.

NOTES

ABBREVIATIONS

BA	Bundesarchiv
Fleck, *Denkstile*	Ludwik Fleck, *Denkstile und Tatsachen: Gesammelte Schriften und Zeugnisse*, ed. Sylwia Werner and Claus Zittel (Berlin: Suhrkamp, 2011)
Fleck, *Genesis*	Ludwik Fleck, *Genesis and Development of a Scientific Fact*, ed. Thaddeus J. Trenn and Robert K. Merton, trans. Fred Bradley and Thaddeus J. Trenn (Chicago: University of Chicago Press, 1981)
DGVG-Ding	Direction Générale des Victimes de la Guerre (Brussels), Ding correspondence, 1934–44
Hirszfeld, *One Life*	*The Story of One Life*, trans. and ed. Marta A. Balinska, ed. William H. Schneider (Rochester: University of Rochester Press, 2011)
HNOC, HLSL	Harvard Nuremberg Online Collection, Harvard Law School Library item no.
IHTP	Institut d'histoire du temps présent, Paris
IPN	Instytut Pamięci Narodowej (Institute of National Remembrance), Warsaw
IWM	Imperial War Museum
Kew	British National Archives–Kew Gardens
Kogon, *Hell*	Eugen Kogon, *The Theory and Practice of Hell: The German Concentration Camps and the System*

	behind Them, trans. Heinz Nordon (New York: Farrar, Straus, 1950)
LFZ	Ludwik Fleck Zentrum, in Archiv für Zeitgeschichte, Zurich
NA	National Archives, Washington, DC
PIA	Pasteur Institute Archives, Paris
RG	record group
Shoah Foundation	USC Shoah Foundation Institute for Visual History and Education
Szybalski, "Genius"	Wacław Szybalski, "The Genius of Rudolf Stefan Weigl (1883–1957), a Lvovian Microbe Hunter and Breeder," in *International Weigl Conference . . . Programme and Abstracts,* ed. R. Stoika et al. (Lviv: Sept. 11–14, 2003), accessed at http://www.lwow.home.pl/Weigl/in-memoriam.html
USHMM	United States Holocaust Memorial Museum
Weindling, *Epidemics*	Paul Weindling, *Epidemics and Genocide in Eastern Europe, 1890–1945* (New York: Oxford University Press, 2000)
YVA	Yad Vashem Archive

Preface

1 **The two insects:** B. P. Olds et al., "Comparison of the Transcriptional Profiles of Head and Body Lice," *Insect Molecular Biology* 21 (2012): 257–68; J. E. Light et al., "What's in a Name: The Taxonomic Status of Human Head and Body Lice," *Molecular and Phylogenetic Evolution* 47 (2008): 1203–16.

1 **Both nourish themselves:** Patrick A. Buxton, *The Louse* (London: Edward Arnold, 1947), 18–19.

2 **"They need particular temperature":** Olga Tarasyuk, interview with author, May 2011.

3 **While working as Weigl's assistant:** Fleck, *Genesis.*

3 **Thomas Kuhn, the famous:** Kuhn, *The Structure of Scientific Revolutions*, 50th anniversary ed. (Chicago: University of Chicago Press, 2012).

4 **Blood had always been:** *Goethe's Faust*, ed. E. J. Turner et al. (London: Rivington's, 1882), 79.

Notes

Introduction

7   **It is a hostile wind:** Shoah Foundation, 50467 Reidar Dittmann.

7   **In the winter:** Pierre D'Harcourt, *The Real Enemy* (London: Longman, 1967), 106.

8   **Their primary target, the Gustloff-II:** Stéphane Hessel, *Danse avec le siècle* (Paris: Éditions du Seuil, 1997), 83–91; David A. Hackett, trans. and ed., *The Buchenwald Report* (Boulder, CO: Westview Press, 1997), 305–6.

9   **The Nazis renamed the place:** *Buchenwald Concentration Camp, 1937–1945: A Guide to the Permanent Historical Exhibition* (Göttingen: Wallstein, 2005), 27.

9   **"Here Goethe rested":** Hackett, *Report*, 32.

9   **As the war dragged on:** Christian Pineau, *La simple vérité, 1940–1945* (Paris: René Julliard, 1960), 482.

10   **"Die, die you beast":** Ludwik Fleck, "The Goethe Oak," accessed at http://www.elmalpensante.com/index.php?doc=display_contenido&id=1025.

10   **The ideas and thinkers:** Fleck, *Genesis*, 133.

11   **Fleck, as a sociologist:** Fleck, "Wissenschaft und Umwelt," in Fleck, *Denkstile*, 329.

11   **Those in the thought collective of Block 50:** Fleck, "Problems of the Science of Science," in *Cognition and Fact: Materials on Ludwik Fleck*, ed. Robert S. Cohen and Thomas Schnelle (Dordrecht: D. Reidel, 1986), 113–25.

Chapter 1: Lice/War/Typhus/Madness

13   **The body louse evolved:** D. Raoult and V. Roux, "The Body Louse as a Vector of Reemerging Human Diseases," *Clinical Infectious Diseases* 29 (1999): 888–90.

13   **In one of the earliest:** Exodus 8:17.

13   **It has even been hypothesized:** J. W. Maunder, "The Appreciation of Lice," *Proceedings of the Royal Society of Medicine* 55 (1983): 1–31.

14   **An account of the 12th-century funeral:** Hans Zinsser, *Rats, Lice and History* (Boston: Little, Brown, 1935), 184–85.

14   **Typhus "will continue to break into":** Ibid., 301.

14   **At the end of World War I:** K. David Patterson, "Typhus and Its Control in Russia, 1870–1940," *Medical History* 37 (1993): 361–63.

15   **The Przemyśl complex:** S. Ansky, *The Enemy at His Pleasure: A Jour-*

ney through the Jewish Pale of Settlement during World War I, ed. and trans. Joachim Neugroschel (New York: Henry Holt, 2002), 123.

15 **It was retaken three:** Brigitte Biwald, *Von Helden und Krüppeln: Das österreichisch-ungarische Militärsanitätswesen im Ersten Weltkrieg* (Vienna: Haupt, 2002), 551. See also Franz Forstner, *Przemysl: Österreich-Ungarns bedeutendste Festung* (Vienna: Österreichischer Bundesverlag, 1987), 277–89.

15 **After passing his:** Szybalski, "Genius." See also Stefan Kryński, "Rudolf Weigl," at http://www.lwow.home.pl/Weigl/human.html.

16 **Thus Weigl was simultaneously:** Gabriel Brzęk, *Józef Nusbaum-Hilarowicz: Życie, prace, dzielo* (Lublin: Wydawn. Lubelskie, 1984), 95–96.

16 **While Fleck earned his doctorate:** Summaries of Fleck's life and work are contained in K. Leszczyńska, "Ludwik Fleck: A Forgotten Philosopher," in *Penser avec Fleck: Investigating a Life Studying Life Sciences*, ed. Johannes Fehr et al. (Zurich: Collegium Helveticum, 2009), 23–39; and Thomas Schnelle, "Microbiology and Philosophy of Science, Lwów and the German Holocaust: Stations of Life—Ludwik Fleck 1896–1961," in *Cognition and Fact—Materials on Ludwik Fleck*, ed. Robert S. Cohen and Thomas Schnelle (Dordrecht: L. Reidel, 1986), 3–38.

17 **Fleck liked to dress:** A. D. Peterkin, *One Thousand Beards: A Cultural History of Facial Hair* (Vancouver: Arsenal Pump Press, 2001), 180–81.

17 **At the other end:** Riza Durmaz et al., "Prevalence of Group A Streptococcal Carriers in Asymptomatic Children and Clonal Relatedness among Isolates in Malatya, Turkey," *Journal of Clinical Microbiology* 41 (2003): 5285.

17 **Although it generally kills:** Didier Raoult and Philippe Parola, eds., *Rickettsial Diseases* (New York: Informa Healthcare, 2007).

18 **More importantly, human:** Zinsser, *Rats*, xiii.

19 **"Tell me, Sir, where":** Accounts of the conversation circulated among Weigl's assistants and are recounted in, for example, Andrzej Wincewicz et al., "Rudolph Weigl, (1883–1957)—A Scientist in Poland in Wartime Plus Ration quam vis," *Journal of Medical Biography* 15 (2007): 112.

20 **"To watch him tenderly":** Hermann Eyer, "In Memoriam Rudolf Weigl," *Zentralblatt für Bakteriologie, Parasitenkunde, Infektionskrankheiten und Hygiene* 171 (1958): 379.

Notes

20 **To add to the confusion:** Jan O. Andersson and Siv G. E. Andersson, "A Century of Typhus, Lice and *Rickettsia,*" *Research in Microbiology* 151 (2000): 143–50.

21 **Typhus bacteria live:** Michael W. Gray, "Rickettsia, Typhus and the Mitochondrial Connection," *Nature* 396 (1998): 109–10.

21 **Sickness typically begins:** David Walker and Didier Raoult, "Typhus Group Rickettsioses," in *Tropical Infectious Diseases: Principles, Pathogens, and Practice,* ed. Richard L. Guerrant (Philadelphia: Churchill Livingstone 2006), 548–56; Walker and Raoult, "Rickettsia," in *Mandell, Douglas and Bennett's Principles and Practice of Infectious Diseases,* 7th ed. (Philadelphia: Churchill Livingstone, 2009), 252–53.

21 **At the peak of illness:** J. M. Mitchell et al., *Typhus Fever, with Special Reference to the Russian Epidemics* (London: Bailliere Tindall and Cox, 1922), 16–17.

23 **Another American, a volunteer:** Peter Englund, *The Beauty and the Sorrow: An Intimate History of the First World War* (New York: Knopf, 2011), 194, 215.

23 **"Although my memory":** Dmitri Pletnev, "Einige Bemerkungen über Flecktyphus nach Beobachtungen während der Moskauer Epidemie 1917–1920," *Zeitschrift für klinische Medizin* (1922): 285–301.

23 **Some hallucinatory motifs:** "Ergebnisse der zweiten Beratendentagung Ost 11/30–12/3, 1942," BA Militärdienst, RH1/23/246.

23 **American famine relief:** Bertrand M. Patenaude, *The Big Show in Bololand: The American Relief Expedition to Soviet Russia in the Famine of 1921* (Stanford: Stanford University Press, 2002), 239.

23 **The journalist John Reed:** "The Last Days with John Reed: A Letter from Louise Bryant; Moscow, Nov. 14, 1920," courtesy of a. nora claypoole [*sic*].

24 **Those who recovered:** Anton Chekhov, "Typhus," in *The Party and Other Stories* (Whitefish: Kessinger, 2004), 291–302.

24 **The Grand Army marched:** Linda Hohamdi and Didier Raoult, "Louse-Borne Epidemic Typhus," in *Rickettsial Diseases* (Boca Raton: CRC Press, 2007), 51–62.

24 **Napoleon's benighted soldiers:** Ludwik Gross, "How Charles Nicolle of the Pasteur Institute Discovered That Epidemic Typhus Is Transmitted by Lice," *Procceedings of the National Academy of Sciences* 93 (1996): 10539–40.

Notes

25 **The hygienic corps of the:** Arthur Allen, *Vaccine: The Controversial Story of Medicine's Greatest Lifesaver* (New York: Norton, 2007), 60.

25 **In Turkey, where the enfeebled:** Weindling, *Epidemics*, 105–12.

25 **"Russia," a Russian officer told:** Ansky, *Enemy*, 83.

26 **Even Aleksandra Piłsudska, wife of:** Aleksandra Piłsudska, *Piłsudski: A Biography by His Wife* (New York: Dodd, Mead, 1944), 243–44.

26 **In Erich Maria Remarque's:** Remarque, *All Quiet on the Western Front* (New York: Ballantine, 1987), 69.

26 **"The only way to obtain":** Accounts of lousiness among British World War I troops were collected by John Simkin at http://www.spartacus .schoolnet.co.uk/FWWlice.htm.

27 **Though no typhus:** Wilhelm His, *A German Doctor at the Front* (Berkeley: National Service, 1933), 75.

27 **It rarely killed:** Richard Strong et al., *Trench Fever: Report of Commission, Medical Research Committee, American Red Cross* (Oxford: Oxford University Press, 1918), 2–3.

28 **Typhus broke out in Serbia:** Hirszfeld, *One Life*, 32; Kenneth Maxcy, *Typhus Fever in the United States* (Baltimore: Williams and Wilkins, 1929), 5–6.

28 **Each laboratory had its:** W. Köhler, "Killed in Action: Microbiologists and Clinicans as Victims of Their Occupation. Part 1: Typhus," *International Journal of Medical Microbiology* 295 (2005): 133–40.

29 **Prowazek protected himself:** Jan. 21, 1915, letter in Austrian Kriegsarchiv, courtesy of Paul Weindling.

29 **Rocha Lima, who fell ill:** Burt Wolbach et al., *The Etiology and Pathology of Typhus: Being the Main Report on the Typhus Research Commission of the League of Red Cross Societies to Poland* (Cambridge: Harvard University Press, 1922), 116–20.

29 **One of the few typhus:** Hans Zinsser, *As I Remember Him: The Biography of R.S.* (Boston: Little, Brown, 1940), 220.

29 **Though evidence of louse transmission:** "Typhus Discovery Described in Paper," *New York Times*, May 17, 1914.

30 **Plotz and his vaccine:** "Mt. Sinai Aids Work on Serbian Typhus," *New York Times*, June 27, 1915.

30 **It was never exactly:** Mitchell et al., *Typhus Fever*, 38.

30 **In 1916, Edmund Weil:** R. Cruikshank, "The Weil-Felix Reaction in Typhus Fever," *Journal of Hygiene* 27 (1927): 64–69.

Notes

30 **Other physicians, including Nicolle:** Albert Besson, *Practical Bacteriology, Microbiology and Serum Therapy* (New York: Longmans, Green, 1913), 847; Maximiliano Ruiz Castañeda, *Escritos y entrevistas* (Toluca: FONAPAS, 1978), 41–43.

31 **To prove that a particular:** Victoria Harden, "Koch's Postulates and the Etiology of Rickettsial Diseases," *History of Medicine and Allied Sciences* 42 (1987): 277–95

32 **The early years of the Russian:** Francis McCullagh, *A Prisoner of the Reds: The Story of a British Officer Captured in Siberia* (London: John Murray, 1921), 31–35.

32 **"A minor setback":** Jerzy Borzęcki, *The Soviet-Polish Peace of 1921 and the Creation of Interwar Europe* (New Haven: Yale University Press, 2008), 15.

32 **"I do not suppose":** Carl Eric Bechhofer Roberts, *In Denikin's Russia and the Caucasus, 1919–1920* (New York: Collins, 1921), 109–10.

33 **The Polish leader Piłsudski:** W. Bruce Lincoln, *Red Victory: A History of the Russian Civil War* (New York: Simon and Schuster, 1989), 403.

33 **Kolchak . . . was routed and fled:** McCullagh, *Prisoner,* 6–35.

33 **"The sights which":** Ibid., 31, 6.

34 **"Comrades," Lenin told:** Vladimir I. Lenin, "Report of the All-Russia Central Executive Committee and the Council of People's Commissars, Dec. 5, 1919," in *Collected Works,* vol. 30 (Moscow: Progress Publishers, 1965), 228.

34 **A German Red Cross:** Peter Mühlens, "Die russische Hunger- und Seuchenkatastrophe in den Jahren 1921–1922," *Zeitschrift für Hygiene und Infektionskrankheiten* 99 (1923): 1–45.

34 **Mutual delousing:** Patenaude, *Bololand,* 236.

34 **Conditions were particularly awful:** Oct. 20, 1920, letter from Harry Plotz to Felix M. Warburg, Joint Distribution Committee, accessed at http://search.archives.jdc.org/multimedia/Documents/NY_AR1921/00022/NY_AR1921_00233.pdf#search='harry plotz kiev'.

35 **Typhus would have a transformative:** McCullagh, *Prisoner,* 321

35 **This demographic impact:** Churchill speech of Nov. 5, 1919, in *Churchill by Himself: The Definitive Collection of Quotations,* ed. Richard M. Langworth (New York: Public Affairs, 2008), 35.

36 **His method of inoculating:** Stanisława Woyciechowska, interview by Ryszard Wójcik, Jan. 7, 1979.

Notes

36 **Weigl had not been:** Weigl, "Der gegenwärtige Stand der Rickettsia-forschung," *Klinische Wochenschrift* 3 (1924): 1638.

37 **"His determination to pursue":** Zbigniew Stuchly, "Wspomnienia o Rudolfie Weiglu" (Recollections of Rudolf Weigl), accessed at http://lwow.home.pl/weigl/stuchly.html.

37 **Even as a student:** Brzęk, *Nusbaum-Hilarowicz*, 270–71.

37 **Weigl published the first:** *Beiträge zur Klinik der Infektionskrankheiten und Immunitätsforschung* 8 (1920): 353–76.

38 **He and a friend were:** Woyciechowska, interview with Wójcik, Jan. 7, 1979.

38 **Health disasters were:** H. L. Gilchrist, "Fighting Typhus Fever in Poland," *University of Cincinnati Medical Bulletin*, Feb. 1922.

38 **Herbert Hoover, whom Wilson:** Alfred E. Cornebise, *Typhus and Doughboys: The American Polish Typhus Relief Expedition, 1919–1921* (Newark: University of Delaware Press, 1982), 15–17; Zbigniew Karpus, *Russian and Ukrainian Prisoners of War and Internees Kept in Poland in 1918–1924* (Torun: Wydawn. Adam Marsalek, 2001), 51–53, 106–12.

39 **Perhaps because lice were:** Zinsser, *Rats*, 187. See also Gilchrist, "Fighting Typhus Fever."

39 **Children were always the first:** Cornebise, *Doughboys*, 63–70.

40 **"The Jews were said to be":** E. W. Goodall, "Typhus Fever in Poland, 1916 to 1919," *Proceedings of the Royal Society of Medicine* (Sect Epidemiol State Med) 13 (1920): 272–73.

40 **Several of the medical:** R. A. Bacot, "Details of the Technique Adopted in Following Weigl's Plan of Feeding Lice Infected with the Virus of Typhus Fever by Rectal Injection," *British Journal of Experimental Pathology* 3 (1922): 72–74.

Chapter 2: City on the Edge of Time

41 **Rajchman, an assimilated:** Marta Balinska, *For the Good of Humanity. Ludwik Rajchman, Medical Statesman* (Budapest: Central European University, 1998), 41–80.

41 **The health agency, known:** Hirszfeld, *One Life*, 66–72.

42 **Soon after Weigl moved to Lwów:** R. A. Bacot, "Details of the Technique Adopted in Following Weigl's Plan of Feeding Lice Infected with the Virus of Typhus Fever by Rectal Injection," *British Journal of Experimental Pathology* 3 (1922): 72–74.

Notes

42 **Like many successful:** Gabriel Brzęk, *Józef Nusbaum-Hilarowicz: Życie, prace, dzielo* (Life and works) (Lublin: Wydawn. Lubelskie, 1984), 55.

42 **She was beautiful:** Wiktor Weigl, "Wspomnienia o moim Ojcu" (Memories of my father), in *Zwyciężyć tyfus—Instytut Rudolfa Weigla we Lwowie. Dokumenty i wspomnienia,* ed. Zbigniewa Stuchly (Wrocław: Sudety, 2001), accessed at http://lwow.home.pl/weigl/turek.html.

43 **Weigl had many affairs:** Wacław Szybalski, interview with author, July 2011, Madison, WI; Stefan Kryński, "Kartki 29," in *Kartki ze wspomnień starego profesora* (Memories of an old professor) (Gdańsk: Akademia Medycyna, 2006), accessed at lwow.home.pl/weigl/krynski.html; Wójcik, interview with Tadeusz Brylak, Nov. 1980.

44 **The family spent:** Wiktor Weigl, "Moim Ojcu."

45 **Lwów was a city of rolling:** Sources examined for the history and geography of the city include Peter Faessler, Thomas Held, and Dirk Sawitzki, eds., *Lemberg-Lwow-Lviv: Eine Stadt im Schnittpunkt europäischer Kulturen* (Cologne: Boehlau, 1993); Ernst Hofbauer, *Verwehte Spuren: Von Lemberg bis Czernowitz: Ein Trummerfeld der Erinnerungen* (Vienna: Ibera, 2004); Hermann Simon, Irene Stratenwerth, and Ronald Hinrichs, eds., *Lemberg: Eine Reise nach Europa* (Berlin: Links Verlag, 2007); John Czaplicka, ed., *Lviv: A City in the Crosscurrents of Culture* (Cambridge: Harvard University Press, 2005); Roman Kaluźa, *Through a Reporter's Eyes: The Life of Stefan Banach* (Boston: Birkhäuser, 1996).

46 **After independence, one:** Simon et al., eds, *Lemberg,* 132.

47 **"We were like ants":** Stanisław Lem, *Highcastle: A Remembrance,* trans. Michael Kandel (New York: Harcourt, Brace, 1995), 133–34.

47 **"We were proud of our city":** Wacław Szybalski, interview with author, July 2011.

47 **Nostalgia for Lwów:** Lem, *Highcastle.*

48 **The city boasted 21:** Andrzej Bonusiak, *Lwów w latach 1918–1939* (Lwów in the years 1918–1939) (Rzeszów: Wydawnictwo Wyższej Szkoly Pedagogicznej, 2000).

49 **It became the most popular:** Olena Onufriv, "Tylko we Lwowie," in Simon et al., eds., *Lemberg,* 214–16.

49 **Every middle-class Lwowite:** Adam B. Ulam, *Understanding the Cold War: A Historian's Personal Reflections,* 2d ed. (New Brunswick: Transaction Publishers, 2002), 4–6.

Notes

49 **"Most of my colleagues":** Leopold Infeld, *Quest: The Evolution of a Scientist* (New York: Doubleday, 1941), 151–52.

50 **Their favorite was at first:** Adam Ulam, *Cold War*, 6–8; Kaluża, *Reporter's Eyes*, 42–48; S. M. Ulam, *Adventures of a Mathematician* (New York: Scribner's, 1976), 50–52.

50 **The Lwów school:** Material on the mathematics circles in Lwów and the story of the Scottish Book are taken from Kaluża, *Reporter's Eyes*; Adam Ulam, *Understanding*; S. M. Ulam, *Adventures*; Mark Kac, *Enigmas of Chance: An Autobiography* (New York: Harper & Row, 1985); and Hugo Steinhaus, *Wspomnienia i zapiski* (Memoirs and jottings) (Wrocław: ATUTA, 2010); S. Ulam, "John Von Neumann," accessed at http://www.ams.org/journals/bull/1958-64-03/S0002-9904-1958-10189-5/S0002-9904-1958-10189-5.pdf; Mark Kac, "Hugo Steinhaus: A Reminiscence and a Tribute," accessed at http://poncelet.math.nthu.edu.tw/disk5/js/biography/steinhaus.pdf.

50 **Steinhaus owed this distinction:** Kac, *Enigmas*, 34–35.

51 **Some of these discussions:** S. M. Ulam, *Adventures*, 34.

53 **The Roma had a character:** Józef Wittlin, *Mein Lemberg*, trans. Klaus Staemmler (Frankfurt: Suhrkamp, 1994), 125.

53 **Of course, daily existence:** Infeld, *Quest*, 86–149.

53 **Ludwik Fleck took a:** K. Leszczyńska, "Ludwik Fleck: A Forgotten Philosopher," in *Penser avec Fleck: Investigating a Life Studying Life Sciences*, ed. Johannes Fehr et al. (Zurich: Collegium Helveticum, 2009), 25–27.

54 **His best friend was the:** Fleck and Olgierd Krukowski, "Oddzialywanie skóry w durze plamistym na odmieńca X₁₉ i prątki pokrwene" (Impact of typhus on X₁₉ and related mycobacteria) *Medycyna doświadczalna i spoleczna* 1 (1923): 98.

54 **A few of his contemporaries:** Thomas Schnelle, "Microbiology and Philosophy of Science, Lwów and the German Holocaust: Stations of a Life—Ludwik Fleck 1896–1961," in *Cognition and Fact—Materials on Ludwik Fleck*, ed. Robert S. Cohen and Thomas Schnelle (Dordrecht: L. Reidel, 1986), 17.

54 **The mathematician Steinhaus:** See Leszczyńska, "Fleck," 27; Fleck, "Briefe an Steinhaus," in *Denkstile*, 387–92; and Steinhaus, *Wspomnienia*, 159–60.

54 **But Fleck was notoriously:** Fleck, *Denkstile*, 548n; recollections of Fleck at "Lublin, Pamięć Miejsca," pamiecmiejsca.tnn.pl.

Notes

54 **Fleck also had regular:** Leszczyńska, "Fleck," 5–18; Eugene Ziskind and Esther Somerfield-Ziskind, "In Memoriam: Peter Jacob Frostig, M.D., 1896–1959," *American Journal of Psychiatry* 117 (1960): 479–80.

55 **In 1927, Fleck, then:** "Transkript des Briefes von Prof. Dr. Joseph Parnas," LFZ, Unterlagen und Notizen von Thomas Schnelle: Allgemeine Korrespondenz und Notizen von Thomas Schnelle 1978–1993, 4.1, Signatur 97.

55 **Upon returning:** Wiktor Weigl, "Moim Ojcu."

55 **The son of an attorney:** Sylwia Werner, "Von Ameisen, Affen und Menschen: Betrachtung fremder Welten im Lemberg der Zwischenkriegszeit," presentation at "Lemberg/L'viv/Lwów um 1900—Aktuelle Forschungen," Herder Institut, Marburg, Germany, April 18, 2012; Werner, "Ludwik Fleck und die Wissenskultur der Lemberger Moderne," in *Vérité, Widerstand, Development: At Work with / Arbeiten mit / Travailler avec Ludwik Fleck,* ed. Rainer Egloff and Johannes Fehr (Zurich: Collegium Helveticum, 2011), 59–65.

55 **Fleck's early work:** Weigl, "Über das Wesen und die Form des Fleckfiebererregers," *Bulletin international de l'Académie Polonaise des Sciences et des Lettres* (1930): 6–21.

56 **By the mid-1920s:** Victoria A. Harden, "Koch's Postulates and the Etiology of Rickettsial Diseases," *Journal of the History of Medicine and Allied Sciences* 42 (1987): 277–95.

56 **He tested the formulation:** "Die Methoden der aktiven Fleckfieber-Immunisierung," *Bulletin international de l'Académie Polonaise des Sciences et des Lettres* (1930): 25–59.

56 **Shortly after returning from Vienna:** "Über einige spezifische Merkmale des ärztlichen Denkens," in Fleck, *Denkstile,* 41–51.

58 **Fleck's work was "probably":** Thomas Schnelle, "Ludwik Fleck and the Influence of the Philosophy of Lwów," in *Cognition and Fact,* 231.

58 **This had to be so:** Fleck, *Genesis,* 47.

59 **Fleck's work anticipated:** Christian Bonah, "'Experimental Rage': The Development of Medical Ethics and the Genesis of Scientific Facts. Ludwik Fleck: An Answer to the Crisis of Modern Medicine in Interwar Germany?," *Social History of Medicine* 15 (2002): 187–207.

59 **"We used to think that science":** Fleck, *Denkstile,* 333.

59 **In debunking the view:** Ilana Löwy, "Ways of Seeing: Ludwik Fleck and Polish Debates on the Perception of Reality, 1890–1947," *Studies in History and Philosophy of Science* 39 (2008): 382.

Notes

60 **Witkiewicz, who had seen:** Polish Philosophy Page, "Stanislaw I. Witkiewicz," at http://web.archive.org/web/20080209021703/http://www.fmag.unict.it/~polphil/PolPhil/Witk/Witk.html#anchor602777.

Chapter 3: The Louse Feeders

61 **The public health authorities:** Weigl, "Über das Wesen und die Form des Fleckfiebererregers," *Bulletin international de l'Académie Polonaise des Sciences et des Lettres* (1930): 1–21; Weigl, "Die Methoden der aktiven Fleckfieber-Immunisierung," ibid., 55.

62 **The first human:** Hélène Sparrow and Charles Nicolle, "Application au cobaye et à l'homme de la méthode de vaccination contre le typhus exanthématique par emploi d'intestins phéniqués de poux," *Archives de l'Institut Pasteur de Tunis* 21 (1932): 25–31.

62 **The labs in Lwów:** Ludwig Anigstein, "Professor Hélène Sparrow-Germa, MD (1891–1970): A Pioneer in World Health," *Polish Medical Science and History Bulletin* 14 (1971): 100–101; R. Debré, "Helena Sparrow: A Polish and French Scientist," *Materia medica Polona* 11 (1979): 79–82.

62 **The trial was a success:** Sparrow and Nicolle, "Application," 29–30.

62 **Rozalia, to everyone's:** Weigl, "Faits d'observation et expériences demontrant l'efficacité du vaccine à rickettsia pour la prévention du typhus," *Archives de l'Institut Pasteur de Tunis* 22 (1933): 318.

63 **One of the visitors:** See, e.g., Jean Lindenmann, "Women Scientists in Typhus Research during the First Half of the Twentieth Century," *Gesnerus* 62 (2005): 261–63.

63 **She was not alone:** Hans Zinsser, *Rats, Lice and History* (Boston: Little, Brown, 1935), 167.

64 **Sikora's personality was:** Hilda Sikora, "Rickettsienfund bei Katzenstaupe," *Zeitschrift für Hygiene und Infektionskrankheiten* 125 (1944): 530–32; "Hilda Sikora," *Angewandte Parasitologie* 11 (1970): 63; "Hilda Sikora," *Angewandte Parasitologie* 19 (1978): 64.

64 **Over a decade:** Weigl, "Über das Wesen," 1–4.

64 **Disregarding the accident:** "Death of Edmund Weil," *Journal of the American Medical Association* 79 (1922): 229.

64 **"A young person was attracted":** Władysław Wolff, "O Profesorze Weiglu i 'Weiglowcach,'" accessed at www.Lwow.com.pl/Wolff/Wolff.html.

65 **The visitor, crossing:** Wiktor Weigl, "Wspomnienia o moim Ojcu"

Notes

(Memories of my father), in *Zwyciężyć tyfus—Instytut Rudolfa Weigla we Lwowie. Dokumenty i wspomnienia*, ed. Zbigniewa Stuchly (Wrocław: Sudety, 2001), accessed at http://lwow.home.pl/weigl/turek.html; G. B. Mathews, "Of Lice and Men," *Twentieth Century* 33 (1943): 227–35.

66 **Elated by the vaccine's:** Jan Rutten, "La mortalité des missionaires avant et après l'emploi du vaccin de Weigl," *Varia Dossiers de la Commission Synodale à Pekin* (1936): 183; Rutten to Weigl, May 9, 1948, at Lwow.com.pl/weigl/rutten.html.

66 **Peter Radło, a Hygiene:** Piotr Radło, "Observations sur la vaccination contre le typhus exanthématique par le vaccin de Weigl," *Archives de l'Institut Pasteur de Tunis* 26 (1937): 667–70.

66 **By 1938, about 68,000 Poles:** Hermann Eyer, "Die durch Läuse übertragbaren Infektionskrankheiten und ihre Bekämpfung," *Medizinische Welt* 14 (1940): 261–64.

66 **Overall, the number:** Friedrich Hansen, *Biologische Kriegsführung im Dritten Reich* (Frankfurt: Campus, 1993), 88–92.

66 **"When he came to our":** Wolff, "O Profesorze."

67 **If there were no:** Wolff, interview with Ryszard Wójcik, March 1984; untitled films in possession of Krystyna Weigl-Albert.

67 **Louse feces in these:** Jan Starzyk, interview with Wójcik, Dec. 1980.

67 **The hygiene teams found:** Hirszfeld, *One Life*, 210–11.

68 **A device known as:** Stefan Kryński et al., "Weigl's Method of Intrarectal Inoculation of Lice in Production of Typhus Vaccine and Experimental Works with *Rickettsia Prowazeki*," *Annales Academiae Medicae Gedanensis* 4 (1974): 19–51; Szybalski, "Genius."

69 **The first vaccination series:** Weigl, "Methoden," 52–55.

69 **The total was reduced:** Eyer, "Rudolf Weigl und die aetiologische Fleckfieberbekämpfung," *Münchener medizinische Wochenschrift* 109 (1967): 2185–91.

69 **By the end of 1933:** Adam Finkel, "Über das zytologische Blutbild bei läusefütternden Personen," *Archiv für Innere Medizin* 25 (1934): 49–66.

69 **"Lice feeders must be":** Sparrow and Maurice Huet, "L'élevage du pou au laboratoire," *Archives de l'Institut Pasteur de Tunis* 37 (1960): 323.

70 **They also had to be:** Finkel, "Blutbild," 64.

70 **Weigl was an idiosyncratic:** Hermann Eyer, "In Memoriam Rudolf Weigl," *Zentralblatt für Bakteriologie, Parasitenkunde, Infektionskrankheiten und Hygiene* 171 (1958): 358.

Notes

71 **He neither requested nor received:** Wacław Szybalski, interview with author, July 2011; Wiktor Weigl, "Moim Ojcu."

71 **If he used the formal:** Stefan Kryński, "Kartki 29," in *Kartki ze wspomnień starego profesora* (Gdańsk: Akademia Medycyna 2006), accessed at lwow.home.pl/weigl/krynski.html.

71 **By then, however, Weigl:** Kryński, "Kartki 29."

72 **As they walked away:** Wiktor Weigl, "Moim Ojcu."

72 **The rooms were painted gold:** Kryński, "Kartki 29."

72 **Armed Poles repaid:** Svjatoslav Pacholkiv, "Zwischen Einbeziehung und Ausgrenzung: Die Juden in Lemberg, 1918–1919," in Alexandra Binnenkade et al., *Vertraut und fremd zugleich: Jüdisch-christliche Nachbarschaften in Warschau—Lengnau—Lemberg* (Cologne: Böhlau, 2009), 172–87.

73 **In Lwów, the delegates found:** Arthur L. Goodhart, *Poland and the Minority Races* (New York: Brentano's, 1920), 24, 142.

74 **Yet the demonstrations were:** Arnon Rubin, *Against All Odds: Facing the Holocaust* (Tel Aviv: Tel Aviv University Press, 2009), 6–10.

74 **People in the procession:** Antony Polonsky, "A Failed Pogrom," in *The Jews of Poland between the Two World Wars*, ed. Yisrael Gutman et al. (Hanover, NH: Brandeis University Press, 1989), 110–19.

74 **But Banach's wife:** Frank Stiffel, interview with author, Jan. 2011; S. M. Ulam, *Adventures of a Mathematician* (New York: Scribner's, 1976), 107.

74 **For Jews, the interwar:** "Interwar Poland: Good for the Jews or Bad for the Jews?," in *The Jews in Poland*, ed. C. Abramsky et al. (Oxford: Basil Blackwell, 1986), 130–39.

74 **Few Jews joined:** Jim Tuck, *Engine of Mischief: An Analytical Biography of Karl Radek* (New York: Greenwood Press, 1988), 3–6.

75 **Up until the start:** Pacholkiv, "Zwischen," 163.

75 **Eleven of 600:** Samuel Drix, *Witness to Annihilation: Surviving the Holocaust: A Memoir* (Washington: Brassey's, 1994), 10–11.

75 **When a nationalist student:** Mark Kac, *Enigmas of Chance: An Autobiography* (New York: Harper & Row, 1985), 34–35.

75 **Yet it is worth:** Christoph Mick, *Kriegserfahrungen in einer multiethnischen Stadt: Lemberg 1914–1947* (Wiesbaden: Harrassowitz, 2011), 411.

75 **The growth of institutional:** Władysław Kunicki-Goldfinger to Schnelle, Aug. 27, 1978, LFZ, Unterlagen und Notizen von Thomas Schnelle; Signatur 100, Fragebogen von Thomas Schnelle, 1978–1979.

Notes

76 **Fleck joined an:** YVA, Concentration Camp Inmates Questionnaire, "Ludwik Fleck, #4934," courtesy of International Tracing Service.

76 **His lectures:** "Records of the Jewish Medical Society, Lwow," USHMM, RG 31.04M, reel 5, various frames.

76 **In 1933, Fleck sent:** Ludwik Fleck, "Briefwechsel mit Moritz Schlick," in *Denkstile*, 561–65.

77 **"Poor Poland, you are":** Wiktor Chajes, *Semper Fidelis: Pamiętnik Polaka wyznania mojzeszowego z lat 1926–1939* (Kraków: Księgarnia Akademicka, 1997), entry for Jan. 12, 1936.

77 **"In that case," Weigl said:** Wiktor Weigl, "Moim Ojcu."

77 **They set up their first:** Ibid.; Szybalski, interview with author.

Chapter 4: The Nazi Doctors and the Shape of Things to Come

79 **In 1935, the year:** BA Signatur DY55/28 Gesch-Z 4/0955; Genzken, "SS Personal Bericht," Signatur VBS286 Archivsignatur 6400041387.

80 **When Himmler heard:** Weindling, *Epidemics*, 338.

80 *Obersturmbannführer* **Joachim:** Florian Bruns, "Staatshygiene und Menschenversuche: Das medizinische Ethos des Joachim Mrugowsky," in *Medizinethik im Nationalsozialismus: Entwicklungen und Protagonisten in Berlin (1939–1945)* (Stuttgart: Franz Steiner, 2009), 135.

80 **Ding spent the better:** Some of Ding's correspondence, 1934–44, is contained in a cache of personal and work-related papers brought to Belgium by a Buchenwald survivor that were found in 2009 at the archive of the Direction Générale des Victimes de la Guerre, in Brussels. This collection is hereafter cited as DGVG-Ding.

81 **Schuler, she told:** Else Braun to Oberstlt. Knothe, Nov. 28, 1915, DGVG-Ding, in brown folder, "personal"; Otto Petersohn to Ding, Dec. 20, 1942.

81 **The Dings adopted Erwin:** BA Signatur DY55/28 Gesch–Z 4/0955.

81 **That year he also:** BA VBS286 Archivsignatur 6400041387; Ding to Lotte Barthel, July 4, 1942, DGVG-Ding, green folder, "Dr. Ding, SS Untersturmführer."

82 **Erwin Ding, 23 years old:** BA Signatur DY55/28 Gesch–Z 4/0955; BA VBS283 Archivsignatur 6055002585.

82 **The Schuler family:** Ding to Genzken, May 12, 1939, DGVG-Ding, in unmarked box.

82 **"From my earliest school days":** Feb. 2, 1938, letter to Interior Minis-

Notes

try, DGVG-Ding, in green folder, "Dr. Ding, SS Untersturmführer." Also see Sept. 3, 1939, letter to Maria von Schuler in same folder.

83 **"Poland was literally sick":** Hirszfeld, *One Life*, 160.

83 **Fleck's friend Chwistek:** "Ein interesantes Buch," in Fleck, *Denkstile*, 606.

84 **In Lwów, Fleck was:** "Records of the Jewish Medical Society," USHMM 31.040M, reel 5.

84 **"The deeper in the woods":** Ilana Löwy, *Medical Acts and Medical Facts: The Polish Tradition of Practice-Grounded Reflections on Medicine and Science* (Kraków: Académie Polonaise des Sciences, 2000), 106.

85 **No matter how science:** Fleck, *Genesis*, 45, 54, 101–2.

85 **Thought collectives consisted of:** Ibid., 105–6.

85 **"The special mood of the thought":** Ibid., 107–8.

86 **Democracy, he said:** Ibid., 105–6.

86 **The parent, meanwhile, would simply:** Ibid., 113–15.

87 **"Every communication and, indeed":** Ibid.

87 **This was more likely:** Ibid., 92–93; Fleck, "Über den Begriff der Art in der Bakteriologie," in *Denkstile*, 91–125.

88 **This was despite the fact:** This and subsequent quotations are from Fleck, *Genesis*, 59–61, 41, 68–77.

89 **Fleck was not the only:** See "Max von Pettenkofer, 1818–1901," at http://ocp.hul.harvard.edu/contagion/vonpettenkofer.html.

89 **But whereas the social:** Weindling, *Epidemics*, 201–3.

89 **Zeiss called his field:** Thomas Werther, "Fleckfieberforschung im Deutschen Reich 1914–1945: Untersuchungen zur Beziehung zwischen Wissenschaft, Industrie und Politik unter besonderer Berücksichtigung der IG Farben" (PhD diss., Marburg University, 2004), 74–75, accessed at http://archiv.ub.uni-Marburg.de/diss/z2008/0157/pdf/dtw.pdf.

90 *Geomedizin* **was exactly:** Fleck, "Wissenschaft und Umwelt" in *Denkstile*, 329.

90 **In a 1944 journal:** Joachim Mrugowsky, "Beiträge zur Geomedizin: Das Seuchenspektrum," *Zeitschrift für Hygiene und Infektions-Krankheiten* (1944): 679–91.

90 **He was responsible for:** Weindling, *Epidemics*, 248–50.

90 **In Eastern Europe, with its:** Werther, "Fleckfieberforschung," 74–75.

Notes

90 **The louse, carrier of:** Alex Bein, "The Jewish Parasite," *Leo Baeck Institute Yearbook* 9 (1964): 3–5, 19–37.

90 **"The Jew is a bacillus":** Werther, "Fleckfieberforschung," 107.

91 **The belief that certain cultures:** Fleck, *Genesis*, 23.

91 *Geomedizin*'s **suggestion that Jews:** Hugh Raffles, "Jews, Lice, and History," *Public Culture* 19 (2007), accessed at publicculture.org/articles/view/19/3/jews-lice-and-history/.

91 **And there were legitimate cultural:** Hirszfeld, *One Life*, xxxii.

92 **Typhus wasn't an inevitable:** Friedrich Hansen, *Biologische Kriegsführung im Dritten Reich* (Frankfurt: Campus, 1993).

93 **He was also a lifelong:** Peter Eyer, interview with author, May 2011; Peter Eyer, personal communications.

93 **As a faculty member:** "Lebenslauf," Dec. 27, 1943, BA-Berlin, VBS1 Signatur 1020025603.

93 **He praised the anti-Semitic:** Hermann Eyer, "Die Gesundheitspflege in ländlichen Grenzgebieten," *Deutsches Ärzteblatt* 68 (1938): 441–45.

94 **After the annexation:** Peter Eyer, interview with author.

49 **Although Germany had been:** Weindling, *Epidemics*, 331–32, 247; Weindling, "Between Bacteriology and Virology: The Development of Typhus Vaccines between the First and Second World Wars," *History and Philosophy of the Life Sciences* 17 (1995): 81–90.

94 **In 1938–39, physicians there:** See http://www.pasteur.fr/infosci/archives/e_blao.html.

94 **At the outbreak of war:** M. Ruiz Castañeda, "Experimental Pneumonia Produced by Typhus Rickettsiae," *American Journal of Pathology* 15 (1939): 467–76; Paul Giroud and Jean Jadin, "Conceptions actuelles concernant les rickettsioses et leur vaccinations," *Annales de la Société Belge de Médicine Tropicale* 3 (1961): 193–206.

94 **Scientists in the United States:** Herald Cox, "Epidemic and Endemic Typhus," *Public Health Reports* 55 (1940): 110–15; Cox, "Use of Yolk Sac of Developing Chick Embryo as Medium for Growing Rickettsiae of Rocky Mountain Spotted Fever and Typhus Groups," ibid., 53 (1938): 2241–49; Joseph Sadusk, "The Immunization of Troops with Typhus Vaccine and the Characteristics of Typhus in Immunized Individuals," *Yale Journal of Medicine and Biology* 21 (1949): 211–32.

95 **In April 1939:** Peter Eyer, interview with author.

95 **At the Red Sea port:** Giacomo Mariani, "La lotta contra le rickettsiosi

umani nell' AOI Africa orientale italiana," *Opere per l'organizzazione civile in Africa orientale italiana* (1939): 59–66; Mariani, "Vaccinazioni contro il tifo esantematico eseguite nel 1938 sull'altipiano etiopico con il vaccino Weigl," *Annali d'igiene* 7 (1939): 316–22.

95 **The same month:** Blanc to Pistoni, PIA, BLA2.

96 **He urged that the Weigl:** Richard Pankhurst, "Some Notes for a History of Typhus in Ethiopia" (unpublished 1975 manuscript at Library of Congress), 1–27.

97 **The possibility of a Nobel Prize:** Kryński, "Cards 28," *Reminiscences of an Old Professor,* accessed at lwow.home.pl/weigl/krynski.html; Wójcik, "Pakt z diablem" (Pact with the devil), *Przegląd tygodniowy* 4 (1994).

97 **The university authorized a paid:** Weigl papers in Lviv University archive, courtesy of Prof. Rostyslav Stoika.

98 **The Italians reported:** Pankhurst, "Notes," 10.

Chapter 5: War and Epidemics

99 **For his state medical:** Erwin Ding, "Der Pavor nocturnus bei Kindern" (MD diss., University of Leipzig, 1937).

99 **With his pregnant wife:** Kogon, *Hell,* 265.

99 **The SS leader Theodor:** Richard J. Evans, *The Third Reich in Power* (New York: Penguin, 2005), 81–90.

100 **The first glimpse:** See, e.g., Ernst von Salomon, *The Captive: The Story of an Unknown Political Prisoner* (London: Weidenfeld and Nicolson, 1961), 108; Shoah Foundation (all testimonies were viewed at the USHMM), 50467 Reidar Dittmann.

100 **"You took off your shoes":** Shoah Foundation, 17900 Horace Hecht.

101 **Prisoners often puzzled:** Waitz, "Auschwitz I Stammlager," in *De l'université aux camps de concentration: Témoignages strasbourgeois* (Paris: Les Belles Lettres, 1947), 438–39.

101 **Himmler himself stated:** See Hugh Raffles, "Jews, Lice, and History," accessed at http://publicculture.org/articles/view/19/3/jews-lice-and-history/.

102 **"A few weeks in Buchenwald":** Walter Poller, *Medical Block, Buchenwald: The Personal Testimony of Inmate 996, Block 36* (Secaucus, NJ: Lyle Stuart, 1960), 244–45, 212, 159–60.

103 **Ding ably carried:** Judith Hahn, *Grawitz, Genzken, Gebhardt: Drei Karrieren im Sanitätsdienst der SS* (Münster: Klemm & Oelschläger, 2008), 161.

Notes

104 **The Reverend Paul Schneider:** Poller, *Medical Block*, 201–6; 106–8; 246–49.

105 **Meanwhile, Ding pressed on:** Ding to Genzken, May 12, 1939, DGVG-Ding.

105 **Three months later:** "Lebenslauf," July 15, 1939, DGVG-Ding.

106 **On November 6, two weeks:** Jochen August, *Sonderaktion Krakau: Die Verhaftung der Krakauer Wissenschaftler am 6. November 1939* (Hamburg: Hamburger Edition, 1997).

106 **Around this same time:** Sworn statements in support of Hermann Eyer's release from British POW status, addressed to University of Bonn Medical School Dean Erich von Redwitz, in possession of Peter Eyer: Ortrud Kristen, Nov. 19, 1946; Robert Kudicke, Jan. 15, 1946; Hermann Eyer, Nov. 8, 1946.

107 **Years later, there:** Memo dated 10-06-1976 from Kraków to Warsaw, IPN Files, Przybyłkiewicz, 9828/II IPN KR 010/9659 Tome I Secret; also personnel file from Sept. 1953 in same folder.

107 **Eyer had been told:** Eyer to Redwitz, Nov. 8, 1946; H. Eyer, "Die Fleckfieberprophylaxe der deutschen Wehrmacht im 2. Weltkrieg," *Wehrmedizin und Wehrpharmazie* (1979): 56–61.

108 **He delivered his first batch:** BA-Freiburg, RH12/23/archivsignatur357; Eyer, Tätigkeitsbericht des Instituts für Fleckfieber- und Virusforschung, 6/1–7/31, 1940.

108 **In an accompanying pamphlet:** Ibid., "Fleckfieber Merkblatt für Soldaten."

108 **Jews, he wrote:** Ibid.; Eyer, "Die durch Läuse übertragbaren Infektionskranheiten und ihre Bekämpfung," *Die Medizinische Welt* 14 (1940): 261–64.

108 **In Polish cities:** Shoah Foundation, 14797 Lusia Hornstein.

109 **The Nazi bombardment:** Stefan Szende, *The Promise Hitler Kept* (New York: Roy, 1945), 1516; Frank Stiffel, *The Tale of the Ring: A Kaddish* (New York: Bantam Books, 1984), 13; Shoah Foundation, 7394 Alex Redner.

109 **The Eastern Trade Fair:** Wacław Szybalski, personal communication.

109 **Three weeks of bombing:** Christoph Mick, *Kriegserfahrungen in einer multiethnischen Stadt: Lemberg 1914–1947* (Wiesbaden: Harrassowitz, 2011), 420.

110 **For many sophisticated:** Szende, *Promise*, 19, 29–31; Stiffel, *Tale*, 30; Shoah Foundation, Hornstein; Kurt I. Lewin, *A Journey through Illu-*

sions (Santa Barbara: Fithian Press, 1994), 28–30; Szybalksi testimony; Karolina Lanckoronska, "Mut ist angeboren," in Hermann Simon, Irene Stratenwerth, and Ronald Hinrichs, eds., *Lemberg: Eine Reise nach Europa* (Berlin: Links Verlag, 2007), 70–73.

110 **Although the invasion was tragic:** Hornstein interview, USHHM; Zygfryd Atlas, *Just One Life* (Caulfield North: Rocham, 1999), 20.

111 **In a kindergarten:** Mali Karl, *Escape a la vida* (Lima: Pueblo Libre, 1989), 36; Nava Ruda, *Zum ewigen Andenken: Erinnerung eines Mädchens aus dem Ghetto Lwows, 1928–1999* (Konstanz: Hartung-Gorre, 2000), 10.

111 **The majority of the 22,000:** Dov Levin, *The Lesser of Two Evils: Eastern European Jewry under Soviet Rule, 1939–1941*, trans. Naftali Greenwood (Philadelphia: Jewish Publication Society, 1995), 50, 196–97.

112 **They lifted bans or limits:** Omer Bartov, *Erased: Vanishing Traces of Jewish Galicia in Present-Day Ukraine* (Princeton: Princeton University Press, 2007), 36–37.

112 **More than 50,000:** Szende, *Promise*, 19–20.

112 **In November, there was a plebiscite:** Ibid., 20–28.

112 **Many died there:** Ibid., 11–36.

112 **Many young Jews:** Stiffel, *Tale*, 30.

113 **Lwów's mathematicians:** S. M. Ulam, *Adventures of a Mathematician* (New York: Scribner's, 1976), 133.

113 **The Soviets must have considered:** YVA, International Tracing Service Documentation, Military Government of Germany, Concentration Camp Inmates Questionnaire: Ludwig [*sic*] Fleck, Inmate 4934; Ilana Löwy, "Ways of Seeing: Ludwik Fleck and Polish Debates on the Perception of Reality, 1890–1947," *Studies in History and Philosophy of Science* 39 (2008): 377; Thomas Schnelle, "Microbiology and Philosophy of Science, Lwów and the German Holocaust: Stations of a Life—Ludwik Fleck 1896–1961," in *Cognition and Fact—Materials on Ludwik Fleck*, ed. Robert S. Cohen and Thomas Schnelle (Dordrecht: L. Reidel, 1986), 18.

113 **Whatever the case:** K. Leszczyńska, "Ludwik Fleck: A Forgotten Philosopher," in *Penser avec Fleck: Investigating a Life Studying Life Sciences*, ed. Johannes Fehr et al. (Zurich: Collegium Helveticum, 2009), 27; Franciszek Groer, "Nachruf auf Ludwik Fleck," in *Denkstile*, 643.

113 **Fleck's rise:** "Ludwig Fleck und die innere Emigration," in *Emigrantenschicksale: Einfluss der jüdischen Emigranten auf Sozialpolitik und Wis-*

Notes

senschaft in den Aufnahmeländern, ed. Albrecht Scholz and Caris-Petra Heidel (Frankfurt: Mabuse, 2004), 351; Plonka-Syroka, personal communication with author, May 2013.

114 **Intriguingly, this deal:** Weindling, *Epidemics*, 333–34.

114 **It is not clear whether Weigl:** Harvard University Archives, Papers of Hans Zinsser, box 2, folder 61.

114 **In February 1940:** M. Sahaydakovskyy and S. Hnatush; "Professor Rudolf Weigl: A Life Dedicated to Science and Humanity" (publication information unknown), accessed at www.lwow.com.pl/weigl/Weigl-ukr.html; Szybalski, interview with author; Danuta Nespiak, "Profesor Rudolf Weigl był Polakiem z wyboru" (Professor Rudolf Weigl—Pole by choice), in *Semper Fidelis* (Wrocław: Towarzystwo Miłośników Lwowa i Kresów Południowo Wschodnich, 1994).

114 **During the 22 months:** Sahaydakovskyy and Hnatush, "Life Dedicated."

115 **"Never join the party":** Szybalski, interview with author.

115 **A Ukrainian professor:** Stefan Kryński, "Kartki 36," in *Kartki ze wspomnień starego profesora*, accessed at lwow.home.pl/weigl/krynski .html.

115 **The Soviet scientist:** Szybalski interview; Sahaydakovskyy and Hnatush, "Life Dedicated."

116 **In the first days:** Mick, *Kriegserfahrungen*, 443.

116 **"They had a good sense":** Szybalski, interview with author.

117 **He was very sage:** Wiktor Weigl, "Wspomnienia o moim Ojcu," in *Zwyciężyć tyfus—Instytut Rudolfa Weigla we Lwowie. Dokumenty i wspomnienia*, ed. Zbigniewa Stuchly (Wrocław: Sudety, 2001), accessed at http://lwow.home.pl/weigl/turek.html.

118 **A November 25, 1939, memorandum:** Christopher R. Browning, "Genocide and Public Health: German Doctors and Polish Jews, 1939–1941," in *The Path to Genocide: Essays on Launching the Final Solution* (Cambridge: Cambridge University Press, 1992), 146.

119 **As the historian Christopher:** Ibid., 149.

119 **Jost Walbaum, a longtime:** Ibid., 149–53.

119 **By the time the Nazis:** Friedrich Hansen, *Biologische Kriegsführung im Dritten Reich* (Frankfurt: Campus, 1993), 93–95.

119 **The German occupation doctors:** Browning, "Genocide," 146–52.

119 **In 1941, the German:** Janina Hera, "*Konkurs na sztukę antytyfusową*," *Pamiętnik teatralny* 46 (1997): 399–409.

Notes

120 **The German medical contribution:** *Kampf den Seuchen: Deutscher Ärzte-Einsatz im Osten* (Kraków: Deutscher Osten, 1941).

120 **One writer, Joseph Ruppert:** Joseph Ruppert, "Die Seucheninsel Polen," in *Kampf*, 25–26.

120 **A Dr. Werner Kroll wrote:** Werner Kroll, "Die Gesundheitskammer im Generalgouvernement," in *Kampf*, 113.

120 **What was needed:** Kroll, "Jüdische 'Wunderdoktoren' Entlarvt!," in *Kampf*, 125–27.

121 **By cramming half a million:** Hirszfeld, *One Life*, 211.

121 **The overcrowded, underfed:** Marcel Reich-Ranicki, *Mein Leben* (Munich: Deutscher Taschenbuch Verlag, 1999), 212.

121 **"There were even lice":** Władysław Szpilman, *The Pianist: The Extraordinary True Story of One Man's Survival in Warsaw, 1939–1945* (New York: Picador, 1999). See also Charles G. Roland, *Courage under Siege* (New York: Oxford University Press, 1992), 121–53.

121 **Over the next 18 months:** Tomasz Cieszyński, "Dzieło Rudolfa Weigla ofiarowane ludzkości i Polsce" (Rudolf Weigl's work for Poland and humanity), 1994, accessed at http://www.lwow.home.pl/weigl/cieszyn ski.html.

121 **Such scientific missions:** Jerzy Chmielowski, interview with author, May 2011.

121 **They delivered it to Ludwik:** Hirszfeld, *One Life*, 267–69; Szybalski, "Genius"; Andrzej Wincewicz et al., "Rudolph Weigl, (1883–1957)—A Scientist in Poland in Wartime Plus Ration quam vis," *Journal of Medical Biography* 15 (2007): 114.

122 **The German doctors Robert:** M. Gromulska, "Państwowy Zakład Higieny w czasie wojny w latach 1939–1944," *Przeglad epidemiologiczny* 62 (2008): 719–25.

122 **Kudicke's private secretary:** Edward Zubik and Irena Gamota, interview with Ryszard Wójcik, 1983.

122 **In Lwów, the Jewish survivor:** Frank Stiffel, interview with author, Jan. 2011.

122 **"Dr Weigel, an outstanding bacteriologist":** Szpilman, *Pianist*, 17–18.

123 **Although the ghetto inhabitants:** Raoul Hilberg et al., eds., *The Warsaw Diary of Adam Czerniakow: Prelude to Doom*, trans. Stanislaw Staron et al. (New York: Stein and Day, 1979), 324.

124 **On July 20, 1941, the mathematician:** Hugo Steinhaus, *Wspomnienia i zapiski* (Wrocław: ATUTA, 2010), 202–3.

Notes

Chapter 6: Parasites

125 **The Soviets abandoned:** Christoph Mick, *Kriegserfahrungen in einer multiethnischen Stadt: Lemberg 1914–1947* (Wiesbaden: Harrassowitz, 2011), 512–13.

125 **The Nazis, meanwhile:** Teresa Prekerowa, "Relief Council for the Jews, 1942–1945," in *The Jews in Poland*, ed. Chimen Abramsky et al. (Oxford: Basil Blackwell, 1986), 163–67; Józef Garliński, *Poland in the Second World War* (New York: Hippocrene Books, 1985), 45.

125 **In the weeks before:** Shoah Foundation, Hornstein.

126 **The Lwów chapter:** Mick, *Kriegserfahrungen*, 520–22.

126 **There he used his skills:** Yitzhak Sternberg, *Under Assumed Identity* (Israel: Ghetto Fighters Press, 1986), 49, 83–87.

126 **More than 130,000 Jews died:** Mick, *Kriegserfahrungen*, 500–501; David Kahane, *Lvov Ghetto Diary*, trans. Jerzy Michalowicz (Amherst: University of Massachusetts Press, 1990), 141–42; Stefan Szende, *The Promise Hitler Kept* (New York: Roy, 1945), 50–51; Eliyahu Yones, *Smoke in the Sand: The Jews of Lvov in the War Years 1939–1945* (New York: Gefen, 2004); Leon W. Wells, *The Death Brigade* (New York: Macmillan, 1963), 123–24.

127 **Before abandoning Lwów for:** Dieter Schenk, *Der Lemberger Professorenmord und der Holocaust in Ostgalizien* (Bonn: Dietz, 2007), 86–87; Eva Szybalski, *Lwów, a City Lost: Memories of a Cherished Childhood*, 130. The book is a first-person account by Szybalski's father, Stanisław, brother of Wacław Szybalski. It is published online at home.comcast.net/~julsta/szybalski.pdf.

127 **A Russian chauffeur who:** Wacław Szybalski, interview with author, July 2011.

127 **Amid plundering and arson:** Schenk, *Professorenmord*, 88–91; Lala Fischman and Steven Weingartner, *Lala's Story: A Memoir of the Holocaust* (Evanston: Northwestern University Press, 1997), 90–91.

127 **Clocks set to:** Mick, *Kriegserfahrungen*, 493.

128 **The first posters went:** Frank Stiffel, *The Tale of the Ring: A Kaddish* (New York: Bantam Books, 1984), 38–39.

128 **The morning of July 3:** Schenk, *Professorenmord*, 11.

128 **"I heard the howling":** Benedikt Friedman, *Ich träumte von Brot und Büchern* (Vienna: Promedia, 1992), 52–53.

128 **Staff at Weigl's . . . "spectacle of death":** Kryński, "Kartki 37," accessed at http://lwow.home.pl/weigl/krynski.html.

Notes

130 **A firing squad:** Shoah Foundation, Hornstein; Kurt I. Lewin, *A Journey through Illusions* (Santa Barbara: Fithian Press, 1994), 30–37; Marek Redner, *Recollections on the Life and Martyrdom of Jewish Medical Doctors in the Lvov Ghetto* (n.p.: A. S. Redner, 2003), 8.

130 **A Nazi propaganda film:** Deutsche Wochenschau, "Lvov/Lemberg massacre; Jews arrested," USHMM, RG-60.0267, tape 201; "Jews beaten, bodies, crowd (Lwow)," RG-60.0328, tape 202B.

130 **"We could see them beating Jews":** Shoah Foundation, Alex Redner.

130 **The number of Jews murdered:** Mick, *Kriegserfahrungen*, 500; Szende, *Promise*, 50–51. See also John-Paul Himka, "The Lviv Pogrom of 1941: The Germans, Ukrainian Nationalists and the Carnival Crowd," in *Canadian Slavonic Papers* 8 (2011): 209–42.

131 **The last order:** Kahane, *Diary*, 10, 32; Janina Opieńska-Blauth, *Drogi i spotkania* (Lublin: Wydawnictwo Lubelskie, 1979), 78–81; Tom Gross, "Goodbye, Golden Rose," *Guardian* (Manchester), Sept. 2, 2011, accessed at http://www.guardian.co.uk/commentisfree/2011/sep/02/ukraine-holocaust-denial-lviv/print.

131 **Hitler had ordered:** Schenk, *Professorenmord*, 114.

131 **Things went differently:** Ibid., 121–24.

132 **The pediatrician Franciszek Groër:** Ibid., 124.

132 **The dapper playwright:** Wanda Ladniewska-Blankenheim, YVA, testimony O.3/3118.

133 **The crime scene was:** Jadwiga Złotorzycka, "Professor Rudolf Weigl (1883–1957) i jego instytut," in *Analecta: Studia i materiały z dziejów nauki* 1 (1998), accessed at http://lwow.home.pl/analecta.html.

133 **Two days later:** Peter Eyer, personal communication with author, Aug. 2011.

134 **"Anyone who witnesses":** Weigl, "Pokoj," in *Zwyciężyć tyfus: Instytut Rudolfa Weigla we Lwowie: Dokumenty i wspomnienia,* ed. Zbigniew Stuchly (Wrocław: Sudety, 2001).

134 **German officials who:** Andrzej Wincewicz et al., "Rudolph Weigl, (1883–1957)—A Scientist in Poland in Wartime Plus Ration quam vis," *Journal of Medical Biography* 15 (2007), 111; Rafal Bubnicki, "Polak z krwi I kości" (Pole of flesh and blood), *Rzeczpospolita* 11 (1994).

135 **When the Nazi invasion began:** Zbigniew Stuchly, Nov. 17, 1994, tape recording by Halina Shepherd of Radio Lviv, courtesy of National Museum Przemyśl.

136 **The institute grew quickly:** Szybalksi, "Genius"; Stanisława Woyciechowska, interview with Ryszard Wójik; Josef Daniels to Erich von
Redwitz, Nov. 19, 1946, courtesy of Peter Eyer.

136 **How many Poles:** Tomasz Cieszyński, "Dzieło Rudolfa Weigla ofiarowane ludzkości i Polsce" (Rudolf Weigl's work for Poland and humanity), 1994, accessed at http://www.lwow.home.pl/weigl/cieszynski.html;
list of feeders at http://www.lwow.home.pl/weigl/weiglowcy.html.

136 **The Poles working:** Szybalski, interview with author.

137 **The regime created a ghetto:** Lviv Oblast Records, USHHM,
RGM31.003; Report from Katzman to Frank; Selected records from the
Lviv State Oblast Archive, RGM 31.001m Vermerk Betrifft: Judenum-
siedlung; "Umsiedlung Lemberger Juden," *Lemberger Zeitung*, Nov. 15,
1941.

137 **The Nazis also set up a:** Wells, *Brigade*, 87–93; Stanisław Lenz, testimony Yad Vashem 0.3/3093. B. 1902; Samuel Drix, *Witness to Annihilation: Surviving the Holocaust: A Memoir* (Washington: Brassey's, 1994),
73–88; Kahane, *Diary*, 51; Philip Friedman, *Roads to Extinction: Essays
on the Holocaust*, ed. Ada June Friedman (New York: Jewish Publications Society, 1980), 303–12.

137 **For a while, doctors:** Redner, *Recollections*, 9.

138 **This was probably:** Dieter Pohl, *Nationalsozialistische Judenverfol-
gung in Ostgalizien 1941–1944: Organisation und Durchführung eines
staatlichen Massenverbrechens* (Munich: Oldenbourg, 1996), 115.

138 **The Nazis confiscated:** Kahane, *Diary*, 21, 70–71; Drix, *Witness*, 34.

138 **Fleck spent the first:** Fleck, "Untersuchungen zum Flecktyphus im
Lemberger Ghetto in den Jahren 1941–1942," in *Denkstile*, 505–14;
Fleck, "Wie wir den Anti-Flecktyphus-Impfstoff im Lemberger Ghetto
hergestellt haben," ibid., 521–25.

139 **It may have been:** Szybalski, interview with author. Fleck is on a
partial list of wartime Weigl employees compiled in 1994 by Tomasz
Cieszyński, Zbigniew Stuchly, Andrzej Nespiak, and Jan Starzyk, accessible at www.lwow.com.pl/weigl/weiglowcy.html.

139 **However, Fleck did meet:** Fleck, "Untersuchungen," 505, 510.

139 **A while later:** Transkript der Handschrift von Frau Dr. Seeman, LFZ,
Unterlagen und Notizen von Thomas Schnelle, Allgemeine Korrespondenz und Notizen von TS 1978–1993, 4.1 Signatur 97; also Shoah Foundation, 26409 Bruno Seeman.

Notes

139 **As the weather turned:** Fleck, "Badania nad tyfusem plamistym w getcie lwowskim" (Typhus research in the Lwów ghetto), Yad Vashem, Marek Dworzecki-Archiv, Sign p. 10/File 52, 366–72.

139 **The outbreak began:** Redner, *Recollections*, 30.

140 **That winter:** Fleck, "Badania," 368.

140 **The pattern had been:** Martin Broszat, *Nationalsozialistische Polenpolitik, 1939–1945* (Frankfurt: Fischer, 1965), 218; Christopher Browning, "Genocide and Public Health: German Doctors and Polish Jews, 1939–1941," in *The Path to Genocide: Essays on Launching the Final Solution* (Cambridge: Cambridge University Press, 1992), 146–61; Wilhelm Hagen, "Krieg, Hunger und Pestilenz in Warschau, 1939–43," *Gesundheitswesen und Desinfektion* 8 (1973): 115.

140 **Frank, the German:** Browning, "Genocide," 154–58.

141 **Hirszfeld, who had been:** Hirszfeld, *One Life*, 182, 191, 252, 259.

141 **On April 24, 1943:** Himmler's speech is reprinted in U.S. Office of Chief of Counsel for the Prosecution of Axis Criminality, *Nazi Conspiracy and Aggression*, vol. 4 (Washington, DC: GPO, 1946), 574.

Chapter 7: The Fantastic Laboratory of Dr. Weigl

143 **"Its base was the farmers":** Mirosław Żuławski, "Weiglówka" {Memories of Lwów), accessed at lwow.com.pl/weiglowka.html.

144 **The tens of millions:** Stefan Kryński et al., "Weigl's Method of Intrarectal Inoculation of Lice in Production of Typhus Vaccine and Experimental Works with *Rickettsia prowazeki*," *Annales Academiae Medicae Gedanensis* 4 (1974): 21.

145 **Vaccine production began:** Ibid., 20–51; Szybalski, "Genius."

149 **The Gestapo arrested:** Mark Kac, *Enigmas of Chance: An Autobiography* (New York: Harper & Row, 1985), 85–89.

150 **Marek Zakrzewski:** Zakrzewski, "Wspomnienia karmiciela wszy" (Memories of a louse feeder), accessed at http://lwow.home.pl/semper/wszy1.html.

150 **Banach usually sat:** Szybalski, interview with author.

152 **Szybalski was particularly:** Szybalski, interview with John J. Greczek, March 2007.

152 **Banach's love for Lwów:** Kac, *Enigmas*, 82.

153 **Szybalski's father, Stefan:** Eva Szybalski, *Lwów, a City Lost: Memories of a Cherished Childhood*, 144, accessed at http://www.yumpu.com/en/document/view/3143300/lwow-a-city-lost-comcastnet.

Notes

153 **In 1943, the Germans:** Martin Broszat, *Nationalsozialistische Polenpolitik, 1939–1945* (Frankfurt: Fischer, 1965), 169–73.

154 **The Nazis were proving:** Benedikt Friedman; *Ich träumte von Brot und Büchern: Zornige Erinnerungen eines jüdischen Österreichers* (Vienna: Promedia, 1992), 90; David Kahane, *Lvov Ghetto Diary*, trans. Jerzy Michalowicz (Amherst: University of Massachusetts Press, 1990), 77.

154 **Wherever Jews went:** Kahane, *Diary*, 70–71.

154 **"The brutality of these":** Kogon, *Hell*, 20.

154 **In the hospital:** Fleck, "Wie wir den Anti-Flecktyphus-Impfstoff im Lemberger Ghetto hergestellt haben," in *Denkstile*, 521–23; Fleck, "Untersuchungen zum Flecktyphus im Lemberger Ghetto in den Jahren 1941–1942," ibid., 505–14.

155 **When relatives got:** Marek Redner, *Recollections on the Life and Martyrdom of Jewish Medical Doctors in the Lvov Ghetto* (n.p.: A. S. Redner, 2003), 31–36.

155 **Samuel Drix:** Drix, *Witness to Annihilation: Surviving the Holocaust: A Memoir* (Washington: Brassey's, 1994), 93–95.

156 **Most of the survivors:** Hirszfeld, *One Life*, 221.

156 **After the war:** "Briefwechsel mit Ludwik Hirszfeld," in *Denkstile*, 574.

158 **News of Fleck's vaccine:** Tadeusz Kielanowski, "My Meetings with Ludwick Fleck in Lublin during the Years 1945–1950," *Kwartalnik historii nauki i technologi* (1983): 582–85.

158 **At the Weigl:** Anna Fabiańska, "Wspomnienia preparatorki" (Memories of a *preparatorki*), accessed at http://lwow.home.pl/weigl/fabianska.html.

159 **Wacław Szybalski's brother:** Eva Szybalski, *Lwów*, 177–79.

159 **"We were one big":** Żuławski, "Weiglówka."

160 **Disease was a permanent:** Alfred Jahn, *Z Kleparowa w świat szeroki* (Wrocław: Zakład Narodowy im. Ossolińskich, 1991), 120–24.

160 **For others, illness:** Żuławski, "Weiglówka."

160 **Stan Szybalski contracted:** Eva Szybalski, *Lwów*, 183.

161 **Weigl's senior staff:** Kryński, "Weigl's method," 19–23.

161 **The Lwów institute teemed:** Jerzy Gardynik, "Rola Instytutu Tyfusowego profesora Rudolfa Weigla w osłonie ludności i konspiracji polskiej w okupowanym Lwowie," accessed at http://lwow.home.pl/semper/tyfus1.html.

162 **Louse feeding was an effective:** Żuławski, "Weiglówka"; Gardynik,

Notes

"Rola"; Elżbieta Lonc and Grażyna Gościniak, "Professors Rudolf Weigl and Ludwik Hirszfeld—In the Meanders of History," *Annals of Parasitology* 58, no. 4 (2012): 194–95.

162 **Jerzy Sokolowski, who:** Sokolowski, interview with Ryszard Wójcik.

163 **The junior Weigl:** Szybalski, interview with author, July 2011.

163 **German officers who:** Josef Daniels to Erich von Redwitz, Nov. 19, 1946; Annemarie Rohrmann to Redwitz, Nov. 16, 1946.

163 **But while it:** Eva Szybalski, *Lwów*, 175–76.

164 **Eyer permitted Weigl:** Starzyk, interview with Wójcik.

165 **Others falsified bills:** Peter Eyer, interview with author, May 2011.

165 **Eyer's deputy in Lwów:** Krystyna Karlicz, interview with Ryszard Wójcik, June 1979.

165 **Six of his lab assistants:** Peter Eyer, interview with author.

166 **For all that:** Testimony by Sofia Bujwid, Aug. 1, 1958, IPN, Przybyłkiewicz file. See also Przybyłkiewicz, "Origin and Development of the Chair of Microbiology at Cracow University," *Polski tygodnik lekarski* 20 (1965): 288–89.

166 **The Jews of Kraków:** *Kampf den Seuchen: Deutscher Ärzte-Einsatz im Osten* (Kraków: Deutscher Osten, 1941), 154–55; BA-Ludwigsburg BA-Mil B162/9805, Eyer Statement in Walbaum Trial, Feb. 9, 1967.

166 **In early 1944:** Jehuda L. Stein, *Jüdische Ärzte und das jüdische Gesundheitswesen in Krakau vom 15. Jahrhundert bis zur Schoáh* (Konstanz: Hartung-Gorre, 2006), 39–56.

167 **After showing the factory owner:** Fleck, "Untersuchungen," 508–9.

167 **A week later:** Fleck, "Wie wir," 522.

168 **A number of Polish and:** Janina Opieńska-Blauth, *Drogi i spotkania* (Paths and encounters) (Lublin: Wydawnictwo Lubelskie, 1979), 78–81.

168 **Finally, after:** Fleck, "Untersuchungen," 505–11; Fleck, "Bericht über den Aufenthalt im KZ Auschwitz," in *Denkstile*, 490n.

168 **The "vaccine trial" came at:** Ernst Hofbauer, *Verwehte Spuren: Von Lemberg bis Czernowitz: Ein Trümmerfeld der Erinnerungen* (Vienna: Ibera, 2004), 69.

169 **A few days later:** Fleck, "Untersuchungen," 510; Redner, *Recollections*, 16–18.

169 **In all, about 50,000:** Mick, *Kriegserfahrungen*, 501.

169 **After the SS:** "Vernehmung Medizinalrat Dr. Wilhelm Dopheide," Sept. 22, 1950, BA-Ludwigsburg, B162/2102 ARZ294/1959, Kolonko u.a.

Notes

169 **Kurzrock survived for:** Fleck, "Bericht," 490n. An alternative version of Kurzrock's fate is in Drix, *Witness*, 155.

170 **On September 7, the ghetto:** Stefan Szende, *The Promise Hitler Kept* (New York: Roy, 1945), 83.

170 **Dr. Franciszek Groër, Fleck's:** Fleck and F. Lille, "Serologic Studies in Blood Cells: On the Serologic Differentiation on White Blood Cells," *American Review of Soviet Medicine* 3 (1945): 174.

170 **One afternoon in 1942:** Tomasz Cieszyński, "Dzieło Rudolfa Weigla ofiarowane ludzkości i Polsce" (Rudolf Weigl's work for Poland and humanity), 1994, accessed at http://www.lwow.home.pl/weigl/cieszyn ski.html.

170 **Smuggling vaccine to Jews:** Danuta Nespiak, "Profesor Rudolf Weigl był Polakiem z wyboru" (Professor Rudolf Weigl—Pole by choice), in *Semper Fidelis* (Wrocław: Towarzystwo Miłośników Lwowa i Kresów Południowo Wschodnich, 1994); M. Sahaydakovskyy and S. Hnatush; "Professor Rudolf Weigl: A Life Dedicated to Science and Humanity" (publication information unknown), accessed at www.lwow.com.pl/ weigl/Weigl-ukr.html.

171 **Moser later recalled:** Meisel to Eyer, Jan. 12, 1957; Meisel to Eyer, Jan. 20, 1972; Eyer to Moser, March 28, 1972; Moser to Eyer, April 4, 1972. All letters are in the possession of Peter Eyer.

171 **Halina Ogrodzińska, an activist:** Ellen Land-Weber, *To Save a Life: Stories of Holocaust Rescue* (Urbana: University of Illinois Press, 2000), accessed at http://onlinebooks.library.upenn.edu/webbin/book/ lookupid?key=olbp21571.

172 **Felicja ended up:** Shoah Foundation, 45624 Felicja Mikolajczyk-Meisela; Wójcik interview with Henryk Meisel, Felicja Mikolajczyk-Meisela, Edward Mikolajczyk, June 1979; Danuta Rymkiwicz, "In Memory of Professor Henryk Meisel," Dec. 15, 1981-dated typescript, courtesy of Peter Eyer; Meisel to Eyer, Jan. 12, 1957; Meisel to Eyer, March 20, 1972.

172 **"Every physician was":** Interview with Peter Eyer.

172 **"I estimate quite conservatively":** Eyer to K. W. Jötten, March 13, 1957, courtesy of Peter Eyer.

173 **The historical record:** Wilhelm Hagen to Bernhard Kläß, Dec. 16, 1975. Peter Eyer possesses numerous letters from German, Polish, and Ukrainian character witnesses for Eyer's wartime behavior, and the dozens of testimonies from Weigl laboratory employees support this.

173 **The Gestapo, many of:** 1972 Testimony by former Gestapo officers Herbert Hamann, Rudolf Koerner, and Kurt Heinmneyer in BA-Ludwigsburg, BA-Mil B162/9805; Az 119f Js 2/72 Beschuldigte Prof Dr Hermann Eyer, u.a.

173 **After the war, these same:** Peter Eyer, interview with author.

173 **Eyer may have been anti-Semitic:** Hirszfeld, *One Life*, 338–39.

174 **Of all the German:** Jakob Gilson, "Prof. Dr. Ludwig Hirszfeld" (PhD diss., University of Munich, 1965), courtesy of Peter Eyer.

174 **The Nazis tolerated Weigl:** The original article, "Das Fleckfieber überwunden; ein Sieg deutscher Wissenschaft in zwölfter Stunde," *Marburger Zeitung*, April 15, 1943, is BA, R55/20912, as are responses from various officials to the error it contains: April 21, 1943, letter to the *Reichsregierung* press department from Behring; June 16, 1943, RKI, Institut fur Infektionskrankheiten, to Kurzel, press department in Reichministerium für Volksaufklärung und Propaganda; Haubold memo, June 26, 1943; Rundspruch, Propaganda Ministry.

174 **In December 1942:** Emil-von-Behring-Bibliothek/Arbeitsstelle für Geschichte der Medizin der Philipps-Universität Marburg, Signatur 230; Weindling, *Epidemics*, 236–37.

176 **Weigl was invited:** Andrzej Wincewicz et al., "Rudolph Weigl, (1883–1957)—A Scientist in Poland in Wartime Plus Ration quam vis," *Journal of Medical Biography* 15 (2007): 113.

176 **Weigl did, however:** Maria Kordas and Paul Weindling, "Working and Payment Conditions at Production of the Vaccine against Typhus by the Weigl Method in Lvov during World War II," 1–8, courtesy of Paul Weindling.

176 **Much as the Germans:** Haas to Weigl, Sept. 10, 1942, Emil-von-Behring-Bibliothek/Arbeitsstelle für Geschichte der Medizin der Philipps-Universität Marburg, Signatur 230.

177 **On February 4, 1943:** Anna Seeman letter to Schnelle, April 2, 1980, in LFZ, 4.4 Unterlagen und Notizen v. Thomas Schnelle, "Fragebogen," Signatur 100; Fleck, "Wie wir" 522; Shoah Foundation, 26409 Bruno Seeman.

177 **The SS man shrugged:** Shoah Foundation, Bruno Seeman; "Testimony of SEMAN Bronislaw, Concentration Camp #103739, provided June 21, 1945," in Zydowski Institut Historyczny (Jewish Historical Institute, Warsaw).

178 **Thus Fleck saved:** Anna Seeman letter to Schnelle; Shoah Foundation, Bruno Seeman.

Chapter 8: Armies of Winter

180 **Hitler's war plan:** Omer Bartov, *The Eastern Front, 1941–45: German Troops and the Barbarisation of Warfare* (New York: St. Martin's, 1986); Bartov, *Hitler's Army: Soldiers, Nazis and War in the Third Reich* (New York: Oxford University Press, 1992), 19–24, 67–77; NA, RG238, ser. M1019, roll 47, Mrugowsky, 1190–94.

181 **To be sure, Germany:** Arthur Felix memo dated Nov. 17, 1941, Kew, FD1/6614; Herbert D. Chalke, "Typhus: Experiences in the Central Mediterranean Force," *British Medical Journal* 1, no. 4460 (June 29, 1946): 979.

181 **By the time:** Arthur Allen, *Vaccine: The Controversial Story of Medicine's Greatest Lifesaver* (New York: Norton, 2007), 141.

18 **But there was:** Bartov, *Eastern Front*, 112.

181 **The number of *living*:** Nuremberg Doctors' Trial, Doc 105, letter from President of the Land Labor Office, Dortmund, Feb. 3, 1942, to the Ruhr Coal Mining District Group.

181 **Thousands more:** Bartov, *Eastern Front*, 107.

182 **Like German soldiers:** Catherine Merridale, *Ivan's War: Life and Death in the Red Army, 1939–1945* (New York: Metropolitan, 2006), 56–59.

182 **In their propaganda:** Leo Gruliow, *Soviet War-Time Medicine* (New York: Russian War Relief, 1942).

182 **At a POW camp:** Büttner to Renoldi, Jan. 18, 1942, BA-Freiburg, RH12/23/187 Büttner, Anlage 5.

183 **On a single day:** Büttner, "Erfahrungsbericht 1. Vierteljahr 1942," BA-Freiburg, RH12/23/187.

183 **"The local difficulties":** Ibid.

183 **Some units tried to:** "Abschrift Nov. 13, 1941," BA-Freiburg, RH12/23/414.

183 **One wrote that:** Gruliow, *Soviet War-Time*; Walther and Vierthaler to "Heeresarzt," Dec. 18, 1941, BA-Freiburg, RH12/23/414.

183 **Typhus seemed to catch:** Herbert Assman memo, BA-Freiburg, RH12/23/187; Kurt Lydtin, "Anlage 3 zum Kriegstagebuch v. 3 – 20/6/42 am Armeearzt 16," BA-Freiburg, RH12/23/188; Lydtin, "Erfahrungen 1. vierteljahr 1942," BA-Freiburg, RH12/23/360.

183 **On January 12, 1942:** Lydtin, "1942 Okt–Dez Fleckfieber," BA-Freiburg, RH12/23/305.

184 **These alarming reports:** Von Stochert, "Die psychischen Störungen bei Fleckfieber," BA-Freiburg, RH1/23/246.

184 **Many German doctors:** "Ergebnisse der zweite Beratendentagung Ost," 11/30–12/3, 1942, BA-Freiburg, RH1/23/246.

184 **The symptoms reminded:** Bansi report, 1942, BA-Freiburg, RH 12/23/187.

184 **In recovery, the patients:** Brinkmann, Heeresgruppe Mitte, "Erfahrungsbericht, 4. Vtlj 1943," BA-Freiburg, RH12/23/187; Stochert, "Die psychische."

185 **To cope with:** Bogendorfer, 2nd Army, "March 1, 1944, Mikatowitschi," BA-Freiburg, RH12/23/187.

185 **The Weil-Felix reaction:** Eyer, at Tagung der beratenden Ärzte, 4/13/42, BA-Freiburg, RH12/23/214; Heinrich Zeiss, "Sammelbericht über Kriegserfahrungen der beratenden Hygieniker," from 1/20/1944, ibid., RH12/23/948; Bieling to O. Qu. Gef., 6/27/1942, Betrift: Fleckfiebererkrankungen bei Schutzgeimpften, ibid., RH12/23/187; Karl Schulze, "Erfahrungsbericht 1.3–30.6.43, ibid., RH12/23/188; Schmitz-Formes, "Erprobung eines neuen Fleckfieber Impfstoffes," ibid., RH12/23/360.

185 **Not knowing whether:** Lydtin, "Tagebuch März 42 bis 7 April," BA-Freiburg, RH12/23/305; Bogendorfer, 2nd Army.

185 **Many Wehrmacht doctors:** Schmitz-Formes, "Erprobung"; Felix von Bormann, experimental report, BA-Freiburg, RH12/23/187; Dr v. Weiss, "Ein Jahr Fleckfieberbehandlung," dated July 31, 1942, ibid., RH12/23/444.

185 **The German soldiers' letters:** Reichspropagandaleitung memo, Jan. 23, 1942, BA-Berlin, NS18/607.

186 **A memo 12 days:** Memo dated Feb. 5, 1942, BA-Berlin, NS18/607.

186 **To combat typhus at the front:** Bormann, report.

186 **Germany's failure:** Gerhard Rose, NA, RG238, ser. M1019, roll 60; David Kinkela, *DDT and the American Century: Global Health, Environmental Politics, and the Pesticide That Changed the World* (Chapel Hill: University of North Carolina Press, 2011), 18–19; Winfried Süss, *Der "Volkskörper" im Krieg, Gesundheitspolitik, Gesundheitsverhältnisse und Krankenmord im nationalsozialistischen Deutschland 1939–1945* (Munich: Oldenbourg, 2003), 227; W. Forth et al., *Men & Fungi: Penicil-*

Notes

*lin Research and Production in World War II German*y (Munich: Zuck-schwerdt, 2000); Lukas Straumann, "Nützliche Schädlinge" (PhD diss., University of Zurich, 2005).

187 **In the winter of 1942:** Albrecht Hase, "Über Entlausung durch Ameisen sowie über die Wirkung der Ameisensäure auf Kleiderläuse," *Zeitschrift für Parasitenkunde* 12 (1942): 665–77.

187 **The more the Germans retreated:** Friedrich Hansen, *Biologische Kriegsführung im Dritten Reich* (Frankfurt: Campus, 1993), 114.

187 **During three years:** Karl-Heinz Leven, "Fleckfieber beim deutschen Heer während des Krieges gegen die Sowjetunion (1941–1945)," in *Sanitätswesen im Zweiten Weltkrieg*, ed. Ekkehart Guth et al. (Herford: E. S. Mittler, 1990), 127–35. See also Alexander Neumann, *"Arzttum ist immer Kämpfertum": Die Heeressanitätsinspektion und das Amt "Chef des Wehrmachtssanitätswesens" im Zweiten Weltkrieg (1939–1945)* (Düsseldorf: Droste, 2005), 223.

187 **At the outbreak of war:** Weindling, *Epidemics*, 331–32.

188 **Gildemeister would work:** François Bayle, *Croix gammée contre cadu-cée: Les expériences humaines en Allemagne pendant la deuxième Guerre mondiale* (Neustadt, 1950), 1148–54, 1179–97, 1241–60, 1275; E. Haagen and B. Crodel, "Versuche mit einem neuen getrockneten Fleckfieberimpfstoff," *Zentralblatt für Bakteriologie* 151 (1944): 369–73. See also Weindling, "Virologist and National Socialist: The Extraordi-nary Career of Eugen Haagen," in *Infektion und Institution: Zur Wis-senschaftsgeschichte des Robert-Koch-Instituts im Nationalsozialismus*, ed. Marion Hulverscheidt and Anja Laukötter (Göttingen: Wallstein, 2009), 232–49.

188 **Meanwhile, IG Farben:** Weindling, *Epidemics*, 344–45.

188 **The leading scientists mistrusted:** Ibid., 331–45. See also Gerhard Rose, NA, RG238, ser. M1019, roll 60, frames 123–46.

188 **The differences were partly:** Eyer, "Die Fleckfieberprophylaxe der deutschen Wehrmacht im 2. Weltkrieg," *Wehrmedizin und Wehr-pharmazie* (1979): 60.

188 **The louse was the:** See interrogation of Gen. Gerhard Rose, NA, RG331, box 93; CIOS Report, item 24, file #XXIV-5/3 Institut für Fleckfieber- und Virusforschung des Oberkommandos des Heeres at Roth, Bavaria, 1945; Nov. 1942 meeting notes, BA-Berlin, R86/4153.

189 **Although Gildemeister:** Rose interrogation, NA, RG238, frames 138–41.

189　**The army medical chief:** Siegfried A. Handloser interview, NA, RG238, ser. M1019, roll 24, 83.

189　**Rose, on the other:** Rose interrogation, NA, RG238, frames 138–40.

189　**By the end of 1941:** File memo on Reich Interior Ministry Conference on Nov. 29, 1941, "The Fight against Typhus," HNOC, HLSL 722. See also Hans Arsperger, "Sonderbericht über den Besuch des Institutes für Fleckfieber- und Virusforschung in Krakau," BA-Freiburg, RH12/23/360, and Eyer, "Fleckfieberprophylaxe," 56–61.

189　**But Behringwerke:** J. Craigie memo, Jan. 1941, Kew, FD1/6614. See also Felicja Meisel-Mikołajczyk, interview by Wójcik.

190　**The Weigl vaccine:** Bieling reports from Feb. 1942, BA-Freiburg, RH12/23/187. See also Fleck, *Denkstile*, 582.

190　**Finally, the shortage:** Reichsministerium des Innern, "Akten betreffend Fleckfieber Impfstoff," Jan. 1942–March 1943, BA-Berlin, R1501/3644.

190　**At the urging of Gildemeister:** See HNOC, HLSL 722.

191　**However, other German officials:** Demnitz affidavit, HNOC, HLSL 721.

191　*Standartenführer* **(Colonel) Joachim:** Ibid.; Bieber note on meeting, HNOC, HLSL 2235; Bayle, *Croix*, 1131–32.

191　**Mrugowsky, who was Erwin:** Florian Bruns, "Staatshygiene und Menschenversuche: Das medizinische Ethos des Joachim Mrugowsky," in *Medizinethik im Nationalsozialismus: Entwicklungen und Protagonisten in Berlin (1939–1945)* (Stuttgart: Franz Steiner, 2009), 147.

192　**After being named in 1938:** Weindling, *Epidemics*, 248–50.

192　**Mrugowsky's staff of 200:** Pierre Joffroy, *A Spy for God: The Ordeal of Kurt Gerstein*, trans. Norman Denny (New York: Harcourt Brace Jovanovich, 1971).

192　**He was responsible:** Weindling, *Epidemics*, 254–57; Bruns, "Ethos des Joachim Mrugowsky," 135–47.

193　**As the scholar Paul:** Weindling, *Epidemics*, 255; Gerhard Peters, general: Himmler memo: BA-Berlin R1501/3644; Degesch shipment in Nov 1941: Staatsarchiv Nürnberg, KV-Anklage, Interrogations REP502 VI Nr P25, courtesy of Paul Weindling; Höss decision: Weindling, *Epidemics*, 294–302, 304–5; Joffroy, *Spy for God*, 258–66.

193　**The Pasteur scientists Paul:** Hélène Sparrow, "Essais d'immunisation avec le virus murin I de Tunis, introduit par la voie nasale," *Comptes* *rendus hebdomadaires des séances de l'Académie des sciences* 201 (1935): 1441.

193 **Durand brought the vaccine:** Paul Giroud and Jean Jadin, "Conceptions actuelles concernant les rickettsioses et leur vaccinations," *Annales de la Société Belge de Médicine Tropicale* 3 (1961); Paul Giroud and René Panthier, "Adaption au poumon de lapin des Rickettsies de Typhus Historique," *Annales de l'Institut Pasteur* 68 (1942): 381–86; Paul Giroud, "Vaccination against Typhus," in *Medical Research in France during the War (1939–1945)*, ed. Jean Hamburger (Paris: Flammarion, 1947), 31–37.

193 **Many tricks were:** Giroud and Panthier, "Adaption"; PIA, DirMIN1, "Reunion de 27 Fevrier 1942 sur le Typhus Examthématique."

194 **In January 1942:** Hubert Duboc, ed., *Barbelés et Typhus* (Luneray: Bertout, 1992), 40–44, 123, annexe 1-12.

194 **The Pasteur Institute, rife:** See Louis Aublant, speech of Nov. 9, 1979, PIA, box DirMIN1.

195 **To give a flavor . . . French POWs:** Trefouel to Ministry of Health, March 7, 1942, PIA, box DirMIN1.

195 **By war's end, Giroud:** "Medical Research in Paris," Sept. 5, 1944, NA, RG331, box 94, CIOS Medical, item 24; "Minutes of 28 Feb 1942 meeting," PIA, box DirMIN1; Memo, "Vaccine anti-Rickettsia delivré gratuitement."

195 **While the typhus vaccine:** Weindling, *Epidemics*, 325–28.

195 **One of the first:** Knapp to Fourneau, July 8, 1942, PIA, DirMIN1.

Chapter 9: The Terrifying Clinic of Dr. Ding

196 **There were really two:** Dov Levin, *The Lesser of Two Evils: Eastern European Jewry under Soviet Rule, 1939–1941*, trans. Naftali Greenwood (Philadelphia: Jewish Publication Society, 1995); Albert Kirrmann, "Buchenwald, la grande ville," in *De l'université aux camps de concentration: Témoignages strasbourgeois* (Paris: Les Belles Lettres, 1947), 67.

197 **Conditions improved:** Kogon, *Hell*, 260–61; Ernst von Salomon *The Captive: The Story of an Unknown Political Prisoner* (London: Weidenfeld and Nicolson, 1961), 118–22; David A. Hackett, ed. and trans., *The Buchenwald Report* (Boulder, CO: Westview Press, 1995), 207.

197 **The work required skill:** Hermann Langbein, *Against All Hope: Resistance in the Nazi Concentration Camps, 1938–1945*, trans. Harry Zohn (New York: Paragon House, 1994), 108.

198 **At times, it went:** Hoven interrogation, NA, RG238, ser. M1019, roll 29, frames 360–85.

198 **Given his erratic behavior:** "Dienstleistungszeugnis für SS-Unterscharführer Waldemar Hoven," June 29, 1939, BA-Berlin, NS19/507; Hoven interrogation, NA, RG238.

198 **Hoven was a rakish:** Hackett, *Report*, 336; Shoah Foundation, 21084 Peter Schenk Sr.

198 **Inmates would sometimes:** Kurt Titz and Herbert Froboess testimony in Buchenwald trial, at NA, RG153, box 255, v. 1, trial rec., pt. 4 (folder 10); ibid., box 246, pt. 8; Kurt Sitte testimony in Buchenwald trial, ibid., box 254, v. 1, trial rec., pt. 2 (folder 2), 366–81; Shoah Foundation, 11111 John Berman (wartime name Hans Baermann).

198 **None of this seemed:** Christian Bernadac, *Les médecins maudits: Dans les camps de concentration, des cobayes humains* (Paris: Michel Lafon, 1996), 188.

199 **Hoven was also known:** Kogon, Hell, 149; Interrogation of Waldemar Hoven by Iwan Devries, Oct. 22, 1946, HNOC, HLSL 221, 19–32; Fritz Rieckert, Affidavit concerning Hoven's work at Buchenwald, HNOC, HLSL 675, 20.

199 **"And what supremacy":** Rudolf Gottschalk, affidavit concerning Hoven's work at Buchenwald, HNOC, HLSL 672, 12.

199 **Arthur Dietzsch:** Salomon, *Captive*, 123–24; Kogon, *Hell*, 158–60.

200 **In November 1941:** Salomon, *Captive*, 118–22.

200 **Ding had studiously courted:** Oskar Hock, Affidavit on SS medical programs, HNOC, HLSL 435, 7. See also, Fritz Kranz, Affidavit on work of Hygiene Institute, HNOC, HLSL 802; Genzken in Bayle, *Croix*, 1221.

200 **Ding had left:** Hygiene Institut der Waffen-SS, Versuche mit Impfstoffen gegen Diphtherie, Fleckfieber, Typhus, Cholera usw 1941–44, BA-Berlin NS33/343 #185.

201 **"Since animal experiments":** Kogon, *Hell*, 156–57.

201 **Shortly after Block:** NA, RG153, box 257, v. 1, trial rec., pt. 7 (folder 2), 3107.

201 **As the nature of:** NA, RG153, box 250, v. 1, clemency, pt. 6 (folders 1 and 2).

202 **The sight of a single louse** Shoah Foundation, 15132 David Dantus; Hackett, *Report*, 65–66; Dietzsch testimony, Buchenwald Trial, NA, RG153, box 257, v. 1, trial rec., pt. 7 (folder 2), 3118–19.

202 **Since there was no:** Salomon, *Captive*, 128–32.

202 **After recovering, Ding:** Carl Blumenreuter, affidavit concerning Genzken's responsibilities in the Waffen-SS medical service, typhus vaccine program, Feb. 6, 1947, HNOC, HLSL 449, 36–37; Bayle, *Croix*, 1191–201.

202 **In November 1942:** Salomon, *Captive*, 128–32; Ernst Klee, *Auschwitz: Die NS-Medizin und ihre Opfer* (Frankfurt: Fischer, 1997), 296–97.

202 **On November 30, 1942:** Hoven quoted in Rieckert, affidavit; Dietzsch testimony, HNOC, HLSL 671, 2.

203 **Haas, sensing:** Salomon, *Captive*, 128–32; testimony by Fritz Kirchheimer, NA, RG153, box 255, v. 1, trial rec., pt. 4 (folder 1), 1149; Shoah Foundation, 41857 Jacobus Van der Geest.

203 **While convalescing at home:** Salomon, *Captive*, 133.

204 **Later subjects were:** Kogon, *Hell*, 156–58.

204 **Ding and Dietzsch:** Waitz, "Au block 46," in *Témoignages strasbourgeois*, 113.

204 **The many vaccines:** *"Tagebuch der Abteilung für Fleckfieber- u. Virusforschung am Hygiene-Institut der Waffen-SS"* (manuscript), HNOC, HLSL 1547.

204 **In practice, though, many of:** Christian Pineau, *La simple vérité, 1940–1945* (Paris: René Julliard, 1960), 381–82.

204 **To get the Block 46:** Waitz, "Au block 46," 109–11.

205 **The prisoners were "stuffed":** Yeo-Thomas, Buchenwald trial, NA, RG153, box 254, v. 1, trial rec. (folder 1), 147.

205 **Said a prisoner who:** Shoah Foundation, 51743 Henryk Mikols.

205 **Having already stuck:** Letter from Dietzsch to Frankfurter Hefte Verlag, IWM, FFEYT3/7.

205 **Stranded in the building:** Dietzsch testimony, Buchenwald trial, NA, RG153, box 257, v. 1, trial rec., pt. 7 (folder 1), 3133.

205 **He could more:** Max Umschweif testimony, NA, RG153, box 258, v. 1, trial rec., pt. 12, 5513–14.

205 **But he also:** Dietzsch testimony, NA, RG153, box 357, v. 1, pt. 7 (folder 2), 3146.

206 **And before long, everyone:** Kogon, *Hell*, 158–60.

206 **One day in the fall:** Willy Bahner, NA, RG253, box 256, v. 1, trial rec., pt. 5 (folder1), 1647–49.

2070 **By the time the camp:** Kogon, *Hell*, 156–57.

207 **Ding knew:** James J. Weingartner, "Law and Justice in the Nazi SS:

The Case of Konrad Morgen," *Central European History* 16 (1983): 276–94; Konrad Morgen testimony at Buchenwald trial, NA, RG153, box 257, v. 1, trial rec., pt. 7 (folder 1), 2797.

207 **He had already:** Morgen affidavit, medical experiments at Buchenwald, HNOC, HLSL 794.

207 **Nothing could have:** Kogon, *Hell*, 156–57.

207 **Despite this, the German:** Bayle, *Croix*, 1173, 1216–38.

207 **The vaccine tests:** Ding's publications—no coauthors were ever listed—include the following: "Zur serologischen und mikrobiologischen Diagnostik des Fleckfiebers," excerpted in *Bulletin of War Medicine* 3 (1942–43): 675; "Über das Ergebnis der Prüfung verschiedener Fleckfieber-Vaccinen gegen das klassische Fleckfieber," *Arbeitstagung Ost der beratenden Fachärzte* 3 (1943): 108; "Über die Schutzwirkung verschiedener Fleckfieberimpfstoffe beim Menschen und den Fleckfieberverlauf nach Schutzimpfung," *Zeitschrift für Hygiene und Infektionskrankheiten* 124 (1943): 670–82; "Fleckfieberrezidiv," *Medizinische Klinik* 39/40 (1944); "Beitrag zur Frage der Tröpfcheninfektion bei Fleckfieber," *Zeitschrift für Hygiene und Infektionskrankheiten* 125 (1944): 431–36.

208 **Typhus was not the only:** Shoah Foundation, 51743 Henryk Mikols.

209 **For some of the prisoners:** Shoah Foundation, 21884 Peter Schenk; Hoven interrogation, NA, RG238, ser. M1019, roll 29, frames 360–62.

209 **Ding also tested:** Stephen H. Lindner, *Inside IG Farben: Hoechst during the Third Reich* (New York: Cambridge University Press, 2008), 311–33; Klee, *Auschwitz*, 296–313; Salomon, *Captive*, 133; Kogon interview, Nov. 28, 1946, NA, RG238, ser. M1019, roll 36, frame 3582.

210 **As the Block 46:** Klee, *Auschwitz*, 304–5.

Chapter 10: "Paradise" at Auschwitz

212 **As part of this shift:** Betty Truck and Robert-Paul Truck, *Médecins de la honte: La vérité sur les expériences médicales pratiquées à Auschwitz* (Paris: Presses de la Cité, 1975), 146.

212 **In November or December:** Mieczysław Kieta, "Das Hygiene-Institut der Waffen-SS und Polizei in Auschwitz," *Die Auschwitz-Hefte* (Weinheim: Beltz, 1987), 213–17.

212 **As he wrote:** Truck and Truck, *Médecins*, 146.

212 **In the weeks before:** Kieta, "Hygiene-Institut," 114; Willy Berler,

Notes

Journey through Darkness: Monowitz, Auschwitz, Gross-Rosen, Buchenwald, trans. Martine Mitrani and Annette Charak (London: Vallentine Mitchell, 2004), 200–204.

212 **The ten members:** Danuta Czech, *Auschwitz Chronicles, 1939–1945* (New York: Henry Holt, 1990), 325.

213 **Perhaps Weber wanted:** Stanisław Lenz testimony, YVA.

213 **Fleck's group:** Bruno Seeman testimony, Shoah Foundation.

213 **On February 11:** Czech, *Chronicles*, 328, 334; Bruno Seeman testimony.

214 **The men entered:** Robert J. Lifton, *The Nazi Doctors: Medical Killing and the Psychology of Genocide* (London: Macmillan, 1986), 264; Fleck, "Aufenthalt im KZ Auschwitz," in *Denkstile*, 487–88.

214 **In March, Fleck and:** Arie Ryszard Fleck, YVA O.3/3521.

214 **Ludwik and Ryszard:** Fleck, "Aufenthalt," 488; Fleck, "Wie wir den Anti-Flecktyphus-Impfstoff im Lemberger Ghetto hergestellt haben," in *Denkstile*, 511.

214 **However, Ryszard was:** Ryszard Fleck testimony.

214 **Fleck's prewar reputaion:** Fleck, "Aufenthalt," 488, and "Wie wir," 523.

215 **The Lwów scientists':** Czech, *Chronicles*, 366; Robert Proctor, "Nazi Doctors, Racial Medicine and Human Experimentation," in *The Nazi Doctors and the Nuremberg Code: Human Rights in Human Perspective*, ed. George Annas and Michael A. Grodin (New York: Oxford University Press, 1992), 21; Vera Laska, "The Stations of the Cross," in *Medicine, Ethics and the Third Reich*, ed. John Michalczyk (Kansas City: Sheed and Ward, 1994), 135–36.

215 **The women—French:** Adelaide Hautval, "Aperçu sur les expériences faites dans les camps de femmes d'Auschwitz et de Ravensbrück," in André Lettich, *Convoi Numero 8* (Paris: Éditions Retour, 2009), 122–25; Hans-Joachim Lang, *Frauen von Block 10: Medizinische Versuche in Auschwitz* (Hamburg: Hoffmann & Campe, 2011), 167–76.

216 **Fleck witnessed these terrible:** Fleck, "Aufenthalt," 488.

216 **During this time, Fleck befriended:** Shoah Foundation, 19441 Magda Blau.

216 **"It was strictly forbidden":** Letter of Hautval to Schnelle, April 2, 1980, LFZ, Allgemeine Korrespondenz und Notizen von Thomas Schnelle 1978–1993, 4.1, Signatur 94.

217 **The windows of Block 10:** Bruno Seeman testimony.

217 **One day, Fleck:** "Aufenthalt," 489. See also Irena Strzelecka, *Medical*

Crimes: The Hospitals in Auschwitz, trans. William Brand (Oświęcim: Auschwitz-Birkenau State Museum, 2008), 12.

218 **Yet even as the gassings:** Hermann Langbein, *Against All Hope: Resistance in the Nazi Concentration Camps, 1938–1945*, trans. Harry Zohn (New York: Paragon House, 1994), 14–15.

218 **Hermann Langbein:** Langbein, *Menschen in Auschwitz* (Vienna: Europa Verlag, 1972), 17.

219 **Langbein, a former:** Langbein, *Against All Hope*, 27

219 **The camp commander:** Rudolf Höss, *Death Dealer: The Memoirs of the SS Kommandant at Auschwitz* (New York: Da Capo, 1996), 323–25.

219 **Arriving at the ramp:** Shoah Foundation, 36554 Louis Micheels.

220 **Langbein was working:** Marc Klein, "Auschwitz I Stammlager," in *De l'université aux camps de concentration: Témoignages strasbourgeois* (Paris: Les Belles Lettres, 1947), 447–48.

220 **Wirths wrote detailed:** Hermann Langbein, *People in Auschwitz*, trans. Harry Zohn (Chapel Hill: University of North Carolina Press, 2004), 371–73.

220 **The reports may have:** Ibid., 552. For information on the SS judicial inquiry at Auschwitz and other camps, see James J. Weingartner, "Law and Justice in the Nazi SS: The Case of Konrad Morgen," *Central European History* 16 (1983): 276–94.

220 **On May 5, 1943, Weber's:** Mieczysław Kieta, "Das Hygiene-Institut der Waffen-SS und Polizei in Auschwitz," in, *Die Auschwitz-Hefte*, vol. 1, 2nd ed. (Hamburg: Rogner und Bernhard, 1995), 213–17.

220 **Inmates were already:** Susanne Heim: *Kalorien, Kautschuk, Karrieren: Pflanzenzüchtung und landwirtschaftliche Forschung an Kaiser-Wilhelm-Instituten 1933–1945* (Göttingen: Wallstein, 2003), 177; Peter Longerich, *Himmler*, trans. Jeremy Noakes and Lesley Sharpe (New York: Oxford University Press, 2012), 685–86.

221 **The United States was:** Mark R. Finlay, *Growing American Rubber: Strategic Plants and the Politics of National Security* (New Brunswick: Rutgers University Press, 2009), 19–20, 162–63, 205–7.

221 **Himmler and Caesar:** Wanda L. Blankenheim, Yad Vashem testimony, RG 0.3/3118.

221 **At Monowitz:** Primo Levi, *Survival in Auschwitz: The Nazi Assault on Humanity*, trans. Stuart Woolf (New York: Simon and Schuster, 1996).

221 **But while the:** See Shoah Foundation, 24748 Rosette Moss, 4616 Ellis Hertzberger, 6370 Simone Floersheim, 653 Gertruda Milchova; and

Notes

Simone Alizon, *L'exercice de vivre* (Paris: Stock, 1996), 264–81, Blankenheim testimony, 15.

222 **The women in the:** Anna Zieba, "Das Nebenlager Rajsko," *Hefte von Auschwitz* 9 (1966): 75–90.

222 **In October 1942, Caesar:** Langbein, *People*, 418; Blankenheim testimony, 13.

222 **The leaders of the:** Alizon, *L'exercise de vivre*, 264–67; *Claudette: Auschwitz-Birkenau, 1942–1945: Recherche en laboratoire*," trans. and ed. Lore Shelley (Chambéry: Jean-Jacques Rousseau, 2002), 1–42.

223 **Fleck and the other:** Zieba,"Rajsko," 75–90; Kieta, "Hygiene-Institut," 213–17.

223 **The walk took:** Louis J. Micheels, *Doctor 117641: A Holocaust Memoir* (New Haven: Yale University Press, 1989), 100.

224 **Arriving at the institute:** Kieta, "Hygiene-Institut," 215; Lettich, *Convoi*; Berler, *Journey*; Léon Poliakov, *Bréviaire de la Haine: Le IIIe Reich et les Juifs* (Paris: René Julliard, 1964), 118–20.

224 **After Josef Mengele:** Kieta, "Hygiene-Institut," 216; Shoah Foundation, 35030 Victor Schnell; Deborah E. Lipstadt, introd. to Lucie Adelsberger, *Auschwitz: A Doctor's Story*, trans. Susan Ray (Boston: Northeastern University Press, 1995), xiii–xvii. For more on Mengele, see Gerald Posner and John Ware, *Mengele: The Complete Story* (New York: Cooper Square, 2000).

224 **On the same floor:** Fleck, "Wie wir," 523.

224 **The dandelion scientist:** Joachim Caesar, NA, RG238, M1019, roll 11.

225 **A general state of:** USHMM, Hygiene Institute der Waffen SS-Polizei, Auschwitz RG 15.108 (30 microfilm reels containing photographed records of serological and bacteriological tests performed by Fleck and others at Rajsko).

225 **In a little room:** Kieta, "Rajsko"; Lettich, *Convoi*; Berler, *Journey*; Shoah Foundation, 6246 William Schiff.

225 **In an attic workshop:** Kieta, "Rajsko."

225 **One day, Weber:** Shoah Foundation, Herzberger.

225 **Their wives had been:** Frank Stiffel, *The Tale of the Ring: A Kaddish* (New York: Bantam Books, 1984), 256–61; Stiffel, interview with author, Jan. 2011.

226 **Despite their celebrity:** Bruno Seeman testimony.

226 **As a Nazi boss:** Blankenheim testimony.

226 **He ran the labs:** Berler, *Journey*.

226 **Micheels said:** Micheels, *Doctor,* 98–104.

226 **Weber was needlessly:** Ibid., 71–76, 84–85.

227 **One irksome task:** Lettich, *Convoi,* 74–76.

227 **Weber enjoyed walking:** Truck and Truck, *Médecins,* 156–57.

227 **Fleck's son, Ryszard:** Imre Gönczi, personal communications, April 2011; YVA O.3/2874; Ryszard Fleck testimony.

228 **"Our relations with the SS":** Klein, "Auschwitz I," 449–50.

229 **In the spring of 1944:** Ian Kershaw, *Hitler, 1936–1945: Nemesis* (New York: Norton, 2000), 628.

229 **"Before that time":** Blankenheim testimony, 13.

229 **Another doctor wrote:** Adelsberger, *Doctor's Story,* 85.

229 **Near the end:** Tadeusz Kielanowski, "In der Angelegenheit des Artikels von Prof. Dr. L. Fleck über ärztliche Experimente an Menschen," in *Denkstile,* 584.

230 **In Lwów, as the war:** Ryszard Wójcik, "Pakt z diabłem" (Pact with the devil), *Przegląd tygodniowy* 4 (617) (1994). Also see the five-part Wójcik series "Kapryśna gwiazda Rudolfa Weigla" (The wayward star of Rudolf Weigl), in *Odra* 9 and 10 (1980–81).

230 **The dilemma:** *Third Part of the Night,* by Andrzej Żuławski, Polski State Film, 1971.

231 **In practice, the Poles:** Szybalski, interview with author.

Chapter 11: Buchenwald: Rabbit Stew and Fake Vaccine

232 **Many of the doctors:** Stanisław Kłodziński, "Sabotaż w buchenwaldz-kim Instytucie Higieny SS; Dr. Marian Ciepielowski" *Przegląd lekarski* 34 (1977): 141–45; François Bayle, *Croix gammée contre caducée: Les expériences humaines en Allemagne pendant la deuxième Guerre mondiale* (Neustadt, 1950), 1177.

232 **Apart from Ding:** Albert Kirrmann, "Les laboratoires du block 50," in *De l'université aux camps de concentration: Témoignages strasbourgeois* (Paris: Les Belles Lettres, 1947), 115.

233 **Mrugowsky from the:** Mrugowsky testimony, NA, RG238, ser. M1019, roll 47, Mrugowsky, frame 1191.

233 **The Giroud vaccine:** Bayle, *Croix,* 1224; Haubold, file memo, HNOC, HLSL 2241.

233 **Ding made two:** Interrogation of Dr. Kogon in NMT trial 4 (Pohl Case), concerning medical experiments at Buchenwald, HNOC, HLSL 453.

Notes

234 **There were plenty of doctors:** Shoah Foundation, 20816 Marko Max Feingold.

234 **Jellinek came to:** Willy Jellinek, interview with Thomas Schnelle, April 8, 1980, in LFZ, Unterlagen und Notizen von Thomas Schnelle: Allgemeine Korrespondenz und Notizen von Thomas Schnelle 1978–1993, 4.1, Signatur 94; author's interview with and personal communications from Howard Cohn, May 2012.

234 **No vaccine experts were:** Kłodziński, "Sabotaż," 141–45.

235 **Ciepielowski, handsome:** Ibid.; Bayle, *Croix*, 1158, Marjan Ciepielowski testimony in Buchenwald trial, NA, RG153, box 255, v. 1, trial rec., pt. 4 (folder 10), 1123–31; photograph of Ciepielowski, courtesy of George Otlowski, Metuchen, NJ.

235 **Perhaps the most:** Hubert Habicht, ed., *Eugen Kogon—Ein politischer Publizist in Hessen* (Frankfurt: Insel, 1982), 7–12.

235 **Kogon's steadfast:** Kogon, *Hell*, 263–65, 283–88.

236 **Before long:** undated document, "Officials of the Concentration Camp at Buchenwald," NA, RG153, box 244; Konrad Morgen testimony, ibid., box 257, v. 1, trial rec., pt. 7 (folder 1), 2758–65.

236 **Kogon maneuvered Ding:** Kogon, *Hell*, 160–61.

236 **The vaccine detail:** Ibid., 160–61, 263–65.

236 **Konrad Morgen, the SS:** Morgen, affidavit concerning medical experiments at Buchenwald, HNOC, HLSL 794, 49–54.

237 **Another political prisoner:** Pierre Julitte, *Block 26: Sabotage at Buchenwald*, trans. Francis Price (Garden City, NY: Doubleday, 1971), 105, 121, 129, 140, 176–77. For confirmation of identities, see Pierre Durand, *Les Français à Buchenwald et à Dora: Les armes de l'espoir* (Paris: Éditions Sociales, 1977).

237 **Block 50 had a well-cared-for:** Julitte, *Block 26*, 100–101.

237 **The building was startlingly:** Kirrmann, "Laboratoires," 115–18.

238 **As Fleck wrote:** Fleck, "Problems of the Science of Science," in *Cognition and Fact: Materials on Ludwik Fleck*, ed. Robert S. Cohen and Thomas Schnelle (Dordrecht: D. Reidel, 1986), 113–27.

238 **Ding pressed the:** Bayle, *Croix*, 1179.

239 **The Block 50 crew:** Mimeographed typed manuscript, DGVG-Ding, green box.

240 **The first samples:** Bayle, *Croix*, 1166.

240 **It was at this moment:** Kogon, interview with Thomas Schnelle, June 2, 1979, LFZ, Unterlagen und Notizen von Thomas Schnelle: Allgeme-

ine Korrespondenz und Notizen von Thomas Schnelle 1978–1993, 4.1, Signatur 94.

240 **Fleck befriended:** Jellinek, interview with Schnelle; Jellinek, letter to Fleck, Oct. 27, 1946, LFZ, Biographisches Material betr. Ludwik Fleck/1.2. Biographische Notizen und Korrespondenzen; Ewa Pleszczyńska, testimony at pamiecmiejsca.tnn.pl.

241 **In 1939, Mrugowsky:** Weindling, *Epidemics*, 231.

241 **He ordered Fleck:** Kielanowski, "My meetings," 582–85; Jellinek interview with Thomas Schnelle, April 8, 1980, LFZ.

241 **Fleck's authority:** Jellinek interview with Schnelle; Kogon interview with Schnelle.

241 **Fleck described:** All quotations below are from Fleck, "Science of Science," 113–27.

244 **Here, Fleck referred:** Klemens Barbarski, "Sabotaż w ampulce," *Przekrój* 99 (1947): 16.

245 **Their lives hung:** Fleck, "In der Buchenwalder Angelegenheit; Kommentar zum Buch F. Bayles," in *Denkstile*, 549–57.

245 **This is also the:** Bayle, *Croix*, 1178–79.

246 **Ding, in short:** Ludwik Fleck testimony, YVA Sign 03/650.

246 **Block 50 produced:** Jerzy Lutowski, "Was ist Leukergie? Wir sprechen mit Professor Fleck," in *Denkstile*, 515–18.

247 **Even Fleck's son:** Ryszard Fleck testimony, YVA.

248 **The men in the block:** Howard Cohn, interview with author.

248 **Hummelsheim, the bilingual:** Julitte, *Block 26*, 176–77.

248 **Following the liberation:** *Vie académique* (1984): 570–73, in ARC037, "Alfred Balachowsky," at IHTP; Balachowsky testimony, PIA,, box LEPC1.

248 **Born in Russia:** Nicolas Chevassus, "Alfred Balachowsky: Un pastorien à Buchenwald," *La Recherche* 370 (2003): 50–52; Alfred Balachowsky, *Titres et travaux scientifiques de Alfred-Serge Balachowsky* (1967); Jean Dorst, "La vie et l'oeuvre d'Alfred Balachowski," *La vie des sciences* 1, no. 6, pp. 567–76.

249 **From there, he was:** Balachowsky at http://avalon.law.yale.edu/imt/01-30-46.asp.

249 **After learning of Balachowsky's:** Julitte, *Block 26*, 174–75; *Vie académique* (1984): 570.

249 **Balachowsky was skeletal:** Julitte, "Allocution de M. Pierre Juliette," in 1972, "Remise de l'épée d'académicien" for Balachowsky, accessed from PIA, BAL1.

Notes

249 **Balachowsky's diaries:** Balachowsky diaries, ARC037, IHTP.

249 **After the war:** Kogon, interview, Nov. 28, 1946, NA, RG238, ser. M1019, roll 36; Fleck, "Angelegenheit," 549–60.

250 **In Block 50:** Balachowsky testimony, PIA, LEPC1.

249 **Fleck conducted bacteriological:** Fleck, "Bericht über den Aufenthalt im KZ Buchenwald," in *Denkstile*, 492–97; Fleck, "Angelegenheit," 549–60.

250 **On one occasion:** Ibid.; Balachowsky diary, Feb. 26, 1945, PIA, BAL1.

250 **The mistrust would:** Fleck, "Angelegenheit," 552.

250 **Kogon, who admired:** ARC037, folder "Alfred Balachowsky, 1901–1983," IHTP; Kogon to Schnelle; interview with Eugen Kogon, NA, RG238, ser. M1019, roll 36; *cross examination of the witness Dr. Kogon*, HNOC, HLSL 454.

250 **Bizarrely, Balachowsky's:** See Eva Hedfors, "Medical Science in the Light of the Holocaust: Departing from a Postwar Paper by Ludwik Fleck," *Social Studies of Science* 38 (2008): 259–83; and the response by the Fleck scholars Olga Amsterdamska et al., "Medical Science in the Light of a Flawed Study of the Holocaust: A Comment on Eva Hedfors' Paper on Ludwik Fleck," ibid., 937–44.

250 **By the summer:** Jellinek interview with Schnelle.

251 **The bombs slightly damaged:** Ding-Schuler to Mrugowsky, Aug. 26, 1944, DGVG-Ding, green folder.

251 **As night fell:** Christian Pineau, *La simple vérité, 1940–1945* (Paris: René Julliard, 1960), 482–84.

251 **"Even today":** Ludwik Fleck, "El Roble de Goethe," *El Malpensante* 97 (May 2009), accessed at http://www.elmalpensante.com/index. php?doc=display_contenido&id=1025.

251 **That night:** Stéphane Hessel, *Danse avec le siècle* (Paris: Éditions du Seuil, 1997), 83–91.

252 **In Kraków, Eyer's:** Eyer to Olga Weigl, March 12, 1944; A. Rohrmann to Eyer, Nov. 16, 1946.

252 **Weigl's older brother:** Weigl to Eyer, Aug. 27, 1966.

252 **After the Warsaw . . . relief:** Heinrich Mückter to Erich von Redwitz, Nov. 19, 1946.

252 **The war was not easy:** Peter Eyer, interview with author.

253 **Just before:** Bruce Marshall, *The White Rabbit* (Boston: Houghton Mifflin, 1953).

253 **Balachowsky sought help:** Ernst von Salomon, *The Captive: The Story*

of an Unknown Political Prisoner (London: Weidenfeld and Nicolson, 1961), 137–49; Marshall, *White Rabbit*, 230–53; Balachowsky testimony, PIA, LEPC1; Hessel, *Danse*, 85–91.

253 **The secrecy:** See NA, RG153, box 250, v. 1, clemency, pt. 6 (folders 1 and 2); Kogon *Hell*, 158–60.

253 **To start the plan:** Salomon, *Captive*, 137–49; Marshall, *White Rabbit*, 230–53; Balachowsky testimony, PIA, LEPC1; Hessel, *Danse*, 85–91; Kogon, *Hell*, 212–18; Durand, *Les Français*, 53–55; report by Balachowsky on events at Buchenwald, IWM, Yeo-Thomas, GB62–xx05, box 1, April 23, 1945.

254 **Ding, whom Kogon:** Yeo-Thomas testimony, Buchenwald trial, NA, RG153, box 254, v. 1, trial rec., pt. 2 (folder 2), 141–44.

254 **The Gestapo telephoned:** Ibid.; Kogon, *Hell*, 214.

255 **At this point:** IWM, Wing Commander FF E Yeo-Thomas, GB62–xx05, box 1; file FFEYT2/3.

255 **The other two cases:** Air Ministry Press conference on Feb. 15, 1946, IWM, Yeo-Thomas, GB62–xx05, box 1.

255 **That left Hessel:** Hessel, *Danse*.

256 **Yeo-Thomas remained:** Yeo-Thomas testimony, 147.

256 **On January 17:** Accounts of the death march here include Shoah Foundation testimonies of Seeman, Milchova, Ryszard Arie Fleck, and Schiff; Freddie Knoller, *Living with the Enemy: My Secret Life on the Run from the Nazis* (London: Metro Publishing, 2005); YVA testimony by Blankenheim; Ryszard Wójcik interviews of Henryk Meisel and Felicja Meisel-Mikolajczyk.

256 **In the beginning:** Shoah Foundation, Bruno Seeman.

257 **The men, separated:** See YVA testimonies of Wonda Blankenheim, Bronisław Seeman, Ryszard Fleck, Henryk Meisel, and Felicja Meisel-Mikolajczyk.

257 **They died by the hundreds:** Pineau, *Simple*, 537.

257 **Alfred Balachowsky's diary:** "Notes faites par A. Balachowsky," in ARC037, IHTP.

258 **The French, sustained:** Pineau, *Simple*, 537–39.

258 **Again, Fleck was:** Jellinek interview with Schnelle.

258 **On February 9, Erwin Ding:** Erwin Schuler, insurance claim, DGVG-Ding, green box.

258 **Increasingly he was plotting:** Bayle, *Croix*, 1172.

258 **In the final days:** Fleck, *Denkstile*, 492.

Notes

259 **As the Americans approached:** Howard Cohn, personal communication; Kogon, *Hell,* 283–88.

259 **On April 11, a crowd:** John Berman testimony.

259 **Ryszard Fleck remembered:** Ryszard Fleck testimony.

259 **"When I walked into":** Shoah Foundation, 44720 Leon Bass.

260 **The Communists put up:** Meyer Levin, *In Search* (New York: Paperback Library, 1961), 216–18.

Chapter 12: Imperfect Justice

261 **About a week:** Ding-Schuler statement, June 18, 1945, NA, RG153, box 252, v. 1, trial rec., pt. 3 (folder 3).

261 **Only a few months earlier:** Ding to Osiander, Aug. 16, 1944, BA-Berlin, VBS283/6055002585.

261 **Just as he won his:** E.g., DVDG-Ding Ordner 1546, Aktenvermerk, March 31, 1945, re "Mittelwerke"; Ordner 1548 "Geheim," Schuler to Mrugowsky, March 18, 1945; Mrugowsky to Lolling, Feb. 10, 1945.

262 **Ding-Schuler had:** François Bayle, *Croix gammée contre caducée: Les expériences humaines en Allemagne pendant la deuxième Guerre mondiale* (Neustadt, 1950), 1178.

263 **If citizen Schuler:** Ibid., 1199–201.

263 **It may have been:** Rose interrogation, NA, RG238, ser. M1019, roll 60, frame 151.

264 **"My wife is alone":** Bayle, *Croix,* 1200.

264 **After the war:** Air Ministry press conference on Feb. 15, 1946, IWM, Yeo-Thomas, GB62–xx05, box 1, file FFEYT2/3; BA-Berlin, D0/1/28859 Standort 51, Magazine M 3 10.

264 **But Irene:** "Allocution de M. Pierre Juliette," in "Remise de l'épée d'académicien" for Balachowsky, 1972, PIA, BAL1.

264 **There were many Nazi:** Gerstein is viewed sympathetically in *A Spy for God: The Ordeal of Kurt Gerstein*, trans. Norman Denny (New York: Harcourt Brace Jovanovich, 1971), and in Robert Proctor, *Racial Hygiene: Medicine under the Nazis* (Cambridge: Harvard University Press, 1988), 290; Wirths's story is in Hermann Langbein, *People in Auschwitz*, trans. Harry Zohn (Chapel Hill: University of North Carolina Press, 2004), 385; Grawitz's end is mentioned in Naomi Baumslag, *Murderous Medicine: Nazi Doctors, Experimentation, and Typhus* (Westport, CT: Greenwood Press, 2005), 180.

264 **Many more tried:** Materials on the investigation of Weber, at Kew,

WO309/469 and W0309/472, including an amusing account of the search by British agents leading to his arrest.

265 **The SS commander of Galicia:** Raul Hilberg, *The Destruction of the European Jews* (New York: Holmes & Meier, 1985), 708.

265 **Several hundred:** Norbert Frei, A*denauer's Germany and the Nazi Past: The Politics of Amnesty and Integration* (New York: Columbia University Press, 2002), 67, 94, 178.

265 **In their declaration at Yalta:** *The Trials of War Criminals before the Nuernberg Military Tribunals* (Washington, DC: GPO, 1949), 8.

265 **The origins of:** "International scientific commission for the investigation of med war crimes," Kew, WO309/471. I thank Paul Weindling for drawing my attention to this file.

265 **The medical war crimes:** Paul Weindling, personal communication; Weindling, "From International to Zonal Trials: The Origins of the Nuremberg Medical Trial," *Holocaust and Genocide Studies* 14 (2000): 367–89.

266 **At a May 15, 1946:** Kew, WO309/471, "International."

266 **In a July 31, 1946, consultation:** "Minutes of meeting to discuss war crimes of medical nature executed in Germany under the Nazi regime. Appendix B: Outline of Principles and Rules of Experimentation on Human Subjects," PIA, box LEP1.

266 **Some, such as:** Paul Weindling, "Human Guinea Pigs and the Ethics of Experimentation," *BMJ* 313 (1996): 1467–70.

266 **Andrew C. Ivy, an American:** Kew, W0309/471, "International."

267 **The Doctors' Trial:** Opening statement of the prosecution, *U.S.A. v. Brandt,* Dec. 9, 1946, HNOC, HLSL 565.

268 **Doctor colleagues of:** Paul Weindling, *Nazi Medicine and the Nuremberg Trials: From Medical War Crimes to Informed Consent* (New York: Palgrave Macmillan, 2004), 204–8.

269 **The latter defended:** *Trials of War Criminals,* 539–54; Herbert D. Chalke, "Typhus: Experiences in the Central Mediterranean Force," *British Medical Journal* 1, no. 4460 (June 29, 1946): 978–80. A fascinating, if revolting, account of the method for production of the Algerian vaccine is at T. E. Woodward, "Rickettsial Vaccines with Emphasis on Epidemic Typhus: Initial Report of an Old Vaccine Trial," *South Africa Medical Journal* (Oct. 1986): 73.

270 **In a crowning irony:** Bayle, *Croix,* 1226–27; Ciepielowski testimony in Buchenwald trial, NA, RG153, box 255, v. 1, pt. 4 (folder 10), 1230–31.

271 **Fleck came to Nuremberg:** Fleck, "Zwei Zeugenaussagen im IG-Farben-Prozess," in *Denkstile*, 497–99.

271 **Fleck was devastated:** Fleck letter to Hirszfeld, in *Denkstile*, 582.

272 **Many other scientists:** Weindling, *Nuremberg*, 216.

272 **Most went back to their old:** See, e.g., Ernst Nauck et al., *Tropical Medicine and Parasitology*, FIAT Review of German Science, 1939–1945 (Wiesbaden: Office of Military Government for Germany, 1948); Rudolf Wohlrab, "Kudicke," *Deutsche medizinische Wochenschrift* 86 (1961): 1882–83. Eyer's obituaries of his racialist colleagues included "Nachruf auf Karl Kisskalt," ibid., 87 (1962): 1473; "Franz Redeker" (Nachruf), ibid., 88 (1963): 1063; "In Memoriam Ernst Georg Nauck," *Archives der Hygiene* 152 (1968): 193; "Ernst Rodenwaldt zum Gedächtnis," *Münchener Medizinische Wochenschrift* 108 (1966): 120.

273 **On January 17, 1945:** Heinrich Mückter to Josef von Redwitz, Nov. 19, 1946.

273 **In the closing:** Institut für Fleckfieber und Virusforschung des Oberkommandos des Heeres at Roth, Bavaria, 1945, NA, RG331, CIOS Report, item 24, file #XXIV-5/3.

273 **The U.S. Army held:** Peter Eyer, interview and communications with author.

274 **Poland is a country:** Ryszard Wójcik, "Pakt z diabłem" (Pact with the devil), *Przegląd tygodniowy* 4 (617) (1994).

275 **The postwar years:** Henryk Gaertner, interview in the documentary film *To Overcome Death: Professor Rudolf Weigl*, dir. Halina Szymura (TV Katowice, 2009); Wójcik interviews with Mr. and Mrs. Giercuszkiewic, Sept. 1979; Wójcik interview with Wojciechowska, Jan. 1979; Wiktor Weigl, "Wspomnienia o moim Ojcu," in *Zwyciężyć tyfus—Instytut Rudolfa Weigla we Lwowie. Dokumenty i wspomnienia*, ed. Zbigniewa Stuchly (Wrocław: Sudety, 2001), accessed at http://lwow.home.pl/weigl/turek.html.

275 **In 1945, he was:** Fryderyk Weigl, interview with Wójcik, 1982; Maciej Bilek, "Krakowskim szlakiem Rudolfa Weigla" (Rudolf Weigl in Kraków), *Alma Mater* (2007): 66–70.

276 **Weigl found himself:** Peter Eyer, interview; Stanisław Kosiedowski et al., "Spór wokół prof. Weigla" (Dispute over Prof. Weigl), accessed at http://lwow.home.pl/weigl/kol.html.

276 **Colleagues over the years:** IPN files, Przybyłkiewicz, 9828/II IPN KR 010/9659.

276 **But a louse:** IPN file, Przybyłkiewicz curriculum vitae.

277 **Przybyłkiewicz was the only:** H. Eyer, Z. Przybyłkiewicz, and H. Dillenberg, "Das Fleckfieber bei Schutzgeimpften," *Zeitschrift für Hygiene und Infectionskrankheiten* 122 (1940): 702.

277 **He also claimed:** Correspondence Przybyłkiewicz-Eyer, 1989, courtesy of Peter Eyer.

277 **Weigl's name started:** Fryderyk Weigl, interview with Wójcik.

277 **Perhaps the most loyal:** Oleksandra Tarasyuk and Iryna Kurhanova, "To the 100th Anniversary of Doctor Henrich Mosing Birthday," *Sepsis* 4 (2011): 19–20.

278 **In March 1948:** Elżbieta Lonc and Grażyna Gościniak, "Professors Rudolf Weigl and Ludwik Hirszfeld—In the Meanders of History," *Annals of Parasitology* 58, no. 4 (2012): 194–95.

278 **"The Germans had offered":** Fryderyk Weigl, interview with Wójcik.

278 **Eyer felt disappointment:** Peter Eyer interview.

279 **Despite all he had done:** Ryszard Fleck testimony.

280 **The fate of Fleck's:** Bruno Seeman testimony.

280 **The Seemans ended up:** Personal communication from Alan Sallwasser, Dec. 2011.

281 **Ciepielowski, the chief:** Klemens Barbarski, "Sabotaż w ampulce," *Przekrój* 99 (1947).

281 **He would marry:** Personal communication, George Otlowski, Oct. 2012.

281 **Another Block 50:** Howard Cohn, personal communications.

281 **Unlikely friendships sprang:** "Action of the Modification Board," NA, RG153, box 259, v. 1. Dietzsch was fingered by Alfred Balachowsky, though the latter knew little of the goings-on in Block 46; see statement concerning the typhus vaccine experiments at Buchenwald, HNOC, HLSL 1797.

281 **The old spy:** Correspondence with Buchenwald inmates, Kew, FFEYT-3/7.

282 **Yeo-Thomas and his wife:** Letter to Yeo-Thomas from AD, April 18, 1957, IWM, FFEYT3/7.

282 **Many of the Buchenwald:** Ibid.; Ernst von Salomon *The Captive: The Story of an Unknown Political Prisoner* (London: Weidenfeld and Nicolson, 1961), 1–2.

282 **"Of all my":** Stéphane Hessel, *Danse avec le siècle* (Paris: Éditions du Seuil, 1997).

Notes

282 **On April 17, 1945:** YVA, concentration camp inmates questionnaire, "Ludwik Fleck, #4934."

283 **Some acquaintances:** Jellinek interview with Schnelle; Eleanor Tarkowska, Lublin Medical Academy, letter to the Polish Academy of Science, Feb. 2, 1954, IPN, Ludwik Fleck file.

283 **The new Soviet:** Christoph Mick, *Kriegserfahrungen in einer multiethnischen Stadt: Lemberg 1914–1947* (Wiesbaden: Harrassowitz, 2011), 545–53.

283 **Where the Lwowites:** Gregor Thum, *Uprooted: How Breslau Became Wrocław during the Century of Expulsions*, trans. Tom Lampert et al. (Princeton: Princeton University Press, 2011).

284 **The Germans who:** Dieter Schenk, *Der Lemberger Professorenmord und der Holocaust in Ostgalizien* (Bonn: Dietz, 2007), 17.

284 **The poet Adam Zagajewski:** Adam Zagajewski, "To Go to Lvov," in *Without End: New and Selected Poems* (New York: Farrar, Straus and Giroux, 2004).

285 **Lublin was a postwar desert:** Fleck, *Denkstile*, 587–91. Audio recordings of recollections of postwar Lublin, and particularly of Fleck, are cached at pamiecmiejsca.tnn.pl.

285 **"Lublin is a true":** Fleck, *Denkstile*, 587.

285 **To save money:** Tadeusz Kielanowski, "My Meetings with Ludwick Fleck in Lublin during the Years 1945–1950," *Kwartalnik historii nauki i technologi* (1983), 584–85; Klingberg, interview with author, May 2012.

286 **In his first lecture:** Ewa Pleszczyńska at pamiecmiejsca.tnn.pl.

285 **Although there are:** Lucie Adelsberger, *Auschwitz: A Doctor's Story*, trans. Susan Ray (Boston: Northeastern University Press, 1995), 131–35.

287 **Fleck traveled:** Irene Rubaszko, Aug. 2, 1978, LFZ, 4.4 Unterlagen und Notizen v. Thomas Schnelle, "Fragebogen," Signatur 100.

287 **A 1954 letter:** Eleanor Tarkowska, Lublin Medical Academy, letter to the Polish Academy of Science, Feb. 2, 1954, IPN, Ludwik Fleck file.

287 **On the streets:** Gusta Dickmann, interview with Schnelle, in LFZ, 4.4 Unterlagen und Notizen v. Thomas Schnelle, "Fragebogen," Signatur 100.

287 **Most of Fleck's assistants:** Ewa Pleszczyńska, interview at pamiecmiejsca.tnn.pl.

287 **He emphasized the:** Kazimerz Gerkowicz, LFZ, 4.4 Unterlagen und Notizen von Thomas Schnelle, "Fragebogen," Signatur 100.

287 **Said another:** Interviews with Pleszczyńska, Borecka, Stein, and Perlinska-Schnejder at pamiecmiejsca.tnn.pl.

288 **After returning:** Fleck, "In der Frage ärztlicher Experimente an Menschen," in *Denkstile,* 538–45.

288 **Ah, to be a Frenchman:** See correspondence from Balachowsky's trip, PIA, BAL1.

288 **Rudolf Weigl, meanwhile:** Henryk Gaertner, "Wspomnienie o Rudolfie Weiglu" (Recollections of Rudolf Weigl), *Alma Mater* (Jagiellonian University) 93 (2007); Gaertner in the documentary film *To Overcome Death: Professor Rudolf Weigl,* dir. Halina Szymura (TV Katowice, 2009).

289 **At Weigl's memorial:** Henryk Mosing, "Rudolf Weigl uczony i człowiek na 50-lecie Jego badań nad tyfusem plamistym" (Rudolf Weigl, scholar and man in his 50 years of research), in *Zwyciężyć tyfus,* ed. Zbigniew Stuchly (Wrocław: Sudety, 2001); Fryderyk Weigl, interview with Wójcik, 1983.

289 **As the service ended:** Fryderyk Weigl, interview with Wójcik.

290 **Thus it was left to Hermann:** Eyer, "In Memoriam Rudolf Weigl," *Zentralblatt für Bakteriologie, Parasitenkunde, Infektionskrankheiten und Hygiene* 171 (1958): 377–79.

290 **Even in 1983:** Lonc and Gościniak, "Meanders of History," 195.

290 **Hermann Eyer, who was ingenious:** Peter Eyer interview. See http://www.mvp.uni-muenchen.de/research.html?&L=34.

290 **In 1956, the year:** Meisel to Eyer, Sept. 17, 1956; Eyer to Meisel, Sept. 28, 1956; Eyer to Meisel, Sept. 6, 1957; Meisel to Eyer March 20, 1972; Eycr to Meisel, Dec. 22, 1975—all courtesy of Peter Eyer.

292 **Fleck spent seven:** Danuta Borecka interviewed on June 14, 2007, Barbara Narbutowicz on March 20, 1979, at pamiecmiejsca.tnn.pl.

292 **Fleck was a wonderful:** Borecka, interview with Lidia Perlińska-Schnejder, March 30, 2007, at pamiecmiejsca.tnn.pl.

294 **While they were living:** Ibid.

293 **Certain colleagues:** Bozena Plonka-Syroka, personal communication.

294 **When Balachowsky's:** Narbutowicz testimony, in LFZ, 4.4 Unterlagen und Notizen von Thomas Schnelle, Signatur 94.

294 **By the time Fleck left:** Klingberg, interview with author; Borecka interview.

294 **Israeli embassy officials:** Klingberg, interview with Thomas Schnelle, May 26, 1979.

294 **From Israel, Fleck:** K. Leszczyńska, "Ludwik Fleck: A Forgotten Phi-

Notes

losopher," in *Penser avec Fleck: Investigating a Life Studying Life Sciences*, ed. Johannes Fehr et al. (Zurich: Collegium Helveticum, 2009), 34.

295 **Although Ness Ziona was:** Fleck and Z. Evenchik, "Latex Agglutination Test with Brucella Antigen and Antiserum," *Nature* 194 (1962): 548–50; interview of David Ben-Nathan and two former Ness Ziona employees who asked not to be identified in Tel Aviv, July 2012.

295 **One of Fleck's best friends:** Aleksander Kohn, interview with Thomas Schnelle, LFZ, 4.4 Unterlagen und Notizen, Signatur 100.

296 **Klingberg recruited:** Klingberg, interview with author.

297 **In 1961, less than:** Interview with Ephrati, May 31, 1979, Schnelle papers.

297 **His body was brought:** Interview with Ben-Nathan and two former Ness Ziona employees, July 2012.

Afterword

299 **When the Germans:** See Charles M. Wheeler, "Control of Typhus in Italy 1943–1944 by Use of DDT," *American Journal of Public Health* 36 (1946): 119–29; see also Arthur Allen, *Vaccine: The Controversial Story of Medicine's Greatest Lifesaver* (New York: Norton, 2007), 140–42.

299 **The Allies came too late:** Naomi Baumslag, *Murderous Medicine: Nazi Doctors, Experimentation, and Typhus* (Westport, CT: Greenwood Press, 2005), 26–27.

300 **according to Weigl:** Rudolf Weigl, "Immunization against Typhus Fever in Poland during World War II," *Texas Reports on Biology and Medicine* 5 (1947): 177–79.

300 **Weigl's lice:** Henryk Mosing, "Rudolf Weigl uchony i człowiek na 50-lecie Jego badań nad tyfusem plamistym" (Rudolf Weigl, scholar and man in his 50 years of research), *Przeglad epidemiolyczny* 20 (1966): 93–100.

300 **About 10,000 descendants:** Iryna Kurhanova, interview with author.

300 **Advances in knowledge:** R. J. Duma et al., "Epidemic Typhus in the United States Associated with Flying Squirrels," *Journal of the American Medical Associoation* 245 (1981): 2318–23.

301 **Nowadays fewer people:** Didier Raoult and Veronique Roux, "The Body Louse as a Vector of Reemerging Human Diseases," *Clinical Infectious Diseases* 29 (1999): 893.

Notes

301 **Typhus outbreaks still:** David Walker, interview with author, UT-Galveston, May 2012.

301 **A year later:** D. Roault et al., "Outbreak of Epidemic Typhus in Russia," *Lancet* 352 (1998): 1151.

301 **Other rickettsial:** Dr. Allen L. Richards, interview with author, Naval Medical Research Center, May 2012.

301 **Flea-carried murine:** Jennifer Adjemian et al., "Murine Typhus in Austin, Texas, USA, 2008," *Emerging Infectious Diseases* 16 (2010): 412–17.

301 **Overall, classical typhus:** Richards interview; Walker interview.

302 **Walker's department:** Walker interview.

303 **Everything passes:** Szybalski, interview with author.

303 **Yet the story:** Żuławski in *To Overcome Death: Professor Rudolf Weigl,* dir. Halina Szymura (TV Katowice, 2009).

303 **". . . people bade goodbye":** Adam Zagajewski, "To Go to Lvov," in *Without End: New and Selected Poems* (New York: Farrar, Straus and Giroux, 2004).

ACKNOWLEDGMENTS

This book could not have been written without the partnership of Izabela Wagner, Waclaw Szybalski, and Peter Eyer. Dr. Szybalski, a stalwart of Weigl's wartime laboratory, has been central to keeping alive his mentor's accomplishments. Szybalski shared his expertise and experiences, and introduced me to Izabela, a brilliant sociologist who joined my search for traces of Weigl and Fleck. She located and translated crucial documents, opened her home, and brought me to Ryszard Wojcik, who generously shared his materials, his astounding life story, and his friendship. Peter Eyer shared papers, letters, difficult evaluations, and (with his wife Gabriele) abundant hospitality. Stanislaw Kosiedowski was generous with time and assistance; his lwow.pl website provides an outstanding service to Polish history. Krystyna Weigl-Albert shared photographs and encouragement.

My agent, Sarah Chalfant has been a wonderful supporter. Angela von der Lippe, Tom Mayer, and Ryan Harrington at W. W. Norton gave me dedication, braininess, and a sense of fun. Basia Bernhardt has been a warm friend who made learning Polish an impossible delight. Marcel and Ania Drimer, Krystyna Boron, and Joris de Mooij helped with translations. George J. Otlowski, Jr., Nancy Zerbe, and Paul Abbey directed me to traces of Marian Ciepielowksi. Ann Hulbert, Jeff Baker,

Acknowledgments

Walt Orenstein, and Paul Offit supported the project from the beginning, and Paul Weindling has been a patient adviser.

My book received generous support from Peter Kovler and the Kovler Fund of the Community Foundation of the National Capital Region, Edward Serrota at the Central Europe Center for Research and Documentation, and the Wellcome Trust's program in the humanities.

The following archivists and scholars offered meaningful assistance: Naomi Baumslag, Johannes Fehr, Sylwia Werner, Irena Steinfeldt, Shaul Ferrero, Amy Schmidt, Daniel Demellier, Dominique Dupenne, Sandra Legout, David Osterbur, Patricia Heberer, Peter Gohle, Udine Beier, Kornelia Grundmann, Marek Jaros, Holm Kirsten, Gert De Prins, Eric W. Boyle, Misha Mitsel, Valerie Hugonnard, Pawel Pluta, Sofia Dyak, Roman Lozynskyi, Anna Cieplinska, Jozefa Kostek, Thomas Schnelle, Marta Balinska, Susana Case, John Parascandola, Ellen Land-Weber, Andrzej Gamian, Rostyslav Stoika, Irina Kurhanova, Olga Tarasyuk, Katharina Kreuder-Sonnen, Jason Francisco, David Lee Preston, Michael Kogon, Arthur Silverstein, David Taylor, Bozena Plonka-Syroka, Christian Barouby, Allen Richards, David Walker, Eric Lohr, Steve Sestanovich, and Pedro Pablo Kuczynski.

My friends Jonathan Skolnik, Natan and Vered Guttman, Masha Belenky, Scott Wallace, Josh Rosenberg, Martha Weiss, Tamara Razi, and Peter Lewis listened and encouraged. Jim Heintz took vacation time to show me around Lviv with cultural and Cyrillic translations. Andreas Biefang, Susanna Weineck, Thomas Wiegold, and Birgit Böhret housed, fed and entertained me with warmth and style. My siblings Emily and Nick provided moral and financial support.

As always, Margaret Talbot gave me the best advice, love, and encouragement along the way.

I thank Ambassador Lee Feinstein for a glorious seder at his residence in Warsaw; Czeslaw Radzikowski and Stanislaw Ulaszewski for friendly tours of Wrocław; Marietta Steinhart for Viennese research; David Ben-Nathan for gathering old Fleck colleagues; Antoinette Nora Claypoole for her work on Louise Bryant; Joerg Dopheide and Alfred

Acknowledgments

Smieszchala for tracing Wilhelm Dopheide; Howard Cohn for the postwar story of his father; Claude Romney for her thoughts about Auschwitz and Fleck; Marcus Klingberg and his daughter Sylvia for clinging to ideals; and Imre Goncze for sharing his painful story with me. And all the other witnesses, and the people they loved.

INDEX

Index

Index

Index

Index

typhus transmission in, 13, 14, 24–25, 26, 29, 32, 33, 67, 91–92, 108, 180–81, 299
coccidiosis, 227
Cohn, August, 234, 248, 251, 281
cold viruses, 17
Cold War, 4, 248, 265–66, 274
Columbia University, 63
comatose conditions, 22
Combiescu, Dr., 244
Combined Intelligence Objectives Subcommittee (CIOS), 265–66
common criminals, 100, 197, 199, 204–6
communism, 4
    in Germany, 99
Communists, 112, 197, 200–201, 222, 234, 235, 249, 251, 259–60, 281, 297
    postwar, 283–84, 296–97
concentration camps, 99, 152, 162–63, 166, 218
    biomedical professionals in, 102–4, 218
    brutality in, 100–104, 137
    clinics in, 102–3
    commandants, 218
    death certificates in, 103–4
    dogs at, 226
    factories at, 218
    industrial-scale murder at, 218–19
    labor policies at, 218
    medical experiments in, 80, 90, 191–92, 201–10, 271
    mortality rates at, 218–19, 299–300
    policies in, 101
    postwar interpreter of, 235
    status and power in, 102, 197–99
Congress of People's Commissars, 34
conscientious objectors, 266
consent, of experiment subjects, 267
contamination, 91, 108
control vaccine, 247
convalescent serum, of typhus patients, 185
"cooties," 26
cordon sanitaire, 35
corpses, 163, 218, 255, 260
    haulers of, 214
    after pogrom, 129–31
corruption, 207, 236
Cottbus, 28

cow flesh, experiments with, 228
Cox, Herald, 94–95
    vaccine of, 181, 190, 299, 300
crematoria, 101
creosote baths, 26, 29
crimes against humanity, 267
crowded conditions, 96, 121, 139, 220
Crusoe, Robinson (char.), 245
cultural explanations for disease, 90–91
cultures:
    bacterial broth for, 228, 234
    for growing typhus, 188, 240
Cumming, Cecilia, 132
Curie, Marie Skłodowska, 38
cyanide gas, 90
Czech Republic, 15
Czerniaków, Adam, 123

Dachau, 99–100, 106, 200, 259, 299
Dana-Farber Cancer Institute, 287
dandelions, research into, 221–22
Daniels, Josef, 165
D-Day, 8
DDT powder, 186–87, 299–300
death, freezing to, 101
death camps, 130, 137, 163
    machinery of, 192
    smells of, 163, 260
    see also concentration camps
death through exhaustion, 218
death trains, 33–34
Degesch, 193
de Kruif, Paul, 58
delirium, 21–22, 34, 37, 107, 155, 185
delousing, 34
    campaigns for, 26, 35, 39, 66–67, 95, 100–101, 108, 140, 181, 193
    machinery for, 192
    resistance to, 39
    in Russian Revolution, 34, 35, 39
    trains for, 39
    in World War I, 26, 27, 180–81
    in World War II, 181, 193, 202, 253
Demnitz, Albert, 175
Denikin, Anton, 33
Denmark, 193, 207
deportations, by Soviets, 110–12, 117, 283
Dessau, 81

Index

Index

Index

Index

Index

Index

Index

Index

Index

Index

Pleszczyńska, Ewa, 287
Plotz, Harry, 29–30, 34–35
pneumonia, 101, 157
pogroms, 34–35, 38, 46, 72–73, 128–31
Pohl, Oswald, 212, 218, 220
poisoning, 250
Poland, Poles, 15–16, 33, 35
  academic world of, 41–42, 50, 106
  anti-Semitism in, 16, 38, 53, 56, 72–77,
    83, 127–31, 283
  Communist Party of, 74
  de-Stalinization of, 294
  government-in-exile, in London, 162
  independence of, 26, 32, 38, 42, 46
  intelligentsia of, 106–7, 131, 283
  interwar period of, 46–47, 53–54,
    72–77, 83
  invasion of, 109–10
  National Academy of, 287, 289
  nationalists of, 46, 72–73, 74–77, 83
  Nazi period in, 3, 60, 105–9, 112, 117–23,
    125–78
  partition of, 46, 50
  population postwar of, 283–84
  postwar life in, 274–79, 283–84
  postwar science in, 288
  prime minister of, 147–48
  public health in, 41–42, 61, 94
  secret police of, 287, 296
  Soviet period in, 110–17
  typhus in, 38–42, 90–91, 95
Polish National Institute of Hygiene (PZH),
  41–42, 62, 64–65, 66, 121, 140, 171,
  278, 288, 294
Polish notation, 50
Polish soldiers, 109–10, 114, 125
Polish-Soviet War, 33, 38, 253
political prisoners:
  of Germany, 99, 100, 197, 219
  as key workers, 197–98, 217
  political significance, of syphilis, 88
Poller, Walter, 102–5
postwar genetics community, 47
poverty, 90–91
POW camps, 181–82
  medical experimentation in, 185, 269–70
  starvation in, 182
  typhus in, 194, 270

POWs:
  of Austria, 23, 28
  of Britain, 248
  of France, 194–95
  of Russia, 2–3, 14–15, 23, 26, 28, 38–39,
    139–40, 144, 181–82, 194
  of Turkey, 23
Poznań, 278
Preminger, Otto, 280
President Warfield, 280
preventive medicine, of Nazis, 193
"Principles and Rules of Experimentation
  on Human Subjects" (Ivy), 267
prison factories, 249
"Problems of the Science of Science"
  (Fleck), 241–45
Promise Hitler Kept, The (Folkmann), 170
propaganda:
  of Nazis, 101
  of Soviets, 182
property, confiscation of, 106, 137–38, 277
protein broth, 228
Proteus OX-19, 30–31
proto-ideas, in medicine, 91, 92
Prowazek, Stanislaus von, 28–29
Prussian army, 25
Prussian virtues, 200
Przemyśl, 15, 110
  lab in, 15, *19*, 36, 41, 170
Przybyłkiewicz, Zdzisław, 107, 166, 288
  Weigl and, 276–77, 279, 290
public health:
  in Germany, 88–89, 93–94, 101
  in Poland, 64–67, 92, 114, 119–20, 140–
    42, 154
Public Health Laboratory, U.S., 94–95
PZH (Polish National Institute of Hygiene),
  41–42, 62, 64–65, 66, 121, 140, 171,
  278, 288, 294

Quarantine, 119–20
quarantines, 90, 95, 100, 140, 141, 185, 202
quintana, 27, 160, 161–61

rabbits:
  at Buchenwald, 234, 237
  as food, 221, 227, 247–48, 251, 259
  typhus research with, 188, 193–94, 237

377

Index

Index

Index

Sobibor, 99, 218
social constructivists, 296
social medicine, 89
sociology of scientific knowledge, 58
sodium evipam, 199
SOE, *see* Special Operations Executive
Sokolowski, Jerzy, 162
Soviet Academy of Medicine, 114
Soviet-Nazi demarcation line, 284
Soviet Ukraine, postwar in, 279, 282–84
Soviet Union, 76, 86, 95, 112
 collaborators and, 278
 Nazi invasion of, 124, 179–81
 passports of, 116
 POWs from, 181, 183, 185, 194
 scientists of, 221
 spy for, 296–97
 tensions with, 265
 typhus in, 180, 277
Sparrow, Hélène, 62, *63*, 193
spastic movements, 21–22
Special Operations Executive (SOE), British, 249, 264, 282
 Buchenwald rescue plot of, 253–56
spotted fever, 20, 24
squirrel-to-person transmission, 300–301
Stalag IV-B, 194
Stalin, Joseph, 109–10, 111, 125, 265, 279, 284
Stalingrad, 179–80, *179*
Stalinism, 86, 115
staph infections, 161
Staraya Russa, 183–84
starvation, 100–101, 121, 131, 138–40, 156, 182, 197, 200, 257, 259–60
Starzyk, Jan, 61, 165, 276
State Institute of Serotherapy (Vienna), 55
statistics, in medical thinking, 57
Steinhaus, Hugo, 50–51, 54, 285
sterilization experiments, 215–16, 266
Stiffel, Frank, 74, 112–13, 122, 225–26
Stockholm, 97
stool tests, 224
Stozek, Włodzimierz, 50, 132, 147–48
Strasbourg, University of, 188
Streicher, Julius, 90–91
Streptococcus pyogenes, 17, 226–27
Strong, Richard, 25

strophanthin, 104, 185, 205
Structure of Scientific Revolutions, The (Kuhn), 3
Stryj, 15, 54
Stryj Park, 47–49, 71
Stubendienst, 102
Stuchly, Zbigniew, 61, 133, 165, 170–71, 231, 294
Sturmabteilung, 81
Stürmer, Der, 90–91
stylet, 21
subsultus tendinum, 22
Sucharda, Edward, 116–17
suicides, 22–23, 205–6
 by Nazis, 264
supply lines, 180, 218
surrealism, 60
swollen testicles, 22
Sympatius (char.), 241–42, 245
symptoms of typhus, 21–22, 36–37, 155, 184, 185, 205–6
syphilis, 88, 200, 224, 225, 227
Szczepko (Kazimierz Wajda), 49
Szeptycki, Andrzej Graf, Archbishop of Lwów, 128
Szpilman, Henryk, 121–23
Szybalski, Stanisław, 153, 159–61
Szybalski, Stefan, 115–16, 152–53
Szybalski, Wacław, 47, 73, 77, 115–17, 127, 137, 139, 162–63, 231, 284
 Weigl lab description of, 147–52, 303

T-4, 138
Tannenberg, Battle of, 25–26
Tarasyuk, Oleksandra, 1–2
Taraxacum kok-saghyz, 221–22
Tarnów, 15
Tarski, Alfred, 51
tattoos, 213, 220
Taylor, Telford, 267–68
Teller, Edward, 50
tents, for delousing, 26, 67
testes, of guinea pigs, 239
tetanus, 31
Texas, University of, at Galveston, 301–2
Theory and Practice of Hell, The (Kogon), 207, 236, 281
Third Army, U.S., 259–61

Index

Index

Index

Index